First World War
and Army of Occupation
War Diary
France, Belgium and Germany

39 DIVISION
117 Infantry Brigade
Headquarters
10 March 1916 - 31 December 1916

WO95/2584

The Naval & Military Press Ltd
www.nmarchive.com
Published in association with The National Archives

Published by

The Naval & Military Press Ltd

Unit 10 Ridgewood Industrial Park,

Uckfield, East Sussex,

TN22 5QE England

Tel: +44 (0) 1825 749494

www.naval-military-press.com

www.nmarchive.com

This diary has been reprinted in facsimile from the original. Any imperfections are inevitably reproduced and the quality may fall short of modern type and cartographic standards.

© Crown Copyright
Images reproduced by permission of The National Archives, London, England, 2015.

Contents

Document type	Place/Title	Date From	Date To
Heading	39th Division 117th Infy Bde Bde Headquarters Mar-Dec 1916		
Heading	39th Division The 39th Division Disembarked In France Between 4th & 8th March 1916 B.H.Q. 117th Infantry Brigade. March 1916		
War Diary	Steenbecque	10/03/1916	10/03/1916
War Diary	Estaires	13/03/1916	13/03/1916
War Diary	Sailly	14/03/1916	20/03/1916
War Diary	Laventie	26/03/1916	26/03/1916
Heading	War Diary 117th Infantry Brigade. (39th. Division). Volume 1. 10.3.16-31.3.16. To/ Officer i/c A.G. Office, Base.		
War Diary	Gonnehem	28/03/1916	30/03/1916
Miscellaneous	Appendix 1. Detail Of 117th Infantry Brigade. Headquarters. Appendix 1		
Operation(al) Order(s)	117th Bde. Order No. 1. Appendix II.	12/03/1916	12/03/1916
Miscellaneous	Training-39th Division. Appendix III	26/03/1916	26/03/1916
Operation(al) Order(s)	117th Infantry Brigade Order No. 4. Appendix IV	27/03/1916	27/03/1916
Heading	39th Division. B.H.Q. 117th Infantry Brigade April 1916 Appendices Attached:- Relief Orders Defence Scheme.		
War Diary	Gonnehem	02/04/1916	15/04/1916
War Diary	Near Locon	16/04/1916	23/04/1916
War Diary	Loisne	24/04/1916	30/04/1916
Operation(al) Order(s)	117th Brigade Order No. 5. Appendix I	04/04/1916	04/04/1916
Miscellaneous	A Form. Messages And Signals.		
Operation(al) Order(s)	117th Infantry Brigade Order No. 7 Appendix 2	15/04/1916	15/04/1916
Operation(al) Order(s)	117th Brigade Order No. 6. Appendix 3	14/04/1916	14/04/1916
Miscellaneous	March Table to accompany 117th Brigade Order No. 6		
Operation(al) Order(s)	117th Infantry Brigade Order No. 8. Appendix 4	21/04/1916	21/04/1916
Miscellaneous	Relief Table of 118th Infantry Brigade By 117th Infantry Brigade. (To Accompany 117th Infantry Brigade Order No. 3, Dated 21st Apl. 1916).	21/04/1916	21/04/1916
Miscellaneous	Table Of Relief Of Posts. To Accompany 117th Infantry Brigade Order No. 3, Dated 21st Apl. 1916	21/04/1916	21/04/1916
Miscellaneous	Provisional. Brigade Defence Scheme. (Festubert Section).	21/04/1916	21/04/1916
Operation(al) Order(s)	117th Infantry Brigade Order No. 9 Appendix 4 A.	22/04/1916	22/04/1916
Operation(al) Order(s)	117th Infantry Brigade Order No. 7. Appendix 5	21/04/1916	21/04/1916
Miscellaneous	Garrisons And Stores-Corre-Essars System. Table A.		
Operation(al) Order(s)	117th Infantry Brigade Order No. 7	21/04/1916	21/04/1916
Miscellaneous	Garrisons And Stores-Gorre-Essars System. Table.		
Operation(al) Order(s)	117th Infantry Brigade Order No. 10. Appendix 6	26/04/1916	26/04/1916
Miscellaneous	Relief Table. To accompany 117th Infantry Brigade Order No. 10, Dated 26.4.16	26/04/1916	26/04/1916
Heading	39th Division. B.H.Q. 117th Infantry Brigade May 1916 Brigade Orders Attached:		
War Diary	Loisne Festubert Section	01/05/1916	10/05/1916
War Diary	Near Locon	10/05/1916	15/05/1916
War Diary	Canal House Near Gorre	17/05/1916	31/05/1916

Operation(al) Order(s)	117th Infantry Brigade Order No. 11. Appendix 1	30/04/1916	30/04/1916
Miscellaneous	Relief Table. To accompany 117th Infantry Brigade Order No. 11, Dated 30.4.16	30/04/1916	30/04/1916
Miscellaneous	Trench Orders. Trench Administration And Discipline. Appendix II	26/04/1916	26/04/1916
Miscellaneous	No. Of Copies		
Operation(al) Order(s)	117th Infantry Brigade Order No. 12 Appendix III	04/05/1916	04/05/1916
Miscellaneous	Relief Table To accompany 117th Infantry Brigade Order No. 12 Dated 4.5.16	04/05/1916	04/05/1916
Operation(al) Order(s)	117th Infantry Brigade Order No. 14. Appendix IV.	07/05/1916	07/05/1916
Miscellaneous	Relief Table of 117th Infantry Brigade By 116th Infantry Brigade. Table A.		
Miscellaneous	Garrisons And Stores-Gorre-Essars System. Table B.		
Operation(al) Order(s)	117th Infantry Brigade Order No. 15. Appendix V	16/05/1916	16/05/1916
Miscellaneous	Relief Table of 118th Infantry Brigade By 117th Infantry Brigade. To accompany 117th Infantry Brigade Order No. 15, Dated 15th May, 1916. Table A.	15/05/1916	15/05/1916
Miscellaneous	Relief Of Posts-Givenchy Section. To Accompany 117th Infantry Brigade Order No. 15. Dated 11th May, 1916. Table B.	11/05/1916	11/05/1916
Operation(al) Order(s)	B Section. Infantry Brigade Order No. 16. Appendix VI	20/05/1916	20/05/1916
Miscellaneous	Small Operation 22.5.16. Appendix VII	22/05/1916	22/05/1916
Miscellaneous	The Following Will Be Added To Trench Orders Issued On The 28th April, 1916 Appendix VIII.	25/05/1916	25/05/1916
Operation(al) Order(s)	117th Infantry Brigade Order No. 17. Appendix IX	24/05/1916	24/05/1916
Miscellaneous	Small Operation 26.6.16. Appendix X	25/05/1916	25/05/1916
Miscellaneous	Provisional Plan Of Defence Of "B" Section (Givenchy) 39th Divisional Section. Appendix XI.	26/05/1916	26/05/1916
Miscellaneous	General Plan In Case Of Attack.		
Miscellaneous	Garrison. Appendix A.		
Miscellaneous	Garrisons And Stores.		
Miscellaneous	Amendment to Plan Of Defence Of "B" Section (Givenchy) Dated 26th May, 1916	26/05/1916	26/05/1916
Miscellaneous	Position Of Machine Guns And Lewis Guns. Appendix C.		
Operation(al) Order(s)	117th Infantry Brigade Order No. 19 Appendix XII	28/05/1916	28/05/1916
Miscellaneous	Issued at 3 p.m. to:-		
Miscellaneous	With reference to Plan of Defence of "B" Section (Givenchy), Dated 26th May, 1916-General Plan in Case Of Attack. Appendix XIII WD.	29/05/1916	29/05/1916
Heading	39th Division. B.H.Q. 117th Infantry Brigade June 1916 Appendices Attached:- Note On Defences. Brigade Orders. Report On Operation 4/5th June. Plan Of Defence Givenchy Secton Plan Of Defence Festubert Section Defence Scheme.		
War Diary	Canal H'se Near Gorre	01/06/1916	04/06/1916
War Diary	Canal H'se	05/06/1916	06/06/1916
War Diary	Essars	07/06/1916	11/06/1916
War Diary	Loisne	12/06/1916	30/06/1916
Miscellaneous	Appendix I	02/06/1916	02/06/1916
Operation(al) Order(s)	117th Infantry Brigade Order No. 20. Appendix II.	01/06/1916	01/06/1916
Miscellaneous	To Headquarters, 39th Division. Appendix III	05/06/1916	05/06/1916
Miscellaneous	Plan Of Defence Of Givenchy Section 39th Divisional Sector Appendix IV.	04/06/1916	04/06/1916
Miscellaneous	General Plan In Case Of Attack.		
Miscellaneous	Garrison. Appendix A.		

Type	Description	Date From	Date To
Miscellaneous	Garrisons And Stores Appendix. B.		
Miscellaneous	Position Of Machine Guns And Lewis Guns. Appendix C.		
Operation(al) Order(s)	117th Infantry Brigade Order No. 21 Appendix V	05/06/1916	05/06/1916
Miscellaneous	Relief Table to accompany 117th Infantry Brigade Order No. 21, Dated 5.6.16	05/06/1916	05/06/1916
Operation(al) Order(s)	117th Infantry Brigade Order No. 22 Appendix VI	09/06/1916	09/06/1916
Miscellaneous	Relief Table of 105th Infantry Brigade By 117th Infantry Brigade. (To Accompany 117th Infantry Brigade Order No. 22 Dated 9.6.16.)	09/06/1916	09/06/1916
Miscellaneous	Table Of Relief Of Position To Accompany 117th Infantry Brigade Order No. 22, Dated 9.6.16	09/06/1916	09/06/1916
Miscellaneous	To/ Officer Commanding 16/Notts & Derby. R. Appendix VII WD	14/06/1916	14/06/1916
Operation(al) Order(s)	117th Infantry Brigade Order No. 25. Appendix VIII	15/06/1916	15/06/1916
Miscellaneous	Table Of Relief Of Posts. To Accompany Brigade Order No. 25, Dated 15.6.16. Table A.	15/06/1916	15/06/1916
Miscellaneous	117th Infantry Brigade Festubert Section Appendix IX General Plan In Case Of Attack.	18/06/1916	18/06/1916
Miscellaneous	117th Infantry Brigade. Table Of Posts In Festubert Section. Appendix. A.		
Miscellaneous	117th Infantry Brigade Distribution Of S.A.A. And Grenades. Right Sub-Section Fest. R. Appendix. B.		
Miscellaneous	117th Infantry Brigade. Addendum To The Brigade Scheme In Case Of Attack.	18/06/1916	18/06/1916
Operation(al) Order(s)	117th Infantry Brigade Order No. 26. Appendix X	22/06/1916	22/06/1916
Operation(al) Order(s)	117th Infantry Brigade Order No. 27. Appendix XI	21/06/1916	21/06/1916
Miscellaneous	117th Infantry Brigade. To Accompany 117th Infantry Brigade Order No. 27, Dated 21.6.16. Table A.	21/06/1916	21/06/1916
Miscellaneous	117th Infantry Brigade. Addendum To The Brigade Scheme In Case Of Attack.	24/06/1916	24/06/1916
Miscellaneous	117th Infantry Brigade. Table Of Posts In Festubert Section. Appendix A.		
Miscellaneous	117th Infantry Brigade Keeps In Front Line System. Appendix C.		
Miscellaneous	117th Infantry Brigade Posts In Village-St. Vaast-Croix Barbee System. Appendix D.		
Operation(al) Order(s)	117th Brigade Order No 28 Appendix XIII	27/06/1916	27/06/1916
Miscellaneous	Amendments.		
Heading	39th Division. B.H.Q. 117th Infantry Brigade July 1916 Appendices Attached:- Brigade Operation Orders. Report On Raid 3/4th July (App II) Reports On Raids 11/12th (App VI) Defences & Dispositions In Case Of Attack Relief Orders.		
War Diary	Loisne	01/07/1916	13/07/1916
War Diary	Cense Du Raux	14/07/1916	20/07/1916
War Diary	Le Hamel	21/07/1916	25/07/1916
War Diary	Canal House	26/07/1916	31/07/1916
Operation(al) Order(s)	117th Infantry Brigade Order No 30 Appendix I	03/07/1917	03/07/1917
Miscellaneous	To O.C. 17Motts O Daily R 16th Rifle Brigade.	30/06/1916	30/06/1916
Operation(al) Order(s)	Amendment to 117th Brigade Order No. 30	02/07/1916	02/07/1916
Miscellaneous	A Form. Messages And Signals.		
Miscellaneous			
Miscellaneous	To/ Headquarters, 39th Division. Appendix II	05/07/1916	05/07/1916
Miscellaneous	To/ Headquarters, 39th Division.	04/07/1916	04/07/1916
Miscellaneous	Advance Report On Raid Carried Out On Pope's Nose.	04/07/1916	04/07/1916

Type	Description	Date From	Date To
Operation(al) Order(s)	117th Brigade Order No. 31. Appendix III.	07/07/1916	07/07/1916
Operation(al) Order(s)	117th Infantry Brigade Order No. 32. (Preliminary Orders For A Minor Appendix 4	09/07/1916	09/07/1916
Operation(al) Order(s)	117th Infantry Brigade Order No 33 Appendix 5	10/07/1916	10/07/1916
Operation(al) Order(s)	Amendment To 117th Infantry Brigade Order No. 33	11/07/1916	11/07/1916
Miscellaneous	To/ Headquarters, 39th Division. Report On Two Small Enterprises Carried Out On The Night Of 11/12th July. Appendix VI	12/07/1916	12/07/1916
Operation(al) Order(s)	117th Infantry Brigade Order No. 35 Appendix Z	14/07/1916	14/07/1916
Miscellaneous	117th Infantry Brigade Ferine Du Bois Section). Appendix VIII.	18/07/1916	18/07/1916
Miscellaneous	Table Of Posts In Ferme Du Bois Section. Appendix A.		
Miscellaneous	Ferme Du Bois Section. Distribution of S.A.A. & Bombs. Right Battalion. Appx. B.		
Miscellaneous	Herewith Appendix C to 117th Infantry Brigade Defence Scheme (Ferme Du Bois Section) issued yesterday, the 18th July, 1916. Appendix IX.	19/07/1916	19/07/1916
Miscellaneous	117th Infantry Brigade. Croix Barbee-St Vaast System, Showing Keeps Occupied By the Support Battalion, With Stores, etc. Appx. C.		
Miscellaneous	Amendments to 117th Infantry Brigade Defence Scheme Appendix 10	19/07/1916	19/07/1916
Operation(al) Order(s)	117th Brigade Order No. 36. Appendix 11	19/07/1916	19/07/1916
Miscellaneous	117th Infantry Brigade. (Relief Table To Accompany 117th Brigade Order 36, Dated 19.7.16).	19/07/1916	19/07/1916
Operation(al) Order(s)	39th Divisional Reserve Order No. 2 Appendix 12	21/07/1916	21/07/1916
Operation(al) Order(s)	117th Infantry Brigade Order No. 37 Appendix 13	23/07/1916	23/07/1916
Operation(al) Order(s)	117th Infantry Brigade Order No. 38 Appendix 14	25/07/1916	25/07/1916
Operation(al) Order(s)	117th Infantry Brigade Order No 39	31/07/1916	31/07/1916
Miscellaneous	A Form. Messages And Signals.		
Operation(al) Order(s)	Amendment to 117th Brigade Order No. 30	02/07/1916	02/07/1916
Miscellaneous	To/ Headquarters, 39th Division.	02/07/1916	02/07/1916
Heading	39th Division. B.H.Q. 117th Infantry Brigade August 1916 Appendices Attached:- Brigade Orders. Defence Scheme. Tracing.		
War Diary	Canal House Near Gorre.	01/08/1916	06/08/1916
War Diary	Canal House.	07/08/1916	09/08/1916
War Diary	Raimbert	10/08/1916	10/08/1916
War Diary	La Thieuloye	11/08/1916	23/08/1916
War Diary	Doullens.	24/08/1916	24/08/1916
War Diary	Vauchelles	25/08/1916	27/08/1916
War Diary	Beaussart	28/08/1916	31/08/1916
Operation(al) Order(s)	117th Brigade Order No. 40. Appendix I	31/07/1916	31/07/1916
Miscellaneous	117th Infantry Brigade. Plan Of Defence Of Givenchy Section. Appendix II.	04/06/1916	04/06/1916
Miscellaneous	General Plan In Case Of Attack.		
Miscellaneous	Showing Dispositions Of Medium And Light Trench Mortars. Appendix A.		
Miscellaneous	Garrisons And Stores. Appendix B.		
Miscellaneous	Showing Machine Gun And Artillery Dispositions. Appendix C.		
Miscellaneous	(Showing Distributions Of Battalions And Companies) Appendix D.		
Miscellaneous	Givenchy Section Signals-117th Infantry Brigade. Visual Signalling. Appendix E.		
Operation(al) Order(s)	117th Infantry Brigade Order No. 41 App III	05/08/1916	05/08/1916

Miscellaneous	117th Infantry Brigade. Relief Table To Accompany 117th Infantry Brigade Order No. 41, Dated 5.6.16	05/06/1916	05/06/1916
Operation(al) Order(s)	117th Infantry Brigade Order No. 43. Appendix IV	09/08/1916	09/08/1916
Miscellaneous	March Table to accompany 117th Infantry Brigade Order No. 43, Dated 9.8.16	09/08/1916	09/08/1916
Operation(al) Order(s)	117th Infantry Brigade Order No. 44. Appendix V	10/08/1916	10/08/1916
Operation(al) Order(s)	117th Infantry Brigade Order No. 46. Appendix VI	11/08/1916	11/08/1916
Miscellaneous	117th Infantry Brigade No. 47. Appendix VII	20/08/1916	20/08/1916
Miscellaneous	The Arrangements For To-Marrow Will Be As Follows.		
Operation(al) Order(s)	117th Infantry Brigade Order No. 48. App VIII	22/08/1916	22/08/1916
Miscellaneous	117th Infantry Brigade Train Table To Accompany 117th Brigade Operation Order No. 48--For "B" Day (24th August, 1916).	24/08/1916	24/08/1916
Miscellaneous	117th Infantry Brigade. March To Accompany 117th Brigade Operation Order No. 48--For "A" Day (23rd August, 1916).	23/08/1916	23/08/1916
Miscellaneous	117th Infantry Brigade. Supply And Transport Table To Accompany 117th Brigade Operation Order 48 (Dated 22nd August, 1916)	22/08/1916	22/08/1916
Operation(al) Order(s)	117th Brigade Order No. 49. App IX	24/08/1916	24/08/1916
Miscellaneous	117th Infantry Brigade. March Table To Accompany 117th Infantry Brigade Order No. 49. Dated 24th August, 1916	24/08/1916	24/08/1916
Operation(al) Order(s)	117th Infantry Brigade Order No. 49 App X.	27/08/1916	27/08/1916
Miscellaneous	117th Infantry Brigade. March Table To Accompany 117th Infantry Brigade Order No. 49, Dated 27.8.16	27/08/1916	27/08/1916
Operation(al) Order(s)	117th Infantry Brigade Order No. 50, App XI	29/08/1916	29/08/1916
Miscellaneous	Time Table To Accompany 117th Infantry Brigade Order No. 50, Dated 28.8.16	28/08/1916	28/08/1916
Miscellaneous	Appendix B. 117th Infantry Brigade Order No. 50 Signal Code Between Aeroplanes And Infantry.		
Operation(al) Order(s)	Appendix C. To Accompany 117th Infantry Brigade Order No. 50 Medical Arrangements.		
Miscellaneous	To Accompany 117th Infantry Brigade Order No. 50. Appendix D.		
Operation(al) Order(s)	Appendix E. To Accompany 117th Infantry Brigade Order No. 50, Dated 29.8.16	29/08/1916	29/08/1916
Operation(al) Order(s)	117th Infantry Brigade Order No. 51 App XII	29/08/1916	29/08/1916
Operation(al) Order(s)	Important Amendment to 117th Brigade Order No. 51. App XIII.	30/08/1916	30/08/1916
Operation(al) Order(s)	Special Orders To G.C., Section, 227 Company R.E., To Accompany 117th Infantry Brigade Order No. 50. App XIV.	30/08/1916	30/08/1916
Operation(al) Order(s)	Amendments And Addenda To 117th Infantry Brigade Order No. 50. App 15	30/08/1916	30/08/1916
Operation(al) Order(s)	117th Infantry Brigade Order No. 52 App 16	31/08/1916	31/08/1916
Map	Section Of		
Map	Section Of Secret Map No. 4		
Heading	39th Division. B.H.Q. 117th Infantry Brigade September 1916 Appendix Attached:- Report On Operation 3rd September 1916. Brigade Orders. Defence Scheme.		
War Diary	Beaussart	01/09/1916	02/09/1916
War Diary	Nr.Hamel.	03/09/1916	03/09/1916
War Diary	Nr. Force-Ville.	04/09/1916	04/09/1916
War Diary	Bertrancourt	05/09/1916	05/09/1916

War Diary	Vitermont	06/09/1916	19/09/1916
War Diary	Sailly Au Bois.	20/09/1916	30/09/1916
Miscellaneous	A Form. Messages And Signals.		
Miscellaneous	To/ Headquarters, 39th Division. App I	03/09/1916	03/09/1916
Miscellaneous	To/ Headquarters, 39th Division.	05/09/1916	05/09/1916
Miscellaneous	Report of Hostile Shell Fire During Operations, 3rd. September.	05/09/1916	05/09/1916
Miscellaneous	To/ Headquarters, 39th Division.	06/09/1916	06/09/1916
Operation(al) Order(s)	117th Brigade Order No. 54. Advance Order For Move Of 117th Infantry Brigade. App II.	04/09/1916	04/09/1916
Operation(al) Order(s)	117th Infantry Brigade Order No. 55. App III.	05/09/1916	05/09/1916
Operation(al) Order(s)	117th Infantry Brigade Order No. 56. App IV	05/09/1916	05/09/1916
Miscellaneous	March And Relief Table To Accompany 117th Brigade Order No. 56		
Operation(al) Order(s)	Amendment to 117th Infantry Brigade Order No. 56 App IV	05/09/1916	05/09/1916
Operation(al) Order(s)	117th Brigade Order No. 57. App V	10/09/1916	10/09/1916
Operation(al) Order(s)	117th Infantry Brigade Order No. 58. App VI	14/09/1916	14/09/1916
Operation(al) Order(s)	117th Infantry Brigade Order No. 59	14/09/1916	14/09/1916
Operation(al) Order(s)	Amendment to 117th Infantry Brigade Order No. 59	16/09/1916	16/09/1916
Operation(al) Order(s)	117th Infantry Brigade Order No. 60	15/09/1916	15/09/1916
Operation(al) Order(s)	117th Infantry Brigade Order No. 62. App VII	18/09/1916	18/09/1916
Miscellaneous	Table "A"-March And Relief Table For The 19th September, To Accompany 117th Brigade Order No. 52		
Miscellaneous	Table "B" March And Relief Table For The 20th September, To Accompany 117th Brigade Order No. 62		
Miscellaneous	117th Infantry Brigade No. 63 App VIII	25/09/1916	25/09/1916
Miscellaneous	117th Infantry Brigade Defence Scheme (Provisional). App IX.		
Miscellaneous	117th Infantry Brigade. Provisional Defence Scheme While The 117th Brigade Is Holding The Serre And Hebuterne Sections.	29/09/1916	29/09/1916
Miscellaneous	Appendix "A" Distribution And Location Of Units Of 117th Infantry Brigade And Units Attached To 117th Infantry Brigade.		
Miscellaneous	Appendix "B" Vickers Machine Gun Emplacements In Serre And Hebuterne Sections.		
Miscellaneous	Appendix "C" Artillery : Heavy, Medium And Light Trench Mortars.		
Miscellaneous	Appendix "D" S.O.S. Signals And Retaliation Scheme.		
Miscellaneous	Appendix "E" Water Supply Arrangements, Trench Trainways, And Bomb, S.A.A. & Ration Stores.		
Miscellaneous	Appendix "F" Serre And Hebuterne Sections Signals Communications.		
Miscellaneous	Appendix "G" Medical Arrangements.		
Operation(al) Order(s)	117th Infantry Brigade Order No. 64. App X.	30/09/1916	30/09/1916
Miscellaneous	Relief Table to accompany 117th Brigade Operation Order No. 64		
Operation(al) Order(s)	117th Infantry Brigade Order No. 65. App XI.	30/09/1916	30/09/1916
Miscellaneous	March And Relief Table To Accompany 117th Brigade Operation Order No. 65		
Heading	39th Division. B.H.Q. 117th Infantry Brigade October 1916 Appendices Attached:- Brigade Orders. Report On Operations 9th October 1916 Report On Operations 21st October 1916. Maps: Tracings etc.		
Miscellaneous	To/ Headquarters, 39th Division.	01/11/1916	01/11/1916

Type	Description	From	To
War Diary	Bertrancourt	01/10/1916	02/10/1916
War Diary	Senlis	03/10/1916	03/10/1916
War Diary	Martinsart	04/10/1916	04/10/1916
War Diary	Passerelle De Magenta	05/10/1916	09/10/1916
War Diary	Senlis.	10/10/1916	15/10/1916
War Diary	Passerelle De Magenta	16/10/1916	24/10/1916
War Diary	Pioneer Road.	25/10/1916	26/10/1916
War Diary	Passerelle De Magenta	27/10/1916	28/10/1916
War Diary	Senlis.	29/10/1916	31/10/1916
Operation(al) Order(s)	117th Brigade Order No. 66. App I.	01/10/1916	01/10/1916
Operation(al) Order(s)	117th Infantry Brigade Order No. 67. App II	02/10/1916	02/10/1916
Operation(al) Order(s)	117th Infantry Brigade Order No. 69 App III	04/10/1916	04/10/1916
Miscellaneous	Relief Table. To accompany 117th Infantry Brigade Order No. 69		
Operation(al) Order(s)	117th Infantry Brigade Order No. 70. App IV.	07/10/1916	07/10/1916
Miscellaneous	117th Infantry Brigade. App V	08/10/1916	08/10/1916
Operation(al) Order(s)	18th Divisional Artillery Order No. 23 By Brig. Gen. S.F. Metcalfe, D.S.O. App. VI.	08/10/1916	08/10/1916
Operation(al) Order(s)	Artillery Order No. 37. App VII.	08/10/1916	08/10/1916
Miscellaneous	Report on Operations Carried Out On The Morning Of The 9th October, 1916. App VIII.	09/10/1916	09/10/1916
Operation(al) Order(s)	117th Infantry Brigade Order No. 71. App. IX.	09/10/1916	09/10/1916
Miscellaneous	117th Infantry Brigade March And Relief Table To Accompany The 117th Brigade Order No. 71		
Operation(al) Order(s)	Amendment To 117th Brigade Order No. 73 App X	16/10/1916	16/10/1916
Operation(al) Order(s)	117th Infantry Brigade Order No. 73	15/10/1916	15/10/1916
Miscellaneous	Relief Table To accompany 117th Brigade Order No. 73		
Operation(al) Order(s)	117th Infantry Brigade Order No. 74. App XI.	18/10/1916	18/10/1916
Operation(al) Order(s)	117th Infantry Brigade Order No. 75. App XII.	19/10/1916	19/10/1916
Operation(al) Order(s)	117th Infantry Brigade Order No. 76. App XIII	19/10/1916	19/10/1916
Miscellaneous	117th Infantry Brigade Report On The German Attack On Point 16 On The Morning Of The 20th October App XV.	20/10/1916	20/10/1916
Operation(al) Order(s)	117th Infantry Brigade No. 77 App XV	20/10/1916	20/10/1916
Miscellaneous	117th Infantry Brigade App XVI	20/10/1916	20/10/1916
Miscellaneous	117th Infantry Brigade. App XVII.	21/10/1916	21/10/1916
Operation(al) Order(s)	117th Infantry Brigade Order No. 78. App XVIII.	20/10/1916	20/10/1916
Operation(al) Order(s)	117th Infantry Brigade Order No. 79 App XIX	22/10/1916	22/10/1916
Operation(al) Order(s)	117th Infantry Brigade Order No. 80	23/10/1916	23/10/1916
Miscellaneous	Table Showing Movements Of Units Of The 117th Infantry Brigade On The 23rd., 24th., And 25th October. (To Accompany 117th Infantry Brigade Order No. 80).		
Operation(al) Order(s)	117th Infantry Brigade Order No. 81	23/10/1916	23/10/1916
Operation(al) Order(s)	117th Infantry Brigade Order No. 82. App XXI.	23/10/1916	23/10/1916
Operation(al) Order(s)	117th Brigade Order No. 83. App XXII.	24/10/1916	24/10/1916
Miscellaneous	Relief Table to accompany 117th Infantry Brigade Order No. 83		
Operation(al) Order(s)	117th Infantry Brigade Order No. 84. App XXIII.	26/10/1916	26/10/1916
Miscellaneous	Relief Table to accompany 117th Infantry Brigade Order No. 84		
Operation(al) Order(s)	117th Infantry Brigade Order No. 85. App XXIV.	27/10/1916	27/10/1916
Miscellaneous	Table Showing Movements Of Units Of The 117th Infantry Brigade On "Y" And "Z" Days (To Accompany 117th Infantry Brigade Order No 85).		

Operation(al) Order(s)	117th Infantry Brigade Order No. 86. App XXIVa.	28/10/1916	28/10/1916
Operation(al) Order(s)	117th Infantry Brigade Order No. 87. App XXIIV.b.	28/10/1916	28/10/1916
Operation(al) Order(s)	117th Infantry Brigade Order No. 88. App XXV.	28/10/1916	28/10/1916
Miscellaneous	Relief Table to accompany 117th Infantry Brigade Order No. 88		
Operation(al) Order(s)	117th Infantry Brigade Order No. 89	31/10/1916	31/10/1916
Map	Operation Trench Map		
Miscellaneous	1 Platoon 11th		
Miscellaneous			
Miscellaneous	A Form. Messages And Signals.		
Map	St Pierre Divion.		
Map	Thiepval		
Miscellaneous	39/G/36/4. II Corps.	12/10/1916	12/10/1916
Miscellaneous	C Form (Original). Messages And Signals.		
Map	Trench Map		
Miscellaneous	A Form. Messages And Signals.		
Heading	39th Division. B.H.Q. 117th Infantry Brigade November 1916		
War Diary	Senlis	01/11/1916	02/11/1916
War Diary	Passerelle De Magenta.	03/11/1916	04/11/1916
War Diary	Senlis	05/11/1916	05/11/1916
War Diary	Passerelle De Magenta.	06/11/1916	07/11/1916
War Diary	Pioneer Road.	08/11/1916	10/11/1916
War Diary	Senlis.	11/11/1916	12/11/1916
War Diary	North Bluffs	13/11/1916	13/11/1916
War Diary	Paisley Dump.	14/11/1916	14/11/1916
War Diary	Warloy.	15/11/1916	15/11/1916
War Diary	Gezaincourt	16/11/1916	16/11/1916
War Diary	Bollezeele	17/11/1916	30/11/1916
Operation(al) Order(s)	117th Infantry Brigade Order No. 89. App I.	31/10/1916	31/10/1916
Operation(al) Order(s)	Amendment to 117th Infantry Brigade Order No. 85. App II.	02/11/1916	02/11/1916
Operation(al) Order(s)	117th Infantry Brigade Order No. 90. App III.	02/11/1916	02/11/1916
Operation(al) Order(s)	117th Infantry Brigade Order No. 91. App IV.	02/11/1916	02/11/1916
Miscellaneous	Relief Table to accompany 117th Infantry Brigade Order No. 91		
Operation(al) Order(s)	117th Infantry Brigade Order No. 92. App V.	04/11/1916	04/11/1916
Miscellaneous	Relief Table to accompany 117th Infantry Brigade Order No. 92		
Operation(al) Order(s)	Amendment to 117th Infantry Brigade Order No. 85. App II.	05/11/1916	05/11/1916
Operation(al) Order(s)	117th Infantry Brigade Order No. 93. App. VI.	06/11/1916	06/11/1916
Miscellaneous	Relief Table to accompany 117th Infantry Brigade Order No. 93		
Operation(al) Order(s)	117th Infantry Brigade Order No. 94. App XII.	07/11/1916	07/11/1916
Miscellaneous	Relief Table to accompany 117th Infantry Brigade Order No. 94		
Operation(al) Order(s)	117th Infantry Brigade Order No. 95. App VIII.	10/11/1916	10/11/1916
Miscellaneous	Movement Table To Accompany 117th Infantry Brigade Order No. 95		
Operation(al) Order(s)	117th Infantry Brigade Order No. 96. App IX.	11/11/1916	11/11/1916
Miscellaneous	Table to accompany 117th Infantry Brigade Order No. 96		
Operation(al) Order(s)	117th Infantry Brigade Order No. 97. App X.	13/11/1916	13/11/1916
Miscellaneous	To/ Headquarters, 39th Division.	16/11/1916	16/11/1916

Miscellaneous	117th Infantry Brigade. Report On Operations Carried Out On November 13th., 1916, By The 16th Notts & Derby Regiment. App 10.a.	14/11/1916	14/11/1916
Miscellaneous	117th Infantry Brigade. Report On Operations Carried Out On November 13th., 1916	13/11/1916	13/11/1916
Operation(al) Order(s)	117th Infantry Brigade Order No. 98. App XII.	14/11/1916	14/11/1916
Miscellaneous	Relief Table to accompany 117th Infantry Brigade Order No. 98		
Miscellaneous	To Headquarters, 39th Division.	18/11/1916	18/11/1916
Operation(al) Order(s)	117th Infantry Brigade Order No. 100. App 12	16/11/1916	16/11/1916
Operation(al) Order(s)	117th Infantry Brigade Order No. 101. App 13	21/11/1916	21/11/1916
Heading	39th Division. B.H.Q. 117th Infantry Brigade December 1916 Appendices Attached:- Brigade Orders.		
Miscellaneous	To/ Headquarters, 39th Division.	01/01/1917	01/01/1917
War Diary	Bollezeele	01/12/1916	11/12/1916
War Diary	Poperinghe	12/12/1916	12/12/1916
War Diary	Canal Bank (West)	13/12/1916	31/12/1916
Operation(al) Order(s)	117th Infantry Brigade Order No. 103	05/12/1916	05/12/1916
Miscellaneous	March Table to accompany 117th Infantry Brigade Order No 103		
Operation(al) Order(s)	117th Infantry Brigade Order No. 104	06/12/1916	06/12/1916
Miscellaneous	Programme For Inspection Of 117th Infantry Brigade By Lieut. General Sir Aylmer Hunter-Weston, K.C.B. D.S.O., Commanding VIII Corps On 8th December, 1916	08/12/1916	08/12/1916
Diagram etc	Ceremonial		
Operation(al) Order(s)	117th Infantry Brigade Order No. 105	09/12/1916	09/12/1916
Miscellaneous	Table "A" To Accompany 117th Infantry Brigade Order No. 105		
Miscellaneous	Table "B" To Accompany 117th Infantry Brigade Order No 104, Showing Movements Of 117th Machine Gun Coy., 117 Trench Battery, Battalion Transport And Animals, Battalion Lewis Gun Teams And Handcarts.		
Miscellaneous			
Operation(al) Order(s)	Further Amendments to 117th Infantry Brigade Order No. 105	10/12/1916	10/12/1916
Operation(al) Order(s)	Amendment to 117th Infantry Brigade Order No. 105	10/12/1916	10/12/1916
Operation(al) Order(s)	117th Infantry Brigade Order No. 106	11/12/1916	11/12/1916
Miscellaneous	Relief Table To Accompany 117th Infantry Brigade Order No. 106		
Miscellaneous	Disposition Table to accompany 117th Infantry Brigade Order No. 106		
Operation(al) Order(s)	117th Infantry Brigade Order No. 107	16/12/1916	16/12/1916
Operation(al) Order(s)	Amendment to 117th Infantry Brigade Order No. 108	20/12/1916	20/12/1916
Operation(al) Order(s)	117th Infantry Brigade Order No. 108	20/12/1916	20/12/1916
Operation(al) Order(s)	117th Infantry Brigade Order No. 109	21/12/1916	21/12/1916
Operation(al) Order(s)	117th Infantry Brigade Order No. 110	24/12/1916	24/12/1916
Operation(al) Order(s)	117th Infantry Brigade Order No. 111	28/12/1916	28/12/1916
Miscellaneous	Routine Orders By Brigadier General R.D.F. Oldman, D.S.O., Commanding 117th Brigade	07/12/1916	07/12/1916
Miscellaneous	Routine Orders By Brigadier General R.D.F. Oldman, D.S.O., Commanding 117th Brigade.	08/12/1916	08/12/1916
Miscellaneous	Routine Orders By Brigadier General R.D.F. Oldman, D.S.O. Commanding 117th Brigade.	14/12/1916	14/12/1916
Miscellaneous	Routine Orders By Brigadier General R.D.F. Oldman, D.S.O., Commanding 117th Brigade.	20/12/1916	20/12/1916

Miscellaneous	Routine Orders By Brigadier General R.D.F. Oldman, D.S.O., Commanding 117th Brigade.	21/12/1916	21/12/1916
Miscellaneous	Routine Orders By Brigadier General R.D.F. Oldman, D.S.O., Commanding 117th Brigade.	23/12/1916	23/12/1916
Miscellaneous	Routine Orders By Brigadier General R.D.F. Oldman, D.S.O., Commanding 117th Brigade.	26/12/1916	26/12/1916
Miscellaneous	Routine Orders By Brigadier General R.D.F. Oldman, D.S.O. Commanding 117th Brigade.	29/12/1916	29/12/1916
Miscellaneous	Routine Orders By Brigadier General R.D.F. Oldman, D.S.O., Commanding 117th Brigade.	31/12/1916	31/12/1916

39TH DIVISION
117TH INFY BDE

BDE HEADQUARTERS

MAR - DEC 1916

39th Division.

The 39th Division disembarked in France
between 4th & 8th March
1916

B. H. Q.

117th INFANTRY BRIGADE.

MARCH 1916

ORIGINAL

Secret.

Army Form C. 2118.

WAR DIARY or INTELLIGENCE SUMMARY

117th Infantry Brigade. (39th Division).

(Erase heading not required.)

Instructions regarding War Diaries and Intelligence Summaries are contained in F. S. Regs., Part II. and the Staff Manual respectively. Title Pages will be prepared in manuscript.

Place	Date 1916	Hour	Summary of Events and Information	Remarks and references to Appendices
STEENBECQUE	10th March		Brigade arrived here intact - attached to First Army, 111 Corps; for detail Brigade see	App. 1.
ESTAIRES	13th do		Brigade moved here (8th Div. Reserve). The rise in temperature from 35% on our arrival in FRANCE to 50% was keenly felt by the troops on the march.	App. 11.
SAILLY	14th do		The Brigade is attached to the 8th Division for Instruction. 16th and 17th Notts & Derby. R. to the 23rd Brigade and 17th K.R.Rif. C. & 16th Rif. Brig. to the 25th Brigade. The instruction to be first individual, then by platoons, companies and battalions in progression.	
SAILLY	20th do		Two companies of each Battalion went up to the trenches at a time the other two resting in billets. During the period of attachment each Battalion had a few casualties, enough to make them realise the real and not enough to upset them. The above arrangements were upset by the move of the 8th Division and of the 39th.	
LAVENTIE	26th do		The Brigade received orders to attack 2 Battalions to the 33rd Division at BETHUNE for instruction.	App. 111.

((1))

SECRET.   ORIGINAL.

                    WAR DIARY.

                117th INFANTRY BRIGADE.
                    (39th. Division).

                       VOLUME 1.

                    10.3.16. — 31.3.16.

        To/
            Officer i/c A.G. Office,
                Base.

Army Form C. 2118

Instructions regarding War Diaries and Intelligence
Summaries are contained in F. S. Regs., Part II.
and the Staff Manual respectively. Title Pages
will be prepared in manuscript.

WAR DIARY
or
INTELLIGENCE SUMMARY

117th Infantry Brigade. (39th Division).

(Erase heading not required.)

Place	Date 1916	Hour	Summary of Events and Information	Remarks and references to Appendices
GONNEHEM	28th March.		Brigade moved from ESTAIRES. 16th Notts & Derby. R. and 16/Rif. Brig. to BETHUNE, to be attached to 33rd Division for Instruction. 17th Notts & Derby. R. and 17th K.R.Rif. C. to Rest billets. 17th Notts & Derby. R. to LA VALLEE and BUSNETTES. Brigade Headquarters, GONNEHEM, 17th K.R.Rif. C. - GONNEHEM. Only 6 men fell out on this march; bands were played and 1½ hours halt made for dinners from Cookers at midday.	App.IV.
do	29th	do	Major-General Commanding 39th Division visited Brigade Headquarters and some billets, with G.O.C. G.O.C. and Bde. Major returned with him to Division Headquarters and saw demonstration of FLAMMENWERFER, which Officers, N.C.O's and men of 17th Notts & Derby. R. and 17th K.R.Rif. C. attended. A very practical demonstration that if men keep low in trench they will not be hurt.	
do	30th	do	G.O.C. left for 33rd Division to see Units carrying out their instruction. Site chosen for 25 yards range for Snipers. Brigade Grenade School started.	

(2)

[signature]
for Brig. Gen.
Commanding 117th Infy Brigade

Appendix 1.

Detail of 117th INFANTRY BRIGADE.

Headquarters.

G.O.C.	Brigadier-General P. HOLLAND, C.B. late Indian Army.	
Bde. Major.	Major C.G. STANSFELD.	8th GURKHA RIFLES.
Staff Captain.	Capt. A.J. STEPHENSON-FETHERSTONHAUGH	6th WORC. R.
Bde Machine Gun Offr	Lieut E. MARSDEN.	MACHINE GUN CORPS
Cmmdg: No.3 Sect. 39th Div. Sig. Co.	2/Lieut. L.W. DELPH.	R.E.

Units.

16th Bn. Notts & Derby. R.	(The Chatsworth Rifles)	Lt Col. C. HERBERT-STEPNEY.
17th Bn. - ditto -	(The Welbeck Rangers)	Lt Col E.B. HALES.
17th Bn. King's Royal Rifle Corps.		Lt Col. E.F. WARD.
16th Rifle Brigade.		Lt Col. H.F. DARELL.
No.3 Section, 39th Div. Signal Co.		2/Lt. L.W. DELPH. R.E.

SECRET.

Appendix II

117th Bde. Order No.1.

Ref. Map. 1/40,000, Sheet 36.A.   12.3.16.

Movements.   1.   The Brigade will march to ESTAIRES on Monday, 13th instant; distance about 12 miles.

Starting Point.   2.   Cross Roads J.2.c.4.8.

2.(a) Units will move to the Starting Point as follows

16/Rif. Brig., followed by 17/K.R.Rif. C. by road opposite Camp through D.25 and via STRENBECQUE STN.
17/Notts & Derby. R., followed by 16/Notts & Derby by road through I.6.a. and b. - D.25.c. and STN.
Brigaded Transport under Lieut. Fishe by MORBECQUE Rd. and D.25.b.

Route.   3.   Route.   Cross roads J.2.c.4.8. LE PARC - LA RUE DES MORTS - PRE A VINS (K.1.c.5.3.) - Cross roads K.15.c.3.2. - Road junction K.16.b.4.2. - VIERHOUCK (K.11.d.) - NEUF BERQUIN - ESTAIRES.

Advanced Guard.   4.
(1 Co. 16/Rif Brig)

Main Body in order of march.

Hd. Qrs.   9.30. a.m.
3 Sig. Sect.
16/Rif. Brig. (less 1 Co.).
17/K.R.Rif. C.   9.36.
17/Notts & Derby. R.
16/Notts & Derby. R. (less 1 Co.)

Rear Guard.
1 Co. 16/Notts & Derby. R.

Halts.   5.   There will be a midday halt for dinners.

Transport.   6.   Four G.S. wagons per Unit will be supplied in addition to the four wagons now with the Train. Blankets will be carried on these wagons and the ground sheet only carried on the man. It is important that the men should not be overloaded.

Ambulances.   7.   Ambulances will march in rear of all Brigade Transport, less 1 with Rear Guard.

Reports.   8.   Reports to Head of Main Body.

                               C. STANSFELD Major
               Brigade Major, 117th BRIGADE.

Issued to the following at 10 a.m. by

Unit		Copy No.
16/Notts & Derby. R.	Orderly	Copy No.1.
17/ do do	do	" 2
17/K.R.Rif. C.	do	" 3
16/Rif. Brig.	do	" 4
3 Sect. Sig. Co.	do	" 5

PTO

3 Sect. Sig. Co.	by Orderly.	Copy No. 5.
H.Q. 39th Div.	do	" 6.
G.O.C.	Personally	" 7.
B.M.	do	" 8.
War Diary.		" 9 & 10.

(COPY).

Appendix III

SECRET. G.S. 197/2.

TRAINING - 39th DIVISION.

The following are the arrangements for the training of the first two Battalions of the 39th Division :-

March 27th: C.O's, Adjutants and Billeting parties arrive.

March 28th: 16th Notts & Derby Regt.) Arrive in BETHUNE and come
            16th Rifle Brigade   ) under the orders of G.O.C.,
) 33rd Division. Both battalions
) billeted at BETHUNE.
Company Commanders visit the trenches.

March 29th: 16th Notts & Derby Regt. comes under the orders of G.O.C 19th Brigade for training by Companies in the AUCHY Section.

16th Rifle Brigade comes under the orders of G.O.C., 98th Brigade for training by companies in the CUINCHY Section.

31/1 April:) Companies come out of trenches into Brigade reserve.
(Night))

April 1st: Rest.

" 2/3rd:) 16th Notts & Derby Regt. begins training as a Battalion
(Night)) in ~~CUINCHY Section~~ AUCHY Section under G.O.C., 19th Bde.

16th Rifle Brigade begins training as a battalion in CUINCHY Section, under orders of G.O.C., 100th Brigade.

April 5/6th: 16th Notts and Derby Regt. and 16th Rifle Brigade
(Night) relieved from the trenches and billet in BETHUNE.

" 6th : 16th Notts & Derby Regt. and 16th Rifle Brigade march out of BETHUNE and cease to be under the orders of G.O.C., 33rd Division.

17th Notts & Derby Regt. and 17th K.R.Rif. C. march into BETHUNE, coming under the orders of G.O.C., 33rd Division

                                                    (Sd.) A. SYMONS, Lieut. Colonel, G.S
                                                             33rd. Division.

26th March, 1916.

SECRET   Appendix IV   Copy No. 7

Ref. Sheet 36.A.   117th Infantry Brigade Order No.4.   27.3.16.
1/40,000.

Movements.
1. Moves for 28th instant are given in attached March Table.
2.   A. Battalion.   17/K.R.Rif. C.
         B.   do   17/Notts & Derby. R.
         C.   do   16/Notts & Derby. R.
         D.   do   16/Rif. Brig.

3. Brigade Headquarters A and B Battalions and No. 3 Co. Div. Train will march as under to GONNEHEM (V. 18) (17/K.R.Rif. C. and Train) and BUSMETTES and LA VALLEE (V. 14.15.16.) (17/Notts & Derby R); distance about 13 miles.

Route.
4. Route. Road N. of River LYS – MERVILLE – LE Gd. PACAUT (K.35.d.) – GALONNE – ROBECQ – MARQUOIS – Road junction P.36.b.1.2. – Cross Roads V.5.b.5.2. – GONNEHEM.

Starting Point.
5. Starting Point – for A and B Battalions and Train, Cross Roads L.28.d. central.

Advanced Guard.
6.

1 Coy. 17/Notts & Derby R

Main body in order of march.

Brigade Headquarters   9.15. a.m.
17/Notts & Derby. R. (less 1 Coy.)
17/K.R.Rif. C. (less 1 Coy.)

     Transport.
No.3 Co. Div. Train.

Rear Guard.

1 Coy. 17/K.R.Rif. C.

Ambulance.
7. 1 Motor Ambulance from No. 134 Field Ambulance will accompany the Rear Guard.

Halts.
8. Cookers may be used en route and a halt will be made for dinners about midday.

Bands.
9. There is no objection to bands playing on the march.

16/Notts & Derby R)
17/Notts & Derby R)
10. The 16/Notts & Derby. R. and 16/Rif. Brig. march under the orders of the Senior Officer under separate instructions to BETHUNE, the former will be attached to the 19th Brigade at ANNEQUIN FOSSE, the latter to the 98th Brigade at LE PREOL.

Reports.
11. Reports to Head of Main Body.

                                 C. STANFELD Major
                          Bde. Major, 117th. BRIGADE

Issued to :-
         O.C. 16/Notts & Derby. R.   1
         O.C. 17/Notts & Derby. R.   2
         O.C. 17/K.R.Rif. C.   3
         O.C. 16/Rif. Brig.   4
         G.O.C.   by hand   5
         B.M.   6
         S.C.   7
         Signals   8
√   War Diary   9

39th Division.

B. H. Q.

117th INFANTRY BRIGADE

APRIL 1916 ::

Appendices attached:- Relief Orders
Defence Scheme.

Army Form C. 2118

WAR DIARY
or
INTELLIGENCE SUMMARY

VOLUME 2.

(Erase heading not required.)

Instructions regarding War Diaries and Intelligence Summaries are contained in F. S. Regs. Part II. and the Staff Manual respectively. Title Pages will be prepared in manuscript.

Original

Place	Date April	Hour	Summary of Events and Information	Remarks and references to Appendices
GONNE-HEM	2nd		Brigadier-General P. HOLLAND is placed on Sick List, Influenza. As the Brigade is split up it was not considered advisable to recall Lieut. Colonel DARELL and the Command of the 2 Battalions here devolved on Lieut. Colonel E.B. HALES, 17/Notts & Derby. R.	
	4th		Lieut. General Sir R.C.B. HAKING, K.C.B., Commanding XIth Corps inspected 17/Notts & Derby. R and 17/K.R.Rif. C.; expressed himself very pleased with the former and said the latter required more drill, and that he would see them again in a month.	
	6th		Brigadier-General HOLLAND is taken off the Sick List. 16/Notts & Derby. R and 16/Rif. Brig. are relieved by the 17/Notts & Derby. R and 17/K.R.Rif. C.	Appendix 1.
	7th		Bde. Major visited 17/Notts & Derby. R in 19th Bde. They seem to be settling down quite comfortably.	
	8th		Bde. Major visited 17/Notts & Derby. R. in 19th Bde. They were cooking in front trench, which does not seem as good as having dinners carried up.	
	9th		Bde. Major visited 17/K.R.Rif. C., attached to 100th Bde. They had just had a bad time from enemy trench mortars, but did not seem to mind much. Bde Major returns to Bde. Headquarters.	
	10th		16/Notts & Derby. R. and 16/Rif. Brig. Inspected by Corps Commander; expressed himself pleased with them. He noticed that the clothing of the former was a good deal stained; this is due to having been accustomed to economise in clothing in England and to absence of cleaning material in the way of acid, etc.	

1875. Wt. W593/826 1,000,000 4/15 J.B.C. & A. A.D.S.S./Forms/C.2118.

Army Form C. 2118

Sheet No. 2.

WAR DIARY
or
INTELLIGENCE SUMMARY
(Erase heading not required.)

Instructions regarding War Diaries and Intelligence Summaries are contained in F. S. Regs., Part II. and the Staff Manual respectively. Title Pages will be prepared in manuscript.

Place	Date April	Hour	Summary of Events and Information	Remarks and references to Appendices
GONNE-HEM	11th		Conference of C.O's of Units here – discussed points requiring attention; training of patrols in night work. Arranged class in wiring with 13th Glosters (Pioneers). Physical training and Bayonet class started under Aldershot Instructors. G.O.C. visited trenches of Right Section, 33rd Division, where 17/Notts & Derby. R. had taken over Right of 98th Bde as a Battalion. All ranks were much interested in their work. A good deal of rifle grenade fire was going on and unfortunately the Battalion lost 1 man killed and 1 wounded by a German rifle grenade. G.O.C. saw a big mine sprung by the Germans, right of 90th Bde Line – no damage done, but big crater formed.	
	12th		Received orders from 39th Division to move on 16th to Div. Reserve LOCON Area. G.O.C. visited trenches of Left Section, 33rd Div., where 17/K.R.Rif. C. had taken over Reserve of 100th Bde, accompanied by G.O.C., 100th Bde. A good deal of bombing had taken place the previous night. This is a difficult line and it took the Battalion some time to find themselves and realise what work was required on defence constructions. Heavy rain all day. Trenches difficult to work in.	
	13th		Bde. Major visited 113th Bde. in LOCON Area to get orders for posts, local orders, etc. Instructors from 13th Glosters (Pioneers) hold day and night class of 4 Officers and 16 N.C.O's from each of 16/Notts & Derby.R. and 16/Rif. Brig. in rapid wiring by day and night.	
	15th		Temporary Brigadier-General R.D.F. OLDMAN, D.S.O. took over Command of the Bde. from Brigadier-General W. J. T. GLASGOW, C.B. A.D.S.A. reinforcement mining party of 500 all ranks is detailed for period	App. 2.

WAR DIARY or **INTELLIGENCE SUMMARY**

(Erase heading not required.)

Army Form C. 2118

Sheet No. 3.

Instructions regarding War Diaries and Intelligence Summaries are contained in F.S. Regs., Part II. and the Staff Manual respectively. Title Pages will be prepared in manuscript.

Place	Date	Hour	Summary of Events and Information	Remarks and references to Appendices
Near LOCON	16th		whilst in Divisional Reserve. Bde. moved to LOCON Area by Battalions and 1s Bde. in Div. Reserve. G.O.C. saw 17/Notts & Derby. R., 17/K.R.Rif. C. and 16/Rif. Brig. on the march. G.O.C. reconnoitred assembly posts in the afternoon.	App. 3.
	17th		G.O.C. visited Headquarters, 118th Brigade and Headquarters, 98th Brigade. G.O.C. inspected Bde. Bombing School.	
	18th		G.O.C. inspected 16/Notts & Derby. R. in billets and visited Div. Headquarters in afternoon. G.O.C. lectured to Coy. Commanders on Trench Administration.	
	19th		G.O.C. visited G.O.C., 118th Bde. G.O.C. inspected 16/Rif. Brig.	
	20th		G.O.C. inspected 17/K.R.Rif. C. Bombers were unable to throw 20 yards. Attended Divisional Conference.	
	21st		G.O.C. inspected posts in GORRE - ESSARS System. Visited 3 Battalion Headquarters and various parts of the line in FESTUBERT Section.	
	22nd		G.O.C. visited Machine Gun Co. training with 118th Bde. Lectured to C.O's and Coy. Commanders. 117th Bde. relieves 118th Bde in "C" (FESTUBERT) Section (Left) front line. 16/Rig. Brig. in Right Subsection "C". 1, 16/Notts & Derby. R. in Left Subsection "C". 2. 17/K.R.Rff. C. in Support, 17/Notts & Derby. R. in Reserve; 116th Bde. on our Right, 105th Bde. on our Left.	App. 4 & 4.A.
	23rd		Permanent garrisons of posts in GORRE - ESSARS System relieved by 118th Bde.	App. 5.

Army Form C. 2118

WAR DIARY
or
INTELLIGENCE SUMMARY
(Erase heading not required.)

Sheet No. 4.

Instructions regarding War Diaries and Intelligence Summaries are contained in F. S. Regs., Part II. and the Staff Manual respectively. Title Pages will be prepared in manuscript.

Place	Date April	Hour	Summary of Events and Information	Remarks and references to Appendices
LOISNE	24th		OPERATIONS. Patrols went out to learn front. WORK. Maintenance and repairs. INTELLIGENCE. Nil. Attitude of enemy quiet.	
	25th		Situation Normal. Slight shelling by enemy. Parapets and dug-outs strengthened. Enemy quiet. L.T.M. Batt. 117/1 receives 4.- 3.7" Trench Mortars.	
	26th		Enemy shelled ISLAND No.3 (A.3.c.7.8.), O.B.L. and BARNTON Rd. Machine gun activity at night. Parapets, etc. repaired and strengthened. Improvement to keeps.	
	27th		O.B.L. lightly shelled. Maintenance and improvements. Observation loophole constructed at A3.c.1.3. Great improvement in communication trenches. Opposite C.l. German working parties seen to go out wiring every night.	App. 6.
			Inter Battalion Relief took place night 27/28th.	
	28th		L.T.M. Batt. 117/2 receives 2 Stokes Mortars 3". Quiet day. Work on fire-steps SHETLAND Rd and improvements to trenches, etc.	
	29th		Slight Artillery activity on both sides. Work of connecting Islands continued and repairs and maintenance of breastworks.	
	30th		Enemy machine guns active at night. Officers' patrol reports enemy wire thick opposite CANADIAN ORCHARD.	

SECRET.   War Diary Appendix I   Copy No.

117th BRIGADE ORDER No. 5.

Ref. Sheet BETHUNE.   4.4.16.

MOVEMENTS.   In accordance with 33rd Division Training Memo G.S. 197/2 of 27th March and 39th Division No.39/G/1/13 of 31st March, 16.

The 17/Notts & Derby. R., 17/K.R.Rif. C. and L.T.M. Batt. 117/2 will march to BETHUNE on the 6th instant, under Lieut. Colonel E.B. HALES, 17/Notts & Derby. R. via OBLINGHEM, to arrive at BETHUNE about 12.30. p.m.

Lieut. Colonel Hales will issue his own orders for the march.

                               Major
                 Brigade Major, 117th. BRIGADE

Issued to the following at 1 p.m. by   Copy No.

O.C. 16/Notts & Derby. R.	Orderly	1
O.C. 17/Notts & Derby. R.	do	2
O.C. 17/K.R.Rif. C.	do	3
O.C. 16/Rif. Brig.	do	4
O.C. 3 Co. Div. Train	do	5
General Staff, 39th Division	do	6
G.O.C.	hand	7
B.M.	do	8
S.C.	do	9
Signals	do	10
War Diary	do	11

"A" Form.　　　　　　　　　　　　　Army Form C. 2121.
MESSAGES AND SIGNALS.

Prefix	Code	m.	Words	Charge	This message is on a/c of:	Recd. at	m.
Office of Origin and Service Instructions.			Sent		......................Service.	Date	
			At......m.			From	
			To		(Signature of "Franking Officer.")	By	
			By				

TO { 39th ...... 16 SE 17 SE
     O.C. 17 K.R.Rif. C. 16 R. B. Brig.
     O.C. 3rd Div Train V.C. Sigs.

Sender's Number.	Day of Month	In reply to Number		AAA
* 117/S/41	4.4.16	—		

Reference Bde Order 5
4th aaq the two Battalions
will march by 33rd Div
March Table of S/194/3 of 4th
and not as therein stated
was

From: 16th
Place: 117/Bde
Time:
The above may be forwarded as now corrected.　(Z)　EK.
　　　　　　　　Censor.　Signature of Addressor or person authorised to telegraph in his name.
* This line should be erased if not required.

SECRET.   Copy No. 13

117th INFANTRY BRIGADE ORDER No. 7.

                                                                 15.4.16.
Ref. Sheet
BETHUNE. 1/40,000.

Working Parties.   1.   A Permanent Mining Working Party will be
                        detailed as under :-
                        The party will be attached to the 13th Glosters
                        Pioneers for rations and discipline and will
                        rendezvous at Headquarters, 16/Rif. Brig.
                        (W.4.c.3.8.) at 10.30 a.m., 17th instant and
                        march under the orders of the Senior Officer to
                        FERME DU ROI (E.6.c.), where they will be billeted.

                        They will be rationed up to and for 18th instant.
                        The Senior Officer of the party will report to Bde
                        Headquarters a detail of the duties required of him,
                        by noon, 18th instant.

                               16/Notts & Derby. R.   250 all ranks.
                               16/Rif. Brig.   250 all ranks.

Medical.   2.   Para. 7 (Medical) of Brigade Order 6 is cancelled:
                        Field Ambulances move as follows :-

                        132nd F. Amb. on 18th, from ROBECQ to BOIS DE
                                                              PACAUT.
                        134th F. Amb. on 18th, from ROBECQ to LES PLEAUX.

                        133rd F. Amb. on 19th, from CALONNE to White House
                                                              near ESSARS.

                                                                     Major
                                         Brigade Major, 117th. BRIGADE.

                        Issued to the following at 6 p.m. IY   Copy No.

                        O.C. 16/Notts & Derby. R.   D.R.   1
                        O.C. 17/Notts & Derby. R.   D.R.   2
                        O.C. 17/K.R.Rif. C.   D.R.   3
                        O.C. 16/Rif. Brig.   D.R.   4
                        O.C. 13/Glos. Pioneers.   D.R.   5
                        O.C. 3 Co. Div. Train   D.R.   6
                        S.O. L.T.M. Batt, 117/1, 117/2.   D.R.   7
                        General Staff, 39th Div.   D.R.   8
                        G.O.C.   Hand   9
                        D.C.   do   10
                        S.C.   do   11
                        Signals   do   12
                        War Diary   do   13

SECRET.   WAR DIARY   Appendix
                                          COPY No.

              117th BRIGADE ORDER No.8.
                                               14.4.16.
Ref Sheet
BETHUNE   Appendix 3
1/40,000.

Information.   1. The 39th Division is to relieve the 38th
                    Division in the GIVENCHY and FESTUBERT Sections,
                    having the 33rd Division on the right and the
                    35th Division on the left.
                    Relief to be completed by 20th April.

Reliefs.   2. 116th Inf. Bde is to hold the GIVENCHY Section.
                    118th   "   " " "   "   " FESTUBERT   "
                    117th   "   " " "   "   be in Divisional Reserve.

Movements.   3. Units of the Brigade will move in accordance
                    with attached move table "A".

Working Parties. 4. While in Reserve a Permanent Mining working party
                    of 500 of all ranks will be found from the Bde.
                    in Divisional Reserve. These will be found
                    from the 16/Notts & Derby. R. and 16/Rif. Brig.;
                    details will be issued later, but the relief will
                    probably be on the 18th.

Permanent   5. The 16/Rif. Brig will find the permanent
Garrisons.   garrison of posts in the GORRE-ESSARS System,
                    relieving a unit of the 116th Brigade on the 15th
                    instant under separate instructions.
                    The 17/K.R.Rif. C. will relieve the 16/Rif. Brig.
                    in those permanent garrisons on the 18th instant
                    under arrangements between C.O's. Relief to be
                    reported when complete in both cases. Lists of
                    Posts have been issued to units concerned.

Supply.   6. Refilling point as at present.

Medical.   7. The 132nd F.A. will move to CANAL HOUSE.
                      " 133rd   "   "   "   " MES PLAUX
                      " 134th   "   "   "   " VIELLE CHAPELLE

Report Centre   8. 39th Div. Report Centre is to close at LESPRE:
                    at 10 a.m. 17th instant and reopen at the same
                    hour at LOCON.
                    117th Bde. Report Centre will close at
                    GORRE at 11 a.m. 16th instant and reopen at
                    W.6.d.4.5. at the same hour.

                                                        Major
                                    Bde. Major, 117th BRIGADE
                Issued to the following
                                by   at 4 p.m. Copy No.
                O.C. 16/Notts & Derby Orderly   1
                O.C. 17/   do   do   2
                O.C. 17/K.R.Rif. C.   do   3
                O.C. 16/Rif. Brig.   do   4
                O.C. 3 Co. Div. Train do   5
                S.C. L.T.M. Batt. 117/1
                       & 117/2   do   6
                General Staff, 39th Div. do   7.
                115th Brigade   do   8
                116th Brigade   do   9
                C.R.E.   Tent   10
                R...   11
                D.C.   do   12
                Signals   do   13
                War Diary   14

Table A

March Table to accompany 117th Brigade Order No.6.

| Date | Unit | Moves. | | Route. | Relieving | Remarks. |
		From	To	Reference Sheet BETHUNE		
16th April	16/Notts & Derby R	BUSNETTES & LA VALLEE	Q.26.b.8.4.	Cross Roads V.2.d.7.2. - BUSNES - LALEAU - MARQUOIS - CARRIN.	14/R.W.F.	Times of moves will be notified later.
	17/Notts & Derby R	BETHUNE	W.17.a.3.8.	Under orders to be issued by Lieut. Colonel HALES.	15/R.W.F.	
	17/K.R.Rif. C.	- do -	W.18.d.5.3.		13/R.W.F.	
	16/Rif. Brig.	GONNEHEM	W.4.c.3.8.	LANOY - HINGES - PONT L'Hinges.	16/R.W.F.	
	Bde. Head Qrs 117/1 L.T.M. Batt (less 1 Section) 117/2 L.T.M. Batt	- do -	W.6.d.4.5.	LANOY - HINGES - HINGETTE - AVELETTE.	H.Q. 113th Inf Bde.	

Billeting Parties can arrive any time on the 16th.

SECRET.

Appendix 4 — W D
15

117th INFANTRY BRIGADE ORDER No. 8.

Reference Map BETHUNE (Combined Sheet). 1/40,000.   21.4.16.

RELIEF.	1.	The 117th Infantry Brigade will relieve the 118th Infantry Brigade in FESTUBERT Section on April 23rd and night 23/24th, in accordance with attached Relief Table A. Posts to be relieved in accordance with attached Relief Table B.
		All details not mentioned to be arranged by C.O's concerned.
LEWIS GUN SECTION	2.	Lewis Gun Sections of 17/Notts & Derby.R and 17/K.R Rif. C. to relieve 1/1 Ches. R. and 1/1 Herts. R. respectively in RICHMOND, COVER TRENCHES and ISLANDS on the night of 22/23rd April under arrangements made by Commanding Officers concerned.
MACHINE GUN Co.	3.	O.C. 117th Bde. Machine Gun Co. will arrange for one Vickers Gun to be placed on each of the following posts :-
		LE PLANTIN - FESTUBERT & FESTUBERT EAST.
FORMATIONS.	4.	Troops moving in the FESTUBERT Area will use the following Formations :-
		West of CANAL DE LA LAWE in formed bodies as usual.
		East of the Canal and West of the road LA COUTURE - LE TOURET - LOISNE - GORRE, in Platoons at 200 yds. distance.
		East of this road by Sections at 100 yards distance.
ADVANCE PARTY.	5.	O.C's 16/Notts & Derby. R. and 16/Rif. Brig. will detail one officer per Company, and one N.C.O. per Platoon to proceed to the trenches on the night of 22/23rd April, and remain there until their Battalions arrive.
MARCHES.	6.	To shorten the march of the 16/Notts & Derby. R. the 17/K.R.Rif. C. will close up their billets so as to leave billets for 2 Coys free from 12 noon 23rd, and 16/Notts & Derby. R. will occupy these from 12 noon till the evening.

Sheet No.2.

COMMAND. 7. Until Relief is complete all Units of 117th Brigade who may be in the 118th Brigade Area will be under the Command of the G.O.C., 118th Infantry Brigade.

DEFENCE SCHEME 8. A copy of the Defence Scheme is attached.

REPORTS. 9. Reports when relief is complete will be made by O.C's Units to Brigade Headquarters at LOISNE (M.26.a.3.7.).

                                          [signature]
                                              Major,
                          Brigade Major, 117th BRIGADE.

Issued at 6.15. p.m.	By.	Copy No.
16/Notts & Derby. R.	D.R.	1
17 do do	D.R.	2
17/K.R.Rif. C.	D.R.	3
16/Rif. Brig.	D.R.	4
O.C. L.T.M. Batt. 117/1 & 2.	D.R.	5
117/Bde. Machine Gun Co.	Personally	6
No.3 Sect. Sig. Co.	do	7
No.3 Co. Div. Train.	D.R.	8
Head Qrs., 39th Div.	D.R.	9
G.O.C.	Personally	10
B.M.	do	11
S.C.	do	12
118th Brigade	D.R.	13
Intelligence Officer	Personally	14
War Diary (2 copies)	do	15
Order File	do	16

SECRET.

RELIEF TABLE of 118th Infantry Brigade by 117th Infantry Brigade.

(To accompany 117th Infantry Brigade Order No.3, dated 21st Apl. 1916)

Date 1916	UNIT	To	Route	Relieving.	Proceeding to	Taking over Billets from	Time	Guides
23/4/16	16/Notts & Derby	Left Front Subsection S.21.a.2.2.	Any convenient	1/1 Cambs R	RIEZ du VINAGE ENLARGING Q.26.b.8.4.	16/Notts & Derby	Notts proceed beyond LE TOURET before 8 p.m.	At LE TOURET CrossRoads I.16. Central. 8 p.m.
23/4/16	17/ do do	LE TOURET (Reserve) I.16.	LOCON	1/6 CHES. R	HINGETTE V.17.a.3.8.	17/ do do	Head of 17/ Notts & Derby to be at LE TOURET by 12 noon	
23/4/16	117/1) T.M Batt 117/2) 117 Bde Machine Gun Co.	LE HAMEL X.20.d.	Any convenient	113/1) T.M.B 113/2) 113 Bde M.G	V.12.a.5.6. V.6.d.4.5.	117/1)T.M. Batt 117/2)	Any convenient before noon.	
23/4/16	117th Bde Hd Qrs	LOISNE X.28.a.3.7.	ditto	118th Bde Hd Qrs.	V.6.d.4.5.	118th Bde H.w.	To reach LOISNE by 3 pm	
23/4/16	17/K.R.Rif. C.	FESTUBERT (Support Line) S.13.d.5.10.	As arranged by C.O'it	1/1 HERTS. R	LES CHOQUAU V.13.d.5.3.	17/K.R.Rif. C.		Junction of RUE DU BOIS and RUE DE L'EPINETTE S.13.c.1.5.
23/4/16	16/Rif. Brig.	Right Front Subsection A.2.b.1.4.	ditto	Black Watch	LA PANNERIE V.6.d.4.5.	16/Rif. Brig.	3 p.m.	FESTUBERT Cross Roads at 3 p.m.

Table

TABLE OF RELIEF OF PO.P.

To accompany 117th Infantry Brigade Order No.3, dated 21st pl. 1916.

Dat.	Post.	Strength.	Unit.	Relieving.	Time.
23/4/16	LE PLANTIN. N. A.2.c.2.5.	1 Platoon. 1 M.G.	17/K.R.Rif. C	1/1 Herts. R.	Day Reliefs as arranged by Commanding Officers.
do	FESTUBERT S.25.d.Cenl	1 Platoon 1 M.G.	do	do	do
do	FESTUBERT S.26.c.4.4.	1 Platoon 1 M.G.	do	do	do
do	CAILLOUX. N. S.25.b.3.7.	1 Platoon.	do	do	do
do	CAILLOUX. S. S.25.b.8.9.	1 Platoon	do	do	do
do	EPINETTE. X.24.a.1.6.	1 F.C.O. and 3 men.	do	do	do
do	ROUTE. A. X.29.b.7.3.	ditto	17/Notts & Derby R	1/5 Ch.s. R.	do
do	TUNING FORK. E. X.29.d.9.2.	ditto	do	do	do
do	LOISNE. N. X.22.a.0.3.	ditto	do	do	do
do	LOISNE. E. X.23.a.6.3.	ditto	do	do	do
do	LE TOURET Cenl X.16.d.2.9.	ditto	do	do	do
do	LE TOURET. E. A.17.c.2.8.	ditto	do	do	do

PROVISIONAL. Copy No.....

BRIGADE DEFENCE SCHEME. (FESTUBERT SECTION).

1. DESCRIPTION. (a) The Section of the Front occupied by the Brigade is divided into two Sub-Sections, namely :- Right Sub-Section, C.1. and Left Sub-Section, C.2., each held by a Battalion which is responsible for ISLANDS and O.B.L. in the Sub-Section.
(b) SUPPORT LINE. - Village Line.
(c) RESERVE. (The position of Assembly. LE TOURET DEFENCES).

2. GARRISON. Four Infantry Battalions.
Three Sections Bde. M.G. Coy. - 12 Vickers Guns.

3. DISTRIBUTION O.B. LINE & ISLANDS :-
Right Front Section, 1 Bn. - 8 Lewis and 2 Vickers Guns.
Left Front Section, ditto ditto ditto
SUPPORT LINE. 1 Battalion. - 3 Vickers Guns.
RESERVE. (In the hands of the G.O.C.) 1 Bn. - 5 Vickers Guns.

4. MACHINE GUNS. The Vickers Guns are distributed as follows :-
O.B.L. Right Front Section .... 2 Vickers.
O.B.L. Left Front Section. .... ditto
FESTUBERT POST. E. .... 1 ditto
FESTUBERT POST .... 1 ditto
LE PLANTIN POST .... 1 ditto
IN RESERVE .... 5 ditto

5. PLAN. In the event of the right Battalion of the Brigade on our left being driven in, SHETLAND ROAD will be occupied in order to protect our left flank. With this in view the O/C Bn. holding left Sub-Section will arrange that SHETLAND ROAD is fire-stepped and a garrison detailed. Similarly, should the left Battalion of the Brigade on our right be driven in, the O/C Bn. holding right Sub-Section will occupy GRENADIER ROAD. He will at once fire-step GRENADIER ROAD for defence and detail a garrison. In the event of a frontal attack on the Bde. Section, it must be clearly understood that every endeavour will be made to hold on to the ISLAND LINE. The O.B.L. should be kept in a state of thorough repair at all times, so as to be available should the enemy succeed in breaking through the ISLANDS, and it will be held at all costs.

The O/C Bn. in Support in the Village Line will understand that the OBLIGATORY Garrisons and the Vickers Guns of the Posts in his area, are not to be moved on any account, but the remainder of his Battalion is available for reinforcing the Battalions in front, if called upon.
The Battalion and five Machine Guns in Reserve will remain in the hands of the G.O.C. and will rendezvous behind the LE TOURET line in X.22.b. and d.
Taking into consideration the above distribution of the Bde. O.C's Units will make up their Local Defence Schemes, and forward them to this office as soon as possible. The G.O.C. wishes it to be clearly understood that the ISLAND LINE is the first line of resistance, and to that end he hopes that all O.C's will work to join up the Islands, and re-establish this line to its former strength as quickly as possible. Battalions in the front line requiring working parties from those in support will report details of party required and work to be done to Bde. Headquarters.

Major
Brigade Major, 117th. BRIGADE

21st April, 1916

SECRET.   Copy No.

117th INFANTRY BRIGADE Order No. 8a
4A

Reference Sheet BETHUNE   22.4.16.
     1/40,000

Routes.   1. The following amendments are made to Table A of Brigade
              Order No.8 of 21st.

              Column 4 Route.

              16/Notts & Derby. R.   Starting Point LOCON central.
              Starting Time. 6.30. p.m. Route. PONT TOURNANT - LES FAUQUIS
              - RUE de BOIS - X.21.c.9.9. thence to LE TOURET Cross Roads
              X.16. central.

              17/K.R.Rif. C.   Starting Point and Route as for 16/Notts &
              Derby. R. to Cross Roads S.13.d.1.5. Starting Time 7.20. pm.

              16/Rif. Brig.   Route. DRAWBRIDGE AVALETTE - LES CHOQUAUX
              - X.13.a.2.9. - LES GLATIGNIES - LE HAMEL - GORRE - R.5. -
              FESTUBERT Cross Roads - not to pass X.13.a.2.9. before 5.30 pm.

              Column 5. 16/Rif. Brig. - for W.6.d.4.5. read W.4.c.8.6.

              Column 9. "Guides", 17/K.R.Rif. C. add 9 p.m.

Road   2. Captain COHEN, Asst. Staff Captain, LOCON Central and
Controls   X.13.a.2.9.

              Lieut. AROLIN - LE TOURET Cross Roads to S.13.d.1.5.

Report   3. The Brigade Report Centre will close at W.6.d.4.5. at 3 p.m.
Centre   and reopen at LOISNE X.23.a.3.7. at the same hour.

                                                    Mansfield   Major
                                            Brigade Major, 117th BRIGADE

              Issued at 6.15. p.m. to   By.   Copy No.

              16/Notts & Derby. R.   D.R.   1
              17/   do   do   D.R.   2
              17/K.R.Rif. C.   D.R.   3
              16/Rif. Brig.   D.R.   4
              S.O. L.T.. Batt. 117/1 & 2.   D.R.   5
              117/Bde. Machine Gun Co.   Personally   6
              No.3 Sect. Sig. Co.   do   7
              No.3 Co. Div. Train   D.R.   8
              Headquarters, 39th Div.   D.R.   9
              G.O.C.   Personally   10
              B.M.   do   11
              S.C.   do   12
              118th Brigade   D.R.   13
              Intelligence Officer.   Personally   14
              War Diary (2 copies)   do   15 & 16.
              Order File   do   17

SECRET

Appendix 5

Copy No. 8

117th INFANTRY BRIGADE Order No.7.

21.4.16.

1. Relief.   Under arrangements with G.O.C., 118th Brigade the 1/1 HERTS.
will relieve the 17/K.R.RIF. C. of the permanent garrisons
of posts in the GORRE – ESSARS System vide attached Table A,
on the 22nd instant.

All details to be arranged between C.O's concerned.

Relief to be reported.

C. Seel, Major
Brigade Major, 117th Brigade

Issued at 9 a.m. to	By	Copy No.
O.C. 17/K.R.RIF. C.	D.R.	1
O.C. 3 Sect. Sig. Co.	Personally	2
G.O.C.	do	3
B.M.	do	4
S.C.	do	5
Headquarters, 39th Div.	D.R.	6
118th Brigade (4 copies Table A)	D.R.	7
War Diary	Personally	8
War Diary	do	9

Garrisons and Stores - Comb - Weak System

	Map reference Sheet 52/NW/4	Maximum Garrison	Machine Guns	Permanent Garrison	
				Prox Reserve Bn at COSHF	Each post contains the following stores :-
1. C AND GROUP (3 works) CHOP Or Pit	F.8.a.c.d.	1 Co.	8		1 Inveray Board
2.	T.1.b.5.2.	1½ Pls.	2		1 Billhook
3. LA HUTTE	X.26.c.4.5.	½ Pl.	1		1 Pick
4. RIVER	X.25.a. central	2 Pls.	4		4 Shovels
5. EAST BRIDGE	W.24.c.8.0.	1 Pl.	1	one N.C.O. and 2 men	1 Maul
6. LONG CORNER	X.23.b.7.2.	1½ Pls.	2		2 Wire-cutters
7. LE RUTOI	X.22.d.7.6.	½ Pl.	1		1 Pair of toes
8. C HAZEL, R...	X.19.b.7.6.	1½ Pls.	2		1 Pump	except posts
9. LAST	X.18.c.7.4.	1 Pl.	1		2 Hose lengths	2,3 & 9.
10. MRS PLACE. ..	X.14.a.6.5.	1 Pl.	1		
11. LE-TUREHAM	U.15.a.5.7.	1 Pl.	2		

SECRET.   Copy No. 9

117th INFANTRY BRIGADE Order No.7.

21.4.18.

1. Relief.   Under arrangements with G.O.C., 118th Brigade the 1/1 HERTS.
              will relieve the 17/K.R.Rif. C. of the permanent garrisons
              of posts in the GORRE - ESSARS System vide attached Table A,
              on the 23rd instant.

              All details to be arranged between C.O's concerned.

              Relief to be reported.

                                                    Chifcul . Major
                                            Brigade Major, 117th Brigade.

Issued at 9 a.m. to   BY   Copy No.

O.C. 17/K.R.Rif. C.   D.R.   1
O.C. 3 Sect. Sig. Co.   Personally   2
G.O.C.   do   3
B.M.   do   4
S.C.   do   5
Headquarters, 39th Div.   D.R.   6
118th Brigade (4 copies Table A)   D.R.   7
War Diary   Personally   8
War Diary   do   9

Table A

Garrisons and Stores - GORRE - ESSARS System.

POST	Map reference Sheet BETHUNE	Maximum Garrison	Machine Guns	Permanent Garrison	
1. GORRE GROUP (3 works)	F.3.b.c.d.	1 Co.	3	From Reserve Sn at GORRE	Each post contains the following stores :-
2. CROIX de FER	F.1.b.5.2.	1½ Pls	2		1 Inventory Board
3. LA MOTTE	X.26.c.4.5.	½ Pl.	-		1 Billhook
4. ESSARS	X.25.a. central	2 Pls.	4		1 Pick
5. LAWE BRIDGE	N.24.c.8.0.	½ Pl.	1		4 Shovels
6. LONG CORNER	N.23.b.7.2.	1½ Pls.	2	One N.C.O. and 3 men	1 Maul
7. LE HAMEL	X.20.d.7.6.	½ Pl.	1		2 Wirecutters
8. LE HAMEL N.W.	X.19.b.7.6.	1½ Pls.	2		1 Plan of Keep
9. LAWE	X.13.c.7.4.	1 Pl.	-		1 Pump
10. LES PLAUX. F	X.14.a.6.5.	3 Pl.	-		2 Hose lengths } except Posts 2,3 &5.
11. LES CAOCHAN	X.16.a.5.7.	1 Pl.	2		

SECRET   Appendix 6.   W.D.
                                                          Copy No. 18

117th INFANTRY BRIGADE Order No.10.

                                                          26.4.16.

Relief. 1. An inter Battalion relief will take place in accordance with attached Relief Table on the night 27/28th.

Dispositions. 2. 16/Notts & Derby. R. become Battalion in Support.
17/Notts & Derby. R. take over "C".1.
17/K.R.Rif. C.   "   "   "C".2.
16/Rif. Brig. become Battalion in Reserve.

Time. 3. Relief will commence at 3.30. p.m. and will be continuous. Companies moving up will not be delayed for rations.
Signallers will be relieved during daylight.
All details not mentioned to be arranged between Commanding Officers concerned.

Trench Stores. 4. Battalion Trench Store Lists will be handed over.

Reports. 5. Completion of relief to be reported to Bde. Headquarters.

                                                          Major
                                    Brigade Major, 117th. BRIGADE

Issued at 3.0. p.m. to

	By.	Copy No.
16/Notts & Derby. R.	D.R.	1
17/Notts & Derby. R.	D.R.	2
17/K.R.Rif. C.	D.R.	3
16/Rif. Brig.	D.R.	4
L.T.M. Batt. 117/1.	D.R.	5
L.T.M. Batt. 117/2.	D.R.	6
117/Bde. Machine Gun Co.	D.R.	7
3 Sect. Signal Co.	Orderly	8
3 Co. Div. Train.	D.R.	9
G.O.C.	Personally	10
B.M.	do	11
S.C.	do	12
Bde. Grenade Officer	do	13
Intelligence Officer.	do	14
H.Q., 39th Div.	D.R.	15
116th Bde.	D.R.	16
Group Cmmdr., R.A.	D.R.	17
War Diary	-	18 & 19
Order File	-	20
105th Bde.	D.R.	21
225 Co., R.E.	D.R.	22

RELIEF TABLE.

To accompany 117th Infantry Brigade Order No.10, dated 26.4.16.

-6-

Date.	Unit.	Relieves.	Position. -6-	Guides.	Route.	Relieved unit proceeds to	Remarks.
27/4/16	17/Notts & Derby. R.	16/Rif Brig.	Right Front Section and ISLANDS.	As arranged by C.O's.	Rd junction K.16.c.9.3. - Rd junction F.4.b.9.5. & then as arranged between C.O's	Reserve Billets at le TOURET.	Relief not to commence before 6.30. p.m.
27/4/16	17/K.R.Rif C	16/Notts & Derby. R	Left Front Section & ISLANDS.	do	As arranged by C.O's.	VILLAGE LINE	do

39th Division.

B. H. Q.

117th INFANTRY BRIGADE

MAY 1916

Brigade Orders attached:

SECRET ORIGINAL

Army Form C. 2118

WAR DIARY
or
INTELLIGENCE SUMMARY
(Erase heading not required.)

Instructions regarding War Diaries and Intelligence Summaries are contained in F. S. Regs., Part II. and the Staff Manual respectively. Title Pages will be prepared in manuscript.

Place	Date May	Hour	Summary of Events and Information	Remarks and references to Appendices
LOISNE FESTUBERT SECTION	1st		A quiet day. BARNTON Road and GEORGE St. lightly shelled. Officers' patrol reports enemy wire thick opposite CANADIAN ORCHARD. Usual work on Maintenance, etc. Inter-Battalion relief on night of 1/2nd May. Our snipers claim one victim.	App. 1. App. 11.
	2nd		Le PLANTIN and OLD GERMAN LINE shelled. NO MAN'S LAND drying up. Trench orders issued.	
	3rd		Enemy working parties seem less active. One German bagged by our snipers. Work of joining Islands 10 and 10.A. continued.	
	4th		FIFE Road - CHESHIRE Road - SHETLAND AVENUE and RICHMOND TERRACE shelled.	
	5th		Enemy snipers more active. Work on Islands and O.B.L. continued.	App.111
	6th to 9th		Inter-battalion relief on night 5/6th. Nothing of interest to record.	
	Night 9/10th		Brigade is relieved by 116th Infantry Brigade and moves into Divisional Reserve Rest Billets near LOCON.	App. IV.
Near LOCON	10th		Brigadier-General R.D.F. OLDMAN, D.S.O. proceeded to ENGLAND on short leave. Lieut. Colonel H.F. DARELL, 16th Rifle Brigade, took over Command temporarily.	
	11th		Draft of 132 arrived as reinforcements.	
	13th		Construction of rifle range started at PONT d'AVELLETTE (W.17 central). 60 reinforcemnets arrive.	

1875 Wt. W593/826 1,000,000 4/15 J.B.C. & A. A.D.S.S./Forms/C. 2118.

Army Form C. 2118

WAR DIARY
or
INTELLIGENCE SUMMARY

(Erase heading not required.)

Page 2.

Place	Date	Hour	Summary of Events and Information	Remarks and references to Appendices
Near LOCON.	14th		Brigadier-General R.D.F. OLDMAN, D.S.O. returns from leave and resumes Command. Specimen trenches marked out on Divisional training ground, to be completed by incoming Brigade.	
	15th		Draft of 32 other ranks arrives.	
Canal House near GORRE	17th		117th Brigade relieves 118th Brigade in GIVENCHY Section. Brigade Headquarters at CANAL HOUSE. 16th Rifle Brigade in Right Sub-section, 16th Sherwood Foresters in Left; 17th King's Royal Rifle Corps in Support, 17th Sherwood Foresters in Reserve. The 98th Brigade, 33rd Division is on our Right, and the 116th on our Left. The trenches are in fair condition although there is still plenty of work to be done. VAUXHALL BRIDGE Road lightly shelled.	App. V.
	18th		Our 4.5" Howitzers and field guns fired on the TORTOISE, breaching the enemy parapet for about 10 yards at A.16.C.5.7. At 7 p.m. we bombarded the enemy trenches opposite the Northern and Southern Craters with rifle grenades. This drew severe retaliation from enemy. Wiring carried on and work on repairing damage done by winter months.	
	19th		Enemy is using considerable machine gun fire against our aircraft. One machine gun located by smoke at A.16.C.5½.7. Our Lewis guns dispersed working parties during the night. The 98th Brigade, 33rd Division is on our Right and the 116th on our Left.	
	20th		Usual rifle grenade activity. Enemy snipers quiet. Our machine guns carry on indirect fire intermittently during the night.	

Army Form C. 2118

WAR DIARY
or
INTELLIGENCE SUMMARY
(Erase heading not required.)

Page 3.

Instructions regarding War Diaries and Intelligence Summaries are contained in F.S. Regs., Part II. and the Staff Manual respectively. Title Pages will be prepared in manuscript.

Place	Date	Hour	Summary of Events and Information	Remarks and references to Appendices
Canal House near GORRE	21st		The enemy exploded a small mine at about A.9.D.7.2. This mine is about 100 yards from our parapet and well within the crater area. The explosion was accompanied by an artillery bombardment but no infantry action followed. Our snipers claim two victims. Effects of lachrymatory gas were felt in the whole section. An inter-battalion relief took place on the night 21/22nd. 17/Notts & Derby. R. now in Right Sub-section, 17/K.R.Rif, C. in Left Sub-section, 16/Notts & Derby. R. in Support and 16/Rif. Brig. in Reserve.	App. VI.
	22nd		A small demonstration was carried out against the German trenches behind the Northern craters. The object was to retaliate for their rifle grenade activity and to do as much material damage as possible. 1 Battery 4.5" Howitzers, 1 - 18pr. Battery, 2 Medium Trench Mortars, 6 Stokes and 3.7" L.T.M.s were employed. The Field Artillery fired 50 rounds shrapnel, 50 H.E. and 25 - 18pr. The medium and light trench mortars fired 20 rounds and 50 respectively. In addition, 2 West guns and 8 rifle grenade batteries fired 490 grenades on different points and trenches. The shoot was successfully carried out. German retaliation was sharp, and consisted of about 40 .77 mm and showers of rifle grenades on our front trenches and about 30 - 4.2" H.E. on GIVENCHY KEEP - MOAT FARM and on communication trenches, but after 15 minutes they gave up the contest and we finished our shoot in peace at 7.20 p.m. Operation Order appended.	App. VII.

1875 Wt. W593/826 1,000,000 4/15 J.B.C. & A. A.D.S.S./Forms/C. 2118.

Army Form C. 2118

WAR DIARY
or
INTELLIGENCE SUMMARY
(Erase heading not required.)

Page 4.

Instructions regarding War Diaries and Intelligence Summaries are contained in F. S. Regs., Part II. and the Staff Manual respectively. Title Pages will be prepared in manuscript.

Place	Date	Hour	Summary of Events and Information	Remarks and references to Appendices
Canal Hse nr. GORRE	23rd		Light shelling and some rifle grenade activity. In the last six days our Battalions in the front line have erected a great number of overhead covers, which have proved singularly effective.	
	24th		Our artillery carried out some wire cutting at A.10.C.1.1. Our medium trench mortars, in conjunction with our 4.5" Howitzers shelled the Northern Craters and believe to have destroyed an enemy machine gun emplacement at A.9.B.1.4. A working party heard erecting wire E. of the Southern Craters was fired on by our Lewis guns and believe to have been dispersed. Supplement to our Trench Orders herewith.	App. VIII.
			The casualties from the 1st May up to this date are - Officers - 1 killed, 2 wounded, 3. Other Ranks - killed 20, wounded 113.	
	25th		Usual rifle Grenade activity. Inter-battalion relief. 16/Notts & Derby. R. takes over Left Sub-section - 16/Rif. Brig. Right Sub-section - 17/Notts & Derby. R. becomes Battalion in Support and 17/K.R.Rif. C. in Reserve.	App. IX.
	26th		A small operation was carried out by means of rifle grenades, medium and light trench mortars, with artillery cooperation. The objective was the DUCK'S BILL area. The operation seemed to have had the desired effect as there is a marked diminution of rifle grenades in this particular front. Operation Order appended.. We hold the upper hand in sniping in this section and knock down their periscopes as soon as they are put up. We have also shot numerous uncautious Germans.	App. X

1875 Wt. W593/826 1,000,000 4/15 J.B.C. & A. A.D.S.S./Forms/C.2118.

Army Form C. 2118

WAR DIARY
or
INTELLIGENCE SUMMARY
(Erase heading not required.)

Page 5.

Instructions regarding War Diaries and Intelligence Summaries are contained in F. S. Regs., Part II. and the Staff Manual respectively. Title Pages. will be prepared in manuscript.

Place	Date	Hour	Summary of Events and Information	Remarks and references to Appendices
Canal Hse nr. GORRE	27th		Enemy working parties were active. 3 of them in different parts of the line were dispersed by our Lewis guns. Enemy aeroplanes, which had been absent from this section for the past week, put in an appearance. This may be due to out increased infantry and artillery activity.	
	28th		Enemy blew a small mine at 6 a.m. this morning. Distance about 30 - 40 yards from enemy wire and situated to the North of the mine blown on the 21st instant. Plan of Defence for GIVENCHY SECTION herewith.	App. XI
	29th		A certain amount of shelling took place on both sides. Beyond slight damage done to our support and communication trenches, no harm was done. Enemy appears to be putting a lot of work into his front line. Working and wiring parties are often heard and whenever possible dispersed by our Lewis Guns. Inter-Battalion relief.	App. XII
	30th		Since the night 26/27th the attitude of the enemy seems to have changed. This may point to a relief or may be influenced by our prompt and vigorous retaliation with rifle grenades. Scarcely 50 rifle grenades have come over during the whole day and in return we have sent over about 150. Memo re Plan of Defence appended.	
	31st		Rifle grenades slightly more active. At 1 a.m. a hostile bombing party threw bombs in the neighbourhood of J and K saps. We replied vigorously and the enemy patrol retired. Several working parties dispersed by Lewis gun fire.	App. XIII

[signature]
Brig. Gen.
Commanding 117th BRIGADE

1875 Wt. W593/826 1,000,000 4/15 J.B.C. & A. A.D.S.S./Forms/C. 2118.

SECRET.   Appendix 1   Copy No... 18 WD

                117th INFANTRY BRIGADE Order No.11.

                                              30.4.1916.

Relief.   1. An inter Battalion Relief will take place in accordance
                   with attached Relief Table on the night 1/2nd May.

Dispositions   2. 16/Notts & Derby. R. take over C.2.
                   17/Notts & Derby. R. become Battalion in Support.
                   17/K.R.Rif. C. become Battalion in Reserve.
                   16/Rif. Brig. take over C.1.

Time.   3. Relief will commence at 6.30. p.m. and will be continuous.
                   Rations will be run up to VILLAGE LINE by hand previous
                   to relief. Small parties only to move during daylight.
                   Signallers will be relieved during daylight.
                   Garrisons of posts found by Reserve and Support
                   Battalions. will be relieved by day.
                   All details not mentioned to be arranged between
                   Commanding Officers concerned.

Trench Stores 4. Battalion Trench Store Lists will be handed over.

Reports.   5. Completion of relief to be reported to Bde Headquarters.

                                                    Major
                                        Bde. Major, 117th. BRIGADE

        Issued at 4 p.m. to
                                               By: Copy No.

        16/Notts & Derby. R.   D.R.   1
        17/Notts & Derby. R.   D.R.   2
        17/K.R.Rif. C.   D.R.   3
        16/Rif. Brig.   D.R.   4
        L.T.M. Batt. 117/1.   D.R.   5
        L.T.M. Batt. 117/2.   D.R.   6
        117/Bde. Machine Gun Co.   D.R.   7
        3 Sect. Signal Co.   Orderly   8
        3 Co. Div. Train   D.R.   9
        G.O.C.   Personally 10
        B.M.   do   11
        S.C.   do   12
        Bde. Grenade Officer.   do   13
        Intelligence Officer.   do   14
        H.Q., 39th Div.   D.R.   15
        116th Bde.   D.R.   16
        Group Cmmdr., R.A.   D.R.   17
        War Diary   -   18 & 19
        Order File   -   20
        105th Bde.   D.R.   21
        225 Co., R.E.   D.R.   22

RELIEF TABLE.

To accompany 117th Infantry Brigade Order No.11, dated 30.4.16.

Date.	Unit.	Relieves.	Position	Guides.	Route.	Relieved Unit proceeds to	Remarks.
/5/16	16/Notts & Derby R.	17/K.R.Rif.	Left Front Section and ISLANDS.	As arranged by C.O's.	As arranged by C.O's.	Reserve Billets at le TOURET.	Relief not to commence before 8.30. p.m.
/5/16	16/Rif. Brig.	17/Notts & Derby. R.	Right Front Section and ISLANDS.	do	Rd junction X.16.c.9.8. Rd junction F.4.b.9.5. & then as arranged between C.O's.	VILLAGE LINE	ditto

Appendix II W.D.

T R E N C H   O R D E R S.   117th INFY. BDE.

No.117/E.E./A.125.

TRENCH ADMINISTRATION AND DISCIPLINE.

1. Wherever possible the Guard system is to be used, i.e. posts will be so selected that the Sentry can see the Platoon front up to the next Sentry on either side and the remainder of the Guard or Group will be at his side awake.

2. The N.C.O. in Command of the Group or Guard must post every Sentry in a formal manner. Sentries should not be on for more than an hour at a time or less in bad weather. The Guard Commander will cause 2 of his Guard to patrol as far as the next Guard periodically during the 4-hour Watch. The 4-hour Watch system should be used, each Sentry of the Guard being up for an hour. Sentries are never to be alone; there will always be 2 men together if it is not possible to carry out the group system.

3. Platoon Commanders are to work out their Rosters for the Guards and work. These should be published each morning as soon after "Stand-to" as possible. The proportion of men to be awake by day is 1 in 6 or 8; by night 1 in 3. These are for Guard duties only and will not include workers.

4. Bombers, being experts, should not be used on bombing posts unless it is absolutely necessary. The ordinary soldier who can throw a bomb can equally well look out on a listening post. The expert should be kept for cases of emergency, such as counter attacks. It may however be necessary to have a bombers post, say in a Crater area.

5. Inspect fire-steps and see that they are the proper height and men can fire over them and know direction they are to fire by night. Also parapet for bullet-proofness. Fire-steps should be kept clear.

6. Guards on being relieved are compulsorily to go to rest.

7. An Officer of the Watch per Coy. and one Sergt. per Platoon is to be detailed.

8. Rifles should be inspected at morning and evening "Stand-to" and when the inspection of Guards takes place on going on duty. At morning

Sheet No.2.

morning and evening "Stand-to" trenches should be inspected for cleanliness and sanitation.

9. Notes of repairs required made. After inspection draw out detail of work and issue to Platoon Commanders.

10. If possible, cooking should be by Platoons or Companies, not by individuals. This system increases cleanliness of trenches and ensures control of smoke.

11. Rum will be kept in possession of an Officer and issued by an Officer and drunk in his presence. No accumulations or stores are allowed in an Officer's dug-out.

12. Feet should be inspected daily by an Officer, and dry socks put on in bad weather.

13. No man is to be allowed in the front trenches without his equipment on. If a man cannot carry out a given task while wearing it, it may be taken off by the order of an Officer and laid by his side.

14. Gas Appliances, Ammunition, S.A.A., Rockets and Grenades are to be inspected daily. Stores and rations should be carried up by Coys. in Support rather than that men should come from the front line for this duty. Careful lists of all stores, S.A.A., etc., on going into the trenches to be made. Ammunition should be so placed that it is easily available but not scattered along a trench, as this leads to a large number of boxes being opened unnecessarily. Pouches should be refilled from the central store at "Stand-to." All Grenades are to be inspected daily and cleaned. Boxes at the back of the store should be used before those in the front so as to ensure turnover.

15. Work on parapets and wire should be continuous.

16. Log Books should be kept showing progress of work and any incidents of interest put in. Located machine gun emplacements and snipers posts in the enemy lines should be recorded.

R.D.F.C.

26.4.16.

For distribution see over.

Issued to :-	No. of copies.
16/Notts & Derby. R.	20
17/ do do	20
17/K.R.Rif. C.	20
16th Rif. Brig.	20
L.T.M. Batt. 117/1.	2
L.T.M. Batt. 117/2.	2
117/Bde. Machine Gun Co.	4
No.3 Sect. Signal Co.	2
Bde. Headquarters.	1
G.O.C.	1
B.M.	1
S.C.	1
B.G.O.	1
Intelligence Officer.	1
War Diary	1
Order File	1

SECRET.   Appendix III   Copy No. 18

117th INFANTRY BRIGADE Order No. 12.

                                              4.5.16.

Relief. 1. An inter-Battalion Relief will take place in accordance with attached Relief Table on the Night 5/6th May.

Dispositions 2. 16/Notts & Derby. R. become Battalion in Reserve.
17/Notts & Derby. R. take over C.1.
17/K.R.Rif. C. take over C.2.
16/Rif. Brig. become Battalion in Support.

Time. 3. Relief will commence at 8.30. p.m. and will be continuous. Rations will be run up to VILLAGE LINE by hand previous to relief. Small parties only to move during daylight.
Signallers will be relieved during daylight.
Skeleton Garrisons of posts found by Reserve and Support Battalions will be relieved by day.
All details not mentioned to be arranged between Commanding Officers concerned.

Trench Stores. 4. Battalion Trench Store Lists will be handed over.

Reports. 5. Completion of relief will be reported to Bde Headquarters.

                                         Major
                            Brigade Major, 117th Brigade

Issued at 4 p.m. to

	by	Copy No.
16/Notts & Derby. R.	D.R.	1
17/Notts & Derby. R.	D.R.	2
17/K.R.Rif. C.	D.R.	3
16/Rif. Brig.	D.R.	4
L.T.M. Batt. 117/1	D.R.	5
L.T.M. Batt. 117/2	D.R.	6
117/Bde Machine Gun Co.	D.R.	7
3 Sect. Signal Co.	Orderly	8
3 Co. Div. Train.	D.R.	9
G.O.C.	Personally	10
B.M.	do	11
S.C.	do	12
Bde. Grenade Officer	do	13
Intelligence Officer	do	14
H.Q., 39th Div.	D.R.	15
118th Bde.	D.R.	16
Group Cmmdr., R.A.	D.R.	17
War Diary	-	18 & 19
Order File	-	20
105th Bde.	D.R.	21
225 Co., R.E.	D.R.	22

RELIEF TABLE.

To accompany 117th Infantry Brigade Order No.12, dated 4.5.16.

Date.	Unit.	Relieves	Position.	Guides	Route.	Relieved unit proceeds to	Remarks.
5/5/16	17/K.R.Rif. C.	16/Notts & Derby. R.	C.2. Left Front Section & ISLANDS.	As arranged by C.O's.	As arranged by C.O's.	Reserve Billets at LE TOURET	Relief no/to commence before 3.30. p.m.
5/5/16	17/Notts & Derby. R.	16/Rif Brig.	C. Right Front Section & ISLANDS.	do	do	VILLAGE LINE	ditto

SECRET. Copy No. 19

117th Infantry Brigade Order No. 14.

Ref. Sheet BETHUNE
1/40,000.
7.5.16.

Relief. 1. The 117th Brigade will be relieved by the 116th Brigade in "C" Section, FESTUBERT on the night 9/10th in accordance with attached Relief Table A.
All details not mentioned will be arranged by Commanding Officers concerned.

Billeting Parties. 2. The 117th Brigade will take over the Billets of the 116th Brigade Units as in attached Table A.
Billeting Officers to take over as arranged by Commanding Officers.

Garrisons. 3. The 17/K.R.Rif. C. will take over the "caretakers" garrison of the Posts in the GORRE – ESSARS System at 4 p.m. on the 9th instant, but will not leave the line before 2 p.m., by which time this party will be relieved in the line by a platoon from the 13/R.Suss. R. For detail see Table B.

Lewis Guns 4. Lewis Guns will be relieved on the night 8/9th under arrangements to be made by Commanding Officers.

Reports. 5. Reports of relief by 116th Brigade to Bde Headquarters, LOISNE.
Reports of arrival in rest Billets To Bde Headquarters at W.6.d.

Chatfield Major
Brigade Major, 117th Brigade

Issued at 8 a.m. to

	BY	Copy No.
16/Notts & Derby. R.	D.R.	1
17/Notts & Derby. R.	D.R.	2
17/K.R.Rif. C.	D.R.	3
16/Rif. Brig.	D.R.	4
L.T.M. Batt 117/1	D.R.	5
L.T.M. Batt. 117/2.	D.R.	6
117/Bde Machine Gun Co.	D.R.	7
3 Sect. Signal Co.	Orderly	8
3 Co. Div. Train.	D.R.	9
G.O.C.	Personally	10
B.M.	do	11
S.C.	do	12
Bde. Grenade Officer.	do	13
Intelligence Officer.	do	14
H.Q., 39th Div.	D.R.	15
118th Brigade	D.R.	16
116th Brigade	D.R.	17
Group Cmdr., R.A.	D.R.	18
War Diary	–	19 & 20
Order File	–	21
105th Brigade	D.R.	22
225 Co., R.E.	D.R.	23

SECRET
Table A.

RELIEF TABLE of 117th Infantry Brigade by 116th Infantry Brigade.

Date 1916	UNIT	To	Route	Relieving	Proceeding to	Taking over billets from	Time
3/5/16	13/R. Suss R	Left Front Subsection S.21.a.2.8.	LOCON Central - PONT TOURNANT - Les FACONS - RUE DES LOIS X.21.a.5.9. Le TOURET Cross Roads.	17/K.R. Rif. C	CHOCQUAUX	12/R. Suss R	To pass Le TOURET Cross Roads at 8.15 p.m. Guides meet at Le TOURET.
3/5/16	11/R. Suss R	Le TOURET (Reserve) X.16.	LOCON	16/Notts & Derby R	RIEZ DU VINAGE	14/Hamps. R	Head of 11/R. Suss R to be at Le TOURET by 12 noon.
3/5/16	116/de M'G Gr Units.	LOISNE S.20.a.3.7.	Any convenient	117/Fde HG Qrs.	W.6.d.4.5.	116/de M'G Hd Qrs.	To reach LOISNE by 5 p.m.
3/5/16	13/R. Suss R	FESTUBERT (Support Line) S.13.b.0.10.	As arranged for 13/R. Suss R to Cross Rds S.13.d.1.5.	16/Rif. Brig.	LA BRIQUE	13/R. Suss R	Le TOURET 3 p.m. Guides meet at Junction of RUE DU BOIS and RUE de l'EPINETTE. S.13.d.1.5. 3.30. p.m.
3/5/16	14/Hamps R	Right Front Subsection A.2.b.1.4.	Les GLATIGNIES - Le HAMEL - GORRE - F.5.	17/Notts & Derby R HERBETTE	A.4.c.2.6.	11/R. Suss R	Guides meet at FESTUBERT Cross Roads at 3.30. p.m.

Table B.

Garrisons and Stores -- GORRE - ESSARS System.

POST	Map reference Sheet BETHUNE	Maximum Garrisons	Machine Guns	Permanent Garrison	
GORRE GROUP (3 works)	F.3.b.c.d.	1 Co.	3	From Reserve Bn. at GORRE - E. Sect.	East post contains the following stores :-
CROIX de FER	F.1.b.5.2.	1½ Pls	2		
LA [illegible]	X.26.c.4.5.	½ Pl.	-		1 Inventory Board
ESSARS	X.25.a. central	2 Pls	4	One N.C.O. and 3 men.	1 Billhook
LAWE BRIDGE	W.24.c.8.0.	½ Pl.	1		1 Pick
LONG CORNET	W.23.b.7.2.	1½ Pls	2		4 Shovels
LE HAMEL	X.20.d.7.6.	½ Pl.	1		1 Maul
LE HAMEL, N.W.	X.19.b.7.6.	1½ Pls	2		2 Wirecutters
LAWE	X.13.c.7.4.	1 Pl.	-		1 Plan of Keep
MES PLAUX. W.	X.14.a.6.5.	½ Pl.	-		1 Pump) except posts
LES CHOQUAUX	W.18.a.5.7.	1 Pl.	2		2 Hose lengths) 2, 3 & 5.

SECRET   Appendix V.   Copy No. 18

117th Infantry Brigade Order No.15.

Ref. Sheet BETHUNE   16.5.16.
1/40,000.

Relief.   1.   The 117th Infantry Brigade will relieve the 118th Infantry Brigade in "B" Section (GIVENCHY) on the night of the 17/18th May, 1916, in accordance with attached Relief Table A. Posts will be relieved in accordance with attached Table B. All details not mentioned will be arranged by Commanding Officers concerned.

Lewis Guns   2.   Lewis Guns will be relieved in B.1. and B.2. on the night 16/17th under arrangements between C.O's.

C.O's will send up Bombers to B.1. and B.2 on the night 16/17th in such numbers as they consider advisable, to learn the Bombing Posts.

Trench Mor-tar Batts.   3.   117/1 and 117/2 Trench Mortar Batteries will relieve 118/1 and 118/2 Trench Mortar Batteries on the night of 16/17th May under arrangements to be made by Commanding Officers concerned. O.C., 117/1 will take over 2 Stokes guns 3" from 118/2.

Machine Gun Co.   4.   The 117th Infy. Bde. Machine Gun Co. (having temporarily become Divisional Troops, whilst attached to 118th Infy. Bde. Machine Gun Co.) will remain in its present position under the command of Capt W. ANDREW, O.C., 118th Infy Bde Machine Gun Co.

Reports   5.   Reports of relief to Brigade Headquarters at F.10.b.4.3.

Report Centre   6.   The Brigade Report Centre will close at W.6.d. at 5 p.m. and reopen at F.10.b.4.3. at the same hour.

                                                         Major
                                    Brigade Major, 117th BRIGADE

Issued at 8.0. a.m. to

	By.	Copy No.
16/Notts & Derby. R.	D.R.	1
17/Notts & Derby. R.	D.R.	2
17/K.R.Rif. C.	D.R.	3
16/Rif. Brig.	D.R.	4

                                                    P.T.O.

	By.	Copy No.
L.T.M. Batt. 117/1.	D.R.	5
L.T.M. Batt. 117/2.	D.R.	6
117/Bde. Machine Gun Co.	D.R.	7
3 Sect. Signal Co.	Orderly	8
3 Co. Div. Train.	D.R.	9
G.O.C.	Personally	10
B.M.	do	11
S.C.	do	12
Bde. Grenade Officer.	D.R.	13
Bde. Intelligence Officer.	Personally	14
H.Q., 39th Div.	D.R.	15
118th Brigade.	D.R.	16
116th Brigade	D.R.	17
War Diary	-	18 & 19
Order File		20
~~225 Co., R.E.~~	~~D.R.~~	~~21~~

SECRET

Table A.

RELIEF TABLE of 118th Infantry Brigade by 117th Infantry Brigade

To accompany 117th Infantry Brigade Order No.15, dated 15th May, 1916.

Date 1916	Unit of 117/Bde.	From	To	ROUTE	Takes over from	Hands over to	Time and Guides
17/5/16	6/Notts & Derby R	RIEZ de VINAGE	E.2.	via 17/K.R.Rif.C. Billets and to follow 17/K.R.Rif.C. Movements in and out by North bank of Canal	1/1 Cambs R	1/1 Herts R	Guides at WESTMINSTER Bridge (F.18.a.4.8) at 9.30. p.m.
17/5/16	7/Notts & Derby R	ENGHIEN	Reserve GORRE	any Convenient.	1/6 Ches. R.	1/1 Cambs. R	Relief to be complete by 4 p.m.
17/5/16	17/K.R.Rif.C.	LES CHOQ -UAUX.	MAXXMXH VILLAGE LINE	LES CHOQUAUX - Le HAMEL -GORRE & N. side of Canal. Not to pass GORRE before 7 p.m.	1/1 Herts R	1/4 B.Watch	Guides at WESTMINSTER Bridge (F.18.a.4.8) at 8.30. p.m.
17/5/16	6/Rif. Brig.	LA PANNERIE	E.1.	Halt for teas at GORRE -to be S. and W of road X.27.c. - GORRE - F.4.c. by 7 p.m. Movements in and out by S bank of Canal	1/4 B.Watch	1/6 Ches R	Guides at VAUXHALL Bridge (A.14.a.0.0.) at 9.30. p.m.
17/5/16	117/Bde. H.Qrs.	F.6.d.	F.10.b.4.3	Any convenient	118/Bde H.Qrs	118/ Bde H.Qrs.	To be clear of present Billets by 5 p.m.
Night 16/17th	117/1)T.M 117/2)Batt	F.12.a. 3.8.	Trenches	Any convenient	118/1)TM 118/2)BT	118/1)TM 118/2)BT	As arranged by C.O's

SECRET   Table B.

RELIEF of POSTS -- GIVENCHY Section.
To accompany 117th Infantry Brigade Order No.15, dated 16th May, 1916.

POST	Map reference Sheet BETHUNE	Garrison	Machine Guns	Found by Bn. in	
1. SPOIL BANK	A.15.c.5.8.	1 Platoon	1	B.1.	This table is to be retained for use during inter-Battalion reliefs.
2. ORCHARD	A.15.a.5.4.	1 Platoon	1	do	
3. MARIE	A.9.c.9½.8.	1 Platoon	1	do	
4. HILDERS	A.9.c.5.4.	1 Platoon	1 (L.G)	do	
5. POPPY	A.9.c.7.9½.	½ Platoon	-	B.2.	
6. MOAT FARM	A.9.c.2½.7.	1 Platoon	1 (L.G)	do	
7. GIVENCHY Keep	A.9.c.6.4.	2 Platoons	2	VILLAGE Line	
8. HERTS	A.8.d.7.3.	½ Platoon	1 (L.G)	do	
9. PONT FIXE. S.	A.14.d.3.7.	4 Platoons	-	do	
10. PONT FIXE N.	A.14.a.2.1.	4 Platoons	-	do	
11. WINDY CORNER	A.8.c.7.4.	2 Platoons	-	do	
12. Le PLANTIN. S.	A.3.a.9.7.	1 Platoon	-	do	
13. MARAIS. E.	F.6.c.0.4.	) 1 N.C.O. &	-	Res. GORRE	
14. WESTMINSTER Bridge	F.18.a.4.8.	) 3 men.	-	do	
15. MARAIS. S.E.	F.11.a.4.3.	)	-	do	
16. TUNING FORK. W.	F.4.b.7.6.	)	-	do	
17. GORRE Group of Wks	F.3.b.c.d.	No fixed Garrison	-	do	

SECRET   "B" SECTION   Appendix VI

Infantry Brigade Order No. 16.

20.5.16.

Relief	1.	An inter-Battalion relief will take place on the night of 21/22 May, 1916.
Dispositions	2.	Battalion from B.1, will take over Billets in GORRE and will become Battalion in Reserve.
		Battalion from B.2, will take over Village Line and will become Battalion in Support.
Time	3.	No movement forward of Village Line before 9 p.m. All details not mentioned to be arranged between Commanding Officers concerned.
Trench Stores	4.	Battalion Trench Store Lists will be handed over.
Reports	5.	Completion of relief will be reported to Brigade Headquarters (F.10.b).O.)

                                        Major
                          Brigade Major, L.C.

Issued at 4 p.m. to :-

	By	Copy No.
L.C.A.	D.R.	1
L.C.B.	D.R.	2
L.C.C.	D.R.	3
L.C.D.	R.R.	4
L.C.E.	D.R.	5
L.C.F.	D.R.	6
L.C.G.	D.R.	7
Y.C.L.	D.R.	8
3 Sect. Signal Co.	Orderly	9
G.O.C.	Personally	10
B.M.	do	11
S.C.	do	12
Bde. Grenade Officer	do	13
Intelligence Officer	do	14
~~36th~~ Brigade on right	D.R.	15
~~154th~~ Brigade on left	D.R.	16
Group Cmmdr., R.A.	D.R.	17
War Diary	-	18 & 19
Order File	-	20
~~237 Co.~~, ~~No.~~ L.E.P.	D.R.	21
~~1 Co.~~, ~~No.~~ L.E.C.	D.R.	22

SECRET ~~Appendix~~ VII W D

Copy No. 10
21.5.16.

Small Operation 22.5.16.

Objective 1. The salient in rear of Northern Craters (A.9.b.).

Plan of operation
2. (a). At 6.45 p.m. 2 WEST Machines and rifle grenades batteries to open on SALIENT. Brigade Bombing Officer to direct.

(b). Whether answered by enemy or not 18 pr. and 4.5. Hows. will open on agreed-on trenches in rear of CRATER Trench both frontally and with enfilade batteries under "B" Group R.A. Commander.

(c). 2 Medium T.M's to fire 20 rounds per gun.
      3 Stokes   "   "   "   50   "   "   "
      3 3.7. T.M's "   "   "   50   "   "   "

on agreed-on communication trenches and German trench running through A.9.b.4½.0. to 9.b. central at ~~7 p.m.~~ 6.50. Captain CORRIE will direct.

3. Sufficient rounds will be in readiness to respond to any enemy retaliation with T.M's. O.C., "B" Group has promised a reserve for similar purpose. Rifle grenades and West machines ready to fire day ~~and~~ & night.

4. Trenches and saps in front line will be cleared from CLARGES St. (61) to HITCHIN Rd (68), both inclusive and men kept under cover. To be clear by 6.30 p.m. O.C., B.2. and O.C., "B" Group, R.A. and O.C., M.T.M's will communicate direct as regards the return of the men to the trenches and any further withdrawal.

Machine Guns 5. Capt. ANDREWS will detail machine guns to cooperate.

5. The operations will only be alluded to on the telephone by a prearranged code issued from Bde. H. Qrs under separate cover.

6. Please acknowledge.

Major
Brigade Major, L.C.

Issued at   p.m. to
 O.C. 16/Notts & Derby. R.   1   (verbally ~~before~~)
 O.C. 17/Notts & Derby. R.   2   Capt ANDREWS   6
 O.C. 17/K.R.Rif. C.   3   117/Bde Machine Gun Co
 O.C. L.T.M. Batt. 117/1   4   Hd. Qrs, 39th Div   7
 O.C. L.T.M. Batt. 117/2   5   Group Cmmdr, R.A   8
 O.C. M.T.M's.   9   War Diary   10 & 11

Appendix VIII

No.117/B.M./250.

25.5.16.

The following will be added to TRENCH ORDERS issued on the 28th April, 1916.

(1). On the night of a relief every Coy. in the front line will have a patrol of at least 1 N.C.O. and 2 men out in front. For inter-Battalion reliefs C.O's will arrange whether patrols are found from the Coys. of the relieved or relieving Battalion. As a rule, they can be sent in advance from the latter. For inter-Brigade reliefs they will be found by our Units when relieving; by relieving Brigade when we are relieved.

(2). Every Guard in the front system will always have a supply of at least 2 boxes of bombs.

(3). Every Platoon in the front system will have a store of 100 sandbags ready filled. These are for use in emergencies and will be replaced at once if used.

R.D.F.O.

Issued at 11 a.m. to:-

	No. of Copies.
16/Notts & Derby. R.	20
17/Notts & Derby. R.	20
17/K.R.Rif. C.	20
16/Rif. Brig.	20
L.T.M. Batt. 117/1.	2
L.T.M. Batt. 117/2.	2
117/Bde. Machine Gun Co.	4
3 Sect. Signal Co.	2
Bde. H.Qrs.	1
G.O.C.	1
B.M.	1
S.C.	1
B.B.O.	1
Bde. Intelligence Officer.	1
War Diary	1
Order File	1

SECRET Appendix IX W D Copy No. 17

117th Infantry Brigade Order No.17.

24.5.16.

Relief   1. An inter-Battalion relief will take place on the night of 25/26th May, 1916.

Dispositions   2. Battalion from B.2. will take over Billets in GORRE and will become Battalion in Reserve.

Battalion from B.1. will take over Village Line and will become Battalion in Support.

Time   3. No movement forward of Village Line before 9 p.m. All details not mentioned to be arranged between Commanding Officers concerned.

Trench Stores   4. Battalion Trench Store Lists will be handed over.

Reports   5. Completion of relief will be reported to Brigade Headquarters (F.10.b.9.e.).

[signature] Major.
Brigade Major, 117th Brigade

Issued at 8 p.m. to.

	By.	Copy No.
16/Notts & Derby. R.	D.R.	1
17/Notts & Derby. R.	D.R.	2
17/K.R.Rif. C.	D.R.	3
16/Rif. Brig.	D.R.	4
117/1 L.T.M. Batt.	D.R.	5
117/2 L.T.M. Batt.	D.R.	6
117/Bde. Machine Gun Co.	D.R.	7
Headquarters, 39th Div.	D.R.	8
3 Sect. Signal Co.	Orderly	9
G.O.C.	Personally	10
B.M.	do	11
S.C.	do	12
98th Brigade.	D.R.	13
118th Brigade.	D.R.	14
Group Cmmdr., R.A.	D.R.	15
O.C., M.T.M's.	D.R.	16
War Diary	–	17 & 18.
Order File	–	19
227 Field Co., R.E.	D.R.	20
234 Field Co., R.E.	D.R.	21

SECRET   Appendix X   Copy No. 9

Ref. Bde. Trench Map I.

Small Operation 23.5.16.

Objective	1.	German Duck's Bill and new work at BILL of BILL EXTENSION. Area of Bombardment A.9.D.8.2. - A.9.D.8.5. - A.10.c.1.5. - A.10.c.2.1.
Operators	2.	Rifle Grenades. Lieut. H.P. STEVENS and Bombing Officer, 16/Rif. Brig.

L.T.M's -- 117/1.   4 - 3.7".   )
) 100 rounds per Batt.
        117/2.   4 - 5" Stokes) for 3 bursts.

M.T.M's.   1 --

"B" Group, R.A.

9 p.m. for 5 minutes	3.	(a). Signal to commence -- 3 guns at 1 second interval. 4th gun 5" later.

Special attention to German trench running through craters and bombers post A.9.D.9½.2.

10.5 p.m. for 5 minutes		(b). Signal to commence -- 3 guns at 1 second interval - repeated after 5" and followed by a single gun after a further 5".

Concentrate on new German work A.9.D.9.2. to A.10.c.2.1.

11.45 p.m. for 5 minutes		(c). Signal to commence -- 3 guns at 2" interval. 4th gun after 5" interval.

A.9.D.6.3. to A.10.c.2.1.

Clearing Trenches	4.	O.C's., B.1. and B.2. will clear trenches from 53 to 60 both inclusive and including close support trench. The trenches to be cleared silently on each occasion leaving the men in the supheads to the last.

Trenches to be cleared by 4.50 a.m.
                          9.50 p.m.
                          11.30 p.m.

O.C., B.1. will be in direct telephonic communication with O.C., B.2., O.C., "B" Group and O.C., L.T.M's; orders for L.T.M's and bombers will be passed by O.C., M.T.M's.   O.C., B.2. will report to O.C., B.1.
O.C., B.1. will arrange his own codes for reporting trenches cleared and will inform both O.C., "B" Group and O.C., M.T.M's that trenches are clear and receive
                                                    reports

2.

reports from both the above before remanning trenches. Watches will be synchronised with O.C., B.1.

R.A. 5. O.C.; "B" Group will arrange for one Battery to "stand by" while trenches are cleared. He will direct fire on certain agreed-on coordinates.

6. The 5 p.m. operation is intended to help the M.T.M's and L.T.M's to get their ranges and may appear to be a leisurely proceeding. The later operations are intended to destroy Germans and their new trenches. Lewis guns should fire for a short while after the 10.5 p.m. operation, but the Bosche must be allowed to get back to his work comfortably by 11.45 pm. The R.A. intend to do some other firing during the night but any such firing at other than the above times will not involve any shift of garrison.

                                            Major
                              Brigade Major, 117th BRIGADE

Issued to :-

	Copy No.
O.C. 15/Rif. Brig.	1
O.C. 16/Notts & Derby. R.	2
O.C. "B" Group	3
O.C. M.T.M's	4
O.C. L.T.M. Batt. 117/1	5
O.C. L.T.M. Batt. 117/2.	6
D.D.G.	7
Head Qrs. 39th Div.	8
O.C. 17/Notts & Derby. R.	(verbally)
War Diary	9
B.M.	10

SECRET ~~Appendix~~ ~~PROVISIONAL~~ Copy No... 15. WD

PLAN OF DEFENCE of "B" SECTION (GIVENCHY).

39th DIVISIONAL SECTOR.

26.5.1916.

GARRISON :- As per Appendix A.

DISTRIBUTION

FRONT LINE :-	1.	Present Trench.
SUPPORT LINE :-	2.	ARTILLERY ROW - BAYSWATER - OXFORD TERRACE - CAMBRIDGE TERRACE - PICCADILLY - PARK LANE - WARE ROAD.
RIGHT PROTECTED FLANK	3.	ARTILLERY ROW AND SPOIL BANK.
LEFT PROTECTED FLANK	4.	WARE ROAD - NEWCUT to its junction with HITCHIN ROAD.
POSTS - Supporting SUPPORT LINE.	5.	(B.1.) - SPOIL BANK - ORCHARD KEEP - MARIE. (B.2.) - MOAT FARM - POPPY.
~~VILLAGE LINE~~ CRITICAL KEEP	6.	The Vital point of the Section is that lying within the following boundaries:- PICCADILLY from its junction with CAMBRIDGE TERRACE and WOLFE ROAD, along PICCADILLY, PARK LANE, SCOTTISH TRENCH to its junction with WARE ROAD; the LEFT Protecting Flank as already stated; and WOLFE ROAD on the RIGHT. This Curtain of Trenches defends GIVENCHY KEEP with its supporting points HILDERS - POPPY - MOAT FARM - HERTS - MARIE REDOUBTS. All cellars in GIVENCHY VILLAGE are being made strong for defence by rifle and Machine Gun fire, by the R.E. Companies.
VILLAGE LINE	7.	A succession of strong posts covered along the entire front by a strong belt of wire entanglements. PONT FIXE S. - PONT FIXE N. - WINDY CORNER - LE PLANTIN S.
SECOND LINE	8.	Line of Breastworks from the LA BASSEE canal along the Irrigation canal at Brigade Headquarters thence in a straight line to TUNING FORK ROAD. Three small posts are connected with this line, WESTMINSTER BRIDGE, and MARAIS E. and MARAIS S.W. Several Batteries R.A. are posted in and near this line.
SPECIAL FEATURES	9.	Mining activities on both sides has resulted in the formation of two Mine Craters called CRATERS S. or (DUCK'S BILL) and CRATERS N. The parapets in these Areas are so broken up that their defence is undertaken by Saps, each of which is garrisoned by a party of Bombers. The parapet between those Crater Areas is held in the usual way, and is protected by wire.
SIDBURY HILL		This underfeature situated 400 yards N.E. of PONT FIXE BRIDGE constitutes an advanced post to the defences of the VILLAGE LINE, and very suitable for Machine Gun defence.
Report Centre.	10.	B3. The Advanced ~~Brigade~~ Report Centre is at FANSHAWE CASTLE (A.14.a.5.5.).

GENERAL PLAN in case of Attack.

To carry out the provisions of the 39th Divisional Defence Scheme, the following will be the action of the Brigade while holding "B" Section.

<u>Front Line</u>

The front line Battalions will hold on to the first and support lines at all costs. The line of Keeps B.1. - STOIL BANK - ORCHARD Farm - MARIE - HILDERS - POPPY - MOAT Farm are manned with their normal garrisons, which will remain in the keeps in any event and are not at disposal of local commanders for counter-attack. If these garrisons are at work near their keeps they will return at once. O.C's, front line Battalions will push forward the reserves in their hands, i.e., in B.1. 3 platoons, in B.2 one a half platoons, so as to be available for immediate counter-attack.

<u>Support Bn.</u>
<u>Village Line</u>

The Battalion in the Village Line is available for the counter-attack in any portion of the Brigade Front, less the following minimum garrisons in the Village Line Redoubts.

(1) GIVENCHY KEEP   2 Pl.   2 M.G's.
(2) HERTS REDOUBT   ½ B1G.   1 L.G. 1½
(3) PONT FIXE S.   1 Pl.   Hilders   1 L.G.
(4) PONT FIXE N.   1 Pl.
(5) WINDY CORNER   1 Pl.
(6) Le PLANTIN S.   ½ Pl.

              Total 6 Pls

thus leaving 10 platoons and 2 ½ Lewis Guns for immediate counter-attack. The O.C., Village Line Battalion will act as circumstances require and attack if necessary without waiting for orders from Brigade. His first efforts will be directed to moving up his men closer to the summit of the ridge into jumping-off places, for which purpose the keeps will offer opportunities. The principle of not using the supporting troops until the right moment and then in sufficient force to gain a decision, must be kept in view.

<u>Reserve Bn.</u>

The Reserve Battalion will get ready to move up the Village Line as ordered by Brigade Headquarters. The Routes to be used are

1.
p.t.o

Sheet No.2

1. Canal Bank to PONT FIXE.
2. Canal Bank - WESTMINSTER BRIDGE Road - WINDY CORNER.
3. TUNING FORKS, - Le PLANTIN.

These will be reconnoitred by all concerned.

L.T.M. Batt. The guns of the L.T.M. Batteries will normally be so disposed as to admit of 2 of each Batt., thereof being available and in the hands of O.C., Sub-section for counter-attack.

Machine Gun Co. The Machine Gun Co. is disposed with 12 guns in keeps and posts and 4 in Reserve at GORRE which will move up to the neighbourhood of Brigade Advanced Report Centre.

Tunnelling Co. 254th Tunnelling Co. are allotted posts for the garrson which will be notified hereafter.

Major
Brigade Major, 117th Brigade

Issued at 8 a.m. by

	By.	Copy No.
16/Notts & Derby. R.	D.R.	1
17/Notts & Derby. R.	D.R.	2
17/K.R.Rif. C.	D.R.	3
16/Rif. Brig.	D.R.	4
L.T.M. Batt. 117/1.	D.R.	5
L.T.M. Batt. 117/2.	D.R.	6
117/Bde. Machine Gun Co.	D.R.	7
O.C., M.T.M's.	D.R.	8
3 Sect. Signal Co.	Orderly	9
Head Qrs., 39th Div.	D.R.	10
G.O.C.	Personally	11
B.M.	do	12
S.C.	do	13
Intelligence Officer.	do	14
War Diary	-	15 & 16
Order File	-	17
B.B.O.	Personally	18
Group Commdr., R.A.	D.R.	19
227 & 234 Field Co., R.E.	D.R.	20 & 21

Appendix A.

GARRISON.

INFANTRY

    Four Battalions

    B.1.   1 Battalion.

    B.2.   1 do

    Village Line.   1 do

    Reserve.   1 do

Machine Guns.   1 Company.

Trench Mortars

    Medium T.M's - not yet allotted.

Light Trench Mortars.

    B.1.   1 Batt.

    B.2.   1 Batt.

Artillery   5. 18 Pr. Batts equals 20 guns.

            4. 4.5" Hows.

GARRISONS AND STORES.

Area.	Posts.	Garrison Platoon	Garrison L.G.'s	S.A.A. Bxs	Hand Grenado Boxes	Meat Boxes	Biscuit	Water Petrol Tns	Tanks W stor	Ammunition Very-boxes	Vermoral Sprayers	Solution jars	Shovels	Picks	Sandbags	Barbed wire coils	Wirecutters	Pumps	L.G. SAA Boxes
B.1.	SPOIL BANK	1	1LG	14	50	2	2	10	2	5	1	4	20	6	100	5	1		6
	ORCHARD	1	1LG	14	50	2	2	20	1	3	1	4	20	6	100	5	1		6
	HARIE	1	1LG	14	50	2	2	10	1	5	1	4	20	6	100	5	1	1	6
	HILDERS	1	1LG	14	60	2	2	20	2	5	1	4	20	6	100	5	1		6
B.2.	HOLY	1	1LG	7	25	1	1	10	1	2	1	4	10	3	10d	5	1		
	OAT PARK	1	1LG	14	50	2	2	20	1	3	1	4	20	5	10d	5	1	1	6
VILLAGE LINE	TRAMS	1	1MG	7	25	1	1	10		2	1	4	10	5	10d	5	1	3	
	GIVENCHY KEEP	4	2MG	60	100	10	10	20	4	25	5	12	30	15	10,000	20	5		12
	FORT PIXE S.	4		56	200	8	8	20	2	12	2	8	50	15	15,000	15	2		
	FORT PIKE R.	2		28	200	8	8	20	2	12	2	8	50	15	15,000	15	2		
	KIRDY CORNER	1		14	100	4	4	10	2	6	1	4	25	8	100d	15	2		
	L. PLANTIN S.	1		14	50	2	2	10	1	5	1	4	20	6	200	10	1		
GORRE Area.	MARAIS E.	1 MG																	
	WEST. INSTEER	and																	
	BRIDGE	3 men																	
	MARAIS S.E.	each																	
	TUNING FORK																		
	GORRE Group																		
	of Works																		

FIRING & SUPPORT LINES

Area		Platoon	L.G.'s	S.A.A. Bxs	Hand Grenade Boxes					Ammunition Very-Boxes	Vermoral	Solution							
B.1.	Firing Line	7		28	200					20	10	40						12	
	Support Line	2		56	200					10	5	20							
	Reserve	3		42	100														
B.2	Firing Line	9		56	200					20	10	40						2	
	Support Line	5½		56	200					10	5	20							
	Reserve	1¼		28	100														

No establishment of stores beyond what is on Inventory Board.

(a) A Platoon (of an assumed strength of 35 All Ranks) is taken as the Unit in compiling this table.
(b) This works out 400 rounds S.A.A. per rifle in keeps.
(c) An extra 6,000 rounds is allowed for each LG or MG.
(d) Rations for two days per rifle is allowed for.
(e) S.A.A. in firing-line is calculated at 1 Box per Section.

SECRET

WD

Copy No. 15.

28.5.16.

Amendment to

Plan of Defence of "B" Section (GIVENCHY) dated 26th May, 1916.

1. Delete "PROVISIONAL" at top of page 1.

2. Add Appendix C. (attached).

   Emplacements for Machine Guns and Lewis Guns.

3. In General Plan in Case of Attack.

   Support Battalion, Village Line.

   To list of Keeps and Posts add - HILDERS, 1 L.G. (Garrison found by Battalion in B.1.). Total 6 Pls. 2 L.G.

   and for 3 Lewis Guns in next line, read "2 Lewis Guns."

Major
Brigade Major, 117th BRIGADE

Issued at 8 a.m. to :-

	Copy No.
O.C. 16/Notts & Derby. R.	1
O.C. 17/Notts & Derby. R.	2
O.C. 17/K.R.Rif. C.	3
O.C. 16/Rif. Brig.	4
O.C. 117/1 L.T.M. Batt.	5
O.C. 117/2 L.T.M. Batt.	6
O.C. Medium Trench Mortars	7
O.C. 117/Bde. Machine Gun Co.	8
Hd. Qrs., 39th Div.	9
3 Sect. Signal Co.	10
G.O.C	11
B.M.	12
S.C.	13
War Diary	14 & 15.
Order File	16
Bde. Intelligence Officer.	17
Group Cmmdr., R.A.	18
B.B.O.	19
227 Co., R.E.	20
234 Co., R.E.	21

SECRET   Appendix C.

Position of Machine Guns and Lewis Guns

Machine Guns

    1. SPOIL BANK   )   A.15.C.5.9.
    2. ORCHARD   )   A.15.A.5.4.
    3. GIVENCHY KEEP   )
    4. GIVENCHY KEEP   )   A.9.C.6.4.

    5. WINDY CORNER   A.8.C.7.4.
    6. A.14.A.9.9.
    7. PONT FIXE N.   A.8.B.2.1.
    8. PONT FIXE S.   A.14.D.3.7.

    9. BARN   A.9.C.9½.?.
  10. BOAT HOUSE   A.9.C.2½.7.
  11. ORCHARD (No.2).   A.15.A.5.4.
  12. FRENCH FARM   A.9.C.9.9.

Headquarters at old Hd. Qrs. B.2. (A.8.C.2.3.).
In Reserve at GORRE - 4 Guns.

Lewis Guns   The Battalion in Support will keep a Lewis Gun as permanent garrison in each of the following :-

        HERTS   1
        HILDERS 1

Appendix XII

SECRET

Copy No. 19

117th Infantry Brigade Order No.19.

28.5.16.

Relief   1. An inter-Battalion relief will take place on the night of 29/30th May, 1916.

Dispositions   2. 16/Notts & Derby. R. will take over Billets in GORRE and will become Battalion in Reserve.

16/Rif. Brig. will take over Village Line and will become Battalion in Support.

Time   3. No movement forward of Village Line before 9 p.m.

All details not mentioned to be arranged between Commanding Officers concerned.

Trench Stores   4. Battalion Trench Store Lists will be handed over.

Reports   5. Completion of relief will be reported to Brigade Headquarters (F.10.B.9.0.).

Major

Brigade Major, 117th BRIGADE

Issued at 3 p.m. to :-

(For distribution see over).

Issued at 3 p.m. to :-

	By	Copy No.
16/Notts & Derby. R.	D.R.	1
17/Notts & Derby. R.	D.R.	2
17/K.R.Rif. C.	D.R.	3
16/Rif. Brig.	D.R.	4
117/1 L.T.M. Batt.	D.R.	5
117/2 L.T.M. Batt.	D.R.	6
117/Bde. Machine Gun Co.	D.R.	7
Medium Trench Mortars	D.R.	8
3 Sect. Signal Co.	Orderly	9
Hd. Qrs., 39th Div.	D.R.	10
G.O.C.	Personally	11
B.M.	do	12
S.C.	do	13
98th Brigade.	D.R.	14
118th Brigade.	D.R.	15
Group Cmndr., R.A.	D.R.	16
227 Co., R.E.	D.R.	17
234 Co., R.E.	D.R.	18
War Diary	—	19 & 20
Order File	—	21

SECRET   Appendix XIII WD   Copy No...15
                                            29.5.16

With reference to Plan of Defence of "B" Section
(GIVENCHY), dated 26th May, 1916 - General Plan in
Case of Attack.

Preliminary Warning

In the event of an attack being expected at any time,
and if the G.O.C. considers information received
sufficiently reliable, the following message will be
sent out by 'phone and D.R. or runner : "Carry out
preliminary arrangements."

On receipt of this message

Bns. in Front Line

2 O.C's., Battalions in front line will, if they have
not already done so, get ready to move up their
Reserve Company.

Support Battalion

O.C., Battalion in Support will assemble working
parties (if out) order stand-to for obligatory
minimum garrisons of keeps, and have his 10 Platoons
and 2 Lewis Guns ready to move without further orders
should he consider the situation demands it.

Reserve Battalion

O.C., Reserve Battalion will get ready to move.

Bde. Headquarters.

Brigade Headquarters will get ready to move to
FANSHAWE CASTLE (A.14.A.5.5.).

254 Tunnelling Co.

The personnel of 254 Tunnelling Co. in the front line
will get ready to move as follows :-

N. Crater, Party 1 proceeds via SCOTTISH TRENCH -
UPPER CUT - CALEDONIAN Road and KING'S Road to
GUNNER SIDING.

N. Crater, Party 2. will take the shortest road to
the AVENUE and thence via KILBY'S WALK - KING'S Road
to GUNNER SIDING.

N. Crater, Party 3 will proceed via BOND St -
PICCADILLY and KING'S Road to GUNNER SIDING.

S. Crater parties will take the shortest road to
HOPE St. - thence across into HATFIELD Road and
WOLFE Road to Assembly Trenches off WOLFE Road
(A.15.A.3.9.).

In all cases they will be under their own officers,
who will report to the O.C., the nearest body of
Infantry.

<u>117/Machine Gun Co.</u>	O.C., 117 Co., Machine Gun Corps will have his Reserve Section ready to move up.
<u>Light Trench Mortars</u>	O.C's., 117/1 & 117/2 will have their personnel in rest as well as any reserve under training ready to move up to their positions, detailing such parties as they require from the above to proceed to Bde. Bomb Store to carry up ammunition.
<u>General</u>	3. On receipt of "Carry out preliminary arrangements" Units will send runners to Bde. Hd. Qrs. as under :-

        Infantry Bn. 4 each to F.10.B.9.0.
                   4 each to FANSHAWE CASTLE.

        117/M.G. Co. 1 to each of above.
        117/1 L.T.M. 1   ditto
        117/2 L.T.M. 1   ditto

                                                                               Major
                                            Brigade Major, 117th BRIGADE.

Issued at 3.30 p.m. to :-

	By	Copy No.
16/Notts & Derby. R.	D.R.	1
17/Notts & Derby. R.	D.R.	2
17/K.R.Rif. C.	D.R.	3
16/Rif. Brig.	D.R.	4
117/1 L.T.M. Batt.	D.R.	5
117/2 L.T.M. Batt.	D.R.	6
Medium Trench Mortars	D.R.	7
117/Bde. Machine Gun Co.	D.R.	8
3 Sect. Signal Co.	Orderly	9
Hd. Qrs. 39th Div.	D.R.	10
G.O.C.	Personally	11
B.M.	do	12
S.C.	do	13
Bde. Intelligence Officer	do	14
War Diary	-	15 & 16
Order File	-	17
B.B.O.	Personally	18
Group Comdr., R.A.	D.R.	19
227 Co., R.E.	D.R.	20
234 Co., R.E.	D.R.	21
254 Tunnelling Co., R.E.	D.R.	22

39th Division.

B. H. Q.

117th INFANTRY BRIGADE

J U N E 1 9 1 6

Appendices attached:-

Note on Defences.
Brigade Orders.
Report on Operation 4/5th June.
Plan of Defence Givenchy Secton
Plan of Defence Festubert Section
Defence Scheme.

ORIGINAL

Army Form C. 2118

WAR DIARY
or
INTELLIGENCE SUMMARY
(Erase heading not required.)

VOLUME IV.

Instructions regarding War Diaries and Intelligence Summaries are contained in F. S. Regs., Part II. and the Staff Manual respectively. Title Pages. will be prepared in manuscript.

Place	Date June	Hour	Summary of Events and Information	Remarks and references to Appendices
Canal H'se near GORRE	1st		The enemy is working on N. side of Northern Craters. This new work may point to renewed mining activity.	
	2nd		The enemy is more active, but we still maintain a superiority in rifle grenades. Our machine guns traversed at night on communication trenches and roads. Amendment to Defence Scheme of GIVENCHY SECTION issued.	App. 1.
	3rd		Renewed rifle grenade activity on the part of the enemy, to which we replied effectively. Inter-battalion relief.	App. 11.
	4th		On the night 4th/5th we effected a raid on the German trenches S. of the DUCK'S BILL at about A.10.c.1.1½. At the same time we exploded two mines at the end of E. Sap at about A.9.d.6.4½. (Combined Sheet BETHUNE). The raiding party, consisting of 4 Officers and 70 Other Ranks of 16/Notts & Derby. Regt., after Artillery, Medium, and Light Trench Mortar preparation succeeded in entering the enemy trench, in spite of meeting with opposition from a hostile bombing party in the German front line trench. We successfully bombed about 80 yards of front line trench and the party then returned, as arranged. We estimate having accounted for 25 Germans in the raid itself, without reckoning the casualties which were undoubtedly caused by our artillery and trench mortar bombardment. Our own casualties were, 1 Officer wounded, 2 O.R. killed, 14 wounded and 4 missing. Detailed account of raid.	App. lVl

1875 W¹. W593/826 1,000,000 4/15 J.B.C. & A. A.D.S.S./Forms/C. 2118.

Army Form C. 2118

WAR DIARY
or
INTELLIGENCE SUMMARY
(Erase heading not required.)

Page 2.

Instructions regarding War Diaries and Intelligence Summaries are contained in F. S. Regs., Part II. and the Staff Manual respectively. Title Pages will be prepared in manuscript.

Place	Date	Hour	Summary of Events and Information	Remarks and references to Appendices
Canal H'se	5th		A very quiet day. Patrol parties went into NO MAN'S LAND during the night and salved some articles that had been dropped there during the raid. The work of consolidating our new craters, commenced during the raid, was continued, and a snipers post is being constructed in the near lip. This post will command an excellent view of the enemy front line trenches in rear of the DUCK'S BILL (Southern) Craters. Revised Defence Scheme issued.	App. IV.
	6th		The Brigade is relieved by the 118th Infantry Brigade. Order attached. We move into Stand-to Billets at ESSARS.	App. V.
ESSARS	7th to 11th		Nothing of interest to record.	
LOISNE.	12th		The 117th Infantry Brigade relieves the 106th Infantry Brigade on night 11th/12th in FESTUBERT SECTION. This Section has been much worked on since our last occupation, but an enormous amount of work still remains to be done, especially in joining up the Islands and in wiring. Enemy snipers active.	App. VI.
	13th		The bad weather prevented any activity on either side. Rain fell in torrents and made patrolling difficult. Our snipers claim one victim. The enemy showed a dummy periscope, which did not succeed in drawing our fire.	
	14th		Our 4.5" Hows. fired at supposed enemy machine gun at S.22.c.4½.7. with apparent effect.	
	15th		Our Machine Gun Co. practised indirect fire at divers targets during the night.	
	16th		A readjustment of dispositions of the Brigade took place on the night 16th/17th. The new front	

1875 Wt. W593/826 1,000,000 4/15 J.B.C. & A. A.D.S.S./Forms/C. 2118.

Army Form C. 2118

Page 3.

WAR DIARY
or
INTELLIGENCE SUMMARY
(Erase heading not required.)

Instructions regarding War Diaries and Intelligence Summaries are contained in F.S. Regs., Part II. and the Staff Manual respectively. Title Pages will be prepared in manuscript.

Place	Date	Hour	Summary of Events and Information	Remarks and references to Appendices
LOISNE	16th		held by the Brigade is from PRINCES ISLAND (A.9.a.6.8.) to CADBURY'S TRENCH (S.16.c.1.3.). (Reference, BETHUNE - Combined Sheet) with 4 Battalions in the line, each having at least one Company in reserve in the VILLAGE LINE. Preliminary Order Move Order.	App.VII "VIII
	17th		Our snipers were active and claim to have hit five of the enemy. The enemy does not have appear to be doing much work on his front line although, isolated wiring parties having been heard or seen. These have always been engaged by our Lewis Guns.	
	18th		Nothing of interest to record. Our machine guns carried out indirect fire during the night. New Defence Scheme issued.	App IX.
	19th		Enemy artillery more active than usual. Islands 29 and 30 bombed during the night, apparently by some mechanical means, probably a catapult.	
	20th		Enemy artillery again active. An enemy working party observed during the day in enemy support line. It was dispersed by rifle fire.	
	21st		On our left the enemy put up a notice-board "Why shoot when peace is so near." Our snipers claim 3 victims. The enemy was much more quiet today and many looked over the parapet. They all had grey round caps. This may indicate a relief, as JAEGERS have been previously reported opposite us.	
	22nd		Orders in case of a sudden move appended. Readjustment of Brigade front took place on night 22/23rd. The 16/Rif. Brig. becomes battalion in support, 17/Notts & Derby. Regt. right battalion,	App X.

1875 Wt. W593/826 1,000,000 4/15 J.B.C. & A. A.D.S.S./Forms/C. 2118.

Army Form C. 2118

WAR DIARY
or
INTELLIGENCE SUMMARY
(*Erase heading not required.*)

Instructions regarding War Diaries and Intelligence Summaries are contained in F.S. Regs., Part II. and the Staff Manual respectively. Title Pages will be prepared in manuscript.

Place	Date June	Hour	Summary of Events and Information	Remarks and references to Appendices
LOISNE	22nd		17/K.R.Rif. C. centre battalion and the 16/Notts & Derby. R. left battalion. A little shelling on both sides, otherwise all quiet.	App.Xl
	23/24th		The attitude of the enemy for these two days seems to have changed. His snipers are less active and the men seldom put their heads above the parapet. A certain amount of work still goes on in the enemy front, support and communication trenches. Addendum to Bde. Defence Scheme issued.	App.Xll.
	25th		Our artillery shelled the POPE'S NOSE (A.3.b.½.5.) and effectively breached the parapet and cut two gaps in wire. These gaps are kept open by intermittent Lewis Gun and rifle fire during the night.	
	26th		Attitude of enemy exceptionally quiet. We again shelled the POPE'S NOSE and enlarged the gaps previously made. The enemy was very active trying to repair his trenches during the night. Our Lewis Guns fired on suspected parties during the night and kept the gaps open.	
	27th		Our artillery bombarded enemy's parapet twice and will at S.28.a.7.4. and cut a partial gap about 6 yards wide. All existing gaps are being kept open. Captain W.G. MAXWELL (GORDON HIGHLANDERS) assumed duty to-day as Brigade Major vice Major C.G. STANSFELD, 8th GURKHA RIFLES, appointed G.S.O. 2, 61st Division.	
	28th		The enemy attempted a small raid on our trenches at Island 30. The raiding party, consisting of about a dozen men came through a gap in our wire and, taking advantage of derelict trenches and ditches approached the Island unobserved. They did not damage and were immediately ejected.	

Army Form C. 2118

WAR DIARY
or
INTELLIGENCE SUMMARY

(Erase heading not required.)

Page 5.

Instructions regarding War Diaries and Intelligence Summaries are contained in F. S. Regs., Part II. and the Staff Manual respectively. Title Pages. will be prepared in manuscript.

Place	Date	Hour	Summary of Events and Information	Remarks and references to Appendices
LOISNE	29th		The 17/K.R.Rif. C. attempted a small raid on enemy trenches at S.28.e.7.3½. They were unfortunately held up by the wire which had been insufficiently cut and the party returned to our side without any casualties. The Brigade on our left attempted an attack near the BOAR'S HEAD (S.16.e.) and in conjection our left battalion created a smoke barrage for about 40 minutes. Operation Order appended.	App Xlll.
	30th		Nothing of interest to report. The enemy quiet after the operation of the 29th. During the occupation of the FESTUBERT SECTION by this Brigade the snipers have done good work, particularly in the left Battalion front.

1st July, 1916.

[signature]
Brig. Gen.
Commanding 117th. INFANTRY BRIGADE | |

1875 Wt. W593/826 1,000,000 4/15 J.B.C. & A. A.D.S.S./Forms/C. 2118.

Appendix I

SECRET

Copy No. 16

2.6.16.

Reference Plan of Defence of "B" Section (GIVENCHY) dated 26.5.16, Page 2 - Support Battalion, Village Line.

List of Redoubts in Village Line with minimum garrison -

add (7) ORCHARD - 1 Pl,

alter Total to 7 Platoons,

and in next line read, "Thus leaving 9 Platoons and 3 Lewis Guns for immediate counter-attack."

In Appendix "B" - Garrisons and Stores -

transfer ORCHARD from B.1. to VILLAGE LINE.

[signature]
Major
Brigade Major, 117th BRIGADE

Issued at 3.30 p.m. to :-

(For distribution see over).

Issued at 3.30 p.m. to :-	By	Copy No.
	D.R.	1
16/Notts & Derby. R.	D.R.	2
17/Notts & Derby. R.	D.R.	3
17/K.R.Rif. C.	D.R.	4
16/Rif. Brig.	D.R.	5
117/1 L.T.M. Batt.	D.R.	6
117/2 L.T.M. Batt.	D.R.	7
117/Bde Machine Gun Co.	D.R.	8
Medium Trench Mortars	Orderly	9
3 Sect. Signal Co.	D.R.	10
Hd. Qrs. 39th Div.	Personally	11
G.O.C.	do	12
B.M.	do	13
S.C.	do	14
Bde. Intelligence Officer	do	15
B.B.O.	-	16 & 17
War Diary	-	18
Order File	D.R.	19
Group Comdr., R.A.	D.R.	20
227 Co., R.E.	D.R.	21
234 Co., R.E.		

SECRET.   Copy No. 19.

117th Infantry Brigade Order No. 20.

1.6.16.

Relief

1. An Inter-Battalion relief will take place on the night 3/4 June, 1916.

Dispositions

2. 17/Notts & Derby. R. will take over Billets in GORRE and will become Battalion in Reserve; one Company in close Reserve as at present.

17/K.R.Rif. C. will take over Village Line and will become Battalion in Support.

Time

3. No movement forward of Village Line before 9 p.m. All details not mentioned to be arranged between Commanding Officers concerned.

Trench Stores

4. Battalion Trench Store Lists will be handed over.

Reports

5. Completion of relief will be reported to Brigade Headquarters (F.10.B.9.C.).

W Rokompal Major
Brigade Major, 117th BRIGADE

Issued at 3.0. p.m. to :-

(For distribution see over)

Issued at 8.0. p.m. to :-

	By	Copy No.
16/Notts & Derby. R.	D.R.	1
17/Notts & Derby. R.	D.R.	2
17/K.R.Rif. C.	D.R.	3
16/Rif. Brig.	D.R.	4
117/1 L.T.M. Batt.	D.R.	5
117/2 L.T.M. Batt.	D.R.	6
117/Bde Machine Gun Co.	D.R.	7
Medium Trench Mortars	D.R.	8
3 Sect. Signal Co.	Orderly	9
Hd. Qrs, 39th Div.	D.R.	10
G.O.C.	Personally	11
B.M.	do	12
S.C.	do	13
106th Brigade	D.R.	14
116th Brigade	D.R.	15
Group Comdr., R.A.	D.R.	16
227 Co., R.E.	D.R.	17
234 Co., R.E.	D.R.	18
War Diary	—	19 & 20
Order File	—	21

SECRET   Appendix III   117th Infantry Brigade
To/   Date 6 JUN 1916
Headquarters,   No 117/O.M/805
    39th Division.

Report on Small Operation carried out on the night 4/5th June.

The object of the operation was a raid on the German trenches S. of the DUCK'S BILL at A.10.c.1.1½. At the same time to organise the craters of two mines to be blown at the end of E. Sap, at about A.9.d.6.45., with the object of getting a little further forward in NO MAN'S LAND and so trying to get observation on the German crater trenches on both N. & S. Craters.

2. At 10.10 p.m. the first mine was blown up. At the same time a brisk artillery bombardment of 1 -4.5" How. Battery and 11 - 18 Pr. guns opened on the German trenches on point of entry and German trenches in rear of new craters. In addition to this artillery 4 - 2" Medium Trench Mortars and 4 Light Stokes Trench Mortars kept up an intense fire on the German trenches, on point of entry and neighbouring trenches. Thereafter the whole lifted to the flanks and rear and formed a barrage during the raiding operation.
It may be said here that the artillery and Trench Mortar shooting was excellent. This continued for 5 minutes and stopped. The 3 Infantry parties who were to bomb to the right and left the German front line trenches for a distance of about 80 yards, left our party, crossed NO MAN'S LAND, and, getting through the wire, which had previously been cut by 18 Prs., entered the German trenches notwithstanding being met by a considerable number of bombs.
The idea was that the leading party should bomb to the right; the second to the left and the third establish itself at the point of entry as a liaison party. The Scheme had been carefully rehearsed over a flagged course and was carried out as a raid. The right party were met by a very considerable obstacle about 60 yards from the point of entry. The German trench had been considerably knocked about by our artillery and trench mortars. They succeeded, however, in killing about 8 Germans and bombing 5 or 6 dugouts.

(1)

(2)

The dug-outs had 7 steps leading down into them and they were all under the parapet. The bombs were thrown well inside the doorways and one was entered in order to get prisoners. Two Germans were got out and brought along the trench with a view to bringing them over, but they were so badly wounded that it was found impossible to get them over and they had to be left in the German wire. The left party bombed along the trench and accounted for another 6 or 7 Germans. 3 Dug-outs also were bombed. The withdrawal then took place as previously arranged. The Liaison Officer sent to the right and left to get the men and evacuated them over the German parapet in good order, and without being molested in any way, either by machine gun or rifle fire.

It is noticeable that all the Germans had taken to their dug-outs doubtless due to the severity of the bombardment. The party actually remained in the German trenches from 10.22 until they regained our trenches at 10.55. p.m.

It is regretted that through an oversight no/special detachment had been told off for the purpose of picking up identifications. All that was obtained was a set of equipment and several rifles. One rifle grenade battery was encountered, constructed to carry 2 rifles. There was no overhead cover to the emplacement. The trenches to the left were very wet and a pump was fixed in one of the fire-bays.

3. The pre-arranged plan for consolidation of the craters went through without a hitch but owing to the absence of the expected lip, I am doubtful as to their tactical value. I visited them this morning but was unable to decide at that time to what extent they would be of use. The D Trench connecting them to Sap E. will be continued to-night and deepened so that daylight observation to-morrow may be possible, to determine to what extent they will be useful.

The total casualties in the raiding party amounted to 1 Officer and 2 O.R. severely wounded; 12 other ranks slightly; 2 O.R. killed. In the crater consolidating party 2 O.R. (included above) were killed, which, as they were working in the open in NO MAN'S LAND only 80 yards away from the German trench without cover of

(3)

high lip are very slight. I claim at least 20 German casualties in their own trenches, and, having regard to the number of dug-outs bombed and the groans and noises heard, there may be more. The barrage placed by the artillery and trench mortars on the flanks of the raiding operation were probably responsible for further casualties.

4. The liaison arrangments were as follows :-

Liaison party in German front trench to liaison party in our front trench where reserve bombers and bombs were placed were connected by telephone to O.C., 16/Notts & Derby. R. in CAMBRIDGE TERRACE, by telephone to Brigade Commander and O.C., Artillery Group at O.P. on right of WOLFE Road near GUNNER Siding, thence by telephone to Advanced Brigade Headquarters and Artillery Group Exchange. Liaison worked admirably. Runners crossed NO MAN'S LAND, coming through without fail. *all liaison was reduplicated by runners.*

5. The cooperation of the artillery and medium and light trench mortars was most admirable and was responsible to a very large extent for the success of the operation. The previous wire-cutting and preparation by the artillery had been very well carried out and will doubtless be the subject of a report from Group Commander.

The German retaliation consisted of a certain amount of shelling of GIVENCHY and the neighbourhood of the AVENUE and PICCADILLY with H.E's and Minnenwerfer. The AVENUE was particularly knocked about. ORCHARD FARM received a few shells but the neighbourhood of the road was comparatively free. The retaliation such as it was, took a considerable time to begin; the best part of 20 minutes.

I consider that the spirit shown by the 16/Notts & Derby. R. was excellent. Without hesitation, they advanced through the German wire, which, although almost completely cut, still was a slight obstacle in the face of the bombs which were thrown by the Germans, since this was the first time they have come into close contact with the Bosche.

I propose forwarding some names for favourable consideration at an early date. The work of the 17/K.R.Rif. C. showed equally

P.T.O

fine spirit in the consolidation of their craters, although the operation was of a less showy nature.

[signature] R.D.F. Oldman
Brig. Gen.
Commanding 117th BRIGADE.

5th June, 1916.

H.H.

Copies to O.C. of orig.
17" KRRC
7" Bde gp R.A. ("R.A.") H.Q.
3 gp Divn. taken by hand

SECRET **Appendix IV** Copy No....16

PLAN of DEFENCE of GIVENCHY SECTION

39th DIVISIONAL SECTOR

4.6.16.

GARRISON :- As per Appendix A.

DISTRIBUTION.

FRONT LINE	1.	Present Trench.
SUPPORT LINE	2.	ARTILLERY ROW - BAYSWATER - OXFORD TERRACE - CAMBRIDGE TERRACE - PICCADILLY - PARK LANE - WARE Road.
RIGHT PROTECTED FLANK	3.	ARTILLERY ROW and SPOIL BANK.
LEFT PROTECTED FLANK	4.	WARE Road - NEW CUT to its junction with HITCHIN Road.
POSTS - Support in SUPPORT LINE	5.	(B.1.) - SPOIL BANK - ORCHARD KEEP - MARIE. (B.2.) - MOAT FARM - POPPY.
CENTRAL KEEP	6.	The Vital point of the Section is that lying within the following boundaries :- PICCADILLY from its junction with CAMBRIDGE TERRACE and WOLFE Road, along PICCADILLY, PARK LANE, SCOTTISH TRENCH to its junction with WARE Road; the LEFT Protecting Flank as already stated; and WOLFE Road on the RIGHT. The curtain of trenches defends GIVENCHY KEEP with its supporting points HILDERS - POPPY - MOAT FARM - HERTS - MARIE REDOUBTS. All cellars in GIVENCHY VILLAGE are being made strong for defence by rifle and machine gun fire, by the R.E. Companies.
VILLAGE LINE	7.	A succession of strong posts covered along the entire front by a strong belt of wire entanglements. PONT FIXE S. - PONT FIXE N - WINDY CORNER Le PLANTIN S.
SECOND LINE	8.	Line of Breastworks from the LA BASSEE Canal along the irrigation canal at Brigade Headquarters - thence in a straight line to TUNING FORK ROAD. Three small posts are connected with this line, WESTMINSTER BRIDGE, and MARAIS E. and MARAIS S.E. Several Batteries R.A. are posted in and near this line.
SPECIAL FEATURES	9.	Mining activities on both sides have resulted in the formation of two Mine Craters called CRATERS S. or (DUCK'S BILL) and CRATERS N. The parapets in these Areas are so broken up that their defence is undertaken by Saps, each of which is garrisoned by a party of Bombers. The parapet between these Craters Areas is held in the usual way, and is protected by wire.
SIDBURY HILL		This underfeature situated 400 yards N.E. of PONT FIXE BRIDGE constitutes an advanced post to the defences of the VILLAGE LINE, and very suitable for Machine Gun Defence.
REPORT CENTRE	10.	The Brigade Advanced Report Centre is at FANSHAWE CASTLE (A.14.a.5.5.).

GENERAL PLAN in Case of Attack.

To carry out the provisions of the 39th Divisional Defence Scheme, the following will be the action of the Brigade while holding GIVENCHY SECTION.

FRONT LINE
The front line battalions will hold on to the first and support lines at all costs. The line of keeps GIV. K. - SPOIL BANK - ORCHARD FARM - HAMIE - HILDENS - POPPY - MOAT FARM are manned with their normal garrisons, which will remain in the their keeps in any event and are not at disposal of local commanders for counter-attack. If these garrisons are at work near their keeps they will return at once. O.C's. front line battalions will push forward the Reserves in their hands, i.e... in GIV. K. 3 platoons, in GIV. L. one and a half platoons, so as to be available for immediate counter-attack.

SUPPORT BN
Village Line
The Battalion in the Village Line is available for the counter-attack in any portion of the Brigade Front, less the following minimum garrisons in the Village Line Redoubts.

(1)	GIVENCHY KEEP	2 Pl.	2 M.G's.
(2)	HERTS REDOUBT	½ Pl.	1 L.G.
(3)	PONT FIXE S.	1 Pl.	
(4)	PONT FIXE N.	1 Pl.	
(5)	WINDY CORNER	½ Pl.	
(6)	Le-PLANTIN S.	½ Pl.	
(7)	ORCHARD	1 Pl.	
(8)	HILDENS	--	1 L.G. (Garrison found by Bn. in GIV.
	Total	7 Pls.	

thus leaving 9 platoons and 2 Lewis Guns for immediate counter-attack. The O.C., Village Line Battalion will act as circumstances require and attack if necessary, without waiting for orders from Brigade. His first efforts will directed to moving up his men closer to the summit of the ridge into jumping-off places, for which purpose the keeps will offer opportunities. The principle of not using the supporting troops until the right moment, and then in sufficient force to gain a decision, must be kept in view.

RESERVE BN
The Reserve Battalion will get ready to move up to the Village Line as ordered by Brigade Headquarters. The rout

Sheet No.3.

to be used are :-

    1. Canal Bank to PONT FIXE.
    2. Canal Bank - WESTMINSTER B'GE Road and WINDY CORNER
    3. TUNING FORKS. - Le PLANTIN.

These will be reconnoitred by all concerned.

L.T.M. Batts. The guns of the L.T.M. Batteries will normally be so disposed as to admit of 2 of each Battery therein being available and in the hands of O.C., Sub-section for counter-attack.

Machine Gun Co. The Machine Gun Co. is disposed with 12 guns in keeps and posts and 4 in reserve at GORRE, which will move up to the neighbourhood of Brigade Advanced Report Centre.

Tunnlg Co. 254th Tunnelling Co. are allotted posts in the garrison vide "Preliminary Warning" below :-

Prelim. WARNING In the event of an attack being expected at any time, and if the G.O.C. considers information received sufficiently reliable, the following message will be sent out by 'phone and D.R. or runner: "Carry out preliminary arrangements."

Bns. in Front line On receipt of this message O.C's, Battalions in Front line will, if they have not already done so, get ready to move up their Reserve Company.

Support Battalion O.C., Battalion in Support will assemble working parties (if out), Order stand-to for obligatory minimum garrisons of keeps, and have his 9 Platoons and 2 Lewis Guns ready to move without further orders, should he consider the situation demands it.

Reserve Battalion O.C., Reserve Battalion will get ready to move.

Bde H.Q. Brigade Headquarters will get ready to move to FANSHAWE CASTLE (A.14.a.5.5.).

254 Tunnlg Co. The personnel of 254 Tunnelling Co. in the front line will get ready to move as follows :-

N. Crater, Party 1 proceeds via SCOTTISH TRENCH - UPPER CUT CALEDONIAN Road and KING'S Road to GUNNER SIDING.

N. Crater, Party 2 will take the shortest road to the AVENUE and thence via KILBY'S WALK - KING'S Road to GUNNER SIDING.

Sheet No.4.

N. Crater, Party 3 will proceed via BOND St. - PICCAD-ILLY and KING'S Road to GUNNER SIDING.

S. Crater Parties will take the shortest road to HOPE St. - thence across into HADFIELD Road and WOLFE Road to Assembly Trenches off WOLFE Road (A.15.a.5.9.).

In all cases they will be under their own officers, who will report to the O.C., the nearest body of Infantry.

117 Co. M.Gun Cps   O.C., 117 Co: Machine Gun Corps will have his Reserve Section ready to move up.

Light Trench Mortars   O.C's, 117/1 & 117/2 will have their personnel in rest as well as any reserve under training ready to move up to their positions, detailing such parties as they require from the above to proceed to Bde. Bomb Store to carry up ammunition.

General   On receipt of "Carry out preliminary arrangements" Units will send runners to Bde. Headquarters as under :-

    Infantry Bn.   4 each to F.10.b.9.0.
                     4 each to FF.SHANE CASTLE (A.14.a.5.5)
    117/M. Gun Co.   1 to each of above.
    117/1 L.T.M.   1   ditto
    117/2 L.T.M.   1   ditto

                                 A/S. Fetherstonhaugh Capt
                                         for Major
                             Brigade Major, 117th Brigade

Issued at 11 a.m. to :-

	By.	Copy No.
16/Notts & Derby. R.	D.R.	1
17/ do do	D.R.	2
17/K.R.Rif..C.	D.R.	3
16/Rif. Brig.	D.R.	4
117/1 L.T.M. Batt.	D.R.	5
117/2 L.T.M. Batt.	D.R.	6
Medium Trench Mortars	D.R.	7
117/Bde Machine Gun Co.	D.R.	8
3 Sect. Signal Co.	Orderly	9
H. Qrs, 39th Div.	D.R.	10
G.O.C.	Personally	11
B.M.	do	12
S.C.	do	13
Bde. Intelligence Officer	do	14
War Diary	-	15 & 16
Order File	-	17
R.B.O.,	Personally	18
Group Comdr., R.A.	D.R.	19
227 Co., R.E.	D.R.	20
234 Co., R.E.	D.R.	21
254 Tunnelling Co.	D.R.	22
116th Brigade	D.R.	23

Appendix A.

GARRISON.

INFANTRY

    Four Battalions

    GIV. R.   1 Battalion.

    GIV. L.   1 Battalion.

    Village Line.   1 Battalion.

    Reserve.   1 Battalion.

Machine Guns   1 Company.

Trench Mortars

    Medium T.M's not yet allotted.

Light Trench Mortars

    GIV. R.   1 Batt.

    GIV. L.   1 Batt.

Artillery   5. 18 Pr. Batts. equals 20 guns.

    6. 4.5" Hows.

Appendix B.

(1) A Platoon (of an assumed strength of 35 All Ranks) is taken as the Unit in computing this table.
(2) This works out 500 rounds S.A.A. per rifle in keeps.
(3) An extra 6,000 rounds is allowed for each M.G. or L.G.
(4) Rations for two days per rifle is allowed for.
(5) S.A.A. in firing-line is calculated at 1 box per section.
(6) The Garrisons shown in this appendix are the minimum obligatory Garrisons. The S.A.A. and stores will be maintained at the strength shown so that provision is always made for a probable increase of Garrison.

	Platoons	Machine Guns	S.A.A. Boxes	Mad Grenade Boxes	Foot Boxes	Biscuit Boxes	Water patrol tins	Tanks, water	Ammunition Very-Boxes	Vermorel Sprays	Solution Jars	Shovels	Picks	Sandbags	Barbed wire (old)	Wirecutters	Pumps	MG. SAA Boxes	Billhooks	Trench Stretchers
GIV. K (SPOIL BANK / CHAPLE / HIDE 5	1 1 1	1 1 L.G	14 14 14	50 50 25	2 2 2	2 2 1	100 200 10	2 1 2	3 3 3	1 1 1	3 4 3	20 20 10	6 6 3	100 100 100	5 5 5	1 1 1	1	6 6 6	1 1 1	1 1 1
GIV. L (POPPY / COT FAR	1 1	1	7 14	25 50	1 2	1 2	40 100	1 1	2 3	1 1	4 4	10 20	3 6	100 100	5 5	1 1	1	6 6	1 1	1 1
Villa... BELFS / GIVENCHY KEEP / KEEP FIRE N / KEEP FIRE W / LINDY CORNER / L. PLQTTH R / L. PLQTTH S	1 2 2 2 2 1 1	1 1 1 1 1 1	17 60 56 56 14 14	100 200 100 100 50 50	1 4 3 3 2 2	1 2 1 1 1	100 200 200 200 50 50	4 3 2 1	2 12 12 6 3 2	1 3 3 1 1	4 12 9 9 4 4	20 50 50 50 25 20	5 15 15 10 5 5	100 1000 1020 1040 200 100	5 20 15 15	1 2 2 2 1	1 3	12 6	1 1 1 1	1 1 1
GOR H (MARS N / ARTILLERY N / JAM. L.S.	1 M.C.O. Hut + 2 shelters in stores.							No hut obligatory, but shelters on inventory boards.												
Area Comdg. Group of the			3 mm ench.																	
FIRING & SUPPORT LINES: Firing Line / Support Line	7 2	25 5	200 100						20 10		15 10 5 20			Load out at store						
GIV K (Firing Line / Support Line	3	12	200 100						20 10		10 20 5 20						12 3			
GIV L (Firing Line / Support Line	1½																			

Appendix C.

Position of Machine Guns and Lewis Guns.

Machine Guns.

1. SPOIL BANK   )   A.15.c.5.9.
2. ORCHARD   )   A.15.a.5.4.
3. GIVENCHY KEEP   )
4. GIVENCHY KEEP   )   A.9.c.6.4.

5. WINDY CORNER   A.8.c.7.4.
6. A.14.a.9.9.
7. PONT FIXE N.   A.3.b.2.1.
8. PONT FIXE S.   A.14.d.3.7.

9. MARIE   A.9.c.9½.½.
10. MOAT HOUSE   A.9.c.2½.7.
11. ORCHARD (No.2)   A.15.a.5.4.
12. FRENCH FARM   A.9.c.9.9.

Headquarters at Old Hd. Qrs. GIVENCHY LEFT (A.8.c.2.3.).
In Reserve at GORRE - 4 Guns.

Lewis Guns — The Battalion in Support will keep a Lewis Gun as permanent garrison in each of the following :-

HERTS   1
HILDERS   1

SECRET   Copy No. 20

117th Infantry Brigade Order No. 21.

Ref. Combined   5.5.16.
Map BETHUNE 1/40,000.

Relief
1. The 118th Infantry Brigade will relieve the 117th Infantry Brigade in GIVENCHY Section on the 6th and night of 6/7th June, in accordance with attached Relief Table.

   All details not mentioned to be arranged between Commanding Officers concerned.

Reports
2. Reports when Battalions are relieved to present Brigade Headquarters at F.10.b.9.0.

   Reports of arrival in new Billets to Brigade Headquarters at ESSARS (X.25.a.5.5.).

Report Centre
3. Report Centre will close at F.10.b.9.0. at 6 p.m. on the 6th and will reopen at X.25.a.5.5. at the same hour.

Transport
4. All Transport to be West of GONRE by 10 p.m.

Work
5. Work is to be carried on during relief. Commanding Officers will arrange for Guides to show relieving Battalions exactly where work is being carried out.

   One laying out Patrol per Platoon of units relieving Right and Left Forward Battalions will report to 117th Infantry Brigade Headquarters, Canal House at 7.30 p.m. O.C., 16/Rif. Brig. and O.C. 16/Notts & Derby. R. will arrange for a Guide from there at that hour.

                                                Brigade Major, 117th. BRIGADE.

Issued at 8 a.m. to :-

	By	Copy No.
16/Notts & Derby. R.	D.R.	1
17/Notts & Derby. R.	D.R.	2
17/K.R.Rif. C.	D.R.	3
16/Rif. Brig.	D.R.	4
117/1 L.T.M. Batt.	D.R.	5
117/2 L.T.M. Batt.	D.R.	6
Medium Trench Mortars	D.R.	7
117/Bde. Mchine Gun Co.	D.R.	8
H.Q., 39th Div.	D.R.	9
3 Sect. Signal Co.	Orderly	10
3 Co. Div. Train	D.R.	11
G.O.C.	Personally	12
B.M.	do	13
S.C.	do	14
Bde. Intelligence Officer	do	15
Bde. Bombing Officer	do	16
118th Brigade	D.R.	17
116th Brigade	D.R.	18
106th Brigade	D.R.	19
War Diary	-	20 & 21
Order File	-	22
227 Co., R.E.	D.R.	23
234 Co., R.E.	D.R.	24

SECRET

RELIEF TABLE to accompany 117th Infantry Brigade Order No.21, dated 5.6.16.

Date 1916	Unit of 118th Bde	Relieves Unit of 117th Bde.	Station.	Route.	Guides.	After relief Unit of 117th Bde moves to
Night 6/7th	4/5 Black Watch	16/Rif. Brig.	GIVENCHY (Right)	South Bank of Canal and VAUXHALL B'GE.	To be arranged between C.O's.	ESSARS
6/7th	1/1 Cambs. R.	16/Notts & Derby R	GIVENCHY (Left)	North Bank of Canal and WESTMINSTER B'GE	ditto	ESSARS
6/7th	1/6 Ches. R.	17/K.R.Rif.C.	Village Line	TUNING FORK	ditto	GORRE Wood (F.3.L.)
6/7th	1/1 Herts. R.	17/Notts & Derby R	Reserve GORRE	Any convenient.	ditto	FERME DU ROI (E.6.c.)
—	118/T.M. Batt. 118/M. Gun Co.	117/T.M. Batt. 117/M. Gun Co.	—	ditto	ditto	ditto
6/7th	118/Bde. H.Q.	117/Bde. H.Q.	Canal House (F.10.b.9.0)	ditto	ditto	ESSARS X.25.a.5.5.

SECRET   Appendix VI D   Copy No. 16

117th Infantry Brigade Order No. 22.

Ref. Map BETHUNE
(Combined Sheet) 1/40,000.   9.6.16.

Relief. 1. The 117th Infantry Brigade will relieve the 106th Infantry Brigade in FESTUBERT Section on the night 11/12th June, in accordance with attached Relief Table A. Posts to be relieved in accordance with attached Relief Table B. All details not mentioned will be arranged between Commanding Officers concerned.

Lewis Guns Section 2. Lewis Guns of 17/Notts & Derby. R. and 17/K.R.Rif. C. will relieve on the 10th instant and will report at 106th Infy. Brigade Headquarters, LOISNE at 2 p.m. on the 10th inst.

Machine Gun Co. 3. 117th Bde. Machine Gun Co. will relieve the 106th Brigade Machine Gun Co. on the 10th instant. All arrangements for relief will be made between Officers Commanding Companies direct.

Formations 4. Troops moving in FESTUBERT area will use the following formations :-
West of CANAL DE LA LAWE - In formed Bodies, as usual.
East of Canal and West of the road LA COUTURE - LE TOURET - LOISNE - GORRE, in platoons at 200 yards distance.
East of the/ road by sections at 100 yards distance.

Advance Party 5. O.C's, 17/Notts & Derby. R. and 17/K.R.Rif. C. will detail one Officer per Company and one N.C.O. per platoon to proceed to the trenches on the night of 10/11th June and remain there until their Battalions arrive. They will take over all details with regard to the wiring, etc. Wiring parties from these two Battalions will be sent up on morning of 11th instant.

Command 6. Until relief is complete, all units of 117th Infantry Brigade who may be in the 106th Brigade area will be under the Command of the G.O.C., 106th Infantry Brigade.

Reports 7. Reports when relief is complete will be made by O.C. Units to Brigade Headquarters at LOISNE (C.28.a.4.7.).

2.

Report Centre   3. The Brigade Report Centre will close at HEBUTERNE
(A.25.a.6.5.) at 6 p.m. and reopen at LORETTE (K.29.a
3.7.) at the same hour.

                                        [signature]
                                            Capt.
                                         For Major
                            Brigade Major, 117th Brigade

Issued at 3 a.m. to :-   By.   Copy No.

16/Notts & Derby. R.   D.R.   1
17/Notts & Derby. R.   D.R.   2
17/K.R.Rif. C.   D.R.   3
16/Rif. Brig.   D.R.   4
117/1 L.T.M. Batt.   D.R.   5
117/2 L.T.M. Batt.   D.R.   6
117/Bde. Machine Gun Co.   D.R.   7
S Sect. Signal Co.   Orderly   8
S Co. Div. Train.   D.R.   9
G.O.C.   Personally   10
B.M.   do   11
S.C.   do   12
Bde. Intelligence Officer   do   13
Bde. Bombing Officer   do   14
H.Qrs., 30th Div.   D.R.   15
War Diary   -   16 & 17
Order File   -   18
108th Brigade   D.R.   19
236 Co. R.E.   D.R.   20

TABLE A

RELIEF TABLE of 102nd Infantry Brigade by 117th Infantry Brigade.

(To accompany 117th Infantry Brigade Order No.28, dated 9.6.16).

Date	Unit of 117th	Proceeds to	Route	Relieving	Guides	Remarks
11/12th	16/Notts & D	Le TOURET (Reserve)	Pt.N.13.a.5.4. – turn right at Pt.N.13.a.2.8 – LES CAUDRIGNIES – Le HAMEL – along RUE du BOIS – LE TOURET.	19/Durham Light Infantry	As arranged between O.C's	Header 16/Notts & Derby R. to be at LE TOURET by 12noon
do	17/ do do	ERQUINGHEM (Right)	North Bank of Canal – Turn N. at Pt.P.5.c.4.3 into GORRE – thence by N. road of TUNING FORK to FETUBERT Cross Roads	19th Royal Scots.	ditto	Not to pass Pt.P.5.b. 4.3. before 9 p.m.
do	117/1)&.2.& 117/2)Batt.	LE HAMEL and Trenches	ECRAMS – LE HAMEL	106/1) L.Y.& 1&6/2)Batt.	ditto	Arrangements for relief to be made between O.C.Batts concerned direct.
11/12th	117/3rd Batt.	ISHN X.28.a.3.7	Any convenient.	1&6/No R...	-	To reach LOISNE by 6 p.m.
11/12th	17/Manstr. C.	FESTUBERT (Left)	Guide – P.5.a.0.7 – R. to House A – thence to "N" do 1'th FIRSTS	17th West Yorks	ditto	Not to pass Pt.N.28 N.B.3 before 8.30 pm Not to be clear of N road of TUNI G FORK by 9 p.m.
11/12th	18/H.L.Inf.	Village Line Support	ECRAMS – Le HAMEL – IND – Cemetery – Cross roads I.3.d.1.4.	18th Highland Light Infantry		No 2 Coy for LE PLANTIN & FESTUBERT Cen'l may use LE HAMEL – LOISNE Rd. – thence via X.22.b.5.3. to USING FORK but not to pass 5.b... at LOISNE before 9.30 p.m.
11/	119/Mch.G.	... H... & Trenches	Any convenient	46/Aus. M Gun Co.	ditto	-

Table B.

TABLE OF RELIEF OF POSTS

To accompany 117th Infantry Brigade Order No.25, dated 9.6.19.

Date	Post	Strength	Left	Relieving	Time
11/12th	Le BANTE R A.P.6.d.2.0.	1 Platoon	16/Mfr. Brig.	15th Highland Light Infy.	Maj Reliefs & s arrang ed by Commanding Officers.
11/12th	BRESLAUX U.25.d.4.cent.	do	do	do	do
11/12th	FLEURBAIX L.28.d.4.1.	do	do	do	do
11/12th	CRILLON R L.29.b.6.7.	do	do	do	do
11/12th	CAILLOUX L L.29.b.8.8.	do	do	do	do
11/12th	EPINETTE R. R.24.a.1.8.	1 N.C.O. & 3 men	do	do	do
11/12th	RUGBY K K.23.b.7.0.	do	16/Incks & Derby. R.	1Platdurham Light Infantry	do
11/12th	TURIN Farm R A.22.d.0.2.	do	do	do	do
11/12th	LORNE R A.22.a.0.3.	do	do	do	do
11/12th	DIEHL K A.22.a.6.5.	do	do	do	do
11/12th	Le TILLET Cent. A.16.d.2.0.	do	do	do	do
11/12th	D. I. O. F. E. A.17.c.2.2i.	do	do	do	do

SECRET

117th. Infantry Brigade
Date 14 JUN 1916
No 117/00/23

To/
Officer Commanding
    16/Notts & Derby. R.   17/K.R.Rif. C.
    17/Notts & Derby. R.   16/Rif. Brig.
    117/2 L.T.M. Battery.   117/Bde. Machine Gun Co.

Headquarters, 39th Division.
    do   104th Infantry Brigade
O.C.   225 Co., R.E.

1. The following readjustment will take place in the Brigade Front probably about the 15th instant :-

16/Notts & Derby. R. will take over the line at present held by the Right Battalion of the Brigade on our Left. Frontage left of 17/K.R.Rif. C. exclusive to S.15.c.1.3. (FARM CORNER).

2 Companies in front line; 2 in Support.

O.C., 16/Notts & Derby. R. will reconnoitre the line to-morrow. Guides will be at Battalion Headquarters at S.14.b.7.3. at 9.30 a.m.

2. The following re-distribution of the Brigade Front will take place on the night of this relief :-

    (a). 17/Notts & Derby. R. will close up to its Right, holding a front in the ISLAND LINE from PRINCES ISLAND to No. 10 ISLAND with 2 Companies, including GEORGE St.

1 Company in Support in the O.B.L; 1 Company in Reserve in LE PLANTIN. The Battalion Headquarters will remain where they are.

    (b). 16/Rif. Brig. will take over ISLAND LINE 10.A inclusive to No.15 ISLAND inclusive with 1 Company.

1 Company in the O.B.L.

2 Companies and Battalion Headquarters in FESTUBERT.

    (c). 17/K.R.Rif. C. will close to its left in the O.B.L. in order to give room to the 16/Rif. Brig., place 1 Company in Reserve at EPINETTE. Battalion H.Q. will remain where they are.

3. The Obligatory Garrisons of the VILLAGE LINE will be held as follows :-

    (a). LE PLANTIN N.   1 Platoon.   17/Notts & Derby R.
         FESTUBERT Central 1   do   16/Rif. Brig.
             do   E. 1   do   16/Rif. Brig.
         CAILLOUX S.   1   do   16/Rif. Brig.
         CAILLOUX N.   1   do   16/Rif. Brig.

    (b). These Obligatory Garrisons correspond exactly to those in the Brigade Defence Scheme.

SECRET   W.D   Copy No...

117th Infantry Brigade Order No.25.

Appendix VIII

15.6.16.

Relief.	1.	Reference this office No.117/O.O./23 of the 13th instant, the readjustment of the Brigade Front will take place on the night of 16th/17th.

With the exception of 16/Notts & Derby. R., Commanding Officers will make their own arrangements for the readjustments.

Relief arrangements for 16/Notts & Derby. R. will be as follows :-

16/Notts & Derby. R. will relieve the 20th Lancashire Fusiliers in the present Right Sub-section of the Brigade on our Left on night of 16th/17th. Guides will be at Junction RUE du BOIS and RUE de l'EPINETTE at 9 p.m. on night of 16th/17th.

All details not mentioned will be arranged between Commanding Officers concerned.

Advance Party.	2.	O.C., 16/Notts & Derby. R. will detail 1 Officer per Company and 1 N.C.O. per platoon to proceed to the trenches on night of 15th/16th June and remain there until their Battalion arrives. They will take over all details with regard to wiring. Guides will be at Cross Roads RUE du BOIS and RUE de l'EPINETTE at 9 p.m. on night of 15th/16th.
Lewis Gun Section.	3.	LEWIS Guns of 16/Notts & Derby. R will relieve on night of 15th/16th. Guides will be at Cross Roads RUE du BOIS and RUE de l'EPINETTE at 9 p.m on night of 15th/16th.
Time.	4.	No movements forward of VILLAGE LINE before 9 p.m.
Posts.	5.	Posts will be relieved in accordance with attached Table A.
Reports.	6.	Reports when relief is complete will be made by Officers Commanding Units to Brigade Headquarters at LOISNE (X.28.a.3.7.).

G.H. Fetherstonhaugh Capt.
for Major
Brigade Major, 117th Brigade.

(For distribution see over).

Issued at 3.30 p.m. :-

	By	Copy No.
16/Notts & Derby. R.	D.R.	1
17/ do do	D.R.	2
17/K.R.Rif. C.	D.R.	3
16/Rif. Brig.	D.R.	4
117/Bde. Machine Gun Co.	D.R.	5
117/2 L.T.M. Battery.	D.R.	6
3 Sect. Signal Co.	Orderly	7
H.Q., 39th Div.	D.R.	8
G.O.C.	Personally	9
B.M.	do	10
S.C.	do	11
Bde. Bombing Officer.	D.R.	12
118th Infy. Brigade.	D.R.	13
116th Infy. Brigade.	D.R.	14
104th Infy. Brigade.	D.R.	15
"C" Group Comdr., R.A.	D.R.	16
225 Co., R.E.	D.R.	17
War Diary.	-	18 & 19
Order File	-	20

SECRET   TABLE A.

TABLE of Relief of posts.

To accompany 117th Infantry Brigade Order No.25, dated 15.6.16.

POST	Strength	Unit taking over	Relieving	Time and Guides.
ROUTE A.	1 N.C.O. & 3 men.	17/Notts & Derby R	16/Notts & Derby R	Day reliefs as arranged by Commanding Officers.
TUNING FORK	do	ditto	ditto	ditto
LOISNE N.	do	118th Inf. Brigade	ditto	⎫ Details of these
LOISNE E.	do	ditto	ditto	⎬ reliefs will be
LE TOURET Central	do	ditto	ditto	⎬ notified later.
LE TOURET E.	do	ditto	ditto	⎭
RUE de l'EPINETTE	do	16/Notts & Derby R	20/Lancs. Fus.	Guides will be at CRoss Roads (X.17.c.6.6.) at 3 p.m. 16th inst.
CHAVATTES	do	ditto	ditto	ditto

SECRET Appendix IX Copy No. 17
117th INFANTRY BRIGADE

References to
Sheet BETHUNE 1/40,000.   FESTUBERT SECTION 18.6.16.
and Trench Map 1/10,000.

DEFENCES and DISPOSITIONS in case of ATTACK.

BOUNDARIES. 1. South. GRENADIER Road (Exclusive) LEES REDOUBT - LE
PLANTIN KEEP E. - A.8.b.1.6. - A.7.b.10.6½. - thence
by road to ESTAMINET Corner F.5.b. Central - F.4.b.3.2.
GORRE WOOD (X.27.c.½.3.) inclusive.
North. QUINQUE RUE Crossing - KINKROO KEEP - SHETLAND
Road - INDIAN VILLAGE (all inclusive) - RUE del'EPINETTE
Post N. (exclusive) - X.18.c.9.3. - RUE DU BOIS inclu
-sive to X.16.d.1.9. - EMPEROR Road (inclusive) to
X.16.b.2.5. - thence West to road junction X.15.b.2.5.
West. From road junction X.27.c.1.5. - X.27.a.7.8. -
X.21.a.9.9. - X.15.c.5.9. - X.15.b.2.5.

Lines of   2. The Lines of Resistance are :-
Resistance.   (a). Front System of Trenches.
FRONT LINE   Islands and Old British Line, with their connections.

Support Line.   (b). VILLAGE LINE consisting of certain posts held
                     by Obligatory Garrisons, vide App.A.

Other Lines.   (c). A third line - TUNING FORK E. to EPINETTE W.
                     continued to GIVENCHY SECTION.

                     (d). A fourth line of continuous breastwork and wire
                     running N. to LE TOURET.
                     In these lines of breastwork or wire there are certain
                     intentional gaps left to form pockets, vide Sketch of
                     System of Corps Defence 1/40,000. (Bde. Hd. Qrs. only).
                     Lines C & D are to be regarded as lines for occupation
                     by reinforcements and not as lines for the Brigade to
                     fall back on.

DISTRIBUTION. 3. Two Battalions in Front System.
Right.   Right Battalion from Southern Boundary to QUINQUE RUE
                  and LOTHIAN Road inclusive.
Left.   Left Battalion QUINQUE RUE and LOTHIAN Road (exclusive)
                  to Northern Boundary.
                  One Battalion in Support in VILLAGE LINE:
                  one Battalion in Reserve LE TOURET.

MACHINE GUNS. 4. 12 Machine Guns disposed as follows :-

                  GEORGE St.   1)
                  FIFE Road junction.   1)
                  Left of BARNTON Road.   2)
                  in O.B.L. near INDIAN VILLAGE   2) 12
                  RICHMOND TERRACE   1)
                  VILLAGE LINE   5) (vide App. A.).
                  Emplacements.
                  There are 18 Machine Gun Emplacements in the O.B.L.
                         and 10   in the VILLAGE LINE.
                         in addition to 7 Battle Emplacements in the latter

LEWIS GUNS.   5. 9 Lewis Guns in Islands.
                  1 Lewis Gun in O.B.L. and right of NEW GEORGE St.

TRENCH   6. 1 Section Light Trench Mortars in O.B.L. and
MORTARS.   CANADIAN ORCHARD Salient.

ARTILLERY.   7. The Section is covered by 16 - 18 Prs. and 8 Hows.
                  In addition 2 - 18 Prs. are placed for enfilade
                  fire from the South and 4 from the North.

Sheet No.2.

MEDICAL.	8.	FESTUBERT Right. AID Post. O.B.L. about A.2.b.4.4½. 　　do　　Left.　AID Post.　　do　　do　S.26.b.7.8. Support Battalion in RUE de l'EPINETTE (S.19.b.0.8½.). Advanced Dressing Station (F.5.c.2.9.).
S.A.A.	9.	Distribution of S.A.A. and Bombs as shown in App. B.
TRAMWAYS.	10.	The Tramway Service is being completed by the R.E. and has been reorganized.
Advanced Report Centre.	11.	Brigade Advanced Headquarters is at S.20.c.8.2.

Sheet No.3.

GENERAL PLAN IN CASE OF ATTACK.

Objective. 1. (A). A probable objective of any enemy attack on the Brigade Front will be the breaking of our line with a view to taking the important GIVENCHY Ridge from a Flank.

This must be prevented at all costs. Attention must be paid to the GEORGE St. (New and old) Defences and FIFE Road in this connection. The organisation for fire of the 4 main avenues, FIFE - BARNTON - PIONEER and SHETLAND Roads will support our flanks in case the Flank Battalions of right and left Brigades are driven in. This work is now being taken in hand.

Line of Resistance. 2. (B). The line of ISLANDS is not a line of outposts, but a line of resistance. Many of the old trench between the ISLANDS and the O.B.L. are of use in the counter-attack for concealment of Lewis Guns and troops which may be pushed up. It is necessary therefore, that a thorough reconnaisance of the intervening ground between the O.B.L. and ISLAND should be made. Counter-attack over the open is the only safe way of turning the enemy out of any Islands he may be in possession of.

(C). Should the enemy attack on the Brigade Front, the ISLAND Line will be held at all costs. Should one or more be lost, counter-attack must be developed immediately. Line of advance over the open :

(a). In FEST. R. Sub-section with BARNTON Road and GEORGE St. as guding lines.

(b). In FEST. L. from Support trenches and RICHMOND TERRACE, and from O.B.L. with PIONEER and SHETLAND Roads as guiding lines.

Support. 2. The Battalion in Support in the VILLAGE LINE (less the Obligatory Garrisons) will be available to assist the two Battalions in front line in driving the enemy out of any positions he may

Sheet No.4.

have won. It is to be clearly understood that the
Obligatory Garrisons are not to leave any of the posts
to which they have been allotted. The O.C., Support
Battalion will use his discretion in sending up
support to the Front Battalion when demanded.
He will report all movements to Brigade Headquarters.

Lines of Advance.

3. For Front Battalions. (a). FEST. R. - FIFE Road and
BARNTON Road. (b). FEST. L - - PIONEER Trench and
SHETLAND Road give the necessary guiding lines for
attack "over the open."

4. From the VILLAGE LINE to the O.B.L. CHESHIRE and
WILLOW Roads - BARNTON Road and PIONEER Trench.
In addition the following lines "over the open" have
been reconnoitred by the Brigade Staff. They are
free from obstacles, afford a certain amount of cover
from view, and should be used in preference to the
above-named communication trenches.

    (a). LLOYDS AVENUE - between YELLOW Road and
    WILLOW Road. (A.2.c.5.2.).

    (b). From A.2.c.1.7. in RUE l'EPINETTE to Battalion
    Headquarters, FEST. R. (A.1.b.2.4.).

    (c). From S.25.b.7.3. by track bearing 75 degrees
    (True) and old tram line to about S.26.b.1.7.
    thence through junction of 3 derelict trenches
    to Right Coy. Hd. Qrs. of Left Battalion in
    O.B.L. about S.26.b.4.3.

    (d). From S.19.b.1.3. by track through INDIAN
    VILLAGE to out left of O.B.L.

5. For the Reserve Battalion from LE TOURET. TUNING
FORK to LE PLANTIN Road - Routes A, B and C and the
RUE DU BOIS. Routes A, B and C will allow troops
being taken "over the open" in Artillery formations
in order to avoid loss from barrage fire.

N.B. O.C's, Units will cause all the above to be
reconnoitred by all Officers and at least 2 N.C.O's
per Platoons

Sheet No.5.

Assembly Positions. Support Bn.	6.	Assembly Positions for the Support Battalion can be found in Keeps of the VILLAGE LINE, whence the counter-attack to Forward Lines will take place.
Reserve Bn.	7.	In case of heavy shelling, Assembly Position for the Reserve Battalion can be found in LE TOURET and LE TOURET E. Posts. Should there be no shelling in Reserve Battalion Area, Companies will fall in on the roads near their Billets and await orders. They should not be drawn up in column of route but transport (S.A.A., Bombs, etc.) is to be ready to hook in at short notice.
Runners.	8.	All Battalions will send 4 runners to Brigade Headquarters at LOISNE and 4 to Advanced Brigade Headquarters at S.20.c.8.2.
Machine Guns.	9.	O.C., Reserve Section Machine Gun Co. will report at Brigade Headquarters, LOISNE.
L.T.M. Batts.	10.	One Officer of Reserve Section will report at Brigade Headquarters, LOISNE.
Report Centre	11.	Brigade Headquarters will be ready to move to S.20.c.8.2.

[signature] Capt.
for Major.
Brigade Major, 117th Brigade.

Issued at ~~~~ p.m. to :-

	By.	Copy No.
16/Notts & Derby. R.	D.R.	1
17/Notts & Derby. R.	D.R.	2
17/K.R.Rif. C.	D.R.	3
16/Rif. Brig.	D.R.	4
117/Bde. Machine Gun Co.	D.R.	5
117 L.T.M. Battery.	D.R.	6
3 Sect. Signal Co.	Orderly	7
G.O.C.	Personally	8
B.M.	do	9
S.C.	do	10
Bde. Bombing Officer.	do	11
H.Q., 39th Div.	D.R.	12
O.C., "C" Group, R.A.	D.R.	13
98th Infy. Brigade.	D.R.	14
116th Infy. Brigade.	D.R.	15
225 Co., R.E.	D.R.	16
War Diary	-	17 & 18
Order File	-	19

SECRET   Appendix. A.

117th INFANTRY BRIGADE.

Table of Posts in FESTUBERT SECTION

System	POST	Map reference	Maximum Garrison Post can accommdate Troops. M.G's.		Obligatory Garrison Troops.	M.G's.	Obligatory Garrison found from.	
	(LE PLANTIN. N.	A.2.c.2.5.	1 Co.	5	1 Pl.	1	Support Bn.	
	(FESTUBERT (Cenl)	S.25.d.	2 Cos.	8	1 Pl.	2	ditto	only 1 M.G. at present.
	(do E.	S.26.c.4.4.	2 Pls.	3	1 Pl.	1	ditto	
VILLAGE	(CAILLOUX S.	S.25.b.8.7.	2 Pls.	2	1 Pl.	1	ditto	
LINE	(do N.	S.25.b.8.9.	2 Pls.	2	1 Pl.	1	ditto	
	(EPINETTE E. (late (INDIAN VILLAGE W)		being constructed - no garrison yet allotted.					
	(TUNING FORK E.	X.29.d 7.2.	1 Pt.	3	Caretakers.	xxxxxxxxxxxx	Caretakers. Reserve Bn.	
3rd Line	(ROUTE A.	X.29.b.7.8.	2 Pls.	4		xxxxxxxxxxxx	do	
	(EPINETTE F.	X.24.a.1.8.	2 Pls.	4	1 N.C.O. and 3 men to each Post.		Support Bn.	
4th Line	(LE TOURET (Cenl)	X.16.d.2..	1 Co.	2				Garrisons not detailed from this Brigade.
	(LE TOURET E.	X.17.c.2.8½	1½ Co.	3			Reserve Bn.	
	(LOISNE E.	X.28.a.8.6.	out of repair.					
5th Line	(LOISNE N.	X.22.a.0.3.	1 Pl.	2				

Appendix. ..

117th INFANTRY BRIGADE

Distribution of S.A.A. and Grenades.

Right Sub-section FEST. R.

	S.A.A. (boxes).	Hand Grenades (boxes)
PRINCES ISLAND.	15	15
1, 2, 3 & 4 ISLANDS.	6	6
5, 6. "	5	4
7, 8 & 9. "	5	6
10. "	2	4
10.A "	2	4
11. "	2	4
12. "	2	4
13. "	2	4
13.A "	2	4
GEORGE STREET	8	25
GROUSE BUTTS.	10	30
LE PLANTIN (Reserve).	85	15
O.B.L. A. Coy.	27	25
do B. Coy.	54	20
do C. Coy.	10	40
do Headquarters.	11	70

Each Machine Gun has a Reserve of 9,000 rounds S.A.A.
These amounts will require amending as ISLANDS become joined up.

Left Sub-section FEST.L.

	S.A.A. (boxes).	Hnad Grenades (boxes).
14 ISLAND.	5	8
15 "	1	4
16 "	1	4
20 "	1	4
22 "	1	4
23 "	1	4
24 "	1	4
25 "	1	2 (H.G.)
26 "	1	3
28 "	1	4
30 "	1	4
30.A "	3	8
31 "	1	4
32 "	1	4
33 "	1	4
34 "	1	4
36, 37, 38 ISLANDS.	4	8
COVER TRENCH (Left)	20	27 (2 Bomb Stores)
do do (Right)	20	21 (Kept in 2 Stores on Right and Left).
RICHMOND TERRACE.	20	50 (Kept in 6 Stores distributed along line

---

	S.A.A. (boxes).	Hand Grenades (boxes)
O.B.L.		Position of Boxes
Right Company.	20	25.d.3½.9. -- 10)
Left Company.	20	26.b.6.7. -- 10) 34
		21.a.½.7½. -- 14)
		70.

Battalion Headquarters.
Advanced D.A.C. Depots (Filled by D.A.C.).
1 (F.5.b.6.3.)   205   232
2 (S.13.d.2.3.) RUE   0   167
l'EPINETTE
D.A.C. at ~~ROUGE-I-HOSARD (X.19.c.3.9.)~~.
R. 32 d. 2. 4.

SECRET   117th INFANTRY BRIGADE.
                                           18.6.16.

         ADDENDUM to the Brigade Scheme in case of Attack.

References to
Sheet BETHUNE 1/40,000
and Trench Map 1/10,000.

DISTRIBUTION.   1. For the present the Troops belonging to the Brigade
                    will be distributed as follows :-

                    (a). 16/Notts & Derby. R. will take over the line
                    from the left of the 17/K.R.Rif. C. exclusive to
                    S.16.c.1.3. - end of CADBURY'S TRENCH - BOURNE-
                    VILLE KEEP - CHOCOLATE POST - CHAVATTE POST -
                    LE TOURET N.E. (all inclusive).
                    2 Companies in Front Line; 2 in Support.
                    In case of attack these 2 Companies are at the
                    disposal of the Battalion Commander (less the
                    following Obligatory Garrisons) :-

                        ROPE KEEP   ½ Platoon.
                        TUBE POST   1   do
                        DEAD COW POST   ½   do
                        BOURNEVILLE STATION   1   do
                        OLD BREASTWORK   1   do

                                        Total 4 Platoons.

                    (b). 17/Notts & Derby. R. will close up to its
                    right, holding a front in the ISLAND LINE from
                    PRINCES ISLAND to No.10 ISLAND with 2 Companies,
                    including GEORGE St. 1 Company in Support in the
                    O.B.L. 1 Company in Reserve LE PLANTI .
                    The Battalion Headquarters will remain where they
                    (c). 16/Rif. Brig. will take over the ISLAND
                    LINE No.10.A inclusive to No.15 ISLAND inclusive
                    with 1 Company. 1 Company in the O.B.L.
                    2 Companies and Battalion H.Q. in FESTUBERT LINE.
                    (d). 17/K.R.Rif. C. will close to its left in
                    the O.B.L. in order to give room to the 16/Rif.
                    Brig., placing 1 Company in Reserve at EPINETTE.
                    Battalion H.Q. remain where they are.

VILLAGE LINE   2.   The Obligatory Garrisons of the VILLAGE LINE will
                    be held as follows :-

(a). LE PLANTIN N.	1 Platoon	17/Notts & Derby R
FESTUBERT Central	1 do	16/Rif. Brig.
do E.	1 do	ditto
CAILLOUX S.	1 do	ditto
do N.	1 do	ditto

(b). These Obligatory Garrisons correspond exactly to those in the Brigade Defence Scheme.

The Reserve Companies, less these Obligatory Garrisons of the Battalion in the front line can be called on for the immediate support of the front line, in the same manner as described in the Brigade Defence Scheme for the VILLAGE LINE Battalion. The O.C., 16/Rif. Brig. will exercise his command in accordance with the Brigade Defence Scheme, as if he were commanding the Support Bn. in the VILLAGE LINE.

Machine Guns. 3. Machine Guns will remain distributed as at present, and 2 guns of Reserve Section will go into Front Line of new sub-section on left.

L.T.M. Batts. 4. 1 Section 117 L.T.M. Batt. remains as it is. The other section in Reserve.

Reserve Companies 5. (a). Reserve Companies in the VILLAGE LINE may take off their boots. O.C's Units will give orders to ensure adequate inlying picquets.

(b). All existing orders with regard to platoon outlying patrols hold good.

ARTILLERY 6. Artillery support will remain as it is, except that 1 extra battery will cover the Left Sub-section.

Advanced Report C. 7. Advanced Report Centre is in the same place as before at S.20.c.8.2.

Orders for Counter-Attack. 8. All the orders in regard to the counter-attack contained in the original FESTUBERT SECTION Defence Scheme remain in force.

A.H. Fetherstonhaugh Capt.
for Major.
Brigade Major, 117th Brigade

Issued at p.m. :-

	By	Copy No.
16/Notts & Derby. R.	D.R.	1
17/Notts & Derby. R.	D.R.	2
17/K.R.Rif. C.	D.R.	3
16/Rif. Brig	D.R.	4
117/Bde. Machine Gun Co.	D.R.	5
117/B.T.M. Battery.	D.R.	6
3 Sect. Signal Co.	Orderly	7
G.O.C., B.M., S.C.	Personally	8,9 & 10
Bde. Bombing Officer	do	11
H.Q., 39th Div.	D.R.	12
H.Q. 98th Bde, H.Q. 116th Bde. & "C" Group RA	D.R.	13,14 & 15
225 Co., R.E.	D.R.	16
War Diary	-	17 & 18
Order File	-	19

SECRET   Appendix X   W D   Copy No. 19

117th INFANTRY BRIGADE ORDER No.26.
22.6.16.

The following are the Orders for Transport in the case of a sudden move of the Brigade.

Ref. Sheet BETHUNE
(Combined Map) 1/40,000.

1. On the message "Move" Transport as per margin will move as follows :-

117 M. Gun Co.
Bde. Hd. Qrs.
in order of march

2 (a) Brigade Headquarters and Machine Gun Co. transport will assemble at Brigade Head Quarters and move by road to X.22.d.4½.5. - thence by ROUTE A. to Cross Roads at F.5.b.7.9½. Head to halt there.

17/K.R.Rif. C.
16/Notts & Derby R
in order of march

(b) From LE HAMEL to Brigade Headquarters, LOISNE - thence to X.22.d.4½.5. turning right-handed to 28.b.9½.5. - thence by ROUTE A. to X.29.b.8.7½. - turning right-handed to Cross Roads F.5.b.7.9½. on to the FESTUBERT Road. Head to remain in rear of Brigade Headquarters transport.

17/Notts & Derby R
16/Rif. Brig.
in order of march

(c) In rear of the above to proceed from LE TOURET to X.22.b.4½.5. and thence by the above route, falling in in rear of 16/Notts & Derby. R. transport.

117th L.T.M. Battery

(d) 117th Light Trench Mortar Battery transport will proceed by the same route as the 17/K.R.Rif. C. and 16/Notts & Derby. R. transport, but assemble in rear of whole Brigade transport.

3. From to-day onward all vehicles will have their normal loads loaded on being finished with for the night.

(b) Water-carts will be filled.

(c) Lewis Gun limbers will be loaded up with ammunition ready to take Lewis Guns. Machine Gun limbers will be fully loaded, room being kept for Machine Gun.

(d) The Transport Officer will see that every vehicle is loaded ready to move by night or by day at 15 minutes notice.

4. On the above Orders being given all Cooks in the Front Line will be sent to FESTUBERT VILLAGE, carrying their empty dixies with them. A small fatigue party will be detailed to help them.
Dixies will immediately be loaded into Cookers at Assembly position for transport.

5. The Brigade Salvage Officer, 2/Lieut. T.C.O. WILLIAMS, 16/Notts & Derby. R. will report to Brigade Headquarters at LOISNE (X.28.a.3.7.) where he will take charge of the Brigade Salvage Section.

6. Orders to Transport Officers will be sent direct from Brigade Headquarters.

A/f Fetherstonhaugh
Capt.
A/Brigade Major, 117th Brigade

Issued at 8 a.m. to :-

16/Notts & Derby. R.
17/Notts & Derby. R.
17/K.R.Rif. C.
16/Rif. Brig.
117/Bde Machine Gun Co.
117 L.T.M. Battery.
3 Sect, Signal Co.
3 Co, Div. Train.
G.O.C.
B.M.
S.C.
Bde, Bombing Officer.
War Diary
Order File

	By	Copy No.
	D.R.	1 & 2
	D.R.	3 & 4
	D.R.	5 & 6
	D.R.	7 & 8
	D.R.	9 & 10
	D.R.	11 & 12
	Orderly	13
	D.R.	14
	Personally	15
	do	16
	do	17
	do	18
	-	19 & 20
	-	21

O'S. C, Units.

These orders are Secret and should only be communicated to those actually concerned in these preparations.
Transport Officers should keep their copies in their pockets ready for instant reference.

Fetherstonhaugh
Capt.
A/Brigade Major, 117th Brigade

22.6.16.

H.H.

SECRET　　　　　　Appendix XI　　　　Copy No. 18

117th INFANTRY BRIGADE ORDER No. 27.

Ref. Map BETHUNE　　　　　　　　　　　　　　21.6.16.
(Combined Sheet) 1/40,000.

1. The following adjustment will take place in the Brigade Front to-morrow night, the 22/23rd June.

    (a). The 16/Rif. Brig. will take over the VILLAGE LINE and become the Battalion in Support, as formerly.

    (b). 17/Notts & Derby. R. will extend to its left, taking over its original Front, as held before the readjustment on the 16th/17th.

    (c). 17/K.R.Rif. C. will extend to its right in the O.B.L. and take over its original Front, the Company at present in EPINETTE relieving one Company of the 16/Rif. Brig. in the O.B.L.

POSTS.   2. Posts will be relieved in accordance with attached Table A. The Obligatory Garrisons in the VILLAGE LINE being found by the Support Battalion.

M. Gun Co.   3. 117/Bde. Machine Gun Co. remains as at present.

L.T.M. Batt.   4. 117th Light Trench Mortar Batt. remains where it is.

Time.   5. No movement East of VILLAGE LINE before 9.30 p.m. All other details of relief will be arranged direct between Commanding Officers concerned.

Reports.   6. Completion of relief will be reported to Brigade Head Quarters, (LOISNE (X.28.a.3.7.).

　　　　　　　　　　　　　　　　　　　A.S. Featherstonhaugh.
　　　　　　　　　　　　　　　　　　　　　　　　　Capt.
　　　　　　　　　　　　　　　A/Brigade Major, 117th Brigade

Issued at 10.30 p.m. to :-

	By	Copy No.
16/Notts & Derby. R.	D.R.	1
17/Notts & Derby. R.	D.R.	2
17/K.R.Rif. C.	D.R.	3
16/Rif. Brig.	D.R.	4
117/Bde. Machine Gun Co.	D.R.	5
117 Light Trench Mortar Battery.	D.R.	6
3 Sect. Signal Co.	Orderly	7
G.O.C., B.M., S.C.	Personally	8, 9 & 10
Bde. Bombing Officer.	do	11
H.Q., 39th Div.	D.R.	12
O.C., "C" Group, R.A.	D.R.	13
98th Infy. Brigade.	D.R.	14
116th Infy. Brigade.	D.R.	15
225 & 227 Cos., R.E.	D.R.	16 & 17
War Diary	-	18 & 19
Order File.	-	20

SECRET

TABLE A.

117th INFANTRY BRIGADE.

To accompany 117th Infantry Brigade Order No.27, dated 21.6.16.

Date 1916	Post	Strength	Unit.	Relieving.	Time and guides.	Remarks
22/23rd	LE PLANTIN	1 Platoon	16/Rif. Brig.	17/Notts & Derby. R.	As arranged between Commanding Officers	
do	ROUTE A.	1 N.C.O. & 3 men.	ditto	ditto	ditto	
do	TUNING FORK	do	ditto	ditto	ditto	

SECRET   117th INFANTRY BRIGADE.   W.D. 17
                                 24.6.16.

ADDENDUM to the Brigade Scheme in case of Attack.

References to
Sheet BETHUNE 1/40,000
and Trench Map 1/10,000.

1. The Brigade Front will be extended to its left, the
   Northern boundary being :-
   S.16.c.1.3. - end of CADBURY'S TRENCH - BOURNEVILLE
   KEEP - CHOCOLATE POST - CHAVATTE POST - LE TOURET
   N.E. (all inclusive).

Appendix XII W.D.   17

Herewith ADDENDUM to 117th Infantry Brigade Defence Scheme.
The former and Appendix A, issued on 18th June, 1916 are to be
destroyed.

                                    A. Fetherstonhaugh
                                           Capt.
                            A/Brigade Major, 117th Bde.
24th June, 1916.

(b) Certain posts will be held by Obligatory
    Garrisons. See Appendices C and D.

VILLAGE LINE 2. The Obligatory Garrisons of the VILLAGE LINE will
                 be held as in the old Defence Scheme. 17.6.5.16

Machine Guns 3. Machine Guns will remain distributed as at present,
                 and 2 guns of Reserve Section will go into Front
                 Line of new sub-section on left.

L.T.M. Batts 4. 1 Section 117 L.T.M. Battery remains as it is.
                 The other Section in Reserve.

ARTILLERY   5. Artillery support will remain as it is, except
                 that 1 extra battery will cover the left subsection.

Advanced   6. Advanced Report Centre is in the same place as
Report Centre   before at S.20.c.8.2.

Orders for   7. All orders in regard to the counter-attack
counter-attack. contained in the original FESTUBERT SECTION Defence
                 Scheme remain in force.
                                    A. Fetherstonhaugh
                                           Capt.
                            A/Brigade Major, 117th Brigade

(For distribution see over).

SECRET   117th INFANTRY BRIGADE.
24.6.16.

ADDENDUM to the Brigade Scheme in case of Attack.

References to
Sheet BETHUNE 1/40,000
and Trench Map 1/10,000.

1. The Brigade Front will be extended to its left, the Northern boundary being :-
S.16.c.1.3. - end of CADBURY'S TRENCH - BOURNEVILLE KEEP - CHOCOLATE POST - CHAVATTE POST - LE TOURET N.E. (all inclusive).
The Southern boundary remains as in the old Defence Scheme. 6.5.16.

(a) 16/Notts & Derby. R. will take over the line from the left of the 17/K.R.Rif. C. (exclusive) to the boundary as indicated above.
2 Companies in Front Line; 2 in Support.
In case of attack these 2 Companies are at the disposal of the Battalion Commander (less the Obligatory Garrisons), vide Appendices C and D.

(b) Certain posts will be held by Obligatory Garrisons. See Appendices C and D.

VILLAGE LINE 2. The Obligatory Garrisons of the VILLAGE LINE will be held as in the old Defence Scheme. 6.5.16

Machine Guns 3. Machine Guns will remain distributed as at present, and 2 guns of Reserve Section will go into Front Line of new sub-section on left.

L.T.M. Batts 4. 1 Section 117 L.T.M. Battery remains as it is. The other Section in Reserve.

ARTILLERY 5. Artillery support will remain as it is, except that 1 extra battery will cover the left subsection.

Advanced Report Centre 6. Advanced Report Centre is in the same place as before at S.20.c.8.2.

Orders for counter-attack. 7. All orders in regard to the counter-attack contained in the original FESTUBERT SECTION Defence Scheme remain in force.

A/H Featherstonhaugh
Capt.
A/Brigade Major, 117th Brigade

(For distribution see over).

8.0 a.m 25th

Issued at 3.30 p.m. to :-

	By	Copy No.
16/Notts & Derby. R.	D.R.	1
17/Notts & Derby. R.	D.R.	2
17/K.R.Rif. C.	D.R.	3
16/Rif. Brig.	D.R.	4
117/Bde. Machine Gun Co.	D.R.	5
117 L.T.M. Battery.	D.R.	6
3 Sect. Signal Co.	Orderly	7
G.O.C.	Personally	8
B.M.	do	9
S.C.	do	10
Bde. Bombing Officer	do	11
H.Q., 39th Div.	D.R.	12
O.C., "C" Group, R.A.	D.R.	13
225 Col, R.E.	D.R.	14
227 Co., R.E.	D.R.	15
War Diary	-	16 & 17
Order File	-	18
Handing Over File	-	19

Appendix A.

117th INFANTRY BRIGADE.

Table of Posts in FESTUBERT SECTION

System	POST	Map reference	Obligatory Garrison Troops I.Gs	Obligatory Garrison I.Gs	Maximum Garrison Post can accomodate. Troops	Maximum Garrison M.G's	S.A.A. Boxes	Grenades Boxes	Tinned Meat Boxes	Biscuits Boxes	Water Tins Boxes	Tanks Water Boxes	Shovels	Picks	Sandbags
	LE PLANTIN N.	A.3.c.2.5.	1 Pl	1	1 Co	5	50	40	2	2	50	1	10	5	500
VILLAGE LINE	FESTUBERT (Genl)	S.25.d.	1 Pl	2	2 Cos	8	50	300	6	6	50	1	50	15	500
	do E.	S.26.c.4.4.	1 Pl	-	2 Pls	5	50	100	2	2	50	-	10	5	500
	CAILLOUX S.	S.25.b.3.7.	1 Pl	1	2 Pls	2	10	40	2	2	50	1	10	5	500
	do N.	S.25.b.5.9.	1 Pl	1	2 Pls	2	10	40	2	2	50	1	10	5	500
	EPINETTE E. (late INDIAN VILLAGE W)		Being constructed - no garrison yet allotted.												
3rd Line	TUNING FORK E.	X.29.d.7.2.	Caretakers 1 N.C.O. and 5 men to each post.		1 Pl	3	5	40	2	2	50	-	10	5	500
	BOURE A.	X.29.b.7.6.			2 Pls	4	10	40	2	2	50	1	10	5	100
	EPINETTE W.	X.24.a.1.9.			2 Pls	2	10	40	2	2	50	-	10	5	-
4th Line	LE TOURET (Genl)	X.16.d.2.0.			1 Co.	3	-	-	-	-	-	-	-	-	-
	LE TOURET E.	X.17.c.2.8.			1 Co		-	-	-	-	-	-	-	-	-
	LOISNE A.	X.22.a.3.5.			out of repair		-	-	-	-	-	-	-	-	-
	LOISNE B.	X.22.a.3.3.			1 Pl	3	-	-	-	-	-	-	-	-	-

X Not occupied by Brigade at present.

Appendix C.

117th INFANTRY BRIGADE

Keeps in Front Line System.

Section	Name of Keep	Map reference	Obligatory Garrison			S.A.A. Boxes	Grenades Boxes	Rations	Water galls	Picks	Shovels	Sand-bags
			Men	M. Guns	L. Guns							
FESTUBERT LEFT	NEW ROPE	S.21.d.6.8.	15	1	-	24	25	-	30	5	10	500
	TUBE STATION	S.21.a.8.6.	30	1	1	70	50	-	150	10	20	500
	DEAD COW	S.15.c.4.2.	20	-	-	24	20	-	30	5	10	500
	CHOCOLATE	S.15.a.2.1.	4	1	-	16	-	-	30	5	10	500
	BOURNEVILLE (Section of Reserve Line)	S.15.a.8.1.	2 Platoons		1	50	20	-	100	8	15	500

Appendix D.

117th INFANTRY BRIGADE.

Posts in VILLAGE - St. VAAST - CROIX BARBEE System.

Section	Name of Post	Map reference.	Maximum Garrison			S.A.A. Boxes	Grenades Boxes	Rations	Water galls	Picks	Shovels	Sandbags
			Platoons	M. Guns	L. Guns							
FESTUBERT	RUE DE L'EPINETTE N.	S.13.d.4.6.	2	1	-	40	25	75	100 15	15	30	500
	CHAVATTES	S.13.b.4.8.	1½	-	-	10	8	-	25	5	10	200

Copy No. 7 **Appendix XIII** Secret.

117th Brigade Order No. 28

27/6/16

(1) The following operations will be carried out on the night June 30th/July 1st by the 16th Notts & Derby R. and the 17th K.R. Rif. Corps and the 117 Bde M. G. Coy.

(2) A smoke barrage will be formed from S 22 c 1.4 to S 16 c 3½ 5 by the following means:—

(a) One 3.7" Mortar at FARM CORNER
    (about S 16 c 2.6)

One 3.7" Mortar at FUNNEL STREET.
    (about S 21 b 7.5)

(b) 4 Catapults throwing P. bombs, equally distributed down front.

(c) P.S. Bombs

(d) Smoke candles.

(3). Throwers, (teams of three) will man every fourth bay. These throwers will, as far as possible be found by ordinary guards. Care will be taken to prevent unnecessary crowding of Fire Trenches.

(4) Timings. Zero will be notified later.

0 to 1 hr Smoke Barrage and Artillery Bombardment

1 hr to 2 h. Artillery Bombardment NO Smoke

2 hr to 3 h. Smoke Barrage with VICKERS & LEWIS GUNS

(5) At 2 hr. 5 the 17th. K.R. Rif. Corps' raiding party will leave our trenches under cover of smoke and bombardment and enter GERMAN TRENCHES about S28 a 7.4 and will remain there not more than 15 minutes.

(6) During whole operation all companies of Left and Centre Battalions in front & support lines will stand to under cover, 1 Company in O.B. Line will stand to under cover, 2 Companies in TUBE & BOURNEVILLE will stand to under cover.

(7) The artillery of "C" group will keep up a heavy Bombardment of the enemy's Trenches on agreed on points and on agreed on Time Table, opposite CANADIAN ORCHARD. The bombardment will be lifted and a barrage established to assist the operation of the 17th K.R. Rif. Corps' raiding party.

(8) Reports to advanced Bde H.Q. S20 c 8.2
(9) Acknowledge.

W Charville Capt.
Bde Major. 117 Inf Bde

Copies to 16 Notts & Derby R
17   do
17 KRRifC
16 Rif. Brig.
117 Bde MG Coy.
Bde Major
Office Copy.

39th Division
116 Inf Bde
O.C. Group RFA
117 LTM

Amendments

Copy 117th T.M.

29/30'

Para (a) Delete whole para and substitute

Timings   2.50am - 3.50am Smoke barrage
          2.58am   3.5am Artly barrage
          3.5am   Advance of Infantry
                   and Lewis Guns

Para (c) Delete 2.8 hrs and add 2.50am

10 pm

117th T.M. Batty

39th Division.

B. H. Q.

117th INFANTRY BRIGADE

JULY 1916

Appendices attached:-

Brigade Operation Orders.
Report on Raid 3/4th July (App II)
Reports on Raids 11/12th (App VI)
Defences & Dispositions in case of attack
Relief Orders.

ORIGINAL

Army Form C. 2118

Page 1.

WAR DIARY
or
INTELLIGENCE SUMMARY
(Erase heading not required.)

Instructions regarding War Diaries and Intelligence Summaries are contained in F. S. Regs., Part II. and the Staff Manual respectively. Title Pages will be prepared in manuscript.

Place	Date	Hour	Summary of Events and Information	Remarks and references to Appendices
LOISNE	1st July		All quiet. Our LEWIS guns fired intermittently during the night at the gaps in the enemy wire at A.3.b.1¾.5 and A.3.b.1¾.4½. (Sheet 36.c.N.W.1) and succeeded in keeping them open.	
	2nd		A German was observed wearing a steel helmet similar in pattern to our own. An enemy sniper wearing a black mask was discovered firing between black sandbags. Our own snipers claim to have hit him. The enemy has tried unsuccessfully to repair his parapet and wire.	
	3rd.		The 16th Rifle Brigade, supported on the right by the 17th Notts & Derby Regt. carried out a raid on the German POPE'S NOSE (A.3.b.1¾.4½). Operation Order and full account appended.	App 1 & 2
	4th		Both sides quiet after last night's raid. Our LEWIS guns continued to fire on gaps in enemy wire during the night.	
	5th		The Brigade on our right (19th Brigade) carried out a successful raid on enemy trenches during the night. The artillery bombarded the enemy trenches and almost immediately the enemy put a barrage on our front island line. We allowed this to continue for a short time in order to keep the enemy in doubt as to point of attack, and then answered by our artillery.	
	6th		Our LEWIS guns continued to keep the gaps in enemy wire open by intermittent firing during the night. The attitude of the enemy remains unchanged. He appears to be nervous as a result of our raids. At the slightest sound he throws bombs and opens rapid fire, and judging from the fire developed and the sound of voices, the front line is strongly held. The enemy appears to "stand-to" all night.	

Army Form C. 2118

Page 2.

WAR DIARY
or
INTELLIGENCE SUMMARY
(Erase heading not required.)

Instructions regarding War Diaries and Intelligence Summaries are contained in F. S. Regs., Part II. and the Staff Manual respectively. Title Pages will be prepared in manuscript.

Place	Date	Hour	Summary of Events and Information	Remarks and references to Appendices
LOISNE	7th		The enemy is busy repairing his parapet in A.3.b. and also SUNKEN Road Trench. The attitude of the enemy remains unchanged.	
	8th		16th Rif. Brig. relieve the 17th K.R.Rif. C. in centre subsection.	App. 3.
	9th		A quiet day. At night our Lewis guns kept open the gaps made by our artillery.	
	10th		Our snipers had a good day and hit about 4 Germans.	
	11th		Two minor enterprises were carried out and met with fair success. One was carried out by 17th K. R.Rif. C. at S.29.c.8.9½ and the other by the 16th Notts & Derby Regt. at S.22.c.6.6. The first party cut the wire with a BANGALORE TORPEDO but were held up by low trip wire hidden in the long grass. The second succeeded in entering the enemy trenches and accounted for a good number of Germans. Preliminary Orders (Order No.32), Order No.33 and Amendment. Full account of the raid.	App 4,5,6.
	12th & 13th		Nothing of interest to report. Some artillery activity on both sides.	
GENSE DU RAUX	14th		The 117th Brigade relieves the 124th Brigade in the FERME DU BOIS Section. The 11th Bn. Royal Sussex Regt. is attached to this Brigade and is in reserve in KING'S Rd., LE TOURET. The frontage now held by the Brigade is from the QUINQUE CROSSING to OXFORD ST. Move Order appended.	App. 7.
	15th		A quiet day. Desultory shelling on either side, fix machine guns fired on the enemy front line and communication trenches during the night.	
	16th		Our artillery registered on a few points in the enemy front line and in retaliation the enemy fired a few .77 mm on our front and support lines.	

WAR DIARY or INTELLIGENCE SUMMARY

(Erase heading not required.)

Army Form C. 2118

Place	Date	Hour	Summary of Events and Information	Remarks and references to Appendices
CENSE DU RAUX	17th		A quiet day. Slight artillery activity on both sides. Our snipers hit 3 Germans in a C.T.	
	18th		The shelling of GIVENCHY brought some retaliation on some of our gun positions and on our Brigade Headquarters. An unusual amount of movement was observed during the day and sounds of transport and heavier traction reported from different parts of Brigade Front. Defence Scheme issued.	App. 8. App. 9.
	19th		Appendix to Defence Scheme issued. On our left the 5th Australian Division and the 61st Divn. carried out an operation in the FARQUISSART DISTRICT and in connection we sent out three strong fighting patrols in order to obtain a prisoner. We were unsuccessful and our parties suffered some slight casualties. Amendment to Defence Scheme.	App. 10.
	20th		116th Brigade relieves the 117th Brigade in this section (FERME DU BOIS). Our Brigade, less two Battalions goes into Divisional Reserve at LE HAMEL (X.20.d.6.3). The two Battalions in question are attached to the 118th and 116th Brigades, the 16th Notts & Derby Regt. to the former and the 17th Notts & Derby Regt. to the latter. Order No.36 appended.	App. 11.
LE HAMEL	21st		The 117th Brigade, less the two Battalions attached to the 116th and 118th Brigades respectively becomes part of the Divisional Reserve, the remainder being the mobile column, consisting of the WESTMORELAND & CUMBERLAND YEOMANRY, 5th Motor M.G. Battery and XIth Corps Cyclist Battalion. The whole comes under the orders of the G.O.C., 117th Brigade. 39th Div. Reserve Order No.2 app.	App. 12
	22nd & 23rd		Nothing of interest to record.	

WAR DIARY
or
INTELLIGENCE SUMMARY
(*Erase heading not required.*)

Army Form C. 2118

Page 4.

Place	Date	Hour	Summary of Events and Information	Remarks and references to Appendices
LE HAMEL	24th		The units of the Brigade move as follows :- 16th Notts & Derby Regt. to BETHUNE, 17th Notts & Derby Regt. to LES CHOQUAUX, 17th K.R.Rif. C. remain at LE HAMEL and 16th Rif. Brig. moves to ESSARS (Order appended).	App-13
	25th		Nothing to record.	
CANAL HOUSE	26th		Brigade takes over the GIVENCHY Section from the 118th Infantry Brigade. The front line is held by 16th Rif. Brig. (right) 17th K.R.Rif. C. (left), 17th Notts & Derby Regt. in support, 16th Notts & Derby Regt. in reserve.	APP. 14.
	27th		The daylight relief of the 118th Brigade was quite successful and no hostile shelling took place at all. The attitude of the enemy seems to be quiet and apparently he would like ours to be the same. Very few rifle grenades were fired at us during the day. By night hostile M.Gs and rifles active. A quiet day. A few .77 mm were fired at our front line and communication trenches and about 25 rifle grenades fell in our front line. In retaliation we sent back 50 rifle grenades.	
	28th		Between 11 and 11.15 p.m. our artillery bombarded the hostile trenches, to which the enemy retaliated heavily on front, support and communication trenches. He also opened heavy rapid rifle/fire but his machine gun fire remained normal. Fighting patrols were out at night but met no enemy patrols.	
	29th		Between 11 and 11.15 p.m. our group artillery again bombarded the hostile trenches and drew some retaliation on our front, support and communication trenches. On the whole the retaliation was weak, but quickly forthcoming.	
	30th		We again bombarded the enemy trenches for 15 minutes (10.45 to 11 p.m.) and drew less	

Army Form C. 2118

WAR DIARY
or
INTELLIGENCE SUMMARY
(Erase heading not required.)

Page 5.

Instructions regarding War Diaries and Intelligence Summaries are contained in F.S. Regs., Part II. and the Staff Manual respectively. Title Pages. will be prepared in manuscript.

Place	Date	Hour	Summary of Events and Information	Remarks and references to Appendices
CANAL HOUSE	30th		retaliation than the preceding day. We have greatly subdued the enemy's rifle grenade activity. Today none whatever fell in the right subsection and for every one that fell on the left subsection we retaliated with eight and fired there a total of 535 rifle grenades.	
	31st		A raid was carried out on German trenches S. of RED DRAGON CRATER at 11.15 p.m. by the 17th Notts & Derby Regt., supported by Group Artillery, Heavy, Medium and Light Trench Mortars. Our bombardment brought heavy retaliation on our front and support lines and even as far back as the VILLAGE LINE. Operation Order appended.	App. 15.

Brig. Gen.
Commanding 117th. INFANTRY BRIGADE.

SECRET.

Appendix I

117th INFANTRY BRIGADE ORDER No 29.

Copy No 14

Orders for a small operation to be carried out on the night 3/4th July.

(1) **OBJECTIVE.** To assault the German Salient at A 3 b 3½ 5½ and penetrate as far as the line parallel to the western face of salient and the trenches leading to the Support line on NORTH & SOUTH for a distance of 100 yds. The German Trenches will be held for an hour and before withdrawal entirely destroyed.

(2) **TROOPS TO BE EMPLOYED :-**
2 Companies 16th RIFLE BRIGADE
1 Officer & 15 men 225 Coy. R. E. (for demolition purposes)
1 Officer & 20 men 17th NOTTS & DERBY R.

(3) **ACTION OF ARTILLERY.**
For ten minutes an intense bombardment will be kept up on the trenches immediately opposite CANADIAN ORCHARD salient on the PARABOLA Trench and Trenches in rear of it. They will then switch to form a barrage on agreed-on points in rear of point of attack and keep the barrage up for the whole time the Infantry are in the German Trenches. On the Infantry withdrawing they will drop to the front German Trench and barrage No Man's Land.

(4) **ACTION OF LIGHT TRENCH MORTARS.**
6 3" Trench Mortars will be placed in rear of Islands 10 & 12a and cooperate with the artillery in keeping up the barrage to the flanks of the infantry assault on points
A 3 b 4½ 1
A 3 b 6½ 3
A 3 b 4 7½

dropping to front trench after the infantry has withdrawn.

(5) **ACTION OF R. E.**
R. E. Demolition party will enter German Trenches after the Infantry have established themselves and demolish the German POPES NOSE.

(6) As the Infantry moves to the assault O. C. 17th NOTTS & DERBY R. will make a demonstration at A. 3 c 5½ 4 thereafter remaining in No Man's Land to guard the right flank of assaulting Infantry. A LEWIS GUN will be put out for this purpose at the arranged point.

(7) **TIMINGS.** ZERO will be notified later.
O. O to O.10 hrs Intense Artillery Bombardment
O. O Assemble of Infantry Parties in No Man's Land
O. 6 Assault of GERMAN TRENCHES
O.10 Demonstration at point 34 by 17th NOTTS & DERBY R.
O.12 Switch of artillery to form barrage
O.12 3" Light Trench Mortars open fire
O.12 Rifle & Lewis Gun fire opened from Islands 22 to 34 on German Trenches opposite
O.55 Withdrawal begins. On "Artillery clear" repeated Artillery drops to front line

Synchronization of watches at 8 p.m. & 10 p.m.

Order No 29 -2-

(8) Garrisons of all Islands & BARNTON T. Trench will "stand to" during the operation. Outlying patrols from Islands 1 to 24 will be withdrawn until the operation is finished. All Companies of the 17th NOTTS & DERBY R. in the O. B. Line will "stand to". The Right Company 17th K. R. Rif. Corps will be in readiness to move. Companies in the O. B. Line will remain under cover.

(9) MEDICAL.   Evacuation of CASUALTIES will be
   1. Over the open down path running along Barnton Rd.
   2. Thence to Regtl. Aid Post in O. B. Line
   3. From there to relay post in FESTUBERT by trolley & wheeled stretcher
   4. For this purpose 8 Trollies taking four cases each will be moved from INDIAN VILLAGE Tramway to BARNTON ROAD Tramway under Brigade arrangements.

(10) TRAFFIC.   O. C. 17th NOTTS & DERBY R will arrange for Control of traffic in BARNTON ROAD. There will be NO traffic UP BARNTON ROAD for an hour before ZERO. During the operation all traffic will be confined to operating troops upwards, NONE downwards

(11) ADVANCED REPORT CENTRE at 17th NOTTS & DERBY R. Battn. H. Q.

(12) ACKNOWLEDGE.

                                    W C Maxwell
                                               Captain,
                   Brigade Major 117th Infantry Brigade.

Copies issued to   Time.
16th Notts & Derby R.
17th   do.
17th K. R. Rif.Corps
16th Rifle Brigade
117Bde. M. G. Coy.
117Bde. L. T. M. B.
Brigade Major
Staff Captain
War Diary
H. Q. 39th Division
225 Field Coy R. E.
Artillery Group Commander
118 Inf. Bde
19 Inf Bde.

Secret ~~Copy~~
~~Office Copy~~

BM/39

To O.C. 17 Notts & Derby R
16th Rifle Brigade.

(1) With reference to raid being carried out on night 3/4th June by the 16th Rifle Brigade, the 17th Notts & Derby R will detail a party for carrying out the Bridges which will be placed in readiness beforehand on the night 2/3rd June, in the Cover trench by the 16th Rifle Brigade. This party will place the bridges in position at a hour (to be settled later) ~~soon after dark as possible~~ under the direction and supervision of an Officer of the 16th Rifle Brigade.

(2) The 17 Notts & Derby R will also detail lying-out patrols to guard these bridges and ensure that they are not interfered with by the enemy.

(3) The greatest care must be taken to escape detection.

(4) The Officer of the 16th Rifle Brigade will report to Batt. HQ. 17th Notts & Derby R at 9.30 p.m.

(5) Any further details will be arranged direct between O.C. 17th Notts & Derby R & O.C. 16th Rif Brig —

(6) Acknowledge

W E Manwell
Capt.
Brigade Major 117 Inf. Brigade.

30/6/16.

SECRET

Amendment to 117th Brigade Order No.30.

Para. (6) for A.3.c.5½.4. read A.3.d.5½.4.

                                                                           Capt.
                                    Brigade Major, 117th Inf. Brigade.

2.7.16.
Issued to :-

16/Notts & Derby. R.	H.Q. 39th Div.	Brigade Major
17/ do do	H.Q. 118th Inf. Bde.	Staff Captain
17/K.R.Rif. C.	"C" Group, R.A.	War Diary (2)
16/Rif. Brig.	225 Co., R.E.	
117/Bde. M. Gun Co.	117 T.M. Battery	

"A" Form.
MESSAGES AND SIGNALS. Army Form C. 2121.

SECRET
D.R.

TO 116th Inf Bde
117th " " (reference his B.M/66 of 1/7/16)

Sender's Number: 39/G.S.S/8/8/2
Day of Month: 2/7
AAA

The Divl Commander approves of two Companies 116th Infty Bde (from battalion at LE TOURET) to be placed in VILLAGE LINE of FESTUBERT Section on the night 3rd/4th July AAA all details to be arranged between Brigade Commanders and locations of Companies reported to Div. H.Q.

From 39 Div.
Place
Time

"A" Form. Army Form C. 2121.
MESSAGES AND SIGNALS.

SECRET.

TO GOC

Sender's Number: BM/95
Day of Month: 3rd
AAA

Ref 117 Brigade Order No 30 para 7
ZERO will be at

Please acknowledge.

From 117th Brigade
Time am

(Z) Welmaxwell Capt
Brigade Major

Timings

Zero = 11.30 p.m.

11.30 p.m. to 12.30 a.m. Arty. bombardment (slow) of German trenches opposite CANADIAN Orchard

12.10 a.m. Assembly of Infy. assault parties.

12.30 a.m. Infy. Assault.

12.35 a.m. Quicken Arty Bombt. of Canadian Enemy trs. opposite Orchard

12.40 a.m. Slow bombardment ready to switch barrage in rear of Poppies wood.

12.2550 a.m. Demonstration of 7" Stokes mortars at Pt. O

12.35 a.m. 3 L.T.M's open in G. emplacement at.

12.35 a.m. Rifle Grenades and Stokes on the German trenches opposite Canadian Orchard & Lewis machine gun fire.

1.35 a.m. Infy. withdrawal begins.

SECRET

Appendix II   W.D

To/
    Headquarters,
        39th Division.

Report on Raid carried out on the night of the 3rd/4th July, 1916
by the 16th Rifle Brigade, 17th Sherwood Foresters and R.E.

OBJECT   1. To enter the German trenches at A,3.b.2½.5. known as the POPE'S NOSE, advance as far as the support line, kill as many Germans as possible, and demolish the trenches. The area of objective was approximately 350 yards radius from the apex of the POPE'S NOSE.

Numbers employed.   2. 2 Companies 16th Rifle Brigade; 1 bombing party of 24 men, 17/Notts & Derby. R., demolition party of R.E. 15 men.

PLAN.   3. In order to deceive the enemy a slow bombardment by the Group Artillery was kept up on the German trenches opposite CANADIAN ORCHARD Salient for upwards of an hour. At the moment of entry of the Infantry assault the bombardment was intensified at this spot. The Infantry assaulted at 12.30. The first 4 parties by way of the Northern face of the Salient where a gap in the wire had been well cut, although there were many loose coils which impeded progress. The enemy were fully alert and waiting at the parapet for the assault. Many casualties occurred as the two leading parties began to enter the German trenches. This they did, however, and according to the pre-arranged plan, moved to the left down the German trenches and to the Eastern face across the open. They were heavily opposed with bombs and rifle fire from this rear face. Shortly after the entry of the main party, a party from Island 10 advanced against the Western face of the Salient, carrying ~~bridging~~ bridges and effectively bridged the 15 foot ditch and cut the wire sufficient to allow them to enter the German trenches. It was known that the wire-cutting here had not been very successful. Again they encountered formidable opposition. This allowed the Southern trenches of the object to be made good. It had been hoped that the main attack would carry this trench, thus giving time for the bridging and wire-cutting

2.

operations of the right attack.

At 12.46 the Group Commander switched the artillery from the CANADIAN ORCHARD objective to form a box barrage in rear of the assaulting troops. The signal was given both by telephone and by a red rocket signal. The rate of fire throughout the operation was easily controlled. Slower rates being given on three occasions. The demolition party apparently lost direction to a small extent but were found by runners and entered the German trenches. A machine gun dugout at the apex of the Salient was demolished, but owing to the severe nature of the fighting it was not possible to do more in the way of demolitions.

While the main operation was going on, in order to cover the right flank and create a diversion, a party of the 17/Notts & Derby. R. (1 Officer and 24 men) advanced through the wire at A.3.d.5¼.4½. MACHENSEN'S TRENCH. It was known that this had not been very well cut, but 2 bombing squads were able to enter the trench and bomb down it for a short distance. They were severely opposed while getting through the wire. Having remained for a few minutes in the German trenches, they withdrew and remained in NO MAN'S LAND at the appointed spot, covering the right flank of their Lewis Gun.

Withdrawal 4. The Officer Commanding the raiding party, who was established with his liaison party at the apex of the salient, gave the order to withdraw at 1.35, having previously telephoned thro' to the Advanced Battalion and Brigade Headquarters in the O.B.L that he was going to do so. The withdrawal was effected in good order, runners being employed to give the order to the assaulting troops in the more forward trenches.

5. During the whole operation the trenches opposite the CANADIAN ORCHARD Salient were kept under Rifle Grenade, Lewis Gun, 3" Mortar and rifle fire, upwards of 600 rifle grenades being fired. A suspected machine gun emplacement at S.27 d.4½.½. was kept under the fire of 3 -3" Mortars, as also Pt.A.3.b. 3½.½. on the right flank.

Enemy retaliation 6. At the beginning of the bombardment a small amount of counter-battery retaliation was made in the direction of the FESTUBERT

3.

battery. Thereafter enemy artillery retaliation confined themselves to the CANADIAN ORCHARD SALIENT. There was no machine gun fire, which is not easily explicable, seeing that he was fully prepared for the attack. All our casualties were incurred from rifle and bomb fire in the hand-to-hand fighting that ensued on entry and while in, the German trenches. A large number of red and green rockets were sent up both from the POPE'S NOSE and trenches opposite the CANADIAN ORCHARD Salient, but from observation they appeared to come from the same localities and their meaning is therefore not easy to deduce.

RESULTS. 7. It is difficult to establish the exact course of the action because all the officers/leaders became casualties immediately on entering the German trenches. All that can be vouched for is that 2 German Officers or Non-commissioned Officers and 15 Other Ranks are definitely known to have been killed. One machine gun emplacement was blown up.

Owing to the severe nature of the fighting, it was not possible to take any prisoners.

I regret to say that our casualties were severe, amounting to 3 Officers killed, 2 missing, 5 wounded and upwards of 80 Other Ranks. The proportion of officers employed seems to be high, but it should be remembered that 2 Companies were employed, which was necessary to make good the objective selected. In point of fact only 2 Officers did not become casulaties.

GENERAL. 8 Had it not been for the loss of the officer leaders at the outset it might have been possible to have inflicted heavier losses on the enemy. It may be fairly said that the men had to fight every inch of their way from the moment they entered the German trenches I cannot speak too highly of the fine fighting spirit displayed by the men, and wish to emphasise the fact that the N.C.O's and men having lost their officers, resolutely advanced to the point of their objective.

I propose to bring to the Divisional Commander's notice several names, but I will mention at the moment the names of Major BRIDGES who commanded the raiding party, and that of 2/Lieut. PAGE for his extremely gallant work in bridging the stream and cutting the wire in face of very heavy opposition.

(Sd) R.D.F. OLDMAN Brig. Gen.
Commanding 117th. BRIGADE.

5th July, 1916.

H.H.

SECRET

To/

Headquarters,

39th Division.

In continuation of my Report on the operation carried out by the 16th Rifle Brigade, I herewith forward for the information of the G.O.C, a brief account of the small operation carried out by the 17th Sherwood Foresters on the night 3rd/4th July, 1916. The party of 5 N.C.O's and 43 men under 2/Lieut. W.R. BIRKIN and 2/Lieut A.J. BULLIVANT, left No.3 Island at 12.30 a.m. to make a raid on the German trench at A.3.d.5½.4½.

On arriving 20 yards from the German wire they encountered a party of the enemy lying out on our side of their wire whom they drove in, with bombs. They then went forward to the wire which was 20 yards deep and only cut half way. While cutting their way through the remaining distance, the Germans opened fire with machine guns and rapid rifle fire.

This part of the trench was held very strongly. In spite of the heavy fire, and under cover of our bombs, twelve men actually got into the German trenches and bombed the Germans with great success. Pte. TAYLOR accounting for a number of the enemy himself.

At 1.10 a.m. the party withdrew under cover of the support party to a selected position in NO MAN'S LAND, where they covered the right flank, with one Lewis Gun which had been left there for this purpose when the party advanced.

At 1.50 a.m. the whole party withdrew on to No.3 Island.

The total casualties were :-

        1 Officer wounded.
        1 man killed.
        1 man missing.
        3 N.C.O's wounded.
        6 men wounded.

(Sd.) R.D.F. OLDMAN,
Brig. Gen.
Commanding 117th. BRIGADE.

4th July, 1916.

SECRET

To/

Headquarters,
    39th Division.

Advance Report on raid carried out on POPE'S NOSE.
----

1. According to order the slow bombardment of enemy trenches opposite CANADIAN ORCHARD took place an hour previous to that fixed for the Infantry assault on the POPE'S NOSE. The Infantry assembled in 5 parties in NO MAN'S LAND opposite the Northern face of the POPE'S NOSE. At the same moment the bombardment of the German trenches opposite CANADIAN ORCHARD was intensified. Infantry then advanced to the assault through a gap in the wire which had been cut during the preceding 7 days. The main wire was fully and well cut but there were many loose coils which impeded progress. The two leading parties fought their way through, notwithstanding severe bombing on the part of the enemy. All the leading officers of the first 3 parties became casualties but nevertheless the 2 leading parties reached their objective in the German trench at A.3.b. $3\frac{1}{2}.4.$ to $A.3.b.3\frac{1}{2}.5\frac{1}{2}.$ or East of the face of the POPE'S NOSE. The third party made good the centre communication trench of the POPE'S NOSE. They were unable to proceed further. An assaulting party directed against the Western face at A.3.b. $2\frac{1}{2}.3\frac{1}{2}.$ was unable to effect an entry owing to the wire not having been fully cut.

2. So far the ascertained results are only 12 Germans killed. No prisoners were taken as the fighting was too severe. In this operation it was unfortunate that every officer with the exception of 3 immediately became a casualty. The men actually in the German trenches were from the point of view of the officer leading, leaderless. The opposition on the German wire was very severe.

    The R.E. party carried out the demolition of one machine gun dugout.

3. At the same time as the above operation was carried out the

17/Notts & Derby. Regt. carried out a demonstration at A.3.d. 5.5. where a partial gap had been cut in the enemy wire. Two bombing squads penetrated the German trenches and accounted for 7 Germans. Their Officer became a casualty on the wire, which we knew would present a difficult obstacle.

4. The German artillery retaliation was negligible all being directed at the point of diversion on CANADIAN ORCHARD, but it is noteworthy that at both points of entry the Germans were ready with bombs and rifle fire.

Further details of the raid will be forwarded later.

Original sd (P.D.F. OLDMAN) Brig. Gen.
Commanding 117th BRIGADE.

4th July, 1916.
(5.0 a.m.).

H.H

Appendix III WAR DIARY

SECRET

Copy No. 7.

7.7.16.

117th BRIGADE ORDER No.31.

1. The 17th King's Royal Rifle Corps will be relieved by the 16th Rifle Brigade to-morrow (July 8th) in the Centre Sub-section, FESTUBERT SECTION.

2. No movement E. of the VILLAGE LINE will take place before 9.30 p.m.

3. All details will be arranged by the Officers Commanding the Battalions concerned.

4. Completion of relief will be wired to Brigade Headquarters, LOISNE by code message "TEEK."

W. Cranwell Capt.
Brigade Major, 117th. Brigade.

Copies issued at 9.30 p.m. to :-

	By	Copy No.
H.Q., 39th Division.	D.R.	1
16/Notts & Derby. Regt.	D.R.	2
17/ do do	D.R.	3
17/K.R.Rif. C.	D.R.	4
16/Rif. Brig.	D.R.	5
117/Bde. Machine Gun Co.	D.R.	6
117 Trench Mortar Battery.	D.R.	7
War Diary	-	8 & 9
G.O.C.	Personally	10
B.M.	do	11
225 Co., R.E.	D.R.	12

SECRET.   Copy No 10

(Appendix 4)

117th INFANTRY BRIGADE ORDER No. 39.

(Preliminary orders for a minor enterprise)

1. **OBJECTIVE**   To bomb down German trenches at points S 28 a 8 9½
                          & S 22 c 6 6 for a distance for 100 yds to the
                          right and left, taking on the short communication
                          trenches where possible.

2. **TROOPS EMPLOYED:** 1 party (about 2 officers & 50 other ranks)
                              17th K. R. Rif. Corps
                          1 party (about 2 officers & 60 other ranks)
                              16th Notts & Derby R.

3. **ARTILLERY ACTION**   For the <u>right</u> attack there will be NONE. The
                          wire will be cut with BANGALORE TORPEDOES.
                          For the <u>left</u> there will be a heavy bombardment
                          for 5 minutes prior to the entry of the assaulting
                          party. The wire will be cut with 2" M.T.M. both
                          during the bombardment and previously on the 10th
                          July.

4. **PRELIMINARY REGISTRATION.** On the 9th & 10th July Artillery will
                          register & cut wire with as many rounds as
                          available at points S 28 a 8 9½, S 22 c 7 4,
                          A 3 b 5½ 9½ and A 3 b 2 5½. The registration
                          of the 2" Medium Trench Mortars will take place
                          on the afternoon of the 10th under cover of fire
                          of 4.5 Howitzers or 18 pdrs as available, at time
                          to be agreed on by O.C. Battery concerned & O.C.
                          M.T.M. Section.

5. **STOKES MORTARS**   6 Stokes mortars will be emplaced and will
                          participate in the preliminary bombardment.

6. **VICKERS MACHINE GUNS** will fire on agreed on points in rear of the
                          line of assault.

7. **TIMINGS**   The order for the exact timings of the operation
                          will be issued on the 10th when the result of
                          registration has been confirmed.

                                           W C Maxwell Capt.
                                    Brigade Major, 117th Inf. Brigade.

Copies issued at 2 P.M. 9th July, 1916 to
39th Division
16th Notts & Derby R.
17th K. R. Rif. Corps
16th Rif. Brig
O.C. "C" Group R.F.A.
O.C. 2" M.T.M.
O.C. 117 M. G. Coy.
O.C. 117 L. T. M. B.
War Diary (2 copies)

Appendix 5 / WAR DIARY

SECRET.   Copy No. 17

Ref. Map 36 S.W. 3 1/10,000

                              117th INFANTRY BRIGADE ORDER No 33

                    (Orders for minor enterprises to be carried out on the
                                    night 11/12th July)

1. PLAN. The right raiding party will rely on surprise tactics
   and cut the German wire with a Bangalore Torpedo. This
   raid will be separate from that of the left party. By
   the arrangement whereby the raids take place at dif-
   -ferent times it is hoped to draw the hostile artil-
   -lery fire in answer to our bombardment on the Canadian
   Orchard area and thus helping the left party. The left
   party will go in according to the Time Table.

2. OBJECTIVES.
   Objective A (Right Assault) To assault German Trench at
   point S XXXXXXX S 28 a 8 9½ and bomb down a distance
   of 100 yards to the right and left taking on the short
   communication trenches where possible.

   Objective B. (Left assault) to assault the German
   Trenches at point S 22 c 6 6 and carry out same pro-
   -cedure as described above for Objective A.

3. TROOPS EMPLOYED
   For Objective A 1 party (about 2 Officers & 50 other
   ranks from the 17th K. R. Rif Corps
   For objective B 1 party (about 2 officers & 60 other
   ranks 16th Notts & Derby R.)

4. ARTILLERY ACTION. For the right assault there will be none.
   The wire will be cut with BANGALORE Torpedoes.
   For the left assault there will be an intense Bombard-
   -ment for 5 minutes prior to the entry of the assaulting
   party. The wire will be cut with 2" Medium Trench Mortars,
   both during the bombardment and previously. Three
   minutes after the Infantry enters the German Trenches
   a box barrage will be formed in rear and to either flank
   of the occupied area and will continue till the with-
   -drawal of the infantry when artillery will drop to
   German Front Line.

5. ACTION OF 2" MEDIUM TRENCH MORTARS. M. T. M s will cut wire and
   bombard German Front Line Trenches at agreed on points
   adhering strictly to the timings assisting in Barrage.

6. ACTION OF LIGHT TRENCH MORTARS (STOKES). L.T.M s will bombard
   German Front Line Trenches at agreed on points and
   assist in Barrage adhering strictly to timings.

7. ACTION OF VICKERS GUNS. One Vickers Gun will fire from Cover
   Trench on or about pt. S 28 a 8 2 from 11.30 p.m.
   till 12.30 a.m.   One Vickers Gun will fire from
   1.20 a.m. till Infantry Reported Clear from about
   junction O. G. Line with Princes Street on ADALBERT &
   & EITEL N. & S. alleys, not west of Line drawn N & S
   through S 22 d 4 0.

- 2 -

8. TIMINGS. Between 12.50 a.m. and 1.50 a.m. 17th K.R. Rif Corps carries out its raid
    1.20 a.m. Intense Bombardment, Artillery, Medium Trench Mortars & Light Trench Mortars
    1.25 a.m. Bombardment ceases and 16th Notts & Derby R. Party enters hostile trenches
    1.28 a.m. Barrage forms. Artillery, Medium & Light Trench Mortars
    1.55 a.m. Withdrawal of 16th Notts & Derby Party.

On Infantry being reported "all clear" Medium & Light Trench Mortars and Artillery drop to Enemy Front Line.

Synchronization of watches at 8 p.m. & 10 p.m.

9. ACTION BY OTHER TROOPS IN SECTION DURING OPERATION.
1 Coy 16th Rifle Brigade will "stand to" in RICHMOND TERRACE & COVER TRENCH,
1 Coy 16th Notts & Derby R. will "stand to" in Front Trench
1 Coy 16th Notts & Derby R. (Tube Keep Coy) will stand to" in Support Line.

10 MEDICAL   Evacuation of casualities will be
(a) For 17th K.R. Rif. Corps Raid via QUINQUE RUE to 17th Notts & Derby Regt. Aid Post in O.B. Line thence by trolley to FESTUBERT Relay Post.

(b) For 16th Notts & Derby R. Raid via ROPE Trench to Battn. Aid Post, thence by Trolley to Kings X and RUE DU BOIS Dressing Station.

O.C. 16th & 17th Notts & Derby R. will ensure that trollies are ready at Regimental aid posts and will tell off parties to push them.

11. ADVANCED REPORT CENTRE will be at TUBE Keep (S21 a 8 7).
The G.O.C., Artillery Group Commander & O.C. 16th Notts & Derby R. will be at advanced Report Centre. O.C. 17th K.R. Rif. Corps will be at Battn. H.Q., Centre Battn.

12. LIAISON. Liaison by runner or telephone for 17th K.R. Rif
(a) Corps will be from 16th Rifle Brigade Left Coy H.Q. in COVER Trench, thence to Battn H.Q. 16th Rif.Brig thence to TUBE Keep.
(b) Liaison by runner or Telephone for 16th Notts & Derby R. will be from Right Coy. H.Q. 16th Notts & Derby R. to TUBE Keep.
(c) Liaison by Telephone to Division from TUBE Keep via Advanced Brigade H.Q. and H.Q. LOISNE.

W. Murdoch. Capt.
Copies issued at: 8pm 10-7-16 Brigade Major, 117th Inf.Brigade.
16th Notts & Derby R.   G.O.C.
17th Notts & Derby R.   Brigade Major
17th K.R. Rif. C.   Staff Captain,
16th Rif. Brig.   War Diary
117 Bde.M.G. Coy   Artillery Group Commander
Section Officer 2" M.T.M 184th Inf. Brigade
O.C. 117 Bde L.T.M.   118th Inf. Brigade
39th Division   A.D.M.S.

Typed & Duplicated by Lt.E.KROLIK.

SECRET.   Copy No.

AMENDMENT TO 117th Infantry Brigade ORDER No 33

Para 8 TIMINGS, Delete para and substitute the following :-

        12.30 a.m. 17th K.R. Rif Corps carries out its raid
        1.30 a.m. Intense Bombardment, Artillery, Medium
                    Trench Mortars & Light Trench Mortars,
        1.35 a.m. Bombardment ceases and 16th Notts & Derby R
                    party enters hostile Trenches,
        1.38 a.m. Barrage forms, Artillery, Medium & Light
                    Trench Mortars,
        2.15 a.m. Withdrawal of 16th Notts & Derby R.

On Infantry being reported "all clear" Medium &
Light Trench Mortars and Artillery drop to enemy
front line.

Synchronization of watches at 8 p.m. & 10 p.m.

ACKNOWLEDGE.

                                            Original Signed
                                                        Captain,
                Brigade Major, 117th Inf. Brigade.

Copies issued at 3.30 p.m., 11/7/16 to
    O.C.16th Notts & Derby R.
        17th Notts & Derby R.
        17th K. R. Rif Corps.
        16th Rif. Brig.
        117 Bde M. G. Coy,
Section Officer 2" M.T.M.
O.C. 117 Bde L.T.M.
H. Q. 39th Division
G.O.C.
Brigade Major,
Staff Captain
War Diary
Artillery Group Commander
184th Inf. Brigade
118th Inf. Brigade.

        Typed and duplicated by Lt.E.TROLIN.

Appendix VIII.D.

To/
Headquarters,
39th Division.

Report on Two Small Enterprises carried out on the night of 11/12th July
----

OBJECTIVE. 1. To enter the German trenches at Pt. S.28.a.8.9½. and S.22. c.6.6., bombing to the right and left and down the short communication trenches for a distance of 100 yards.

PLAN. 2. (a). The Plan was as follows :- The right party were to cut the German wire by means of a BANGALORE Torpedo relying on surprise tactics and entirely unassisted by artillery.

(b). The 1st enterprise was separate and distinct from the 2nd. The 2nd enterprise was as follows :- An hour after the 1st enterprise had begun a heavy bombardment with 4 -18 pdrs. batteries, 6 - 4.5" Hows., 4 M.T.M's and 6 - 3" L.T.M's was opened on the selected point. The object of the heavy bombardment in addition to killing and forcing the German to earth was to cover the wire-cutting operations of the 2" Trench Mortars. 5 minutes before this bombardment an extensive smoke barrage was put over the south of the Section from Island 1 to 12 in order to divert some of the hostile artillery fire. In this it was quite successful. On the previous days before the operation the artillery had fired slightly on 4 or 5 points in the Bde. Front. The above plan was dictated almost entirely by the necessity for cutting wire other than by means of 18 pdrs. which, owing to their paucity in numbers and position cannot successfully do the work.

The length of the grass in this section makes wire-cutting by observation an exceedingly difficult task. It was hoped that the action of the ruse would be as follows :-
The surprise attempt would draw artillery fire southward of the second objective. The smoke would divert a portion of the hostile artillery; the heavy bombardment would cover the wire-cutting operations of the 2" mortars, which were bound to alarm the enemy as they have not

previously been used in this section for some time.

Result. 3. (a). In the first enterprise the Torpedo was successfully placed, one line of wire having been cut by hand. It exploded well and made a good gap. The party then advanced to the assault, but found themselves hopelessly held up by a line of low knife-rests concealed by the front wire and the long grass. The enemy immediately lined the parapet and opened a heavy rifle and bomb fire on the party, who replied vigorously. There was nothing left for them to do but return. No hostile artillery fire was, of course, drawn by this short operation.

(b). In the second enterprise the 3 parties who were going to enter the trenches successfully assembled in NO MAN'S LAND during the bombardment, exactly on its termination, the first party rushed to the assault and entered the German trenches. The second party, unfortunately, lost touch with the 1st party and failed to follow in their steps, which meant that the third or liaison party who were responsible for identifications also never reached their objective. The first party on entry immediately bayonetted 4 Germans. 2 German Officers were seen to take shelter in one of the dugouts, 4 of which were found, ~~and 4 of~~ which were bombed successfully, 1 of them being set on fire, a fact which was clearly observable as well from my observation station. Altogether 14 Germans were accounted for and it is hoped ~~that~~ the 2 officers who had gone inside the dugout. The wire was extremely well cut by the 2" Trench Mortars and the men of the raiding party state that they found several dead Germans as a result of the artillery bombardment.

Artillery. The cooperation of the artillery was excellent and extremely easily controlled by the Group Commander, who was with me. I have already mentioned the excellent work done by the wire-cutting medium trench mortars. The bombardment must have been responsible for many casualties to the Germans.

PLAN 2. (Continued) Troops employed in the two enterprises were :-
2 Officers and 62 O.R. 2nd enterprise 3 Officers and 61 O.R exclusive of Reserves in our trenches.

3.

Casualties. 4. We sustained the following casualties :-

<u>1st party.</u> 1 Officer and 12 O.R. wounded; 3 O.R. missing.

<u>2nd party.</u> 1 Officer and 2 O.R. killed or missing.

1 Officer and 18 O.R. wounded.

General. 5. In the second enterprise the enemy placed a very heavy barrage on our front trenches, breaching them in several places slightly to the North of the point of exit of our party. It may be due to this fact that touch with the leading party was lost by the second party and emphasises the necessity for the use of a tape or other means of liaison. The ruse employed met with a fair measure of success, but, of course, did not do all it was hoped in diverting the artillery barrage. There is no doubt that the Germans are very much on the alert all along their line. The parapets are instantly manned and very large quantities of lights are used. Red and green lights were immediately put up on the commencement of our bombardment. Barrage was put on NO MAN'S LAND opposite the smoke screen, the Red "Very" lights which we used evidently confusing the Germans very considerably. It is clear that the enemy has at least re-doubled his guards, if indeed he does not keep his trench garrisons standing-to most of the night. It would seem almost impossible in the flat ground of this section to cut the enemy wire and enter his trenches without receiving hostile artillery retaliation. The absence of mine craters and undulations, the presence of which affords protection to flanks and gives a certain facility for a little manœuvre is undoubtedly/unfavourable to such operations.

Although the operation was not successful in its entirety I have gone into the plan and ruses attempted, and the results obtained, rather fully, as they may produce some useful deductions for future raids.

The second enterprise just missed being a highly successful one.

N.B. The Germans lit fires on his parapet and evidently thought gas was being used.

12/7/16

SECRET   Appendix 7   Copy No...16.. W D

117th INFANTRY BRIGADE ORDER No.35.

Ref. 1/40,000
BETHUNE (Combined Sheet)   14.7.16..
(56.A. S.E, S.W.   )
(56.B. N.E, 56 c.N.W.)

1. 117th Brigade will relieve 184th Brigade in FERME DE BOIS Section.

2. The 118th Brigade will relieve two Battalions in the Right and Centre Subsection of the FESTUBERT Section.

3. The double relief will be carried out as follows :-
   17th Sherwood Foresters will be relieved by a Battalion 118th Brigade (1/1 CAMBS. Regt.). For this relief guides will be at the end of BARNTON Road at 9.30 p.m. On completion the Battalion will move by companies to RICHEBOURG ST VAAST and remain as Support Battalion, taking over the six posts at present held by the 2nd BUCKS Regt.
   Route to be followed. FESTUBERT CENTRAL to S.13.d.1.4. - RUE DE BOIS to S.14.c.5.9. - thence direct to RICHEBOURG ST VAAST.

4. 16th Rifle Brigade. will be relieved by the Battalion 118th Brigade (1/1 HERTS Regt.) and take over the section of the new line from FARM CORNER (S.16.d.3½.6.) to the present Left of the 5th GLOUCESTERSHIRE Regt. *Guides for 1/1 HERTS at FESTUBERT Central.*
   Route to be followed. Companies at present in the COVER Trenches and ISLAND LINE will move by the Front Trenches through the 16th Sherwood Foresters. Companies in the O.B. Line through TUBE STATION Post thence upwards. Movement by companies on completion of relief by Battalion, 118th Brigade.

5. 17th King's Royal Rifle Corps will move from the VILLAGE LINE and take over the front held by the 4th OXFORD & BUCKS Regt. Light Infantry, their Left resting on 15th STREET.
   Route to be followed. Any convenient. Commencement of move at 9.30 p.m. One Officer and 1 N.C.O. for each Post will be left to hand over to the incoming Battalions of the 118th Brigade and then rejoin their Battalion.

6. 16th Sherwood Foresters. will remain as they are except that they will extend their Left as far as FARM CORNER (S.16.d.3½.6) sending up a platoon from the support company to effect this.

7. 117th Bde. Machine Gun Co. will take over gun for gun from the 184th Bde. Machine Gun Co. and 2 at present in 16/Notts & Derby Regt. front, and two in Reserve at RICHEBOURG ST VAAST.

Time for move and route to be followed will be notified later.

8. 117th Trench Mortar Battery will take over gun for gun from the L.T.M. Battery of 184th Brigade. 1 L.T.M. will remain at ROPE KEEP. Commence to move at 8.30 p.m.

9. TRANSPORT. Transport of 16th Sherwood Foresters and 17th King's Royal Rifle Corps will move to LE TOURET.

10. BRIGADE Headquarters will be at CSE. DE RAUX (X.23.a.5.9.). Report Centre will open there at 10 p.m. and close at X.23.a.2.8. (LOISNE) at 12 midnight.

11. CODE for Relief. The Code for relief complete in the present FESTUBERT Section will be "GOOD NEWS OF SOMME BATTLE RECEIVED." For the relief in FERME DE BOIS Section "HIS MAJESTY'S ORDER of the DAY PROMULGATED."

12. MISCELLANEOUS. All other details, guides, stores, etc. will be arranged by Battalion Commanders.

13. Attachment to 117th Brigade. The 11th ROYAL SUSSEX Regt. will take over the Subsection from 15th STREET to OXFORD Street at present held by a Battalion of the 182nd Brigade.

W.F.Maxwell Capt.
Brigade Major, 117th. BRIGADE.

Copies issued at 3.30 p.m. to :-

	By	Copy No.
16/Notts & Derby. Regt.	D.R.	1
17/ do do	D.R.	2
17/K.R.Rif. C.	D.R.	3
16/Rif. Brig.	D.R.	4
117/Bde. Machine Gun Co.	D.R.	5
117/Bde. T.M. Battery.	D.R.	6
3 Sect. Signal Co.	Orderly	7
G.O.C.	Personally	8
B.M.	do	9
S.C.	do	10
39th Division	D.R.	11
184th Brigade	D.R.	12
118th Brigade	D.R.	13
"C" Group, R.A.	D.R.	14
225 Co., R.E.	D.R.	15
War Diary	-	16 & 17
Order File	-	18

SECRET   *Appendix VIII D*   Copy No..10.

~~117th INFANTRY BRIGADE.~~

18.7.16.

(FERME DU BOIS Section).

Reference to
BETHUNE 1/40,000
Trench Map 1/10,000.

Defences and Dispositions in case of Attack.

Salient Features. 1. The salient features of the German Front are few; in front of the Right Subsection the FERME COUR D'AVOUE dominates NO MAN'S LAND up to the BOAR'S HEAD Salient, where the opposing trenches run in close proximity, about 80 yards at their closest. Northwards the line swings back in front of the BOIS DE BIEZ, a very strong point.

Description of Section and Boundaries. 2. The Brigade Section consists of :-

(a). A front line of continuous breastwork from CADBURY'S Trench to OXFORD Street.

(b). A support line, which is a prolongation of the OLD BRITISH Line in the FESTUBERT Section; but not yet completed. It runs as follows :- A continuous breastwork through TUBE STATION Post, BOURNEVILLE STATION, 300 yards North of this occurs a gap until PALL MALL is reached, thence by GUARDS Trench turning Northward at S.10.a.9$\frac{2}{5}$.3. to HEAD Street, across EDGWARE Rd, and on into the next Brigade Section. That portion between GUARDS Trench and HEAD Street is not yet completed. The whole line remains to be wired.

(c). The front line system of posts held by one Company of the supporting Battalion with OBLIGATORY Garrisons (see Appx. A). This includes TUBE, DEAD COW and BOURNEVILLE obligatory garrisons found by right battalion.

(d). A second line system :- The Village St VAAST - CROIX BARBEE System - occupied by the supporting Battalion, but the garrisons of which

Sheet No.2.

are in the hands of the Officer Commanding this Battalion for support of the front line as ordered by the Brigade.

Action in case of attack.

3. In case of attack :-

Right Battalion. O.C., the Right Battalion has two Companies, less obligatory garrisons, at his disposal for the counter-attack, 4 platoons in all.

Centre Battalion. O.C, the Centre Battalion has three platoons at his disposal.

Left Battalion. O.C, the Left Battalion has six platoons at his disposal.

Company Commanders will immediately counter-attack in case the Companies on their flanks are driven in, using their support platoons (if they have any).

Counter-attack parties are as hitherto to be told off every night, and will be so disposed as to be in the Company Commander's hands, i.e., in dug-outs, close to his headquarters.

Similarly, Os.C, Battalions will use their support companies in like manner. All counter-attacks will be launched without waiting for orders from, but reports of action taken will be sent to, the next higher authority.

Brigade Support. Brigade Support consists of 4 companies (less obligatory garrisons) and will normally remain in the hands of the Brigade Commander, but even in this case the O.C, Support Battalion has discretion to launch a counter-attack without waiting for orders.

Reserve Battalion. The Reserve Battalion will also remain in the hands of the Brigade Commander, and is at present billeted in KING'S Road.

Lines of advance

4. Lines of advance for the counter-attack of Battalion support companies are as follows :-

Right Battalion. Over the open, with ROPE Trench as a guiding line.

Centre Battalion, BOND Street, VINE Street, HAZARA and PLUM Streets will act as guiding lines, but the going is very bad and requires careful reconnaisance for lines over the open.

Sheet No.3.

Left Battalion. LANSDOWN Communication Trench - PORT ARTHUR Communication Trench - LA BASSEE Road - HUM and OXFORD Street - offer guiding lines, but the going is very bad.

Os.C., Battalions will cause all the above lines over the open to be carefully reconnoitred and a report will be sent in to Brigade Headquarters as to their practicability. Sketches will accompany the reports.

Artillery. 5. Battery of 18 pdrs ("C" Group) covers the Right Battalion.
4 Batteries 18 pdrs ("F" Group) cover the Centre and Left Battalions.
2 Batteries 4.5" Hows. cover the Section.

L.T. Mortars. 6. Offensive Emplacements are situated at :-

   (1). S.22.c.1.4.
   (2). S.16.a.3.2. (Bay 47) (Emplacements for two mortars).
   (3). S.10.c.4.½. (Bay 86)
   (4). S.10.c.7.4. (Bay 92)
   (5). S.10.c.9.5. (Bay 6)
   (6). S.10.d.½.6. (East and HAZARA Street).
   (7). S.10.d.2½.7½ (East end of PLUM Street, Bay 13).
   (8). S.10.d.5.9½.

Defensive Emplacements are being made at :-

   (1). ROPE KEEP (S.21.d.7.7.)
   (2). WATERS KEEP (S.15.d.7.5.).
   (3). COCKSPUR Street (S.9.d.6.1.).
   (4). BOND Street (S.9.d.9¾.5½.)
   (5). HAZARA Street (S.10.a.7.3.).
   (6). JUNCTION ROW (S.4.d.7.½.).

The teams of these L.T. Mortars live at their emplacements. Company Commanders can call on them at any time for retaliation, reporting at once to their Os.C, Battalions.

Vickers M. Guns. 7. Vickers Machine Guns are disposed as follows :-

   (1). S.22.c.0.7.
   (2). S.16.c.3.1.
   (3). S.16.c.3½.7.
   (4). S.16.a.1.5.
   (5). S.9.d.6.2½. FACTORY.
   (6). S.10.c.5.8. COPSE.
   (7). S.11.a.½.6½.
   (8). S.4.d.8.½.) PORT ARTHUR
   (9). - ditto -)
  (10). S.4.b.9½.0. OXFORD.
  (11). S.4.a.9½.9½. PONT LOGY
  (12). S.3.d.9.8½. LANSDOWN
  (13). S.9.b.½.8. EDWARDS
  (14). S.14.b.5.8. ORCHARD
  (15). S.2.c.2.8½.) RICHEBOURG
  (16). - ditto -) Two reserve guns.

Coy. H.Q. X.17.d.8.9.

Sheet No.4.

Lewis Guns	8.	It is to be noted that in no case will Lewis guns be told off as obligatory in the garrisons of Posts and Keeps.
Medical.	9.	Right Battalion. Aid Post RUE DU BOIS (S.14.b.6½.2.) Advanced Dressing Station RUE DU BOIS (S.17.d.5.8.).
		Centre Battalion Aid Post. S.9.d.2.8. Advanced Dressing Station RUE DU BOIS (S.17.d.5.8.).
		Left Battalion. Aid Post. S.5.c.4.9. Advanced Dressing Station RUE DU BOIS (S.17.d.5.8.).
S.A.A & Bombs.	10.	Distribution as shewn in Appx. B.
Tramways.	11.	for Right Battalion. KING's Road Tramway from Railhead about S.14.a.4.2. to TUBE STATION (about S.21.a.6.6.).
		for Centre Battalion. ST VAAST Tramway.
		for Left Battalion. ST VAAST Tramway (extension).
Report Centres	12.	There are two Advanced Brigade Report Centres, viz - LANSDOWN House (S.3.d.6.8.).
		House in ALBERT Road (S.15.c.2.6.).
		These are alternative and will be used according to the tactical situation.
		Brigade Headquarters is at CSE. DU RAUX (X.25.a.6.8.).

Capt.
Brigade Major, 117th. Brigade.

Copies issued at 3 p.m. to :-

	By	Copy No.		By	Copy No
16/Notts & Derby Regt	D.R.	1	War Diary	-	10 & 11
17/ do do	D.R.	2	Order File	-	12
17/K.R.Rif. C.	D.R.	3	H.Q., 39th Div.	D.R	13
16/Rif. Brig.	D.R.	4	"C" Group, R.F.A.	D.R	14
117/Bde M. Gun Co.	D.R.	5	"F" Group, R.F.A.	D.R	15
117/T.M. Battery.	D.R.	6	227 Co., R.E.	D.R	16
G.O.C.	Personally	7	118th Inf. Bde.	D.R	17
B.M.	do	8	94th Brigade.	D.R	18
S.C.	do	9			

Appendix A.

Table of Posts in FERME DU BOIS Section.

Name of Keep	Map reference	Obligatory Garrison Troops	Obligatory Garrison M. Guns	S.A.A. boxes	Bomb boxes	Tinned Meat	Biscuit boxes	Water Tins	Picks	Shovels	Sand-bags
TUBE STATION	S.21.a.8.3.	1 Pl	-	70	50	-	-	120	10	20	500
DEAD COW	S.15.c.4.2.	1 Pl	-	24	50	-	-	30	5	10	500
BOURNEVILLE	S.15.a.8.1.	2 Pls	-	50	20	-	-	100	8	15	500
CATS	S.15.a.7.8.	½ Pl	-	30	25	-	-	50	5	10	500
ORCHARD	S.14.b.4½.8.	1 Pl	1	24	10	50	50	50	3	6	200
ALBERT	S.8.d.3½.3½.	½ Pl	-	8	10	50	50	30	5	6	200
DOGS	S.9.c.5.9.	½ Pl	-	24	10	50	50	30	5	10	300
EDWARDS	S.9.d.0.7½.	½ Pl	1	24	10	50	50	30	5	10	300
HENS	S.3.d.2.5½.	½ Pl	-	8	8	50	50	50	5	10	300
LANSDOWN	S.3.d.8½.8½.	1 Pl	1	62	10	120	120	100	20	40	1000
Keeps in FRONT System.		Garrisons									
ROPE	S.21.d.6.8.	1 Pl	1	24	25	-	-	30	5	10	500
FACTORY	S.9.d.3½.4.	1 Pl	1	10	30	35	35	35	25	20	1400
COPSE	S.10.c.4½.9½.	1 Pl	1	5	15	35	35	35	10	10	700
PORT ARTHUR	S.4.d.9.2.	1 Pl	2	9	50	60	60	60	15	15	1200

Appx. B.

FERME DU BOIS SECTION.

Distribution of S.A.A. & Bombs.

RIGHT BATTALION

Front Line	S.A.A.	Mills.	Rifle Grenades.
Right Coy.	42,000	852	200
Left "	29,000	924	160
ROPE TRENCH	Nil	240	40
PIPE TRENCH	Nil	300	120
CADBURY TRENCH	Nil	300	100

Second Line.			
ROPE KEEP	26,000	312	-
TUBE KEEP	70,000	720	400
DEAD COW	23,000	240	-
CHOCOLATE	16,000	-	-
OLD BREASTWORK	32,000	240	-
BOURNEVILLE	61,000	564	80
Bn. Advd. Store	3,000	1464	120
Bn. Hd. Qrs.	44,000	1080	60

KEEPS.

RUE DE L'EPINETTE R.	40,000	300	
CHAVATTES	10,000	96	

CENTRE BATTALION.

Front Line.			
"A" Platoon Stores.	56,000	920	716
"B" Company Stores			
Front Line Fish Tail		1800	196
Jc Front Line & BOND	20,000	1200	200
" " " & VINE St	20,000	1200	196
" " Line & COPSE	20,000	1200	196
" do & HAZARA St	20,000	2004	196
" do & COCKSPUR St	15,000	996	196

Second Line.			
Jc of GUARDS St & BOND St.	20,000	1800	392
do do & VINE St	20,000	3600	392
do do & HAZARA St	20,000	3600	Nil
do do & PLUM St	20,000	600	200
STRAND		648	110
PALL MALL		432	110
BUTE STREET		192	280
Bn. Hd. Qrs.	18,000	1018	400

KEEPS

FACTORY Post	10,500	624	80
COPSE Post	5,250	500	40

Appx. B. (Cont'd).

LEFT BATTALION.

	S.A.A.	Mills.	Rifle Grenades.
FRONT LINE		N I L	
Right Coy	30,000	2304	416
Left "	42,000	1176	100
Jc LANSDOWN Trench and GUARDS Support.	-	300	-

SECOND LINE.

	S.A.A.	Mills.	Rifle Grenades.
LANSDOWN TRENCH		1200	70
HUN Street		300	280
Bn. Hd. Qrs.	30,000	1368	360

KEEPS

	S.A.A.	Mills.	Rifle Grenades.
PORT ARTHUR	9,000	480	200
LANSDOWN	15,000	432	Nil
HILLS Post	6,000	480	80

SUPPORT BATTALION

	S.A.A.	Mills.	Rifle Grenades.
CAT Post	5,250	120	40
ORCHARD Post	10,500	120	70
ALBERT "	5,250	120	40
DOG "	5,250	120	40
EDWARDS "	10,500	120	70
MONS "	5,250	120	40
SCOTTS	5,250	120	40
HUNTERS	5,250	120	40
RICHEBOURG	10,500	144	70
RAGS	5,250	Nil	40
BONES	5,250	Nil	40
GROTTO)	5,250	60	
ANGLE)	5,250	60	
ST VAAST	1,000	1320	140
BRIGADE STORE (S.8.a.9½.5).	100,000	1200	600

SECRET   W.D

Herewith Appendix C to 117th Infantry Brigade Defence Scheme (FERME DU BOIS Section) issued yesterday, the 18th July, 1916.

                                                      W C Maxwell   Capt.
                                    Brigade Major, 117th. BRIGADE.

19th July, 1916.

Apx. C.

117th INFANTRY BRIGADE.

CROIX BARBEE - ST VAAST System, shewing Keeps occupied by the Support Battalion, with Stores, etc.

Name of Keep	Map reference	Garrison Troops	M. Guns	S.A.A Boxes	Bomb Boxes	Rations Tinned Meat	Rations Biscuit Boxes.	Water galls.	Picks.	Shovels.	Sandbags
SCOTT	S.8.a.2.0.	½ Pl	-	10	8	75	75	25	5	10	200
HUNTER	S.8.a.2.5.	½ Pl	-	10	8	75	75	25	5	10	200
RICHEBOURG	S.2.c.3.1.	2 Pls & Coy H.Q.	-	32	8	100	100	100	10	20	500
RAGS	S.2.c.3.7.	½ Pl	-	5	8	75	75	25	5	10	500
BONES	S.2.c.3.8½.	½ Pl	-	5	8	75	75	25	5	10	500
GROTTO	S.2.c.3.7½.	½ Pl	-	10	8	75	75	25	5	10	300
ANGLE	S.2.a.4.10.	½ Pl	-	10	9	75	75	25	5	10	300
CHAVATTE	S.13.b.4.8.	1 NCO & 4 men	-	14	10	30	30	-	7	8	-
LE TOURET	X.15.b.5.8.	½ Pl	-	-	-	-	-	-	-	-	-
ST VAAST	S.3.d.1.10.	2 Pls	-	32	10	120	120	100	10	20	500

SECRET   Appendix 10   Copy No....16   19.7.16.   W.D.

Amendments to 117th INFANTRY BRIGADE Defence Scheme

(RUE DU BOIS Section).

Para. 2.   <u>Description of Section and Boundaries.</u>

para. (a). This para. should read

"A front line of continuous breastwork from LA QUINQUE RUE (S.22.c.2.3½) to OXFORD Street, both inclusive."

Para. 9.   <u>Medical.</u>   Map reference of Advanced Dressing Station RUE DU BOIS is X.17.d.5.8. and not S.17.d.5.8.

                         W.G. Maxwell   Capt.
                   Brigade Major, 117th. BRIGADE.

Issued at 3.30 p.m. to :-

	By	Copy No.
16/Notts & Derby Regt.	D.R.	1
17/ do do	D.R.	2
17/K.R.Rif. C.	D.R.	3
16/Rif. Brig.	D.R.	4
117/Bde. Machine Gun Co.	D.R.	5
117/Trench Mortar Battery.	D.R.	6
G.O.C.	Personally	7
B.M.	do	8
S.C.	do	9
H.Q., 39th Div.	D.R.	10
227 Co., R.E.	D.R.	11
"C" Group, R.A.	D.R.	12
"F" Group, R.A.	D.R.	13
118th Infantry Brigade.	D.R.	14
94th Infantry Brigade	D.R.	15
War Diary	-	16 & 17
Order File	-	18

SECRET Appendix 12 W D Copy No. 57

117th BRIGADE ORDER No. 36.

19.7.16.

Ref. Map BETHUNE
Combined Sheet 1/40,000.

RELIEF. 1. The 117th Brigade will be relieved to-morrow (20th July) in the FERME DU BOIS Section by the 116th Bde. The 117th Brigade, less two Battalions (16th and 17th Notts & Derby Regts) will go into Divisional Reserve, in accordance with attached relief table.

New Distribution and Billets. 2. (a). Two Battalions of the Brigade - the 16th and 17th Notts & Derby Regts - will be attached to the 118th and 116th Brigades respectively.

(b). The 16th Notts & Derby Regt. will become Battalion in Brigade Reserve for the 118th Brigade and will be billeted at TUNING FORK with Battalion Headquarters at CANAL HOUSE (F.10.b.3.3).

(c). The 17th Notts & Derby Regt will remain where they are at RICHEBOURG ST VAAST becoming Battalion in Brigade Support for the 116th Brigade.

(d). The 17th K.R.Rif. C. will billet at LE HAMEL.

(e). The 16th Rif. Brig. will billet at LE TOURET.

(f). The 117th Bde. Machine Gun Co. will billet at X.3.d. Central.

(g). The 117th Bde. Trench Mortar Battery will billet at LE TOURET (X.16.b.20) after being relieved.

(h). 117th Bde. Headquarters will be at LE HAMEL (X.20.d.6.3).

Lewis Guns Snipers &c 3. The relief of Lewis guns, Snipers, Observers, Bombing posts, etc., will be carried out under the arrangements of Os.C, Battalions with Os.C relieving Bns.

Machine Gun Co. 4. O.C, 117th Bde. Machine Gun Co. will arrange all details with O.C, 116th Bde. Machine Gun Co. Machine guns will continue to fire on gaps until relieved.

T.M. Batt. 5. The 117th Bde. T.M. Battery will arrange all details with O.C, 116th Bde. T.M. Battery.

Guides. 6. All details regarding guides will be arranged by Os.C, with the units relieving them.

Report Centre. 7. Brigade Report Centre will open at LE HAMEL at 9.30 p.m.

Sheet No.2.

Code for relief.   8. Code sentence "Great attack entirely successful" will be used to denote relief complete.

                                             Featherstonhaugh
                                                               Capt.
                                           for Brigade Major, 117th Bde

Issued at 11 p.m. to :-

	By	Copy No.
16/Notts & Derby Regt.	D.R.	1
17/ do do	D.R.	2
17/K.R.Rif. C.	D.R.	3
16/Rif. Brig.	D.R.	4
117/Bde. Machine Gun Co.	D.R.	5
117/T.M. Battery.	D.R.	6
3 Sect. Signal Co.	Orderly	7
227 Co., R.E.	D.R.	8
G.O.C.	Personally	9
B.M.	do	10
S.C.	do	11
H. Qrs, 39th Div.	D.R.	12
94th Inf. Bde.	D.R.	13
118th Inf. Bde.	D.R.	14
116th Inf. Bde.	D.R.	15
"F" Group, R.F.A.	D.R.	16
War Diary	-	17 & 18
Order File	-	19

117th INFANTRY BRIGADE.

(Relief Table to accompany 117th BRIGADE Order 36, dated 19.7.16).

Date	Unit of 117th Bde (present disposition)	After relief proceeds to	ROUTE	Relieved by	Guides for incoming units.	Remarks
20th	16/Notts & Derby R (Right Subsection)	TUNING FORK with H. Qrs at CANAL HOUSE (F.10.b.3.3).	via FESTUBERT – LE PLANTIN Rd or any other route convenient.	12th & 13th Bns R. Suss. Regt.	As arranged between C.Os.	Becomes Battalion in Brigade Reserve for 118th Brigade.
20th	17/Notts & Derby R (Battalion in Support).	R E M A I N S	I N	P R E S E N T	B I L L E T S .	Remains Battalion in Brigade Support for 116th Brigade.
20th	17/K.R.Rif. C. (Left Subsection)	LE HAMEL	Any convenient.	11/R. Suss Regt	As arranged between C.Os.	
20th	16/Rif. Brig. (Centre Subsection)	LE TOURET	ditto	14/Hants Regt.	ditto	
20th	H.Q. 117th Bde. (GENSE DU RAUX)	LE HAMEL (X.20.d.6.3)	ditto	116th Bde H.Q.	As arranged between C.Os.	
20th	117th M. Gun Co. (H.Q.X.17.d.8.9)	X.3.d. Central	ditto	116th M. Gun Co.		
20th	117/T.M. Battery (H.Q.S.9.a.9.5).	LE TOURET (X.16.b.2.0).	ditto	116th T.M. Battery	ditto	

Incoming Battalions of 116th Brigade will not move East of Line CORNER HOUSE (S.14.c.5.9) and WINDY CORNER (S.9.a.5.10) till 9.30 p.m.
All movements East of this Line will be by Sections at 200 yards interval and Rest by/platoons at 200 yards interval.

SECRET   Appendix 12. D   Copy No. 12

39th Divisional Reserve Order No.2.
                                                    21.7.16.
(Divisional Reserve Order No.1 is cancelled)

1. The Divisional Reserve is divided into two portions.

    (a). 117th Brigade (less two Battalions at present attached to 116th and 118th Brigades respectively) with Brigade Headquarters at LE HAMEL (X.20.d.6.3) and two Battalions billeted at LE HAMEL and LE TOURET, Machine Gun Co. at X.3.d. Central, L.T.M. Battery at LE TOURET (X.16.b.2.0).

    (b). Mobile Column consisting of :-

    Westmoreland & Cumberland Yeomanry with Headquarters at ESSARS (X.25.a.4.5).

    5th Motor Machine Gun Battery with Headquarters at LOCON (X.7.b.5.7).

    XIth Corps Cyclists Battalion, less Detachments, with Headquarters at LOCON (W.6.d.5.3).

    Commander, Lt. Col. BEDDINGTON, Westmoreland & Cumberland Yeomanry.

    (c). The whole Divisional Reserve is under command of the G.O.C., 117th Infantry Brigade with Divisional Reserve Headquarters at LE HAMEL (X.20.d.6.3).

2. The Divisional Reserve will be ready to move at 4 hours notice from 7 a.m. to 8 p.m. and at 2 hours notice from 8 p.m. to 7 a.m daily.

3. On receipt of orders Orders "Stand-to" all units will fall in at their present billets and await orders, at once sending an officer to report to Divisional Reserve Headquarters. Transport will be harnessed up but not hooked in.

4. By night adequate inlying piquets will be provided.

5. All roads leading to the Front System of trenches in the Divl. area and those to the Divisions on the flanks will be reconnoitred.

                                        W. _____ Capt.
                            Brigade Major, 117th. BRIGADE
                            S.O. to Divisional Reserve.

Copies to :-

17/K.R.Rif. C.	H.Q., 39th Div.	G.O.C.
16/Rif. Brig.	West & Cumb Yeomanry	B.M.
117/Bde. M. Gun Co.	5th M.M. Gun Co.	S.C.
117/T.M. Battery.	XIth Corps Cyc. Bn.	War Diary (2 copies)
		Order File

WD SECRET   Appendix 13.   23.7.16.   War Diary

117th INFANTRY BRIGADE ORDER No.37.

Reference BETHUNE
(Combined Sheet) 1/40,000.

1. On the night of the 24th/25th the boundaries held by the 39th Division will be as follows :-

    On the Right   -   LA BASSEE CANAL.

    On the Left.   -   QUINQUE RUE Crossing.

2. Consequent on the shortening of the Front held by the Division, the following moves will take place in the 117th Brigade to-morrow, 24th July.

    (a). The 16th Notts & Derby Regt. will move from Brigade Reserve, 118th Brigade to billets in BETHUNE.

    (b). The 17th Notts & Derby Regt. will move from Brigade Support, 116th Brigade to billets at LES CHOQUAUX.

    (c). The 17th K.R.Rif. C. will remain where they are at present, except that one Coy. now billeted at LE TOURET will billet in LE HAMEL or ESSARS.

    (d). The 16th Rifle Brigade will move from LE TOURET to ESSARS.

    (e). The 117th Machine Gun Co. will move from X.3.d Central to billets or bivouac at LE HAMEL.

    (f). The 117th Bde. L.T.M. Battery will move from LE TOURET to billets at LE HAMEL.

    (g). Brigade Headquarters will remain where they are at LE HAMEL.

    Moves described in sub-paras (c) (d) (e) and (f) will not start before 2 p.m. to-morrow. Those in (a) and (b) after authority to move has been obtained from G.OsC. 116th and 118th Brigades.

3. The necessary billeting parties from each Battalion, 117th Machine Gun Co. and 117th L.T.M. Battery will rendezvous at LE HAMEL at X.20. d.4.7. at 9.0 a.m. to-morrow, where the Staff Captain will give further instructions re billets.

4. Completion of these moves will be reported to Brigade Headquarters and map references of new Battalion, Machine Gun Co. and L.T.M. Battery Headquarters will be included.

5. Acknowledge.

          (Sd.) W.G. MAXWELL, Capt.
          Brigade Major, 117th Brigade

16/Notts & Derby Regt	117th Machine Gun Co.	116th Brigade
17/ do do	117th T.M. Battery.	118th Brigade
17/K.R.Rif. C.	S.C.	B.M.
16/Rif. Brig.	H.Q. 39th Division.	War Diary (2 copies).

SECRET   Appendix 14   Copy No. 14

117th INFANTRY BRIGADE ORDER No.38.

Ref./BETHUNE (Combined Sheet)   25.7.16.
1/40,000.
Trench Map 1/20,000.

1. The 117th Infantry Brigade will relieve the 118th Infantry Brigade in the GIVENCHY Section on the 26th July.

2. The distribution of the Brigade will be as follows :-
All Units will take over the same dispositions as are now held by Units of 118th Brigade.

   (a). <u>Front System</u>. (1). <u>Right Battalion</u>. From LA BASSEE Canal to BOYAU 57 (inclusive). 16th Rifle Brigade. Relieves 4th/5th BLACK WATCH. Battalion H.Q. A.14.a.9.9.

   <u>Left Battalion</u>. From BOYAU 57 Front (exclusive) to junction of KGNR Line and GRENADIER Road (inclusive). 17th King's Royal Rifle Corps. Relieve 1/1st CAMBS Regt. Battalion H.Q. HITCHIN Road.

   (b). <u>Battalion in Support</u>. VILLAGE LINE. 17/Notts & Derby Regt. Relieve 1/6th CHESHIRE Regt.

   (c). <u>Battalion in Reserve</u>. TUNING FORK. 16/Notts & Derby Regt. Relieve 1/1st HERTS Regt.

   (d). Brigade Headquarters will be at CANAL HOUSE (F.10.d.8.9).

3. The 117th Bde. Machine Gun Co. and 117th Trench Mortar Battery will take over from their opposite numbers in the 118th Brigade before 2 p.m. on the 26th July.

4. All arrangements for guides will be made between the Officers Commanding Units, with the Units they relieve.

5. There will be no movement East of the VILLAGE LINE (PONT FIXE - WINDY CORNER - LE PLANTIN) before 2 p.m. except as in para. 3. The most convenient routes will be used.

6. As the relief is taking place in daylight, an interval of at least half an hour will be kept between each Company during the relief. Movement East of Line indicated in para. 5 will be by sections at 400 yards interval, West of this Line by platoons at 200 yards interval.

7. All 1st Line Transport will be at GORRE.

8. The necessary reconnaisances will be carried out this afternoon (July 25th) under Battalion arrangements.

P.T.O.

Sheet No.2

9. Relief complete = HAGGIS.

                                                  Capt.
                           Brigade Major, 117th. BRIGADE

Copies issued to : -   at 9.45 a.m.

	By	Copy No.
16/Notts & Derby Regt.	D.R.	1
17/ do do	D.R.	2
17/K.R.Rif. C.	D.R.	3
16/Rif. Brig.	D.R.	4
117/Bde. Machine Gun Co.	D.R.	5
117th Trench Mortar Battery	D.R.	6
G.O.C.	Personally	7
B.M.	do	8
S.C.	do	9
H.Q. 39th Division.	D.R.	10
118th Infantry Brigade.	D.R.	11
3 Sect. Signal Co.	Orderly	12
War Diary	-	13 & 14
Order File	-	15

SECRET.

Ref. Trench Map 1.10.000.   Copy No.

117th INFANTRY BRIGADE ORDER No 39.

(Orders for Minor Enterprise on the night 31st July/1st August.)

(1) OBJECTIVES, in order of merit:
    (a) to bring back prisoners,
    (b) to kill Germans,
    (c) to destroy two mine shafts.

(2) PLAN: (a) The Infantry raiding party (strength 1½ Companies 17th Notts & Derby R. and an R.E. demolition party will enter the German Trenches at A 10 c $\frac{3}{4}$ 3 and bomb according to plan up the trenches of the area of objective remaining there for approximately two hours.
The signal for retirement will be given from Front Line and Cambridge Terrace by red rockets sent up in bouquets of four in the direction of the German Trenches.

(b) Artillery Action, will be as follows :-
(1) Heavy Trench Mortars will bombard area of objective and then switch to the Northern Craters,
(2) Group Artillery, Heavy & Medium Trench Mortars will bombard NORTHERN Craters. Group artillery will then switch to DUCK'S BILL CRATERS,
(3) Light Trench Moratrs will remain on fixed targets on flanks of objective area and fire on Northern Craters with remainder of guns as ordered.

(c) R.E. action. The demolition party will follow the raiding party after establishment in enemy's trenches and destroy the first two mine shafts encountered.

(d) Machine Gun action,
(1) Vickers Guns will fire on CANTELEUX ALLEYs N. & S. and PRUSSIAN WAY as arranged.
(2) Lewis Guns of the right battalion will keep up fire along their whole front.

(3) TIMINGS.   Zero will be notified later. *Heavy*

0.0 to 0.25	~~Medium~~ Trench Mortars Bombard area of objective,
0.25	Heavy Trench Mortars & Medium Trench Mortars bombard Northern Craters slowly and continue,
0.25 to 0.35	Group Artillery bombards Northern Craters,
0.28 to 0.38	Infantry raiding party assembles in No Mans Land
0.36 to 0.38	Group Artillery bombards area of objective, under which Infantry advances,
0.40	Box Barrage established in rear of area of objective
2.40	Signal for withdrawal.

(4) CLEARANCE OF TRENCHES.

Saps and Front Line trenches from POYAU 54 to REGENT St will be cleared and then re-occupied at O.25.
Troops withdrawn will be placed not further in rear than the support line to right of COVENTRY STREET.
At O.30 troops from Saps and Front Line, from Half-Moon Street to Rifleman's Redoubt (A 10 a 8 3) and troops occupying the parts of PICCADILLY and PARK LANE within these Limits will be withdrawn and put in the GIVENCHY cellars until the end of the Heavy Trench Mortar Bombardment. O.C. Left Battalion is responsible for this.
O.C. 16th Rif. Brig will arrange to build up sandbag passing out places according to the wishes of O.C. 17th Notts & Derby R.

(5) LIAISON. Liaison Officer 17th Notts & Derby R. will be at LEFT Coy. H.Q. Right Battalion and Liaison will be by runner & telephone to 16th Rif. Brig. H.Q. in Village Line thence by special wire to advanced Brigade H.Q.

(6) MEDICAL. Stretcher Cases via WOLFE'S RD. to A.D.S. Village Line thence to Dressing Station LONE FARM.

(7) SUPPORTS 1 Company 16th Notts & Derby R. will proceed to SIDBUR. Hill and be ready to move at short notice during the operations.

(8) TRAFFIC. WOLFE'S ROAD & FINCHLEY ROAD are placed at the disposal of O.C. 17th Notts & Derby R. No traffic will take place for one hour before Zero.
O.C. 16th Rifle Brigade is responsible for Traffic Control.

(9) REPORT CENTRE. During the operations 117th Brigade Report Centre will be at the DISTILLERY, Pont Fixe N 9A 14 b 6 0).

                                      Capt.
                        Brigade Major, 117th Brigade.

Copies issued at 11.45am to :
O.C. 16th Notts & Derby R. — 1
     17th Notts & Derby R. — 2
     17th K. R. Rif. Corps — 3
     16th Rif. Brig. — 4
     117 Bde. M.G. Coy. — 5
     117 Bde. L.T.M.B. — 6
✓ B Group R.F.A. — 7
     Heavy Trench Mortars — 8
     Medium Trench Mortars — 9
     254th Tunnelling Coy. R.E. — 10
G.O.C. — 11
Brigade Major, — 12
Brigade Signalling Offr. — 13
War Diary (2 Copies) — 14, 15
✓ H.Q. 39th Division, — 16
   ✓ 23rd Brigade, — 17
     116th Brigade. — 18

Typed & Duplicated by Lt. E. KROLIK.

"A" Form.
MESSAGES AND SIGNALS.
Army Form C. 2121.

Prefix	Code	Words	Charge	This message is on a/c of:	Recd. at ___ m.
Office of Origin and Service Instructions.		Sent At ___ m. To ___ By ___		Service. (Signature of "Franking Officer.")	Date ___ From ___ By ___

Secret

TO — Office Copy

Sender's Number: BM/380
Day of Month: 31st
In reply to Number:
AAA

Ref 117th Bde Order No 39 received 11.15/a

acknowledge

From: 117th Brigade
Place:
Time: 9.45 a.m.

(Z)

SECRET

Amendment to 117th Brigade Order No.30.

Para. (6) for A.3.c.5½.4. read A.3.d.5½.4.

                                                                              Capt.
                                  Brigade Major, 117th Inf. Brigade.

2.7.16.
Issued to :-

16/Notts & Derby. R.	H.Q. 39th Div.	Brigade Major
17/ do do	H.Q. 118th Inf. Bde.	Staff Captain
17/K.R.Rif. C.	"C" Group, R.A.	War Diary (2)
16/Rif. Brig.	225 Co., R.E.	
117/Bde. M. Gun Co.	117 T.M. Battery	

SECRET

To/

    Headquarters,

        39th Division.

Attached Amendment to 117th Brigade Order 30, for information.

                                          (Sd.) W.G. MAXWELL, Capt for
                                                        Brig. Gen.
                                           Commanding 117th. BRIGADE.

2nd July, 1916.

                                                                        H.H.

39th Division.

B. H. Q.

117th INFANTRY BRIGADE

AUGUST 1 9 1 6

Appendices attached:--

Brigade Orders.
Defence Scheme.
Tracing.

Original.

Army Form C. 2118

Page 1.

WAR DIARY
or
INTELLIGENCE SUMMARY
(Erase heading not required.)

Instructions regarding War Diaries and Intelligence Summaries are contained in F.S. Regs., Part II. and the Staff Manual respectively. Title Pages will be prepared in manuscript.

Place	Date	Hour	Summary of Events and Information	Remarks and references to Appendices
CANAL HOUSE Near CORRE.	1st Aug.		Inter battalion relief took place. The 17th Notts & Derby Regt. is now holding the right subsection, the 16th Notts & Derby Regt. the left. The 16th Rifle Brigade is in support, the 17th K.R.R.Corps in reserve.	App. 1.
	2nd.		Our bombardment of the previous night has greatly damaged the enemy's trenches in rear of the NORTHERN CRATERS. Two large pipes, evidently leading from a mine shaft, are visible and water seen coming out.	
	3rd.		Our L.T.M's and M.T.M's bombarded the two pipes mentioned yesterday. We exploded a small defensive mine at A9d3.8 (approx.), but consolidation was useless. Some rifle grenade activity on the left. On the right things are quiet.	
	4th.		Evidently in retaliation for our H.T.M's the enemy has brought up a heavy minenwerfer and did considerable damage, knocking out a rifle grenade stand, and blowing in the parapet in places. Plan of defence of GIVENCHY Section issued.	App. 2.
	5th.		During the Brigade's tour in the trenches, it can claim to have subdued the hostile rifle grenade activity to a great degree. The system of immediate retaliation with rifle grenade Batteries for any rifle grenades that come over has been very successful. We have always given the enemy three times as much as he gives us, and very often a great deal more.	
	6th.		The Brigade is relieved by the 116th Infantry Brigade, and becomes Brigade in Divisional	

1875 Wt. W593/826 1,000,000 4/15 J.B.C. & A. A.D.S.S./Forms/C. 2118.

Army Form C. 2118

Page 2.

WAR DIARY
or
INTELLIGENCE SUMMARY
(Erase heading not required.)

Instructions regarding War Diaries and Intelligence Summaries are contained in F. S. Regs., Part II. and the Staff Manual respectively. Title Pages will be prepared in manuscript.

Place	Date	Hour	Summary of Events and Information	Remarks and references to Appendices
CANAL HOUSE.	7th		Reserve. Headquarters at 14, RUE GAMBETTA, at BETHUNE.	App.3.
	8th		BETHUNE is shelled by a 38 cm. gun. About 7 shells fell doing considerable damage.	
	9th		Nothing of interest to report.	
	10th		Move order published for Brigade to move to AUCHEL on the 10th.	App.4.
RAIMBERT.			Brigade moved to AUCHEL according to programme, and the Brigade Headquarters are established at RAIMBERT. Move orders published for Brigade to march to area LA THIEULOYE - MONCHY BRETON - MAGNICOURT-EN-COMTE - ORLENCOURT.	App.5.
	11th		Brigade moved as in Appendix 5, and Brigade Headquarters established at LA THIEULOYE. 17th K.R.R.Corps, 117th M.G.Coy., and 117th L.T.M.Battery, to move on 12th as in Appendix 6.	App.6.
LA THIEULOYE.	12th			
	13th			
	14th			
	15th		Training in MONCHY-BRETON area.	
	16th			
	17th			
	18th			
	19th			

WAR DIARY or INTELLIGENCE SUMMARY

(Erase heading not required.)

Army Form C. 2118

Page 3.

Instructions regarding War Diaries and Intelligence Summaries are contained in F. S. Regs., Part II. and the Staff Manual respectively. Title Pages will be prepared in manuscript.

Place	Date	Hour	Summary of Events and Information	Remarks and references to Appendices
LA THIEULOYE.	20th		The Brigade carries out a practice attack on dummy trenches, Order No. 47.	App. 7.
	21st		Training.	
	22nd		Training.	
	23rd		16th Notts & Derby Regt., 17th K.R.R.Corps, 117th M.G.Coy., and 117th T.M.Battery, together with all the wheeled transport of the Brigade, leave for DOULLENS Area by march route. The night of the 23rd is passed in the BUNEVILLE Area. The remainder of the 117th Brigade, i.e. the 17th Notts & Derby Regt., the 16th Rifle Brigade, and Brigade Headquarters, together with the 11th Batt. Royal Sussex Regt., and the 1/4th Batt. The Hampshire Regt., to proceed under Brig.-General R.D.F.OLDMAN, D.S.O., to DOULLENS Area on the 24th., part of the journey to be performed by train.	App. 8.
DOULLENS.	24th		Move to DOULLENS Area took place in accordance with programme. Order No.49 issued for Brigade to move to AUTHIE and VAUCHELLES Area.	App. 9.
VAUCHELLES.	25th		Brigade moved in accordance with orders and Brigade Headquarters are established at VAUCHELLES.	
	26th		The Brigade rests.	
	27th		Brigade receives orders to move to BEAUSSART and BERTRANCOURT.	App. 10.
BEAUSSART.	28th		Brigade Headquarters established here.	

1875 W: W593/826 1,000,000 4/15 J.B.C. & A. A.D.S.S./Forms/C. 2118.

Army Form C. 2118

WAR DIARY
or
INTELLIGENCE SUMMARY

Page 4.

(Erase heading not required.)

Instructions regarding War Diaries and Intelligence Summaries are contained in F.S. Regs., Part II. and the Staff Manual respectively. Title Pages will be prepared in manuscript.

Place	Date	Hour	Summary of Events and Information	Remarks and references to Appendices
BEAUSSART	29th		Orders issued for the Division to attack the German Front, Second and Third line trenches on "A" day. The front allotted to this Brigade is from Pt. 91 to Pt. 13 (ref. map BEAUMONT HAMEL) Amendments and addenda to Attack order issued.	App.11. App.12. App.13. App.14. App.15.
	30th		Ground is continued to be reconnoitred by Officers, N.C.O's, and men, of the Brigade.	
	31st		Move order issued. This was not carried out on appointed day under orders of the Division.	App.16.

[signature]

Brig. General,
Commanding 117th INFANTRY BRIGADE.

Signifies Appendix attached to "Original" copy only.

1875 Wt. W593/826 1,000,000 4/15 J.B.C. & A. A.D.S.S./Forms/C. 2118.

SECRET Appendix I   WD   Copy No... 14

117th BRIGADE ORDER No. 40.

31.7.16.

Map ref. 1/40,000
THUNE (Combined Sheet).

1. On the night 1/2nd August the following inter-battalion reliefs will take place :-

2. 16th Rifle Brigade (Right Subsection) will be relieved by 17th Notts & Derby Regt. (Support Battalion, VILLAGE LINE). 17th K.R.R. Corps (Left Subsection) will be relieved by the 16th Notts & Derby Regt. (Reserve Battalion, TUNING FORK). After relief the 16th Rifle Brigade will take over billets, Keeps, etc. vacated by 17th Notts & Derby Regt. and 17th K.R.R. Corps will take over billets and posts vacated by 16th Notts & Derby Regt.

3. All details of relief will be arranged by Commanding Officers concerned.

4. There will be no movement East of the VILLAGE LINE (WINDY CORNER - PONT FIXE) till 9.30 p.m.

5. Relief complete = CANAL.

W.E. Maxwell
Capt.
Brigade Major, 117th. BRIGADE.

Copies issued at 3.30 p.m. to :-

	By	Copy No.
16th Notts & Derby Regt.	D.R.	1
17th do do	D.R.	2
17th K.R.R. Corps.	D.R.	3
16th Rif. Brig.	D.R.	4
117th Machine Gun Co.	D.R.	5
117th Trench Mortar Battery	D.R.	6
H.Q., 39th Division.	D.R.	7
G.O.C.	D.R.	8
B.M.	D.R.	9
S.C.	D.R.	10
Bde. Signal Officer.	Orderly	11
118th Infantry Brigade.	D.R.	12
24th Infantry Brigade.	D.R.	13
War Diary	-	14 & 15
Order File	-	16

Appendix II

SECRET   Copy No... 13

117th INFANTRY BRIGADE.

PLAN OF DEFENCE OF GIVENCHY SECTION.

(Combined ... t)   (39th Divisional Sector).
 1/40,000.   4.8.16.
Trench Map 1/10,000.

Front System. (1). The Front System consists of a Front Line running from the CANAL through the South and North Craters to SCOTTISH TRENCH, which is not connected up to the nearest (PRINCE'S) "Island" of the Brigade Section on our Left.

Support Line. (2). A Support Line running from the CANAL along BAYSWATER - OXFORD and CAMBRIDGE TERRACES to PICCADILLY - thence to PARK LANE where it runs into SCOTTISH TRENCH. There is a gap on the left of CAMBRIDGE TERRACE where a new trench is being dug to join up PICCADILLY. The following posts form part of the Support Line :- SPOIL BANK - ORCHARD KEEP - MAIRIE - MOAT FARM and POPPY.

Flank Defences of Section. (3). The Right Flank is protected by the CANAL, the TOWPATH of which has one or two indifferent trenches across it and by 2 machine gun positions on the South Bank belonging to the Brigade on our right.
There is a machine gun emplacement at A.15.c.6.9 on our side of the CANAL which protects the Northern Bank.
The Left Flank is protected by WARE Road and NEW CUT which are well organised for defence.

Central Keep Defences. (4). The Central portion of the defensive system is that of GIVENCHY Village, which is protected by MAIRIE - HILDERS - POPPY - MOAT FARM Keeps centralized on GIVENCHY Keep, which is a badly sited work at A.9.c.6.5 with poor field of fire. The cellar system in the village is quite fair but not yet sufficiently connected up.

Village Line. (5). A succession of strong posts covered along the entire front by a strong belt of wire entanglements.- PONT FIXE S. - PONT FIXE N. - WINDY CORNER - LE PLANTIN S.

Sheet No.2.

Second Line. (6). Line of Breastworks from the LA BASSEE CANAL along the irrigation CANAL at Brigade Headquarters - thence in a straight line to TUNING FORK Road. Three small posts are connected with this line; WESTMINSTER BRIDGE - MARAIS E and MARAIS S.W. Several Batteries R.F.A. are posted in or near this line.

Mining Area. (7). Mining activities on both sides have resulted in the formation of two mine areas called CRATER S. or DUCKS BILL and CRATERS N.
The usual saps run out to these craters. The largest is that known as the RED DRAGON CRATER which is probably not surpassed in size anywhere.

Report Centre (8). The Brigade Advanced Report Centre is at FANSHAWE CASTLE (A.14.a.5.5.).

GENERAL PLAN IN CASE OF ATTACK.

To carry out the provisions of the 39th Divisional Defence Scheme the following will be the action of the Brigade while holding GIVENCHY SECTION.

Front Line. The front line Battalions will hold on to the first and support lines at all costs. The line of Keeps GIV. R. - SPOIL BANK - ORCHARD FARM - FAIRIE - HILDERS - POPPY - MOAT FARM are manned with their normal garrisons, which will remain in their Keeps in any event and are not at disposal of local commanders for counter-attack. If these garrisons are at work near their keeps they will return at once. Os.C, Front Line Battalions will push forward the reserves in their hands, i.e., in GIV. R. 1 Company, in GIV. L. 2 platoons, so as to be available for immediate counter-attack.

SUPPORT BN. The Battalion in the Village Line is available for the counter-
Village Line attack in any portion of the Brigade Front, less the following minimum garrisons in the Village Line Redoubts :-

(1)	GIVENCHY KEEP	2 Pl.	1 V.H.G.
(2)	HERTS REDOUBT	½ Pl.	1 L.G.
(3)	PONT FIXE S.	1 Pl.	
(4)	PONT FIXE N.	1 Pl.	
(5)	WINDY CORNER	1 Pl.	
(6)	ORCHARD	1 Pl.	
(7)	HILDERS	1 Pl.	1 L.G.
(8)	MOAT FARM	1 Pl.	
(9)	LE PLANTIN S.	½ Pl.	
	Total	9 Pl.	

thus leaving 7 platoons and 4 Lewis guns for immediate counter-attack. The O.C, Village Line Battalion will act as circumstances require and attack if necessary, without waiting for orders from Brigade. His first efforts will be directed to moving up his men closer to the summit of the ridge into jumping-off places, for which purpose the keeps will offer opportunities. The principle of not using the supporting troops until the right moment, and then in sufficient force to gain a decision, must be kept in view.

RESERVE BN. The Reserve Battalion will get ready to move up to the Village Line as ordered by Brigade Headquarters. The routes to be used are :

1. Canal Bank to PONT FIXE.
2. Canal Bank - WEST MINSTER BRIDGE Road and WINDY CORNER.
3. TUNING FORK S. - LE PLANTIN .

These will be reconnoitred by all concerned.

Sheet No.4.

Artillery Support	"B" Group, R.F.A. covers the section. It consists of

A/170.	XXXXX.	(4 guns)	18-prs.
A/174.	XXXXX.	(4 guns)	ditto
C/179.	XXXXX.	(6 guns)	ditto
B/179.	XXXXX.	(4 guns)	ditto
D/174.	XXXXX.	(4 guns)	4.15 Hows.

for night lines and gun position see Appendix C.

L.M. Batts — The guns of the L.T.M. Batteries will normally be so disposed as to admit of 2 of each Battery therein being available and in the hands of O.C. Subsection for counter-attack (See App A).

Medium Mortars — For dispositions of these mortars see Appendix A.

Machine Gun Co. — The Machine Gun Co. is disposed with 12 guns in keeps and posts and 4 in reserve at GORRE, which will move up to the neighbourhood of Brigade Advanced Report Centre (See also App.A).

Tunnelling Co. — 254th Tunnelling Co. are allotted posts in the garrison vide "Preliminary Warning" below :-

Preliminary Warning. — In the event of an attack being expected at any time, and if the G.O.C. considers information received sufficiently reliable, the following message will be sent out by 'phone and D.R® or runner :"Carry out preliminary arrangements."

Battns in Front Line. — On receipt of this message, Os.C. Battalions in Front Line will, if they have not already done so, get ready to move up their Reserve Company.

Support Battalion. — O.C. Battalion in Support will assemble working parties (if out) under "stand-to" for obligatory minimum garrisons of keeps, and have his 7 platoons and 4 Lewis guns ready to move without further orders, should he consider the situation demands it.

Reserve Battalion. — O.C. Reserve Battalion will get ready to move.

Bde. H.Qrs. — Brigade Headquarters will get ready to move to FANSHAWE CASTLE (A.14.a.5.5).

254 Tunnlg Company — The personnel of 254 Tunnelling Co. in the front line will get ready to move as follows :-

N. Crater. Party 1 proceeds via SCOTTISH TRENCH - UPPER CUT CALEDONIAN Road and KING'S Road to GUNNER SIDING.

N. Crater. Party 2 will take the shortest road to the AVENUE and thence via KILBY'S WALK - KING'S Road to GUNNER SIDING.

Sheet No.5.

N. Crater, Party 3 will proceed via BOND St - PICCADILLY and KING'S Road to GUNNER SIDING.

S. Crater Parties will take the shortest road to HOPE St. thence across into HADFIELD Road and WOLFE Road to Assembly Trenches off WOLFE Road (A.15.a.3.9).

In all cases they will be under their own officers, who will report to the O.C., the nearest body of Infantry.

117 M. Gun Co O.C, 117th Machine Gun Co. will have his reserve section ready to move up.

Light Trench Mortars O.C. 117th Trench Mortar Battery will have his personnel in rest as well as any reserve under training ready to move up to their positions, detailing such parties as they require from the above to proceed to Brigade Bomb Store to carry up ammunition.

General. On receipt of "Carry out preliminary arrangements" Units will send runners to Brigade Headquarters as under :-

Infantry Bn.   4 each to F.10.B.3.3.
              4 each to FANSHAWE CASTLE (A.14.a.5.5).
117 M.Gun Co. 1 to each of above.
117th T.M. Batt 1 to each of above.

F. C. Maxwell Capt.
Brigade Major, 117th. BRIGADE.

Issued at 11 to :-

	By	Copy No.
16th Notts & Derby Regt.	D.R.	1
17th do do	D.R.	2
17th K.R.R. Corps	D.R.	3
16th Rif. Brig.	D.R.	4
117th Machine Gun Co.	D.R.	5
117th T.M. Battery.	D.R.	6
Medium Trench Mortars	D.R.	7
3 Sect. Signal Co.	Orderly	8
H.Q., 39th Division.	D.R.	9
G.O.C.	Personally	10
..M.	do	11
S.C.	do	12
War Diary	-	13 & 14
Order File	-	15
Bde. Bombing Officer	Personally	16
Group Comdr., R.A.	D.R.	17
225 Co., R.E.	D.R.	18
234 Co., R.E.	D.R.	19
254 Tunnlg Co. R.E.	D.R.	20
Handing-over File	-	21

Appendix A.

Shewing Dispositions of Medium and Light Trench Mortars.

Medium Trench Mortars.   At present there are 11 Medium Trench Mortars
                          emplaced as follows :-

        2 STRATHCONA WALK.
        3 CAMBRIDGE TERRACE
        2 AVENUE
        1 UPPER CUT
        3 WARE Road.

The following additional emplacements exists.

        2 in Support Trench about A.15.d.8.8. (nr CHEYNE WALK).
        1 in WOLFE Road.
        2 in AVENUE.
        3 in UPPER CUT.

Light Trench Mortars.

Offensive Emplacements.	Targets	Remarks
A.15.d.$7\frac{1}{2}$.7.	about A.16.c.$7\frac{1}{2}$.9.	not finished.
A.15.d.$8\frac{1}{4}$.9.	" A.16.c.5.5.	do
A.9.d.$5\frac{3}{4}$.0.	" A.10.c.$2\frac{1}{2}$.2.	completed.
A.10.a.6.$\frac{1}{2}$.	" A.10.c.$1\frac{1}{2}$.$1\frac{1}{2}$.	do
A.9.d.$6\frac{1}{2}$.1.	2 A.10.c.$2\frac{2}{3}$.3. and A.9.d.$9\frac{1}{4}$.5.	do
A.9.d.$4\frac{1}{4}$.$2\frac{1}{2}$.	" A.10.c.$2\frac{1}{4}$.$\frac{3}{4}$. and A.9.d.7.7	do
A.9.c.$8\frac{3}{4}$.$9\frac{3}{4}$.	" A.9.b.3.$2\frac{1}{4}$.	do
A.9.a.8.1.	" A.9.b.5.$\frac{1}{4}$.	do
A.9.a.6.$1\frac{3}{4}$.	" A.9.b.4.5.	do

Defensive Emplacements.	Points on our front line guns are registered on.	
A.9.d.$3\frac{1}{2}$.2.	A.9.d.$7\frac{1}{2}$.$\frac{1}{2}$.	Proposed.
A.9.c.$8\frac{1}{4}$.$6\frac{3}{4}$.	A.9.b.1.3.	completed.
A.9.a.$7\frac{1}{2}$.$1\frac{3}{4}$.	A.9.d.$2\frac{1}{2}$.$8\frac{1}{2}$.	do
A.9.a.6.$1\frac{3}{4}$.	A.9.b.$2\frac{1}{4}$.$\frac{1}{2}$.	do
A.15.b.8.$9\frac{1}{4}$.		Proposed.
A.15.b.9.5.		do
A.9.d.$4\frac{1}{2}$.$5\frac{1}{4}$.		do

Much work is still required for the building of these emplacements with suitable shell stores near by.

Appendix 2.

(a) A Platoon (of an assumed strength of 35 All Ranks) is taken as the Unit in compiling this table.
(b) This works out 400 rounds S.A.A. per rifle in keeps.
(c) An extra 6,000 rounds is allowed for each M.G. or L.G.
(d) Rations for two days per rifle is allowed for.
(e) S.A.A. in firing-line is calculated at 1 box per Section.
(f) The garrisons shown in this Appendix are the minimum obligatory garrisons. The S.A.A. and stores will be maintained at the strength shown so that provision is always made for a probable increase of garrison.

GARRISONS AND STORES

AREA	POST	Platoons	Machine Guns	S.A.A. Boxes	Hand Grenade Boxes	Meat Boxes	Biscuit Boxes	Water petrol tins	Tanks, Water	Ammunition Very-Boxes	Vermoral Sprays	Solution Jars	Shovels	Picks	Sandbags	Barbed wire coils	Wirecutters	Pumps	H.G. SAA Boxes	Billhooks	Trench Stretchers
GIVENCHY Right	SPOIL BANK	1	1	14 MG	50	2	2	10	2	3	1	4	20	6	100	5	1	–	6	1	1
	MAIRIE	1	1	14 LG	50	2	2	20	1	3	1	4	20	6	100	5	1	–	6	1	1
	HILDERS	1	1	14 LG	50	2	2	10	2	3	1	4	20	6	100	5	1	–	6	1	1
GIVENCHY Left	POPPY	1	–	–	–	–	–	–	–	–	–	–	–	–	–	–	–	1	–	–	–
	MOAT FARM	½	1	7 LG	25	1	1	10	1	2	1	4	10	3	100	5	1	–	6	1	1
	HERTS	1	–	14	50	2	2	20	1	3	1	4	20	6	100	5	1	–	6	1	1
Village Line	GIVENCHY KEEP	½	1	7	25	1	1	10	–	2	1	4	10	3	100	5	1	1	6	1	1
	PONT FIXE S.	2	2	60 MG	100	10	10	20	4	25	3	12	30	10	1000	20	5	3	12	2	2
	PONT FIXE N.	1	1	56 MG	200	8	8	20	2	12	2	8	50	15	1000	15	2	–	–	–	–
	WINDY CORNER	1	1	56 MG	200	8	8	20	2	12	2	8	50	15	1000	15	2	–	–	–	–
	ORCHARD	1	1	14 MG	100	4	4	20	2	6	1	4	25	8	1000	10	1	–	–	–	–
	LE PLANTIN S.	1	1	14 MG	50	2	2	20	1	3	1	4	20	6	100	5	1	–	6	1	1
GORRE Area	MARAIS E.	½	–	14	50	2	2	10	1	3	1	4	20	6	200	10	1	–	–	–	–
	WESTMINSTER BRIDGE	1 N.C.O. and 3 men each																			
	MARAIS S.W.																				
	TUNING FORK																				
	GORRE Group of Wks												No establishment of stores beyond what is on Inventory Board								
FIRING AND SUPPORT LINES	Firing Line	7		28	200			20		20	10	40						12			
V. R.	Support Line	2½		56	200					10	5	20									
	Reserve	3		42	100																
	Firing Line	9		36	200			10		20	10	40						2			
V. L.	Support Line	4		56						10	5	20									
	Reserve	12		90	100																

Appendix C.

Showing Machine Gun and Artillery Dispositions.

Vickers Machine Guns.

(1)	SPOIL BANK	A.15.c.5.9	(open emplacement)
(2)	ORCHARD	A.15.a.5.4.	do
(3)	ORCHARD FARM	A.15.a.5.4.	do
(4)	FRENCH FARM	A.9.c.9.9.	(closed emplacement)
(5)	GIVENCHY KEEP	A.9.c.6.4.	do
(6)	WINDY CORNER	A.8.c.7.5.	do
(7)	Junction of VAUXHALL Bge Rd and Village Line.	A.14.a.9.9.	do
(8)	PONT FIXE North	A.14.b.5.3.	do
(9)	do do South	A.14.d.3.7.	do
(10)	MAIRIE REDOUBT	A.9.c.9½.10	(open emplacement)
(11)	do do	A.9.c.9½.10.	do
(12)	MOAT HOUSE	A.9.c.2½.7.	(closed emplacement)

Vickers machine guns are actually emplaced at these positions.
The remaining 4 guns are in reserve at GORRE.
In addition to the above emplacements there are many others closed
and open, chiefly in square A.14.d. (PONT FIXE Defences).
A closed emplacement is required firing N.N.E. from MAIRIE REDOUBT
with belt of fire intersecting belt of fire of gun firing S.E. from
FRENCH FARM.

LEWIS GUNS.

The Battalion in support will keep a Lewis gun as
permanent garrison in each of the following :-

HERTS 1 gun.   HILDERS 1 gun.

Artillery Support. The Batteries of the covering Group are responsible
for sections of the German defences as under, within the following
Zones :-

Battery Position.		Zones.
A.7.d.7.2.	4 guns	Canal A.16.c.5½.6 to A.16.a.3½.7½.
F.11.d.2.4.	6 guns	A.16.a.3½.7½ to A.9.d.8½.7.
F.10.d.7.5.	2 guns	A.9.d.8½.7. to A.9.b.3½.1.
do	2 guns	A.9.b.6½.6. to A.9.b.6.9½.
A.24.c.6.7.	4 guns	A.9.b.1½.4½. to 6½.6.
F.5.c.6.7.	4 guns	A.16.c.5½.6. to A.9.b.6.9½.

Appendix D.

GARRISONS (showing distributions of Battalions and Companies).

Right Subsection.	Right Company.	
From LA BASSEE Canal (A.15.d.10.7) to A.9.b.9.0.	From LA BASSEE Canal (A.15.d.10.7) to A.15.b.8½.½.	2 Pls Front Line. 1 Pl SPOIL BANK. 1 Pl GUNNER SIDING.
	Centre Company, from A.15.b.8½.½ to A.15.b.8.7.	2 Pls Front Line 1 Pl OXFORD TERRACE 1 Pl ORCHARD KEEP (obligatory).
	Left Company, from A.15.b.8.7. to A.9.d.9.0.	2 Pls Front Line. 1½ " CAMBRIDGE TERRACE ½ " HAIRIE REDOUBT (obligatory).
	Reserve Company.	4 " Village Line.

Battalion Headquarters A.14.c,8½,9½.

Left Subsection.	Right Company.	2 Pls Front Line and Saps.
From A.9.d.9.0. to Junction of GRENADIER Rd and Front Line.	From A.9.d.9.0. to A.9.d.4.5.	2 Pls Support Line.
	Centre Company, from A.9.d.4.5 to A.9.b.1½.1.	2½ " Front Line 1½ " Support Line. and Sa
	Left Company, from A.9.b.1½.1. to Junction of GRENADIER Rd with Front Line.	3½ " Front Line. ½ " Support Line.
	Reserve Company.	2 " Village Line. 1 " HARE Road. 1 " POPPY REDOUBT (obligatory).

Battalion Headquarters A.8.d.8.5.

Support Battalion.
"A" Company.   (1 Pl.MOAT FARM (obligatory).
                (2 Pl GIVENCHY KEEP (obligatory)
                (1 Pl HILDERS REDOUBT (obligatory)
                 1 Pl HERTS REDOUBT (½ Pl obligatory).
"B" Company.   4 Pl PONT FIXE South (1 Pl obligatory).
"C"   do   3 Pl PONT FIXE North (1 Pl obligatory)
                1 Pl ORCHARD KEEP (obligatory).
"D"   do   1 Pl LE PLANTIN South (½ Pl obligatory).
                3 Pl WINDY CORNER (1 Pl obligatory).

This leaves 7 platoons in all available for counter-attack.

Battalion Headquarters. A.14.c.9.6½.

Reserve Battalion.   Reserve Billets TUNING FORK.

Battalion Headquarters. F.4.a.5.2.

Appendix E.

GIVENCHY SECTION

SIGNALS - 117th INFANTRY BRIGADE.

VISUAL SIGNALLING.

The following Visual Stations have been established on this front :-

RIGHT BATTALION. A.15.c.4.8½ to corner of VAUXHALL BRIDGE Road and
PONT FIXE Road.

LEFT BATTALION.
SPY REDOUBT to Battalion Headquarters at A.8.d.9½.5½.
Battalion Headquarters to Advanced Brigade Headquarters Station at A.14.a.5.5.

SUPPORT BATTALION.
GIVENCHY KEEP to Advanced Brigade Headquarters Station.
Advanced Brigade Headquarters is in visual communication with Brigade Headquarters.

A test message will be sent each evening addressed to the Brigade and will originate from the front line stations. The time the messages are to be sent will be fixed by the Brigade Signal Officer. The messages will be acknowledged by wire.

As much protection as possible must be afforded to these Stations to keep them immune from hostile fire and observation, and to protect the lamp against bad weather conditions.

Battalions on being relieved must make clear to incoming Units the positions of these Stations and the time fixed for sending test messages.

It is to be clearly understood that communication by lamp is for emergency only and will not, with the exception of the test message, be used unless communication breaks down.

In the event of telephonic communication breaking down either from Brigade to Battalion or from Battalion to Front Line, the Stations in the affected area will at once be manned by 3 men in each Station who will stand by for messages, until communication by wire is re-established.

The Advanced Brigade Headquarters Station at A.14.a.5.5 will be manned by the Support Battalion with 5 men, who will receive the test messages each evening and will deliver them by runner to Advanced Brigade Headquarters for transmission to Brigade. In the event of communication breaking down between Brigade and Battalions, the Support Battalion will be notified by the operator on duty at Advanced Brigade Headquarters, and they will at once man the Station and will stand by to receive messages until communication is re-established.

SECRET   AM IV   WD   Copy No...

Ref. Map BETHUNE   117th INFANTRY BRIGADE Order No.41.
(Combined Sheet) 1/10,000.
and Trench Map 1/10,000.   5.8.16.

1. 117th Infantry Brigade will be relieved in the GIVENCHY Section by the 116th Infantry Brigade during the day of August 6th and the night 6th/7th August, in accordance with attached Relief Table.

2. All details not mentioned will be arranged between Officers Commanding concerned.

3. O.C., 117th Machine Gun Co. will arrange relief direct with O.C., 116th Machine Gun Co.

   O.C., 117th Trench Mortar Battery will arrange relief direct with O.C., 116th Trench Mortar Battery.

4. All specialists, including Lewis gunners, will be relieved by daylight.

5. Defence Schemes, Maps and Aeroplane photos will be handed over and receipts obtained.

6. Billeting parties will report to Headquarters of the Battalion from whom they are taking over billets at 2 p.m. on August 6th.

7. On completion of relief Brigade Headquarters will move to No.14 RUE GAMBETTA, BETHUNE.

8. Reports of completion of relief to Brigade Headquarters, CANAL HOUSE.
   Relief complete = BARGE.
   Reports of all in billets to No.14 RUE GAMBETTA, BETHUNE.

Acknowledge.

                                               Capt.
                                 Brigade Major, 117th. BRIGADE.

Copy No.			
1.	16/Notts & Derby R.	7. G.O.C.	13. 39th Division
2.	17/ do do	8. B.M.	14. 24th Brigade
3.	17/K.R.R. Corps	9. S.C.	15. 118th Brigade
4.	16/Rif. Brig.	10. War Diary	16. 116th Brigade
5.	117th M. Gun Co.	11. do do	17. 234 Co. R.E.
6.	117/T.M. Battery.	12. Order File	18. 225 Co. R.E.
			19. "B" Group, R.A.

LECHET

117th INFANTRY BRIGADE.

SKELETON TABLE to accompany 117th Infantry Brigade Order No.41, dated 5.3.16.

Unit	From	To	Relieved by	House for incoming and outgoing battalions	Guides (1 per Platoon)	Remarks
16/Notts & Derby R.	RICHEBOURG (Left)	LE HAMEL (Billets now occupied by 12/R.Suss.R.)	14/Hants Regt	TUILERIES - LE PLANTIN - TIDY CORNER.	WINDY CORNER 9 p.m.	
do	GIVENCHY (Right)	ESSARS (Billets now occupied by 13/R.Suss.R.)	11/R.Suss.R.	CANAL BANK.	VAUXHALL BRIDGE 9 p.m.	
17/R.R. Corps.	TUILING FOR (Bn in Reserve)	LES CHOQUAUX (Billets now occupied by 14/Hants).	13/R.Suss.R.	Any convenient.	NIL	Relief to be completed by 9 p.m. Billeting parties from 13/R.Suss. R. will precede the batt.
AC/Fld. Brig.	Village Line. (Bn in Support)	Ecole de Jeunes Filles BETHUNE (now occupied by 11/R.Suss.R.)	12/R.Suss.R.	Incoming Bns via FUMING FOR. - LE PLANT -IN. Outgoing Bn. Any convenient.	TIDY CORNER 9 p.m.	
117 ... Bur Co.	The Line.	Ecole de Jeunes Filles BETHUNE.	116 M. Gur. Co.	Any convenient.	As arranged between C.Os concerned.	Relief to be completed by 7 p.m.
118 T.M. Batter.	The Line.	do do	116 T.M. Battery	do do	ditto	ditto 7 p.m.

All movements East of GORE by sections at 100 yards interval.

SECRET   Appendix IV   WD   Copy No...15.

117th INFANTRY BRIGADE ORDER No.43.

Ref. BETHUNE (Combined Sheet) 1/40,000.
"   HAZEBROUCK 5.a. 1/100,000.   9.8.16.
"   LENS. 1/100,000.

1. The 117th Brigade, 133rd Field Ambulance and No.3 Coy, 39th Div Train will leave present billets and will move in accordance with attached march table to area RAIMBERT - AUCHEL. The G.O.C, 117th Infantry Brigade will be in command of this area, with Brigade Headquarters at AUCHEL.

2. The 16th Notts & Derby Regt. will be clear of present billets at LE HAMEL by 5 p.m. on the 9th August and will move to ECOLE de JEUNES FILLES, BETHUNE.

3. All movement of units on August 10th will be in accordance with attached march table and the Brigade will move by Battalions - and not as a Brigade.

4. Dress will be marching order - Packs, Steel Helmets. Waterproof sheet and spare underclothing will be carried in the pack.

5. The rate of marching will be 2½ miles per hour, including halts.

6. Each unit will hand over all billet stores, and any special orders applying to the particular billets they occupy to O.C, incoming unit.

7. Two motor lorries per unit will be provided - greatcoats only will be carried on the lorries.

8. On arrival report "all in billets" will be sent to Brigade Headquarters.

                                                   L E Maxwell   Capt.
                                         Brigade Major, 117th. BRIGADE

Issued at 11.30 a.m. to :-
Copy No.1   16/Notts & Derby Regt   Copy No.10. Bde Sigs. Offr.
"   2.   17/   do   do   "   11.   G.O.C.
"   3.   17/K.R.R. Corps.   "   12.   B.M.
"   4.   16/Rif. Brig.   "   13.   S.C.
"   5.   117th Machine Gun Co.   "   14.   War Diary.
"   6.   117th T.M. Battery.   "   15.   War Diary
"   7.   H.Q. 39th Division.   "   16.   Order File
"   8.   133rd Fld Amb.
"   9.   No.3 Coy. A.S.C.

SECRET   MARCH TABLE to accompany 117th INFANTRY BRIGADE Order No.43, dated 9.8.16.

Unit	From	To	Route	To be clear of present billets by	Billeting parties.	Remarks
16/Notts & Derby Regt.	ECOLE de JEUNES FILLES, BETHUNE	AUCHEL	ANNEZIN - LA BEUVRIERE - LA PUGNOY & MARLES-LES-MINES	Start 4 p.m. exactly.	Meet Staff Captain Town Major's Office AUCHEL; pm 9th inst	
17/ do do	ESSARS	do	ditto	4 p.m.	ditto	
17/K.R.R Corps	LES CHOCQUAUX	do	VENDIN-LEZ-BETHUNE - CHOCQUES - MARLES-LES-MINES	4 p.m.	ditto	
16/Rif. Brig.	ECOLE de JEUNES FILLES, BETHUNE	do	ANNEZIN - LA BEUVRIERE - La PUGNOY - MARLES-LES-MINES	5 p.m.	ditto	
117 M. Gun Co.	ditto	do	VENDIN-LEZ-BETHUNE - CHOCQUES- MARLES-LES-MINES	4.30 p.m.	ditto	
117 T.M. Batt.	ditto	do	ANNEZIN - LA BEUVRIERE - LA PUGNOY - MARLES-LES-MINES	4.30 p.m.	ditto	Marches with Bde. H.Q.
117th Bde F.C.	LA RUE GAMBETTA BETHUNE	do	ditto	4.30 p.m.	ditto	
153rd Fld Amb.	BETHUNE	do	Any convenient.	--	Obtain billets from Town Major AUCHEL.	Moves off 11th inst. CLARENCE River at CHOCQUES to be crossed by 6.30 p.m.
No 3 Coy A.S.C 39th Div Train	PONT D'AVELETTES RAIMBERT		VENDIN-LEZ-BETHUNE - CHOCQUES - MARLES-LES-MINES - CHOCQUES	12 noon	ditto	

NOTE. One Officer and small rear party from each Battalion will remain in billets to clean up and hand over to the incoming units of the 21st Bde. This officer will obtain a written acknowledgment from O.C. the incoming unit that the billets were left clean and in good order. 21st Bde billeting parties will arrive to take over billets at 2 p.m. on 10th August.

SECRET   Appendix IV   W D   Copy No. 14

117th INFANTRY BRIGADE ORDER No. 44.

Ref. HAZEBROUCK 5.a. 1/100,000.
LENS. 1/100,000.
                                        10.8.16.

1. The 117th Brigade will continue their march South on August 11th, and will take up billets in the area LA THIEULOYE - MONCH BRETON - MAGNICOURT-EN-COMTE - ORLENCOURT. The Bde. will move by the following route - Forks Rds ¼ mile South of the S. in St. LEONARD - CALONNE RICOUART - Cross roads ¾ mile West of S. in STA. (CALONNE RICOUART) - DIVION - OURTON - DIEVAL - LA THIEULOYE.

2. **Starting point.** Fork Rd junction ¼ mile S. of the S. in St. LEONARD.

Commander
Lt Col MILWARD
17/Notts & Derby R.
(less two Coys).

117th Bde. H.Q.

2 Coys 17/Notts & D.R
17/K.R.R. Corps.
16/Rif. Brig.
16/Notts & Derby R.
(less 1 Coy).
117th M. Gun Co.
117th T.M. Battery.
Echelon B. (brigaded).

Commander
Major CONSTABLE
1 Coy 16/Notts & D.R

3. Advanced guard as per margin will keep ¼ mile in front of the main body.

4. Main body in order as per margin. The head of the main body will pass the Starting point at 5 p.m.

5. Rear party as per margin will keep ¼ mile in rear of the main body.

6. TRANSPORT. (a). Echelon A consisting of SAA and Tool limbers, Lewis gun limbers, Water-carts and Maltese carts, will march in rear of their respective Battalions.

(b). Echelon B (brigaded) under Lt FISHE, 16th Rifle Brigade consisting of all G.S. baggage waggons, mess carts and Field Cookers will march in rear of the main body; prior to marching off, Echelon B will park in AUCHEL at 4.30 p.m. at suitable place to be selected by Lt. FISHE, who will inform units direct as to place selected.

Sheet No.2.

    (c). All pack animals will march in rear of their Coys.

7. A distance of 100 paces between units will be observed throughout the march.

8. Rate of marching will be 2½ miles per hour. If state of road demands it, units themselves will be opened out, but further orders on this will be issued.

9. During each halt a mounted Officer from each unit will report at Brigade Headquarters "all correct", or otherwise, with reference to pace of column and condition of transport.

10. Billeting parties from each unit will meet the Staff Capt. at LA THIEULOYE CHURCH at ~~10 a.m.~~ 12 noon on August 11th. One guide from each party will meet units as they pass LA THIEULOYE CHURCH on the afternoon of the 11th and conduct them to allotted billets in the area.

11. Brigade Headquarters will march at the head of the main body. On arrival in area, Brigade Headquarters will be at LA THIEULOYE. Report Centre at AUCHEL will close at 4.30 p.m. and reopen at LA THIEULOYE at the same hour.

12. Watches will be synchronized at Brigade Headquarters, AUCHEL at 2 p.m. on the 11th, an officer from each unit attending for this purpose.

13. Acknowledge.

                                                                          Capt.
                                       Brigade Major, 117th. BRIGADE.

10.30
Issued at ~~8~~ p.m. to :-

	By	Copy No
16th Notts & Derby Regt.	D.R.	1
17th do do	D.R.	2
17th K.R.R. Corps.	D.R.	3
16th Rif. Brig.	D.R.	4
117th Machine Gun Co.	D.R.	5
117th T.M. Battery.	D.R.	6
Bde. Signal Officer.	Orderly	7
Major CONSTABLE, 16/Notts & Derby R.	D.R.	8
Lt. FISHE, 16/Rif. Brig.	D.R.	9
G.O.C.	Personally	10
B.M.	do	11
S.C.	do	12
War Diary	-	13 & 14
Order File	-	15
H.Q., 39th Division.	D.R.	16

SECRET Appendix VI W.D.   Copy No. 11

117th INFANTRY BRIGADE ORDER No.46.

Ref. LENS 1/100,000 and Sheet 36.b.   11.8.16.

(1).   The following moves will take place to-morrow, August 12th.
       In all cases, except where stated otherwise, troops will be
       clear of present billets by 9 a.m.

   (a). 17th K.R.R. Corps from MONCHY BRETON to MAQUAY.
   (b). 117th Machine Gun Co. from ROCOURT to ORLENCOURT.
   (c). 117th T.M. Battery from ROCOURT to ORLENCOURT.
   (d). 227 Field Coy. will be billeted in BAILLEUL-AUX-CORNAILLES
        by 11 a.m. and Billeting Officer will meet Staff Capt.
        there at 10 a.m.
   (e). No.3 Coy. A.S.C. from MONCHY BRETON to BAILLEUL-AUX-
        CORNAILLES.
   (f). 132 Field Ambulance from MAGNICOURT to TINCQUETTE.

(2).   All other units of the 117th Brigade not mentioned in para. (1)
       will remain where they are billeted to-night.

(3).   Completion of all moves will be reported to Brigade Head
       Quarters, giving map reference of new Headquarters.

(4).   Brigade Headquarters will remain at LA THIEULOYE (N.30.a.6.4).

                                            (Sgd) W. Carwell Capt.
                                         Brigade Major, 117th. BRIGADE

Issued at 11.45 p.m. to :-
                                                By   Copy No1
16th Notts & Derby Regt.   D.R.   1
17th   do   do   D.R.   2
17th K.R.R. Corps.   D.R.   3
16th Rif. Brig.   D.R.   4
117th Machine Gun Co.   D.R.   5
117th T.M. Battery.   D.R.   6
39th Division.   D.R.   7
G.O.C.   Personally   8
B.M.   do   9
S.C.   do   10
War Diary   -   11 & 12
Order File   -   13
132 Field Ambulance.   D.R.   14
227 Field Coy. R.E.   D.R.   15
No.3 Coy. A.S.C.   D.R.   16
Bde. Signal Officer   Orderly   17

SECRET   Appendix VII W.D   Copy No.... 13

Ref. BEAUCOURT (Sheet 1/5,000) Portion of 57.d.S.E. 1 & 2.

20.8.16.

117th INFANTRY BRIGADE No. 47.

Exercise to be carried out by 117th Brigade on 21st August.

1. The Brigade will attack the section of the enemy trenches from Q.17.b.9.1 (inclusive) to Q.17.b.1.3 (inclusive).

    1st Objective. German 1st line from Q.17.b.9.1 (inclusive) to Q.17.b.1.3 (inclusive).

    2nd Objective. German 2nd line from Q.17.b.9.3 (inclusive) to Q.17.b.3.6 (inclusive).

    3rd Objective. German 3rd line from Q.17.b.10.4 (inclusive) to Q.17.b.6.8 (inclusive).

    (a). 16th Rifle Brigade will attack on right; 17th Notts & Derby Regt. on left. Limits of Battalion Subsections are as follows :

    Right Battalion from Q.17.b.9.1 (inclusive) to Q.17.b.4.1 (inclusive).
    Left Battalion from Q.17.b.4.1 (exclusive) to Q.17.b.1.3 (inclusive).
    Dividing Line between Battalions in the objectives is

    through Q.17.b.4.1, Q.17.b.4.3, Q.17.b.6.6.

    17th K.R.R. Corps will be in support.

    16th Notts & Derby Regt. will be in reserve.

    (b). <u>Machine Gun Company</u>.

    1 Section is allotted to 16th Rifle Brigade.
    1 do do do 17th Notts & Derby Regt.
    3rd Section in support at
    4th Section in reserve in GABION AV. in dugout about Q.17.d.8.5.

    (c). <u>Light Trench Mortars</u>. 2 are allotted to 16th Rifle Brigade.
    3 " " " 17th Notts & Derby R.
    3 in reserve in CARMALEA (Q.17.c.½.5).

    <u>NOTE</u>. As only the front system of the British Trenches are dug, support and reserve positions will be imaginary.

2. <u>ASSEMBLY</u>. 16th Rifle Brigade in GORDON & ROBERTS Trenches from LOUVERCY Sap (inclusive) to BEDFORD St. (inclusive).

    17th Notts & Derby Regt. in GORDON & ROBERTS Trenches from RECTOR St. (inclusive) to LONG SAP (inclusive).

    17th K.R.R. Corps. 2 Coys. will hold the Brigade Front from LOUVERCY Sap to LONG Sap (both inclusive) and on being relieved will withdraw - Right Coy by LOUVERCY Sap to WINCHESTER St. Left Coy. by POND St to VICTORIA St.

    <u>N.B.</u> These Coys will resume their positions directly assault troops have gone over.

Assembly for 16th Rifle Brigade will be upwards by BEDFORD St only.
for 17th Notts & Derby Regt. upwards by LONG Sap only.

16th Notts & Derby Regt. will assemble in KNIGHTSBRIDGE and trenches adjoining QUEEN'S Road, leaving FORT JACKSON free.

Machine Gun Co. Reserve Section in GABION AV. in dugouts about G.16.d.8.5.

Light Trench Mortars. Reserve guns in dugouts in CARNALEA at G.17.c.$.5.
R.E. and Pioneers

Complete silence by all ranks will be observed during the assembly.

3. PLAN. Assaulting troops will deploy parallel to objective as close as possible to barrage in NO MAN'S LAND; advance to the assault, making good each objective as met with: troops in rear pass through those in front. On the left flank, trenches will be blocked up to the line of the defensive flank as soon as each enemy line is reached. A defensive flank will be formed running from point 05 through 36 to 68. A separate Coy will be told off for this alone.

Strong points will be made at the following points :-

  Right Battalion. 91. 93. 04. 62.
  Left Battalion. 05. 36. 68. 56.

These points indicate the approximate positions only, which will be determined on the ground.

  TIME TABLE.

4. 50 mins. before O.O. Assembly begins.
O.O. Deployment in NO MAN'S LAND begins.
O.4. Barrage lifts from front enemy trench to 2nd line.
O.10. Barrage lifts from 2nd line to 3rd line.
O.20. Barrage lifts from 3rd line to dugouts in hillside.

5. Communication will be by cable run out from our trenches, visual and pigeons. A contact-patrol aeroplane will be in attendance, whose attention will be attracted by flashing vigilant glasses upwards, smoke candles and red flares. These measures should be used by troops in the most advanced line and troops destined for the furthest objective will wear tin discs on their backs.

6. DUMPS. (1). In our own lines.
    This will not be practised tomorrow but on a subsequent date, probably the 22nd.
  (2). In ~~German~~ lines.

Sheet No.3.

7. One Coy 17th K.R.R. Corps will be in readiness to carry over stores from Battalion dumps, and is allotted as follows :-

½ Coy at left green flag. ½ Coy at Right green flag.

8. <u>Stores to be carried by assaulting troops.</u>

2 Bombs per man)
250 S.A.A.   ) imaginary.

2 Sandbags.
1 pick or shovel per every 3 men.
Leading assaulting waves should not carry these tools.

Carrying parties from assaulting troops will carry :-

Extra tools.
Wire.
Stakes.
Sandbags.

T.C.Glencross, Capt.
Brigade Major, 117th. BRIGADE.

Copies issued to :-
16th Notts & Derby Regt.
17th do   do
17th K.R.R. Corps.
16th Rifle Brigade
117th Machine Gun Co.
117th Trench Mortar Battery.
39th. Division.
G.O.C.
B.M.
S.C.
Lt. WINN, R.F.C.
War Diary (2 copies).
Order File.

<u>NOTE</u> The exact position of Brigade Headquarters and Hours for Synchronization of Watches will be notified later.

WD Copy No. 13

The arrangements for to-morrow will be as follows.

1. All Units of the Brigade will train on the dummy trench area, i.e., in squares O.34.c., O.34.d., U.3.b, U.4.a. Care will be taken not to interfere with the 116th Brigade.

2. The dummy trench system is allotted to the 16th Notts & Derby Regt and 17th K.R.R. Corps, from 9 a.m. to 10.30 a.m.

3. Zero will be at 11.30 a.m.

4. There will be no bombing or other classes to-morrow; Physical Training and Bayonet Fighting will be carried out as usual.

5. Another Scheme embracing the carrying of stores from Battalion and Brigade Dump will be carried out on the 22nd.

                                           Capt.
                           Brigade Major, 117th Brigade

Copies issued to :-
   16th Notts & Derby Regt.
   17th do   do
   17th K.R.R. Corps
   16th Rifle Brigade.
   117th Machine Gun Co.
   117th Trench Mortar Battery.
   39th Division.
   G.O.C.
   B.M.
   S.C.
   Lt. WINN, R.F.C.
   War Diary (2 copies)
   Order File

117th INFANTRY BRIGADE ORDER No.48.

22.8.16.

1. The 117th Brigade and Troops in the present 117th Brigade Area will move South to the MARIEUX Area under the following arrangements :-

2. "A" Day. 23rd August. (a). The 16th Notts & Derby Regt. 17th K.R.R. Corps, 227 Field Co. R.E., 133rd Field Ambulance, No.3. Coy. Train, 117th Machine Gun Co., 117th Trench Mortar Battery, and all wheeled transport and animals (except Lewis gun carts) will vacate 117th Brigade Area and march to the DOULLENS Area, in accordance with the attached March Table.

(b). These Troops will be known as "B" Group, and will be under the command of Lieut. Colonel C. HERBERT-STEPNEY, Comdg. 16th Notts & Derby Regt.

(c). Units will make their own arrangements regarding the despatch of their billeting parties to their destination; except NUNCQ, where they will meet Captain COHEN at Church at 11 a.m.

(d). The Officers' kits of the 117th Trench Mortar Battery will be carried on the Brigade baggage waggon, and should be stacked ready for loading at ORLENCOURT Cross roads (T.6.a.9.6) by 11 a.m. Two men will be left in charge to load kits as the Brigade waggon passes.

(e). "B" Group Headquarters will be at BUNEVILLE and Report Centre will open there at 4 p.m.

3. "B" Day. August 24th.

(a). The 117th Brigade Headquarters, 11th Royal Sussex Regt, 14th Hants Regt. 17th Notts & Derby Regt, 16th Rifle Brigade will proceed by tactical trains on the 24th of August, in accordance with the attached Train Table.

(b). No transport or animals will proceed by train; all transport will leave on the 23rd (vide preceding paragraph and march table).

(c). Lewis gun hand-carts will be taken by train.

(d). The 117th Brigade will have the use of one motor lorry for the purpose of carrying dixies, Officers' kits, and mess boxes to the entraining station. Officers' kits must be as laid down in

Sheet No.2

War Establishments, and mess boxes will be limited to 5 per Battalion. Battalions must make their own arrangements to send for these dixies on arrival of the trains at BOUQUEMAISON.

(e). The motor lorry for the 117th Brigade will go round billets and collect dixies, at central places, as follows :-

16th Rif. Brig.   7.30 a.m.   Rd junction, LA THIEULOYE (N.30.b.2.5).
17th Notts &   8.0 a.m.   Cross rds, ORLENCOURT (T.6.a.9.6).
   Derby Regt.

After unloading kits, etc., at entraining station, the lorry will return to Brigade Headquarters, LA THIEULOYE.

The 116th Brigade will make their own arrangements.

(f). 117th Brigade Report Centre will close at LA THIEULOYE at 8.30 a.m. on 24th August and reopen at DOULLENS about 5 p.m. 24th August.

For arrangements regarding rations, see attached table.

                                                             W.E.Maxwell Capt.
Brigade Major, 117th. BRIGADE.

Copies issued at 8.30 p.m. to :-

16th Notts & Derby Regt.	H.Q. 116th Bde.	H.Q. 39th Division.
17th do do	11t R. Suss Regt.	G.O.C.
17th K.R.R. Corps.	14th Hants Regt.	B.M.
16th Rifle Brigade.	No.3 Coy A.S.C.	S.C.
117th Machine Gun Co.	227 Field Co.R.E.	War Diary (2 copies)
117th T.M. Battery.	133rd Fld. Amb.	Order File
	Bde. Signal Officer.	

117th INFANTRY BRIGADE.

TRAIN TABLE to accompany 117th Brigade Operation Order No.48 -- for "B" Day (24th August, 1916).

Unit.	Hour units must arrive at entraining station.	No. of train	Hour of departure of trains.	Hour of arrival of trains	Composition of each train.	Remarks
117th Bde. H.…	10 a.m.	"A" Train.	10.59 hrs	13.15 hrs	"A" Train. Commander Brig.Gen. Oldman, D.S.O. 117th Inf Bde H.Q. 17th Notts & Derby R 16th Rif. Brig.	1. On arrival at destination all units will march independently to billets & billet -ing representatives for each unit will meet them at the station & conduct them to billets.
17th Notts & Derby Regt.	10 a.m.					2. Lewis gun handcarts will be placed in the brakevans.
16th Rif Brig.	10.30 a.m.					
11th R. Suss. Regt.	10.40 a.m.	"B" Train.	11.44 hrs	13.45 hrs	"B" Train. Commander Lt Col. Hickey. 11th R. Suss R. 14th Hants Regt.	3. The Commander of each train will be responsible for the police arrangements of the train and will detail a train guard.
14th Hants Regt.	11.15 a.m.					4. Dixies, etc., will be stacked in the brakevans.

The Entraining Station in all cases will be LIGNY ST FLOCHEL.
The Detraining   do   do   do   BOUJEMAISON.

An Officer from each Battalion will report to an Officer of the 117th Bde. Staff at 10 a.m. on the platform at LIGNY ST FLOCHEL.

Ref. LENS Sheet, 1/100,000.   **117th INFANTRY BRIGADE.**
MARCH TABLE to accompany 117th Brigade Operation Order No.48 -- for "A" Day (23rd August, 1916).

Unit	Present Billets.	To be clear of present billets by	Destination	ROUTE	Remarks
16th Notts & Derby Regt	LA THIEULOYE	11 a.m.	BUNEVILLE	via ROELLECOURT - FOUFFLIN - RICAMETZ and MAISNIL ST POL.	
17th K.R.R Corps.	MARQUAY.	11 a.m.	NUNCQ.	via ROELLECOURT - FOUFFLIN - RICAMETZ - MAISNIL ST POL. - BUNEVILLE.	
117th Machine Gun Co.	ORLENCOURT.	11 a.m.	MAISNIL ST POL	via ROELLECOURT - FOUFFLIN - RICAMETZ - MAISNIL ST POL - BUNEVILLE.	
117th T.M. Battery.	ditto	11.10 a.m.	NEUVILLE.	via ROELLECOURT - FOUFFLIN - RICAMETZ - MAISNIL ST POL.	
No.3 Coy A.S.C.	BAILLEUX-aux-CORNAILLES.	to pass cross rds just N. of the T in ROELLECOURT by 11 a.m.	NUNCQ.	via ROELLECOURT and FOUFFLIN - RICAMETZ - MAISNIL ST POL - BUNEVILLE.	
227 Field Co R.E.	ditto	DITTO by 10 a.m.	NEUVILLE AU CORNET.	via ROELLECOURT - FOUFFLIN - RICAMETZ - MAISNIL ST POL.	
133rd Fld Amb	ORLENCOURT.	11 a.m.	NUNCQ.	OSTREVILLE - ST POL - PREVENT. Thence by main ST POL Road.	
Transport 17th Notts & Derby R	ditto	10.30 a.m.	NUNCQ.	as for 17th K.R.R. Corps.	Join 17th K.R.R. Corps at MARQUAY & march in rear under the orders of 17th K.R.R. Corps.
do 16 Rif Brig	L. THIEULOYE	11 a.m.	NUNCQ.	as for 16th Notts & Derby R	To march in rear & under orders of 16th Notts & Derby Regt.
do 117 Bde H.Q.	ditto	11 a.m.	NUNCQ.	DITTO	

117th INFANTRY BRIGADE.

SUPPLY and TRANSPORT TABLE to accompany 117th Brigade Operation Order No.48 (dated 22nd August, 1916).

Unit.	23rd Aug.	24th Aug.	25th Aug.	26th Aug.
117th Inf. Bde.	R.P. no change. R.H. no change.	R.P. NUNCQ Area. R.H. no change.	R.P. BOUQUEMAISON. R.H. BOUQUEMAISON.	R.P. LOUVENCOURT. R.H. BELLE EGLISE.
No.3 Coy Train.	No.3 Coy Train moves to MAISNIL ST POL and issues breakfast rations for 24th to Bde. H. Qrs. & 17th Notts & Derby Regt. & 16th Rifle Brigade before leaving.	No.3 Coy Train moves to BOUQUEMAISON Area.	No.3 Coy Train moves to VAUCHELLES-LES-AUTHIE Area with supplies for 117th Inf. Bde., 227 Field Co. R.E., 133 Fld Amb.	No3 Coy Train remains in VAUCHELLES-LES-AUTHIE Area.

SECRET   App IX W D   Copy No. 15

Ref: 1/100,000 LENS Sheet.
                                                24.8.16.
117th BRIGADE ORDER No.49.

1. The 117th Brigade and Divisional Troops attached will vacate the DOULLENS Area to-morrow morning, 25th August and march to billets at AUTHIE and VAUCHELLES.

2. All Units will move in accordance with attached march table. After passing Cross Roads just N. of the S. in FRESCHVILLIERS units will march as a group.

3. Billeting parties (on cycles) will report to the Staff Captain at 9 a.m. at the Church AUTHIE.
   The Staff Captain will allot billets or bivouacs in AUTHIE and VAUCHELLES LES AUTHIE.

4. Guides will meet units at the road junction N.W. of the S. in SARTON and conduct them to billets. Guides will be at this spot by 11.30 a.m.

5. The position of Brigade Headquarters will be notified later.

6. Units will remain in VAUCHELLES LES AUTHIE and AUTHIE billets on the 26th.

                                    W.E.Maxwell.   Capt.
                                Brigade Major, 117th. BRIGADE

Issued at 7.0 p.m. to :-

Copy No.1. 16th Notts & Derby Regt.   Copy No.8. 227 Field Co.R.E.
"   2. 17th   do   do   "   9. 133rd Fld. Amb.
"   3. 17th K.R.R. Corps.   "   10. No.3 Co. Div. Train
"   4. 16th Rifle Brigade.   "   11. G.O.C.
"   5. 117th Machine Gun Co,   "   12. B.M.
"   6. 117th T.M. Battery.   "   13. S.C.
"   7. H.Q. 39th Division.   "   14,15 War Diary (2 copies)
                                        "   16. Order File

SECRET
Ref. LENS Sheet 1/100,000.

117th INFANTRY BRIGADE.

March Table to accompany 117th Infantry Brigade Order No.49, dated 24th August, 1916.

Unit.	Present billets.	Leave present billets at.	ROUTE	Destination.	Remarks
117th Bde H.Q.	DOULLENS.	9.10 a.m.	via DOULLENS		
16th Notts & Derby Regt.	NEUVILLETTE.	7.25 a.m.	Cross roads just		
17th do do	DOULLENS	9.15 a.m.	N.E. of last S.	VAUCHELLES LES AUTHIE or AUTHIE.	
17th K.R.Rif.C	BOUQUEMAISON	7.55 a.m.	in FRESCHVILLERS		
16th Rif Brig.	DOULLENS	9.23 a.m.	- SARTON.	Billets not yet allotted.	
117th M.G. Co.	La CLOSERIE F⁼.	7.45 a.m.	Thence either to		
117th T.M. Batt	NEUVILLETTE.	7.40 a.m.	AUTHIE or VAUCH		
227 Fld Co.RE	DOULLENS	10 a.m.	-ELLES. LES AUTHIE,		
No.3 Co. Train	HAUTE VISEE	Any convenient time, but not to interfere with march of other units.	according as bill -ets are allotted		NOTE. No.3 Coy Divl. Train will billet at LOUVENCOURT under arrangements to be made by O.C. Divl.Train.
133rd Fld Amb.	LE MARAIS SEC.	10 a.m.			

NOTE. The Timings of the March Table must be strictly adhered to. The pace of marching will be at the rate of 2½ miles per hour, which rate must not be exceeded.

SECRET   Copy No. 13.

Ref. Map FRANCE 57.d. 1/40,000.   27.8.16.

117th INFANTRY BRIGADE ORDER No.49a.

1. The 117th Infantry Brigade will move to-morrow, 28th August in accordance with attached March Table.

2. All Units of the Brigade will march independently.

3. In case Os.C, Units wish to communicate with their Billeting Officers who have gone on, instructions have been given for Billeting Officers to call at the Town Major's Office, BERTRANCOURT at 10 a.m. to-morrow.

4. The 16th Notts & Derby Regt. will billet at BEAUSSART and not at BERTRANCOURT, and the 16th Rifle Brigade at Y Camp, BERTRANCOURT, and not at BEAUSSART, as previously arranged.

5. Brigade Headquarters will close at VAUCHELLES-LES-AUTHIE at 2 p.m. and reopen at BEAUSSART at 5 p.m.

                                 W.G. Maxwell. Capt.
                           Brigade Major, 117th Brigade.

Copies issued at 8 p.m. to :-

	By	Copy No.
16th Notts & Derby Regt.	D.R.	1
17th do do	D.R.	2
17th K.R.R. Corps.	D.R.	3
16th Rifle Brigade	D.R.	4
117th Machine Gun Co.	D.R.	5
117th Trench Mortar Battery.	D.R.	6
H.Q. 116th Brigade.	D.R.	7
H.Q. 39th Division.	D.R.	8
Bde. Signal Officer.	Orderly	9
G.O.C.	Personally	10
B.M.	Do	11
S.C.	do	12
War Diary	&	13 & 14
Order File	-	15

SECRET   Ref. Map FRANCE 57.d. 1/40,000.

117th INFANTRY BRIGADE.

March Table to accompany 117th Infantry Brigade Order No.49, dated 27.8.16.

Date	Unit	Present Billets.	To be clear of present billets by	Destination.	Route.	Remarks.
28th Aug.	117th Bde. H.Q.	VAUCHELLES-LES-AUTHIE.		BEAUSSART	via LOUVENCOURT & BERTRANCOURT.	(1). 3 minutes interval between Companies will be observed.
ditto	16th Notts & Derby Regt.	AUTHIE.	2 p.m.	BEAUSSART	via BUS-LES-ARTOIS & BERTRANCOURT.	(2). Units will make their own arrangements for guides to meet them as they approach billets.
ditto	17th do do	VAUCHELLES-LES-AUTHIE.	2 p.m.	Z.Camp. BERTRANCOURT	via LOUVENCOURT.	
ditto	17th K.R.R. Corps	AUTHIE.	2.30 p.m.	X. Camp. BERTRANCOURT	via BUS-LES-ARTOIS	
ditto	16th Rifle Brigade	VAUCHELLES-LES-AUTHIE.	2.30 p.m.	Y. Camp. BERTRANCOURT	via LOUVENCOURT	
ditto	117th M.Gun Co.	VAUCHELLES-LES-AUTHIE.	3 p.m.	Z. Camp. BERTRANCOURT	via LOUVENCOURT	
ditto	117th T.M. Battery	VAUCHELLES-LES-AUTHIE.	3.30 p.m.	Z. Camp. BERTRANCOURT	via LOUVENCOURT	
			3.45 p.m.			

SECRET   Copy No. 19

117th INFANTRY BRIGADE ORDER No.50.

Sumprint Tracing.   29.3.16.
Ref. 1/15,000 BEAUCOURT Trench Map 57.d.SE. 1 & 2.
     1/20,000 Sheet 57.d.S.E.

NOTE. In these orders the day of attack is referred to as "A" Day
      throughout.

Intention.   1.   The Brigade will attack the GERMAN Front Line System
                   on a front from Pt.91 (inclusive) to Pt.13 (inclus-
                   ive). The 116th Brigade attacks from River ANCRE
                   to Pt.91 (exclusive).

Objectives.   2 (a) German 1st line from Pt.91 to Pt.13 (both inclusive).
                (b) German 2nd line from Pt.93 to Pts.35 & 36 (both
                    (inclusive).
                (c) German 3rd line from Pt.04 to Pt.68 (inclusive).

                   A defensive flank will be formed on the left from Sap
                   in our trenches at Q.17.a.8.3 to Pt.05 through Pts. 35
                   and 36 to Pt.68.

Assaulting   3 (a) The 16th Rifle Brigade will attack on the right.
Battalions
                   BOUNDARY OF OBJECTIVE ON RIGHT - the communication
                   trench running through Pts.91,93 to Pt.94 (all
                   inclusive).
                   Battalion H.Q. will be at corner of LOUVERCY St.
                   and SLOANE St. (Q.17.d.2½.1).

                (b) 17th Notts & Derby Regt. will attack on left with
                   its right resting on Dividing Line, as below.
                   BOUNDARY OF ITS LEFT - Sap at CHARING Cross running
                   from our trenches along the defensive flank as in
                   para. (2). Battalion H.Q. will be near junction of
                   POND & VICTORIA St. at Q.17.c.4.8.
                   DIVIDING LINE OF BATTALIONS. Pt.41 (inclusive) to
                   Pt.43 (exclusive) to Pt.66 (exclusive).

Support Bn.   (c) 17th K.R.R. Corps will be in support, 1 Coy. holding
                   front line trenches, which will move up directly
                   assault has taken place.
                   On the night previous to the operation 17th K.R.R.
                   Corps will relieve 1 Battalion of the 118th Infy.
                   Brigade in the front of attack.

Sheet No.2

                Orders will be issued separately for this.

                Battalion H.Q. will be near junction of POND &
VICTORIA St. at Q.17.c.4.8.

<u>Reserve Bn</u> (d) 16th Notts & Derby Regt. will be in Reserve at KNIGHT
-SBRIDGE and FORT MOULIN. Battalion H.Q. will be at
KNIGHTSBRIDGE. O.C. will be with Infantry Brigade H.Q.

<u>Plan of Attack.</u> 4. (A). (a). <u>Infantry</u>. Each wave of Infantry will capture the German trenches in the order of the Objectives mentioned in para. (2), waves at 50 paces distance.

      (b) Captured trenches will be immediately consolidated, special attention being paid to the consolidation of the 2nd line. Troops consolidating the 2nd line will be reinforced, if necessary, for this purpose on information being received that its capture is complete.

      (c) Strong points will be constructed in the neighbourhood of the following points :-

          1st line. points 91 - 41 - 13 and 05.
          2nd "   "   93 - 43 - 33 - 35 and 36.
          3rd "   "   04 - 94 - 66 - 68.

A deep dugout should be included in each strong point if possible. Regard must be paid to their existence when planning the strong point.

At least one Vickers gun will be allotted to each of the following strong points :-

          2nd line. 9.3 - 43 - 35.
          3rd ".   04 - 68.

VICKERS GUN Crews have prior claim to dugout accomodation.

      (d) Definite clearing parties are to be told off in each wave and not less than 2 sentries placed on the door of each dugout. "P" Bombs should not be thrown into the dugouts unless the enemy cannot be disposed of by other means.

      (e) Care must be taken that no communication trenches are left unblocked.

      (f) Company carrying parties follow immediately behind their Companies.

Sheet No.3.

Machine Gun Co. B. Forward Vickers guns as a general principle will be emplaced in the 1st and 2nd captured lines.

    1 Section is allotted to 16th Rifle Brigade.
    1   do   "   "   " 17th Notts & Derby Regt.

These assemble under orders of Os.C, Battalions and get across to the German trenches as early as possible with assaulting waves.

3rd section in support in dugouts at FRENCH Trench and SHOOTERS HILL. 4th section at FORT JACKSON. O.C. Machine Gun Co. will be with the 3rd section. For Infy. carry parties see Appx D.

L.T.M. Battery C. 2 guns are allotted to 16th Rifle Brigade.
    3 " " " " 17th Notts & Derby Regt.
    3 " will be in Reserve at FORT JACKSON.

Assembly and passage of forward mortars will be arranged by Os.C. Battalions as for forward Machine Gun sections. For Infantry carry parties see Appx.D.

D.(a) 1 Section, R.E., less 1 N.C.O. and 10 [15 crossed out] men will advance with the 3rd assaulting wave of the 17th Notts & Derby Regt. to assist in making good the defensive flank.

(b) 1 N.C.O. and 10 men will be attached to the 16th Rifle Brigade and advance in the same manner. Special orders will be issued to O.C, R.E. Sec'n.

E. ½ Coy. 13th Gloucester Regt. (Pioneers). will follow the R.E. and get to work on the tunnels on right and left of LONG SAP. Directly the situation permits, work will be started on a communication trench in the open. (see para 8).

ASSEMBLY. 5. (1). (X). Preliminary Instructions to be carried out before Assembly. Special operation order will be issued for this, dealing with cutting of lanes in our wire, etc. Areas of Assembly are as follows.

2.(a) 16th Rifle Brigade - GORDON & ROBERTS Trenches from

Sheet No.4.

LOUVERCY Sap (exclusive) to RECTOR St. (exclusive).

(b) 17th Notts & Derby Regt. - GORDON & ROBERTS Trenches from RECTOR St. (exclusive) to WORCESTER Trench (incl.).

(c) 17th K.R.R. Corps - GIPSY HILL - VICTORIA St. and Southern portion of RIDGE Trench.

NOTE. 2 Coys 17th K.R.R. Corps not in front trenches will be in their assembly area 2 hours before Zero.

(d) Brigade Machine Gun Co. (forward Sections) with Infy. carriers under orders of assaulting Battalions.

(e). Light Trench Mortar Battery (forward Mortars) under orders of Os.C. assaulting Battalions. Reserve Mortars at FORT JACKSON.

(f) R.E. Section and 1 platoon, 16th Notts & Derby Regt. in POND St. from its junction with LONG SAP & REGENT St. in rear of 16th Rifle Brigade.

(g) ½ Coy. 13th Gloucester Regt. (Pioneers) in REGENT ST. from its junction with POND St. to GABION Avenue via GABION Avenue in rear of R.E. Section.

(h). Four sub-divisions R.A.M.C. which are to follow the assaulting troops will move up to their place of assembly at RIDGE Trench - via GABION Avenue in rear of 13th Gloucester Regt. (Pioneers).

(i). 16th Notts & Derby Regt. H.Q. and 2 Coys in KNIGHTS-BRIDGE Barracks. 2 Coys (less 1 platoon, see Appx. D) FORT MOULIN.

NOTE. Brigade will assemble in the above order, an Officer of each unit reporting to Brigade Headquarters 1 hour before arrival at KNIGHTSBRIDGE and HYDE PARK CORNER.

3. (a) Routes of Assembly. (see map). Assembly will start at 1½ hours before Zero. This hour may be altered on an experiment being carried out to test time required.

(b) 17th Notts & Derby Regt. and 16th Rifle Brigade will start assembly from HYDE PARK CORNER and junction of GABION Avenue and KNIGHTSBRIDGE respectively.

16th Rifle Brigade will assemble via GABION Avenue and

Sheet No.5.

BEDFORD St.

17th Notts & Derby Regt. will assemble via PICCADILLY JAMES St. LONG ACRE and WORCESTER Trench.

(c) The relieved Companies of the 17th K.R.R. Corps will regain their assembly positions via LONG SAP, POND St, i.e. turning inwards.

Artillery 6(a) Artillery barrages are shewon on the attached Appx. A Time Table. Every Officer and N.C.O. should be in possession of a copy of this Time Table, which is to be strictly adhered to.

(b) The 1st barrage starts 50 yards short of German 1st line.

(c) Only percussion shrapnel will be fired for the last minute prior to each lift.

(d) A liaison officer will accompany each assaulting Bn.

(e) The "S.O.S." Signal is THREE RED ROCKETS.

TRAFFIC 7 (A series of traffic control posts will be established throughout Brigade Area under Asst. Staff Captain. (See Traffic Map and Appx. D). They will wear a green brassard. Up to ½ hour before ZERO upward movement will be allowed by all trenches; after that no movement contrary to the arrows will be allowed from ½ hour before ZERO, except runners with the proper armlet on, or a bona-fide message. All other stragglers will be turned back into GORDON & ROBERTS Trenches, where they will be collected by officers of the 17th K.R.R. Corps and forwarded to the German trenches. Traffic control posts will shoot any straggler disobeying these orders. None but reliable men will be selected for the work. O.C. 16th Notts & Derby Regt. will find 1 Officer and 54 men, with a proportion of N.C.Os. (see Appx. D). Date and time of reporting will be communicated later.

Prisoners 8. Not more than 10 prisoners should be collected in one place. One man to each 10 will be detailed as escort; it is however, to be noted, that each man so detailed is a fighting man lost.

Sheet No.6.

<u>No prisoners are to be allowed in communication trenches; they must go over the top.</u> Prisoners will be collected at Advanced Bde. H.Q., KNIGHTSBRIDGE Barracks, whence they will be escorted by the Provost Establishment of the 16th Sherwoods to railway crossing just West of MESNIL at Q.28.c.4.8.

Communication

9. (a) <u>Liaison Officers</u>. O.C. 16th Notts & Derby Regt. will detail one Captain to report to Divl. H.Qrs. 2hrs before Zero on "A" Day. Capt. HEAGERTY and 2 runners from the 16th Notts & Derby Regt. will report to 116th Brigade H.Q. at the same time.

O.C. 16th Notts & Derby Regt. will also detail 1 Offr and 2 runners to report to 144th Brigade H.Q. at same time.

(b) Communication from front to rear will be by the following means :-

(1) <u>Telephone</u>. Each Battalion H.Q. is connected with the Brigade with unburied cable. These lines will be liable to break down. Two lines of D.1 cable will be taken forward by assaulting Battalions.

(2) <u>Runners</u>. All Battalion and Brigade runners will wear a brassard of blue, with a narrow white stripe on the right arm, above the elbow.

The following will report to Brigade H.Q. for duty at 6 p.m. on day previous to operation :-

```
From each Battalion -        4 runners.
  "  117th Machine Gun Co.   2 runners.
  "  117th T.M. Battery.     1 runner.
  "  ½ Coy. 13th Gloucesters 1 runner.
```

(3) <u>Visual</u>. Should other means fail, every effort will be made to establish visual by flag or disc, shutter or lamp.

There will be two Divl. Visual Stations in 144th Brigade Area near SHAFTESBURY Avenue.

(4) <u>Aeroplane</u>. During the attack one aeroplane (distinguishing mark - a broad black band continued on a streamer under each bottom plane) will be

Sheet **No. 7.**

employed as Contact Patrol. This aeroplane will pick up the positions of Battalion H.Q. and receive signals by panel from Battalion and Inf. Bde. H.Q.

The signal code for aeroplane signalling is given in Appx. B.

NOTE. Men of Company for third objective will wear tin discs and carry vigilants and smoke candles on a ratio of 1 packet to every three men. Four selected N.C.Os. in each platoon will carry one flare. They will be used to denote platoon's capture of each objective.

(5) Pigeons. Four trained pigeoners with one basket of pigeons each will accompany the H.Qrs of each assaulting Battalion.

Dress & Equipment.   10. Skeleton march order. 120 rds S.A.A. plus 1 bandolier extra. 4 Mills Grenades. 2 Sandbags.

Each Coy Bomber 6 Mills Rifle Grenades in lieu of Mills Bombs. See also para. (q), sub-para. (b) 4, Footnote. Unexpired portion of day's rations, one iron ration, water bottle filled.

1 man in every 2 will carry a pick or shovel, which is to be properly slung on the back. Rear rank only carry these.

No maps of any description shewing our own trenches will be taken over, but there is no objection to map shewing German system being taken.

Carriage of stores   11. Arrangements for carriage of stores. (See Appx. d & E and map shewing dump). The system is as follows :-

Brigade carrying parties will carry forward stores from the forward Brigade dumps to dumps to be formed at Pts. 61 and 21 in German trenches.

Battalion and Company carrying parties which have already carried over a proportion of stores with assaulting waves will carry up from these points to their Coys.

A Reserve Bde. carrying party will replenish forward Brigade dumps from Divisional dump at ENGLEBELMER (Q.25. a.5.8).

Sheet No. 8.

NOTE. all carriers will wear red brassards.

Stores to be carried by carrying parties with assaulting Companies.

```
           4 shovels per man.              1
           6 picks (2 per man).            3
          30 Iron screw stakes (6 per man). 5
           4 coils B. Wire (1 per man).    4
           6 boxes Bombs at 2 per man.     3
           2 coils Fr. wire at 1 per man.  2
                                          --
                                    Total 18
                                          --
```

8 Red Rockets will be carried by each Coy. carrying party distributed among the men.

Medical. 12. See Appx. C.

An extra Medical Officer will be attached to each assaulting Battalion. These Officers will cross NO MAN'S LAND with the 3rd Coy. of assaulting Battalions and establish Regimental Aid Posts in shelters in the German front line trench. They will take with them and erect necessary sign posts to assist casualties to find these Posts.

Synchronization of watches 13. Synchronization of watches. Each unit, i.e, all four Battalions, 117th Machine Gun Co., 117th T.M. Battery, Officer ½ Coy. 13th Gloucesters and Section Officer R.E. will send one Officer provided with a reliable watch to synchronize at Brigade H.Q. at 9 p.m. (punctual) on day before operations.
Same Officers will parade again at 2 hrs before Zero at Brigade H.Q. for re-synchronization. After synchronization, officers will on each occasion go straight back to their respective Battalion H.Q. to attend the Battalion or unit synchronization, which must be most carefully carried out down to N.C.Os.

Too much stress cannot be laid on the greatest possible care being observed in getting correct synchronization.

Report Centre. 14. Throughout the operations Brigade H.Q. and Report Centre will remain at KNIGHTSBRIDGE Barracks.

Hour of Zero. 15. The hour of Zero will be notified later.

16. Acknowledge.

W.E. Maxwell Capt.
Brigade Major, 117th. Brigade.

Copies issued at 3.0 p.m. to :- (See over).

Copies issued at 3.0 p.m. to :-

16th Notts & Derby Regt.	227 Field Co. R.E.	G.O.C.
17th do do	13th Gloucester Regt.	B.M.
17th K.R.R. Corps.	A.D.M.S. 39th Div.	S.C.
16th Rifle Brigade.	H.Q. 116th Brigade.	War Diary
117th Machine Gun Co.	H.Q. 118th Brigade.	(2 copies)
117th T.M. Battery.	H.Q. 144th Brigade.	Order File.
H.Q. 39th Division.	Bde. Signal Officer	
H.Q. 39th Divl. R.A.		

Appix A

TIME TABLE to accompany 117th INFANTRY BRIGADE ORDER No.50, dated 28.8.16.

Time	Infantry.	Artillery.
ZERO. 0.00.	Infantry commence crossing parapet and getting out into NO MAN'S LAND.	Intense shrapnel barrage 50 yards short of German front line.
0.0½.		Intense shrapnel barrage lifts on to enemy front line.
0.01.	xxxxxxxxxxxxxxxxxxxxxxxxxxxxxxxxxxxx	Heavy Artillery lift on to German Reserve Line.
0.02.	Infantry continue advance across NO MAN'S LAND.	Trench Mortars lift on to German Support Line.
0.03.	**Infantry** advance as close as possible to our **barrage.**	Intense percussion (only) Shrapnel barrage on German front line. 60-prs. open intense Gas shell barrage on STATION ROAD from R.ANCRE to QUARRY (Q.11.d.4.8).
0.04.	Infantry assault German front line.	Intense shrapnel barrage lifts 50 yards, reverts to time shrapnel and continues lifting at the rate of 25 yards every 30 seconds until 2nd barrage line is reached.
0.10.		Heavy Trench Mortars lift on to German Reserve Trench. 2" Trench Mortars cease fire.
0.12.	Second companies of assaulting battalions close up to our barrage.	Heavy Howitzers concentrate on German Reserve Trench.
0.13.	Second companies of assaulting battalions as close as possible to our barrage.	Intense percussion (only) shrapnel barrage on German Support line.
0.14.	Infantry assault German Support line.	Intense shrapnel barrage lifts 50 yards, reverts to time shrapnel and continues lifting at the rate of 25 yards every 30 seconds until 3rd barrage line is reached.
0.33.		60-pr intense gas shell barrage slows down to a quick rate. Heavy artillery lifts off German Reserve line and barrages at Q.17.a. 85.90 - Q.11.d.40.40. - Q.11.d.45.20 - Q.11.d.00.95 - Q.18.a.95.50 BEAUCOURT STATION and STATION ROAD at a steady rate of fire. Heavy Trench Mortars cease fire.

Time.	Infantry.	Artillery.
		Intense percussion (only) shrapnel barrage on German Reserve line.
0.35.	Third companies of assaulting battalions advance as close as possible to our barrage.	
0.36.	Infantry assault German Reserve line.	Intense shrapnel barrage lifts 50 yards, reverts to time shrapnel and continues lifting at the rate of 25 yards every 30 seconds until 4th barrage line is reached.
0.51.		Intense shrapnel barrage ceases and is replaced by bursts of intense fire at uncertain intervals.

Appendix D.

To accompany 117th Infantry Brigade Order No.50.

Shews number of carrying and other parties required and their duties &c.

No. of Pty	Unit	Numbers	Time	Rendezvous	Nature of work	To whom report
1	16/Notts & Derby Regt	2 N.C.Os & 40 men. 1 N.C.O. & 20 from each Bn.	2 hrs before Zero.	Bomb Dump Fort JACKSON	Carry Bombs to replenish front Stores. (1) On the Right. Bomb Store at junction SLOANE St & LOUVERCY St. (2). On the Left. Bomb Store at junction POND St. & LONG SAP.	Store-man
2	16th do	1 N.C.O. & 20 men	2 hrs before Zero.	Left Forward Bomb Store. (Q.17.c.4.9)	Carrying bombs up to Left Bn Dump (German Line) at Pt.21.	do
3	16th do	1 N.C.O & 20 men	2 hrs before Zero.	Right Forward Bomb Store. (Q.17.d.2.2)	ditto Right Bn Dump. Pt. 61.	do
4	16th do	1 N.C.O. & 20 men	do	Reserve Stokes Bomb Store (Q.16.c.9.2½)	To supply right or left forward dump as req'd.	do
5	16th do	do	do	Right Fwd Stokes mortar Store GIPSY HILL (Q.17.c.6.4)	To supply Stokes guns. With Rt. Bn. as req'd.	do
6	16th do	do	do	Left Fwd Stokes Mortar store, BUCKINGHAM PALACE Rd. (Q.17.c.1.8)	To supply Stokes guns with Left Bn as Reqd	do
7 A.	16th do	do	do	Bde R.E Dp. (Q.16.c.9.1)	Supplying stores to either Right or Left fwd. R.E. Dump as req'd.	do
8	16th do	do	do	Left Fwd R.E Dump. (Q.17.c.3.7)	Carrying stores up to Left Bn. Dp. in German line at Pt.21	do
9	16th do	do	do	Right Fwd R.E Dump (Q.17.c.4.4)	Carrying stores up to Right Bn Dp. in German line at Pt.61.	do

These parties begin carrying forward on order of Os.C. assaulting Units, or Brigade H.Q.

B.

No. of Pty	Unit	Numbers	Time	Rendezvous	Nature of work	To whom report
10.	16 N & D	1 NCO & 20 men.	2 hrs before Zero.	SAA Dump junction of CONSTITUTION HILL - KNIGHTS -BRIDGE.	Carrying up to Front Line Bn. (left Bn)	
11	do	do	do	SAA DUMP Ft JACKSON	ditto (Right Bn)	do
12	do	do	do	Brigade Water store (Q.16.d.2.8).	Carrying up water to Rt or Left fwd water store as req'd.	do
13	do	do	do	Right fwd water store (Q.17.d.2.2)	to carry water fwd to Rt Bn.	do
14	do	do	do	Left Fwd. water Dump. (Q.17.c.3.7)	To carry water fwd. to Left Bn	do

NOTE. These parties must be told off from the Companies in KNIGHTS-BRIDGE Barracks and earmarked ready to act instantly on receipt of a message from Brigade Headquarters.

No. of Pty.	Unit	Numbers	Time	Rendezvous	Nature of work	To whom report
15	16 N & D (see para 8 (F)	1 Platoon	Hr to be not -ified later.	Report to Lt ELLEN Secn Off 227 Co.R.E. in present billets.	Carrying for R.E.	Secn Offr R.E. at billets.
16	16 N & D	54 (proportion of NCOs)	5 p.m day before Zero.	Bde. H.Q. KNIGHTS-BRIDGE.	Trench Police	Capt COHEN
17	16 N & D	32	Hr to be not -ified later.	117th. M.G. H.Q present billet	Carry for assault M.G Secns	O.C. 117 M.G. Coy
18	16 N & D	50	do	L.T.M. in present billet.	Carrying shells for fwd. T.M. Batt.	O.C. 117 T.M. Battery

Appendix E.

To Accompany 117th Infantry Brigade Order No.50, dated 29.2.16.

Positions and Quantities of Dumps.

1. S.A.A.

    Distributed in front trenches.   100 boxes.
    Junction of CONSTITUTION HILL and KNIGHTSBRIDGE   100 "
        Barracks.
    FORT JACKSON.   100 "
    Divl. Reserve. ACHEUX WOOD (P.8.d.8.8).

2. Grenades.

    Near junction POND St. - LONG SAP (Q.17.c.4.9)   5000 "
    Near junction LOUVERCY St - SLOANE St (Q.17.d.2.2) 5000 "

    Divl. Depots. No. (1). Q.28.a.7.7. (2). Q.16.d.0.2.

3. Water

        Q.17.d.2.2.   400 galls.
        Q.17.c.3.7.   400 "
        Q.16.d.2.8.   1000 "

4. Very Lights.

    FORT JACKSON.   10 boxes.

5. Stokes Mortar Ammunition.

    BUCKINGHAM PALACE.   1000 rds.
    GIPSY HILL.   1000 "
    Q.16.c.9.2½.   2000 "
    Divl. Reserve. (P.8.d.8.8).

6. Rations.

    Near junction CONSTITUTION HILL & KNIGHTSBRIDGE (Q.16.d.3.7)
                                4500.

7. R.E. Stores.

    Left Forward Dump (Q.17.c.3.7). Right Forward Dump (Q.17.c.4.4).

    Brigade Dump. (Q.16.c.9.1). Divisional Dump, ENGLEBELMER
                                                (Q.25.a.5.8).

8. Stores.

    The Reserve Brigade have a supply of the following at Pt. 18.c.
                                                            8.0.
        RATIONS.
        S.A.A.
        GRENADES.
        STOKES MORTAR AMMUNITION.

SECRET   Copy No. 16

117th Infantry Brigade Order No.51.
                                                    29.2.16.
Ref: 1/40,000 Map.
     1/20,000 Map.

1. Brigade will move tomorrow, 30th, as follows :-

   (A). **17th K.R.R. Corps.** take over trenches from 1/1st CAMBS Regt.
        Relief to commence at 3.30 p.m. Lewis guns will meet guides at
        KNIGHTSBRIDGE Battalion H.Q. at 2.30 p.m.
        All details of relief to be arranged between Os.C, Battalions
        concerned.
        O.C, 17th K.R.R. Corps will occupy Battalion H.Q. in POND St.
        O.C 17th K.R.R. Corps will make the following arrangements
        on taking over :-

      (a). Cut lanes in our wire in front of GORDON & ROBERTS Trenches
           cutting gap of 10 yards in every 15 yards.
           Wire so cut to be wrapped round the posts and not left
           trailing.
           This must be completed by 4 a.m.

      (b). In consultation with O.C, 17th Notts & Derby Regt. and
           16th Rifle Brigade cut our requisite number of steps in
           the assembly trenches.

      (c). See that the Trench Boards said to have been carried up today
           by 118th Brigade are placed at 10 yards intervals the
           whole length of GORDON Trench at the bottom of the trench.

   (B). 17th Notts & Derby Regt. and 16th Rifle Brigade will leave
        present billets at 5 p.m. and rest until 1.00 a.m. in temporary
        billets in VITERMONT (part of ENGLEBELMER).
        These Battalions will be supplied at VITERMONT with Bombs,
        Sandbags, and Rifle Grenades, Smoke Candles, Red Flares, Picks
        and Shovels in conformity with 117th Brigade Order No.50, para.
        10. (String must be provided by units for the shovel slings).
        One Officer per unit will reconnoitre these billets and will
        meet Lt. KROLIK at Q.19.b.5.5. at 3 p.m. to look over billets.

   (C). 16th Notts & Derby Regt. will leave their present billets, and
        march to their points of assembly in time to arrive there by
        1 hr. & 20 minutes before Zero on the night 31st/1st, making
        their own arrangements for meals. Carrying parties will report

Sheet No.2.

according to Appx. D, 3 hrs before Zero.

(D). O.C, Machine Gun Co. will arrange to march forward machine guns with their respective Battalions.

Support and Reserve Sections will follow in rear of Brigade and stay in ENGLEBELMER in Square Q.19.b. ready to move to assembly according to 117th Brigade Order No.50, para. 4 (sub-para. (b)).

(E). Light Trench Mortar Battery. Os.C, 17th Notts & Derby Regt and 16th Rifle Brigade will place at the disposal of O.C, Light Trench Mortar Battery one limber each to carry up STOKES MORTARS to KNIGHTSBRIDGE and HYDE PARK CORNER. They will conform to the movements of their Battalions in order to reach the assembly position according to 117th Brigade Order No.50.

Routes to be followed :-

(a). ASSAULTING BATTALIONS.

The Road - Cross roads P.12.c.9.0 - MAILLY MAILLET - Pt.117 (Q.13.b) - Cross roads Q.19.b.7.0 (VITERMONT) - track junction at Q.21.c.0.7 - Q.27.b.4.6 - thence to MESNIL by track.march up Rly. through square Q.22.c. & A, and Q.16.c. & B to GABION Avenue and HYDE PARK CORNER.

NOTE. One Officer from each Battalion will reconnoitre the route.

(b). Other Units. same route as far as VITERMONT, thence via GABION Avenue.

Hr of Assembly 3. Assembly begins at 3 hrs before Zero (which will be notified later).

Order of march 4. Order of march will be :-

17th Notts & Derby Regt - 16th Rifle Brigade - 16th Notts & Derby Regt.

Hot Meal 5. A hot meal and rum will be served to the Brigade prior to the start for the assembly under orders of O.C, unit.

Details & 1st L.T 6. Details and 1st Line Transport will remain in present billets and bivouacs.

Report Centre 7. Bde. H.Q. will open Report Centre in KNIGHTSBRIDGE at 5.30 p.m. and close at BEAUSSART at same hour.

8. Acknowledge.

Maxwell. Capt.
Brigade Major, 117th. Brigade.

Copies issued at 1 p.m. to :-

No. 1. 16th Notts & Derby Regt.
 2. 17th   do   do
 3. 17th K.R.R. Corps.
 4. 16th Rifle Brigade.
 5. 117th Machine Gun Co.
 6. 117th T.M. Battery.
 7. H.Q. 39th Division.
 8. H.Q. 116th Brigade.
No. 9. 118th Brigade
 10. 144th Brigade.
 11. Bde. Signal Officer.
 12. G.O.C.
 13. B.M.
 14. S.C.
 15. War Diary.
 16. War Diary.
 17 Order File

SECRET   Copy No. 15

30.8.16.
Important Amendment to 117th Brigade Order No.51.

Para. 1, sub-para. (c). For 31st/1st, read 30/31st.

Acknowledge.

                                            Capt.
                        Brigade Major, 117th. Brigade

Issued at 8.30 a.m. :-
 1. 16th Notts & Derby Regt.
 2. 17th   do   do
 3. 17th K.R.R. Corps.   H.Q. 118th Brigade
 4. 16th Rifle Brigade   10. 114th Brigade
 5. 117th Machine Gun Co.   11. Bde. Signal Officer.
 6. 117th T.M. Battery.   12 G.O.C.
 7. H.Q. 39th Division.   13 B.M.
 8. H.Q. 116th Brigade   14 S.C.
                                15 War Diary
                                16   do do
                                17 Order File

SECRET.   Copy No. 10

Special orders to O.C., Section, 227 Company R.E., to
accompany 117th Infantry Brigade Order No. 50.

30.8.1916.

1. Your section will be divided into 2 parties to work with the 2 assaulting Battalions.

   1 section (less 1 N.C.O. and 10 men) will be attached to 17th Notts and Derby.

   1 N.C.O. and 10 men to the 16th Rifle Brigade.

   They will accompany the rear assaulting wave of each Battalion across NO MAN'S LAND.

2. On arrival in the German trenches they will at once begin the construction of Strong Points at Points 04, 33 and 36 working in three parties in conjunction with available Infantry at those spots.

3. The O.C. Section should as far as the situation allows of it give help and advice to the Infantry in the construction of the other strong points laid down in Infantry Brigade Order No.50, para 4(c).

4. The section will march from ENGLEBELMER in Rear of 16th Rifle Brigade. O.C. Section should report to O.C., 16th Rifle Brigade not later than 5 hours before Zero in VITERMONT Q.19.b.

5. 1 Platoon, 16th Notts and Derby, will join your section at ENGLEBELMER at 5 p.m.

6. Acknowledge.

                                                    Captain,
                                       Brigade Major, 117th Brigade.

Issued at 12.30 p.m.
No.1. H.Q., 39th Division.
No.2. C.R.E.
No.3. 17th Notts & Derby Regt.
No.4. 16th Rifle Brigade.
No.5. 227 Company, R.E.
No.6. G.O.C.
No.7. B.M.
No.8. S.C.
No.9. War Diary.
No.10. War Diary.
No.11. Order file.

SECRET.   Appx 15 W.D.   Copy No. 11.

Amendments and Addenda to 117th Infantry Brigade Order No. 50.
--30.8.1916.

1. Para 4 ('Plan of attack') sub para E, at end of para delete words "(see para 8)".

2. Para 4A(c) add "Os.C., Assaulting Battalions will select beforehand the approximate positions in German lines to which they will probably move.   Brigade Headquarters to be informed".

3. Para 6(e) para should read "The 'S.O.S.' signal is three Green Rockets".   (Battalions have already been informed).

4. Para 8, Line two, for word "one" substitute word "two". After word "lost" add "so no more than Two should be allotted".

5. Para 9 in fourth Line of NOTE, sentence "Four selected N.C.Os in each platoon will carry one Flare" should read "Four selected N.C.Os. in each platoon will carry four Flares each".

6. Para 9(4) NOTE - delete sentence "They will be used to denote platoon's capture of each objective" and substitute "The contact patrol aeroplane will fly at 2 hours, 4 hours, and 8 hours after ZERO and flares will be lit at these hours by all advanced troops.   For this purpose four flares will be carried by each of four selected N.C.Os in each assaulting platoon".

7. Para 10. First sentence should read "120 rounds S.A.A., plus 120 rounds extra, 2 Mills Grenades, 2 Sandbags", instead of 50 rounds extra and four Mills Grenades".

8. Para 11. In the first sentence after the word "Trenches" add "Petrol Tins containing water will be carried up under Brigade arrangements to Points 61 and 21 in the captured trenches. They must be carried forward from these points by Company carrying parties to Company Headquarters."

9. Para 11, after sentence ending with words "ENGLEBELMER (Q25 a 5.8)" add new sentence as follows:-

P.T.O.

"As soon as the Infantry have reached their final objective, the Brigade Bombing Officer will go forward to the German trenches, and select Bomb Stores at Points 93, 33 and 36. He will be responsible that these stores are filled. Whenever possible these Bomb Stores will be selected in Strong Points (see Para 4(c))".

10. Para 12, note, for "8 Red Rockets" read "8 Green Rockets".

11. Acknowledge.

Maxwell, Captain,
Brigade Major, 117th Brigade.

Issued at 8 p.m.

No. 1. 16th Notts and Derby Regt.
2. 17th do do.
3. 17th K.R.R.Corps.
4. 16th Rifle Brigade.
5. 117th Machine Gun Coy.
6. 117th T.M.Battery.
7. H.Q., 39th Division.

No. 8. G.O.C.
9. B.M.
10. S.C.
11. War Diary.
12. War Diary.
13. Order file.

SECRET. Appx II WD. Copy No. 17

117th Infantry Brigade ORDER No. 52.

31.8.1916.

Ref: 1/40,000 Map.)
     1/20,000 Map.)

This order cancels 117th Brigade Order No. 51 dated 29.8.16.

1. The Brigade will move today, 31st., as follows:-

   (A) <u>17th K.R.R.Corps</u> take over trenches from the 1/1st CAMBS Regt. Relief to commence at 3.30 p.m. Lewis Guns will meet guides at KNIGHTSBRIDGE Battalion H.Q. at 2.30 p.m. All details of relief to be arranged between Os.C., Battalions concerned.

   O.C., 17th K.R.R.Corps will occupy Battalion H.Q. in POND Street.

   (B) 17th Notts & Derby Regt., and 16th Rifle Brigade, will leave present billets at 2.30 p.m., arriving at ENGLEBELMER at 4.15 p.m. Here they will rest till 5.30 p.m. They will leave ENGLEBELMER and march to the position of Assembly.

   These Battalions will be supplied at Cross Roads, VITERMONT (Q.19.b.5.4.) with Bombs, Sandbags, Rifle Grenades, Smoke Candles, Red Flares, Picks and Shovels, in conformity with 117th Brigade Order No. 50, para 10. (String must be provided for the Shovel Slings).

   (C) 16th Notts & Derby Regt. will leave present billets in sufficient time to be in their Assembly positions by 12 midnight.

   Carrying parties will report as directed in 117th Brigade Order No. 50, app. D, by 8 p.m.

   (D) O.C., Machine Gun Coy. will arrange to march forward Machine Guns with their respective Battalions. Support and reserve sections will follow in rear of the Brigade and remain in ENGLEBELMER in square Q.19.b., leaving ENGLEBELMER in time to be in their Assembly position by 12 midnight.

   (E) OsC., 17th Notts & Derby Regt., and 16th Rifle Brigade, will place at the disposal of O.C., Light Trench Mortar

<u>P.T.O.</u>

Battery one Limber each to carry up STOKES MORTARS to KNIGHTSBRIDGE and HYDE PARK Corner.

They will conform to the movements of their Battalions in order to reach their Assembly position by 12 midnight.

(F) Section of 227th Field Coy., R.E.. will march from ENGLE-BELMER in rear of the 16th Rifle Brigade. O.C. Section should report to O.C., 16th Rifle Brigade, not later than 4.30 p.m. in VITERMONT (Q.19.b.)

The platoon of 16th Notts & Derby Regt. will join the R.E. Section at 227th Field Coy., R.E., H.Q., at P.24.c.2.1., at 3 p.m.

(G) The ½ Coy. 13th Gloucester Regt. will be clear of GABION Avenue by 8 p.m., and will be all in the Tunnelled Saps in GORDON Trench by 10.30 p.m.

2. Route to be followed.

Assaulting Battalions and all units of the Brigade will use the following Route:-

The Road - Cross roads P.12.c.9.0 - MAILLY MAILLET - Pt 117 (Q.13.b.) - Cross roads Q.19.b.7.0. (VITERMONT). Thence by Track to entrance to GABION Avenue to junction of KNIGHTS-BRIDGE and GABION Avenue and HYDE PARK Corner, thence by trenches detailed in 117th Brigade Order No. 50 (3(b)).

NOTE. Movements in the Open East of ENGLEBELMER during daylight will be by platoons at 100 yards interval.

3. Hour of Assembly.

All troops will be in their Assembly positions by 12 midnight on the night 31st/1st.

Assembly will start directly on arrival.

A report that Assembly is complete will be furnished by all units to Brigade Headquarters.

4. Cutting Lanes and Steps, etc.

The two Assaulting Battalions will be responsible for completing

Sheet No. 2.

the following arrangements before Zero:-

    (a) Cutting Lanes in our wire in front of GORDON and ROBERTS Trench, cutting a gap of 10 yards in every 15 yards. Wire so cut to be wrapped round the posts and not left trailing.

    (b) Cutting the requisite number of steps in the Assembly Trenches.

    (c) See that the Trench Boards are in position of readiness in GORDON Trench and placed at 10 yards interval the whole length of the Trench.

A report that these Tasks have been carried out in their entirety will be sent to Bde. H.Q.

Order of March.

Order of March will be:- 17th Notts & Derby Regt., 16th Rifle Brigade, 16th Notts & Derby Regt.

Hot Meal.

A Hot Meal and Rum will be served to the Brigade prior to the start for the Assembly under order of Os.C. Units.

7. Details and First Line Transport.

Details and First Line Transport will remain in present billets and bivouacs.

8. Report Centre.

Brigade Headquarters will open Report Centre in KNIGHTSBRIDGE at 5.30 p.m., and close at BEAUSSART at same hour.

9. Acknowledge.

                                                T.S.Maxwell. Captain,
                                Brigade Major, 117th Brigade.

Copies issued at 11.30 a.m. to:-

No.1.	16th Notts & Derby Regt.	No.10.	H.Q., 116th Brigade.
2.	17th do do	11.	H.Q., 118th Brigade.
3.	17th K.R.R.Corps.	12.	H.Q., 144th Brigade.
4.	16th Rifle Brigade.	13.	G.O.C.
5.	117th Machine Gun Coy.	14.	B.M.
6.	117th T.M.Battery.	15.	S.C.
7.	H.Q., 39th Division.	16.	War Diary.
8.	227th Field Coy., R.E.	17.	War Diary.
9.	13th Gloucester Regt.	18.	Order File.
		19.	Bde Signal Officer.

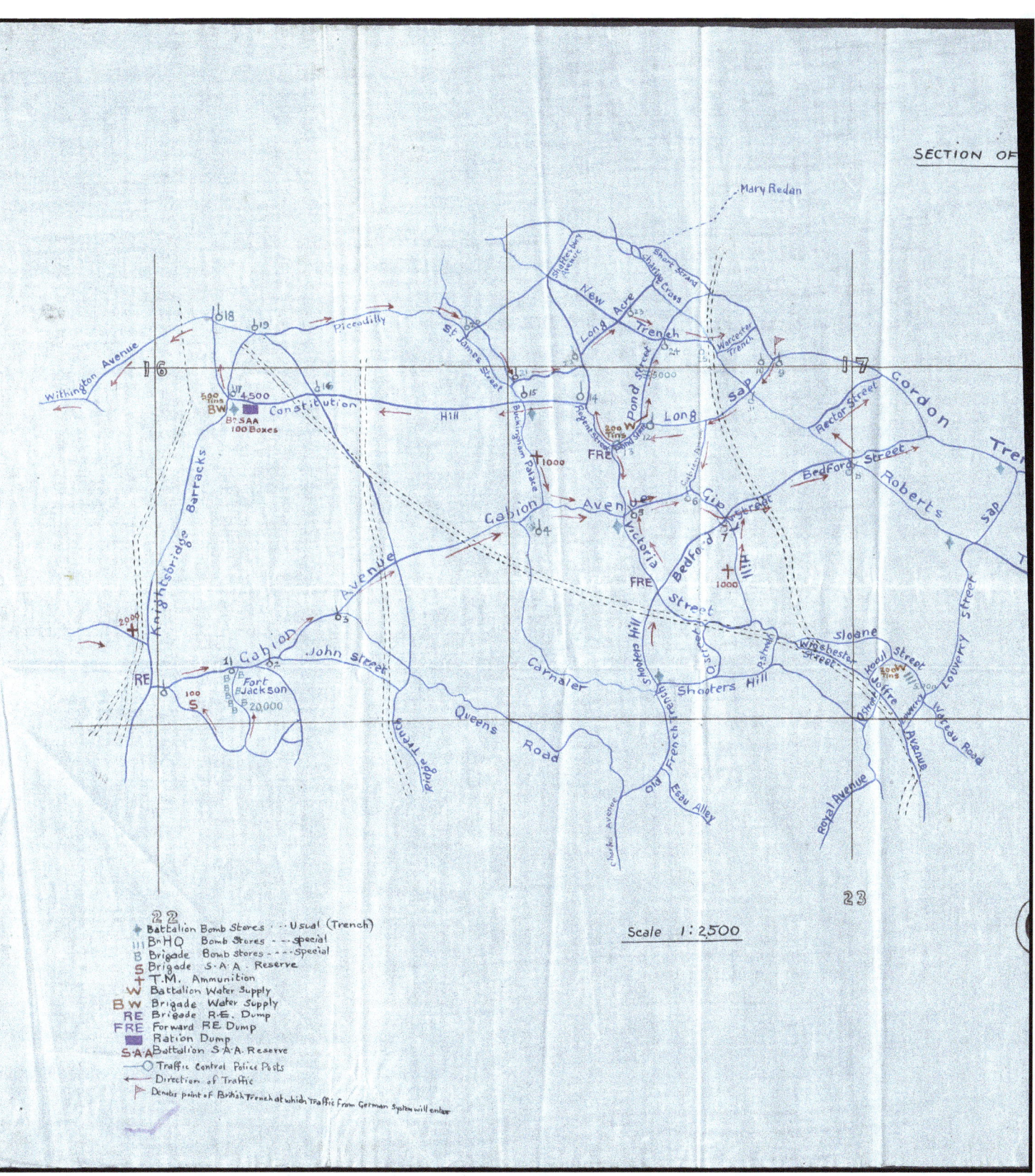

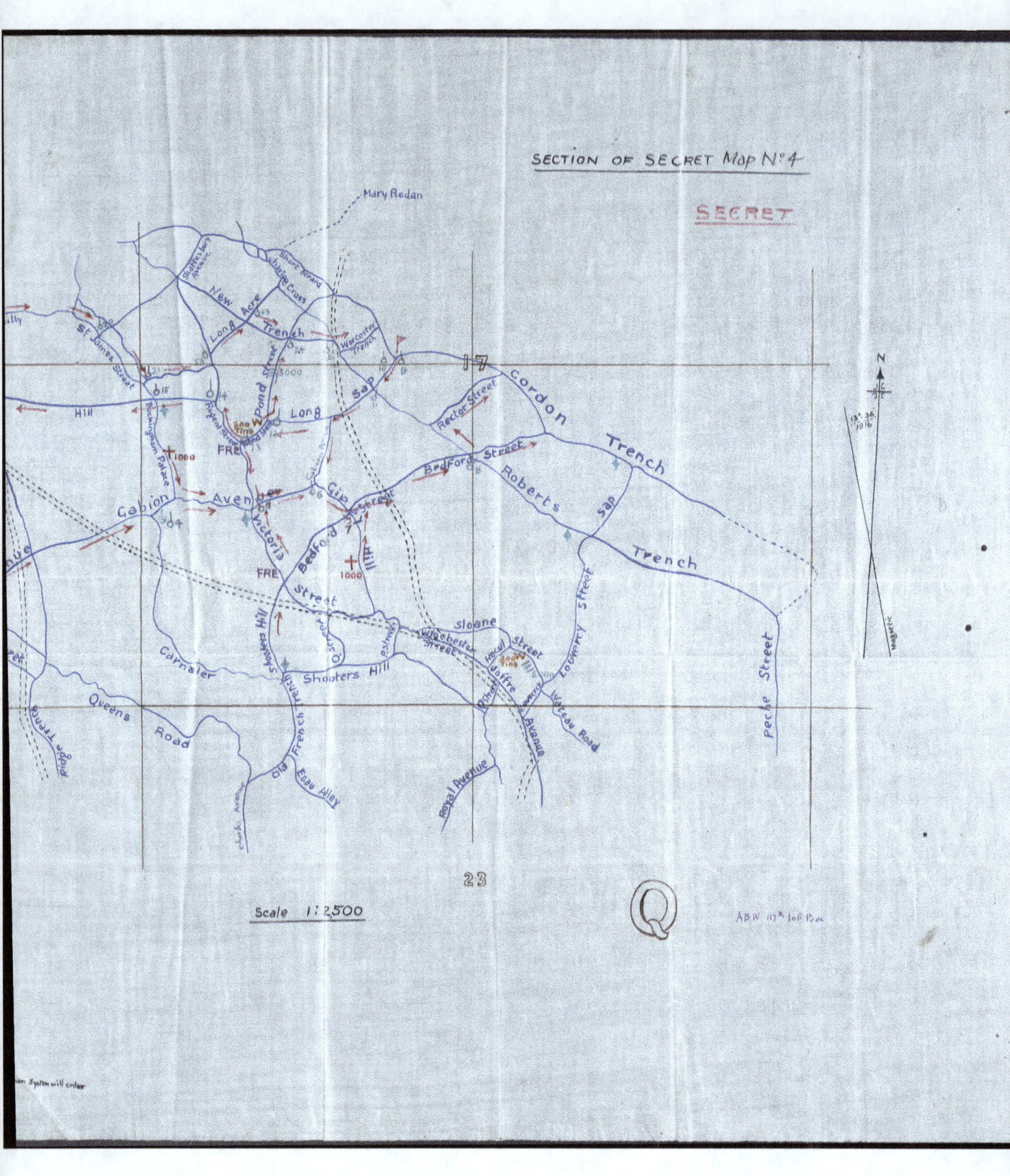

39th Division.

B. H. Q.

117th INFANTRY BRIGADE

SEPTEMBER 1 9 1 6

Appendices attached:-

Report on Operations 3rd September 1916.
Brigade Orders.
Defence Scheme.

Army Form C. 2118

WAR DIARY
or
INTELLIGENCE SUMMARY
(Erase heading not required.)

Page 1.

Instructions regarding War Diaries and Intelligence Summaries are contained in F.S. Regs., Part II. and the Staff Manual respectively. Title Pages will be prepared in manuscript.

Place	Date	Hour	Summary of Events and Information	Remarks and references to Appendices
BEAUSSART	1st Sept.		Nothing of interest to report.	
	2nd		Brigade moves to assembly positions in BEAUCOURT Section.	
Nr. HAMEL.	3rd		In accordance with Brigade Order No.51 (Appendix 12, Volume VI) and amendments, the Brigade attacked on German Trenches North of River ANCRE. Full account appended.	App. I.
Nr. FORCE-VILLE.)	4th		The Brigade comes out of the Line, and moves to BERTRANCOURT.	App. 2.
BERTRAN-COURT.)	5th.		Rest. Orders issued for Brigade to relieve 144th Infantry Brigade in Section LONG ACRE (inclusive) – BROADWAY (exclusive)	App. 3. and App. 4.
VITERMONT.	6th		The 117th Brigade relieves two Southern Battalions of the 144th Infantry Brigade in Sector LONG ACRE (inclusive) – BROADWAY (exclusive) in accordance with Brigade Orders 55 and 56 and Amendment. On our right – 118th Infantry Brigade. On our left – 145th Infantry Brigade.	
	7th		Hostile shelling by 5.9's. The following trenches damaged :- "D" Street, BOND Street, HAYMARKET and NEW FIRING LINE. A few gas shells fell in ENGLEBELMER. Our artillery active all day	
	8th		Our artillery active all day. Very little retaliation from the enemy. A Machine Gun Emplacement suspected at Q.10.d.5.7. Between 5.30 and 6.30 p.m. ten or twelve miniature balloons were sent over our lines by the enemy. It is reported that they dropped pamphlets and journals (in French) calculated to stir up discontent among the French.	
	9th		A quiet day and night.	

Army Form C.2118

WAR DIARY
INTELLIGENCE SUMMARY
(Erase heading not required.)

Page 2.

Instructions regarding War Diaries and Intelligence Summaries are contained in F. S. Regs., Part II. and the Staff Manual respectively. Title Pages will be prepared in manuscript.

Place	Date	Hour	Summary of Events and Information	Remarks and references to Appendices
VITERMONT.	10th		The 116th Infantry Brigade relieved the 145th Brigade on our left. Order for Inter-Battalion relief to take place on the 12th were issued (Brigade Order 57).	App.5.
	11th		Our Artillery and Trench Mortars shot for 10 minutes on enemy support line without any retaliation from the enemy. A quiet day and night.	
	12th		Inter-Battalion relief in accordance with Brigade Order 57 (App.5). The 17th Notts & Derby Regiment, and 16th Rifle Brigade, now become the Battalions in the line, the 16th Notts & Derby in Support in Wood at P.18.b., the 17th K. R. R. Corps in Reserve at MAILLY MAILLET. VITERMONT heavily shelled with 5.9's - very little damage done.	
	13th		VITERMONT and ENGLEBELMER again shelled. Our trenches received attention from H.T.Mortars - we believe our artillery have put it out of action.	
	14th.		ENEMY very quiet. We fired our Lewis and Vickers guns on his wire, also L.T.Mortars on Communication Trenches, but failed to provoke retaliation. Orders were issued for the Brigade to co-operate in the general attack "South" - Brigade Orders Nos 58 and 59, and 60.	App.6.
	15th.		In co-operation with the Attack further South, at 5.35 a.m. Vicker and Lewis Guns, and Rifles, opened fire on German Lines. Smoke was not discharged as wind was not favourable. Fire ceased at 6 a.m. The enemy put a slight barrage on our left support line, doing very little damage,	

Army Form C. 2118

WAR DIARY
of
INTELLIGENCE SUMMARY

(Erase heading not required.)

Page 3.

Instructions regarding War Diaries and Intelligence Summaries are contained in F. S. Regs., Part II. and the Staff Manual respectively. Title Pages will be prepared in manuscript.

Place	Date	Hour	Summary of Events and Information	Remarks and references to Appendices
VITERMONT.	15th(contd)		killing two and wounding two. On our right there was scarcely any damage barrage, and then generally well behind our support line. No damage whatever was done in this Section. The enemy was exceptionally quiet in this Section for the rest of the day. During the night he shewed greater activity with his machine guns.	
	16th		At 12.30 a.m. a small raid was attempted by the 17th Notts & Derby Regiment, the object being an identification. It was, however, unsuccessful.	
	17th		A quiet day. Advance Orders were issued for the Brigade to be relieved in the Line by two Battalions of the 118th Brigade, and for this Brigade to relieve the Left and Centre Brigades of the 2nd Division in the SERRE and HEBUTERNE Sections.	
			A raiding party of the 16th Rifle Brigade left our trenches at 8.15 p.m. The object being an identification. The party was surrounding two Germans working on his wire when the Medium Trench Mortars on our left opened fire on the German front line, killing the two Germans, and wounding several of the raiders.	
	18th		A quiet day. Brigade Order No.62 for relief of Front Line Battalions by 1/4th Black Watch and 1/1st Herts for the 19th issued, and for the 117th Brigade to relieve the 6th and 99th Brigades on the 20th in the SERRE and HEBUTERNE Sections.	App.7.
	19th		Brigade relieved in the "Y" ravine Section by the 1/4th Black Watch and 1/1st Herts in accordance	

WAR DIARY
INTELLIGENCE SUMMARY

(Erase heading not required.)

Army Form C. 2118.

Page 4.

Place	Date	Hour	Summary of Events and Information	Remarks and references to Appendices
VITERMONT	19th (contd)		with Brigade Order No. 62. The Brigade went into billets at BEAUSSART and BERTRANCOURT. Brigade Headquarters remaining at VITERMONT.	
SAILLY AU BOIS.	20th		The 117th Brigade relieved the 6th and 99th Brigades of the 2nd Division in the SERRE and HEBU-TERNE Sections in accordance with Brigade Order No.62. The Brigade now holds the Line from FLAG Avenue to the 16 Poplars. The 116th Brigade is on our right. the 51st Brigade on our left. Brigade Headquarters at SAILLY AU BOIS.	
	21st		The enemy blew a small mine on the front occupied by the 17th Notts & Derby Regiment, doing very little damage. Immediately afterwards they put up a barrage on our support line, and included in this were some heavy trench mortars, one of which destroyed our L.T.M. emplacement, killing one man.	
	22nd		A quiet day. German aeroplanes very active, flying lower than usual.	
	23rd		Enemy shewed more activity with rifle grenades than usual. Very little shelling except at a battery very close to Brigade Headquarters.	
	24th		An organised bombardment by artillery, heavy, medium and light trench mortars, was carried out against the hostile lines opposite our right centre. Retaliation was very weak.	
	25th		A quiet day. The 1st K.R.R.Corps attempted a raid at 10 p.m. on the German lines opposite our front. The attempt did not succeed.	

1875 W: W593/826 1,000,000 4/15 J.B.C. & A. A.D.S.S./Forms/C. 2118.

Army Form C. 2118.

WAR DIARY
INTELLIGENCE SUMMARY

(Erase heading not required.)

Page 5.

Instructions regarding War Diaries and Intelligence Summaries are contained in F. S. Regs., Part II. and the Staff Manual respectively. Title Pages will be prepared in manuscript.

Place	Date	Hour	Summary of Events and Information	Remarks and references to Appendices
SAILLY AU BOIS.	26th		In order to assist important operations on our right a heavy bombardment with artillery and trench mortars was carried out during the day in accordance with Brigade Order No.63. Our Vickers guns carried out bursts of fire throughout the day on enemy communications.	App. 8.
	27th		Very little hostile activity. We retaliated four times during the day with organised bombardment in reply to Minenwerfer.	
	28th		Enemy somewhat more active with artillery and trench mortars. We replied effectively.	
	29th		117th Infantry Brigade Defence Scheme (Provisional) issued. Orders received that Units in SERRE Section, except 117th T.M.Battery, are to be relieved on the 30th by 99th Infantry Brigade.	App. 9.
	30th		Orders received Units in HEBUTERNE Section are to be relieved on 1st October by 6th Inf.Brigade. 117th Infantry Brigade Order No.64 issued for relief of SERRE Section. 117th Infantry Brigade Order No.65 issued for relief of Brigade in HEBUTERNE Section, and 117th T.M.Battery in SERRE Section, and for Brigade to move into BERTRANCOURT. Brigade relieved in SERRE Section by 99th Infantry Brigade.	App. 10. App. 11.

Brigadier General,
Commanding 117th Infantry Brigade.

"A" Form.　Army Form C. 2121.
MESSAGES AND SIGNALS.
No. of Message..........

Prefix....Code....m.	Words	Charge	This message is on a/c of:	Recd. at....m.
Office of Origin and Service Instructions.				Date..........
	Sent		.......Service.	From..........
	At....m.			
	To			
	By	(Signature of "Franking Officer.")	By..........

TO — 39th Divn.

Sender's Number.	Day of Month.	In reply to Number.	
BM/175	5th		A A A

Herewith further report on Operations on 3rd Sept.

From — 117th Bde
Place
Time — 2pm.

The above may be forwarded as now corrected. (Z) W P Maxwell Capt
Censor.　Signature of Addressor or person authorised to telegraph in his name.

To /.
Headquarters,
39th Division.

App I

B.M./856.
Rg.

The following is the account of the action carried out by my Brigade between 5 a.m. and 12 noon on the 3rd September. It is compiled from reports received from the following sources:-

    (i) Unit Commanders;
    (ii) Brigade O.P.;
    (iii) Brigade on my left;
    (iv) Divisional Headquarters.

It contains very little narrated by Officers who actually went into the German trenches as there are not many of these left who are unwounded.

At 5.25 a.m. Brigade O.P. reported "I can see smoke candles in what looks like German second line, enemy machine gun fire very active on the left flank. There seems a considerable flow of men from Gordon and Roberts trench going across "No man's land".

At 5.33 an unconfirmed report by a wounded man states that Right Battalion had gained its objective with little or no opposition. The report received a little later from the Brigade O.P. that the Right Battalion had entered second objective. During this time the report had been received from the Left Battalion that they had reached the first line by 6 a.m., and machine gun fire was very heavy from the German second line, asking urgently for reinforcements in order to maintain the position in the first line, at the same time stating that the O.C. thought that remaining Companies had failed to attain their objective and were wiped out. Orders were sent to O.C., 17th K.R.R.Corps to send one Company of the Support Battalion to reinforce the Left Battalion in the front line. This was carried out promptly, and the Company joined the IVth Notts & Derby's on the left. In the meanwhile glowing reports from the Brigade O.P. seemed to indicate that the Right Battalion had been very successful, which was not in fact the case. It appears that the

- 1 -

Right Battalion had met with considerable opposition in their initial attack, and although isolated parties may have gained the second line, there is no clear evidence at present that they did so in any numbers. The O.C. Unit reported at 7.50 that a good many men had come back into our front line trenches who had failed to get into the first German line. He said he was reorganising his Battalion with a view to further attack in order to support those who had gone over and were believed to be still in the trenches. Reports still came in that parties had even been seen in the third line trench. This report emanated I believe from Air Observation. I then ordered O.C., Right Battalion, to carry out this attack at once, and reinforced his men with one Company of the Support Battalion, and ordered him to carry it out at once, i.e. 10.30. I had received information that the Left Battalion was still holding out in the German first line with difficulty. In addition there were parties of the 116th Brigade Right Battalion, and Left Battalion, reported to be holding out in the German first line on their front. The O.C., my Right Battalion, had in the meantime consulted the OsC., 13th Sussex and 14th Hampshire Battalions, and agreed, on his own initiative, with them to push on and try and fill up the gap thus created between my Left Battalion and the Right Battalion of the 116th Brigade. I then sent orders that I approved of this attack being carried out, and desired that it should be organised to start by 11.30, at the same time informing the artillery what I proposed to do, and that I would ask for heavy barrage between given points when the attack was ready. I had heard from G.O.C., 116th Brigade, that it was reported to him that his Left Battalion was still holding out in some strength in the German first line. This decided me that the attack was justifiable without delay or preparation other than a heavy bombardment for three minutes.   Before the organisation of this attack I consulted the G.O.C., 116th Brigade, on the telephone, and he agreed that it was the best thing to do in order to fill this gap and reinforce the small parties known to be in the German first line.   I then received information that the 17th Sherwoods (Left Battalion's) situation, (reinforced by one Company of the 17th K.R.R. Corps,) was critical, and that they did not think that they could hold out any longer, and even doubted whether there were many of our men left alive in the German trenches.   At about 11.30 I received this information, and thereupon sent an urgent message to the O.C., Right Battalion, to attack no more.   I reported the situation to Divisional Headquarters, and informed them that I did not now propose to try and fill this gap as it was doubtful whether any of our troops were still in the German line on the left.   My message, however, to stop the attack was received too late, and the effort was made meeting with temporary success as the waves penetrated the German first line.   They were, however, bombed out, and together with two small parties whom they found in the German first line trench, consisting of my own men and the Brigade on my left, retired back to our own trenches.   This took place about 12.10 p.m., and after that no further attacks were made.

Orders were given to withdraw all advanced detachments and reorganise.

R D F Oldman

3.9.1916.
Brig.General,
Commanding 117th Infantry Brigade.

To / Headquarters,
    39th Division.

B.M./864.

I have already sent in a report giving an account in chronological order of the Operations of this Brigade on the 3rd September. In the light of further information this has not altered in any particular. The following is an account of details not alluded to therein:-

In the Right Battalion Attack it is clear that the flanks of the Battalion got as far as the second line. In the centre of the Battalion the attack was held up, and only small parties succeeded in establishing themselves in the German first line. The cause of the centre not attaining its object appears to have been due to their being met with bombs and rifle fire. The Germans were clearly seen to have manned their parapet at this spot. Parties entered on the flanks the second objective and there is evidence to show that one party started digging itself in towards the Right Battalion's right flank in the second line. On the left the first objective was reached apparently without much difficulty, but the waves destined for the second and third lines, while crossing between the first and second German lines, were subjected to very heavy machine gun fire, which is said to have come from the German second line, especially Northwards about the top of the Ridge, i.e. in the neighbourhood of Points 33 and 36. In this case also small parties penetrated and started to establish themselves in the second line.

The advance parties of both Battalions were compelled to give ground by the German counter attacks which took the form of bombing parties of 20 to 30 men advancing from the flanks over the top. This was especially the case on the left in front of the Left Battalion. I think the evidence that this was the form of counter attack is clear as a detail, in which both Units agree, states that the Germans were in shirt sleeves and without equipment. The stick bomb was used, and it is said also the Egg bomb. No one admits that the Germans out-ranged us with their bombs. I have not been able to find out the numbers of parties which were comprised in the German counter attack. The timing mark on the bomb was 5½ seconds. I am unable to find out whether any counter attacks were delivered in the German first line by bombing parties issuing from the dug-outs. There is no doubt that there were bombing fights in the German first line, but it appears probable they were parties which had advanced over the top from the second line into the first. It is noticeable that no one is able to say that he met with a dug-out in the German first line. The trench was very much knocked about, and this may have accounted for their not having been discovered, entrances being closed up. The Left Battalion especially emphasises the condition of the trench, and N.C.O's report large number of German dead lying therein. It is stated that machine gun fire was responsible for about 25% of casualties.

All reports agree that very little S.A.A. was used, and two requests were received from the German lines for more bombs. In the case of the Left Battalion extra supplies were actually sent up.

The Company carrying parties with both Battalions reached the German trenches as material was seen lying about in them. They immediately became, however, on arriving there fighting men.

I offer the following opinions:-

The failure of the attack was due almost entirely to shell and trench mortar fire. The effect of the machine gun fire would not have stopped the waves from entering the second line trenches in greater numbers. I cannot find from any report the exact hour at which the German barrage was put down on to the German first line, but it is in the neighbourhood of 5.20. There was no barrage established in our own front trenches except on GORDON Trench, which received a large number of trench mortar bombs and shrapnel, certain points and trenches only being shelled. These have been communicated separately.

- 3 -

I think it would be better to include no one in the assaulting waves such as carrying parties, light trench mortars, and machine guns. It would be better to wait until definite information has been received that the assaulting infantry has attained their objective, and then send them over. If the infantry can hold their position in spite of the German shell fire, these detachments will be able to get up, and need not fear to be cut off by the German barrage. In an attack on an organised system of trenches, in contra distinction to an attack on hastily dug trenches, it seems advisable to carry more bombs and less S.A.A.

I think it would be better to place in our own front trenches only just sufficient men to hold them after the attack has gone over, supporting battalions can remain any distance further to the rear where suitable and protected position offers. The extra length of time involved in getting them up to the front as reinforcements is more than compensated for by their being immune from shell fire directed at our own front trenches. In the present case the trenches were terribly congested, and a large number of casualties no doubt incurred in that manner.

On the whole I think it would be better to assemble in "No man's land" when the light is strong enough for at least the length of a whole Company front to be seen. In this case touch was lost to a small extent in one portion of the Right Battalion as the assembly was not square to the right objective.

Finally, the non-success of the operation may be said to be entirely due to hostile shell fire. Machine guns did not have the effect of stopping our men. This points to the necessity for more counter-battery work by the heavier Howitzers. I think the inclusion of 6" Howitzers in the preliminary bombardment, and subsequent barrages, is highly desirable, as the Field Artillery does not seem capable of driving the enemy into his dugouts. There is much evidence to show that his front line trenches were strongly manned at the time of attack.

(Sd) R. D. F. OLDMAN,
Brig.General,
5.9.1916.   Commanding 117th Infantry Brigade.

B.M./863.

Report of Hostile Shell Fire during Operations,
3rd. September.
----

1. From information from all sources it appears that the majority of shelling was from the 5.9" Howitzer.
    There were also a fairly large number of 8" shells sent over.
    No shells of larger calibre than 8" were observed.

2. The proportion of 4.2" Howitzer and 77 MM was very small.

3. The trenches which received the most attention from the German gunners are as follows:-

    <u>On the Right:</u>   LOUVERCY SAP and LOUVERCY STREET.
                    SLOANE STREET and VICTORIA STREET.
                    GORDON and ROBERTS Trenches.
                    SHOOTERS HILL.

    <u>On the Left:</u>   VICTORIA STREET.
                    LONG SAP.
                    POND STREET.
                    REGENT STREET.
                    GORDON and ROBERTS Trench, and RECTOR STREET.
                    Eastern end of CONSTITUTIONAL HILL.

    Many of these trenches were quite obliterated.
    Perhaps the most intense fire was centred on SLOANE STREET, SHOOTERS HILL, and POND STREET.

4. From the reports received, and from the promptitude of the German barrage, it would appear that the Germans had previously registered their own front line trench.

5. The form of barrage used by the Germans was not the usual curtain fire on our front line trench and "No man's land", but was an intense fire by 5.9" Howitzers distributed very

evenly on all important communications from rear to front, and on support and reserve trenches.

6. The proportion of blinds appeared to be small.

7. Medium minenwerfer fired throughout the operations on GORDON Trench.

[signature]

Brigadier General,
Commanding 117th Infantry Brigade.

5.9.1916.

No. 1 Copy

To
   Headquarters,
      39th Division.

864.
B.M./871.

There are two further points which I have elucidated with regard to operations on 3rd instant:-

1. The distance the Right Battalion of my Brigade had to go was greater than could be accomplished in four minutes. An Officer states that he walked quickly and got within 30 yards of the German parapet, but that his men were 50 yards behind him. This was due to their (i) carrying more weight, (ii) were not as determined as the Officer, (iii) were not square to their objective.

    <u>Deduction</u>: Would it be wiser to increase the barrage to to five minutes to legislate for these events, which are in_herent.

2. The Right Battalion arrived at the German trenches "thin". The cause may have been loss of direction and men hanging back, but the O.C. is of opinion that his front was too long (160 yards).

    <u>Deduction</u>: Would it have been better to have had another Battalion in on a narrow front. The Left Battalion had the greater success as they were on a 90 to 100 yards front (one of their Companies being earmarked for the defensive flank) and reached the German first line without difficulty, though subsequent waves suffered from Machine Gun fire.

Two men, one 17th Notts & Derby Regiment and one 16th Rifle Brigade, have come in this morning. They are too done up to interrogate today, but I will do so tomorrow morning.

                                      Brig.General,
6.9.1916.   Commanding 117th Infantry Brigade.

SECRET.   117th Brigade Order No. 54.   Copy No. 12

Advance Order for Move of 117th INFANTRY BRIGADE.

                                                4.9.1916.
Ref: Map 1/20,000
     Map 1/40,000.

1. The Brigade will move at once to area BERTRANCOURT - BEAUSSART.

2. Units, who will march independly as soon after the receipt of this order as convenient, will take over same Camps and Billets as they occupied before, i.e. 16th Notts & Derby Regt., BEAUSSART; 17th Notts & Derby Regt., "Z" CAMP, BERTRANCOURT; 17th K.R.R.Corps, "Y" CAMP, BERTRAN-COURT; 16th Rifle Brigade, "X" CAMP, BERTRANCOURT; Machine Gun Coy. and Trench Mortar Battery, "Z" CAMP, BERTRANCOURT.

   Brigade Headquarters will move from P.22.b.5.0. to BERTRANCOURT CHATEAU.

3. Report centre at P.22.b.5.0. will close at 5 p.m., reopening at BERTRANCOURT CHATEAU at the same hour.

4. A report on completion of these moves will be sent to Brigade Headquarters.

5. Acknowledge.

                                    T of Maxwell. Captain,
4.9.1916.   Brigade Major, 117th Brigade.

Copies issued at 4 p.m. to:-
 No.1. 16th Notts & Derby Regt.   8. H.Q., 116th Brigade.
    2. 17th Notts & Derby Regt.   9. G.O.C.
    3. 17th K.R.R.Corps.   10. B.M.
    4. 16th Rifle Brigade.   11. S.C.
    5. 117th Machine Gun Coy.   12. War Diary.
    6. 117th T.M.Battery.   13. War Diary.
    7. H.Q., 39th Division.   14. Order file.

SECRET. W.D. A/V/VIII Copy No. ...

117th Infantry Brigade Order No.55.

(Advance Order for the Relief of 144th Brigade on the 6th.,
and evening of 6th/7th Sept.)

Ref: 1/40,000 Map, and   5.9.1916.
Auchonvillers Trench Map.

1. On the 6th, and evening of 6th/7th September, the 117th Brigade will take over line now held by the two Southern Battalions of the 144th Brigade, in the Sector LONG ACRE (inclusive) - BROADWAY (exclusive).

2. The Brigade will be disposed as follows:-

(a) **16th Notts & Derby Regt.**

    Right Front Company: 1 platoon - WELLINGTON (with its left on S. Alley).

                                  1 platoon - OLD FIRE TRENCH (between its Junctions with PICCADILLY and WELLINGTON).

                                  1 platoon - REGENT Street (between Junctions with PICCADILLY and OLD FIRE TRENCH).

                                  1 platoon - OLD FIRE TRENCH (between Junctions with REGENT Street and S. Alley).

    Centre Front Company: 1 platoon - WELLINGTON (between N. & S. Alleys).

                                  2 platoons - NEW FIRING LINE (between N. & S. Alleys).

                                  1 platoon - OLD FIRING LINE (between MARYLEBONE Road and No. 2 Sap).

    Left Front Company: 1 platoon and 2 Lewis Guns - WELLINGTON (between N. Alley and "D" Street).

                                  3 platoons - FETHARD Street (about Q.10.c.8.2.)

    Support Company: Distributed at the discretion of O.C., 16th Notts & Derby Regt., in:-   JOHN Street,
                                                     BROOK Street,
                                                     Piccadilly and St.JAMES Street.
                                                     FORT WITHINGTON,
                                                     FETHARD Street.

    Coy. Lewis Guns: Will be with their Companies.

    Battn. Lewis Guns: Will be with the Support Coy.

    Battalion H.Q.:   - 1 -   P.T.O.

- 2 -

<u>Battn.Headquarters</u>: St.JOHN'S Road, midway between CARLISLE and UXBRIDGE.

<u>Boundaries of Battalion Sector</u>:-

<u>South</u>: Point of MARY REDAN - LONG ACRE (inclusive) - CONSTITUTIONAL HILL - KNIGHTSBRIDGE - GABION (all exclusive).

<u>North</u>: "D" Street (exclusive).
"B" Street (exclusive).

(b) <u>17th K.R.R.Corps</u>.

<u>Front Company</u>: 1 platoon and 2 Lewis Guns - WELLINGTON (between "D" Street and BROADWAY).

3 platoons - ESSEX Street and FETHARD Street, about Q.10.c.8.6.

<u>Support Coy</u>: 3 platoons and 2 Lewis Guns - in FETHARD Street and ESSEX Street.

1 platoon - POMPADOUR.

<u>Reserve Coy</u>: POMPADOUR and St.JOHN'S ROAD.

<u>Battn.Headquarters</u>: HAYMARKET. (Q.10.c.3.3.)

<u>Northern Boundary</u>: BROADWAY (exclusive).

(c) <u>17th Notts & Derby Regt</u>: In support - AUCHONVILLERS.

(d) <u>16th Rifle Brigade</u>: In reserve - MAILLY MAILLET.

(e) <u>117th Machine Gun Coy</u>: 1 Section in support at AUCHONVILLERS, remainder in the line taking over GUN for GUN from the 144th Brigade.

(f) <u>117th T.M.Battery</u>: Two Guns in the line. Remainder of personnel at MAILLY MAILLET.

(g) <u>Brigade Headquarters</u>: ~~will be notified later~~.

Brigade Headquarters will be at VITERMONT.

3. Os.C., Units, will arrange for proportion of Officers and N.C.O's to reconnoitre the trenches and billets into which they will move at the earliest opportunity.

4. Operation Orders for the relief will be issued later.

5. Acknowledge.

T. T. Maxwell Captain,
Brigade Major, 117th Brigade.

5.9.1916.

Copies issued at 2.30 p.m. to:-
No.1. 16th Notts & Derby Regt.
2. 17th do do
3. 17th K.R.R.Corps.
4. 16th Rifle Brigade.
5. 117th Machine Gun Coy.
6. 117th T.M.Battery.
7. H.Q., 39th Division.
8. 144th Brigade.
9. G.O.C.
10. B.M.
11. S.C.
12. War Diary.
13. War Diary.
14. Order file.

SECRET.   Copy No. 16.

117th Infantry Brigade Order No.56.

Ref: 1/40,000 Map.
     1/20,000 Map,   5.9.1916.
     Auchonvillers Trench Map.

1. The Brigade will take over tomorrow, 6th September, the line now held by the two Southern Battalions of the 144th Brigade in the Sector LONG ACRE (inclusive) - BROADWAY (exclusive). The 116th Brigade will take over present billets tomorrow afternoon.

2. All moves will be in accordance with the Advanced Order issued today (117th Brigade Order No.55) and the attached "March and relief tables", and all details of relief not mentioned in the Table will be arranged direct between Commanding Officers.

3. The Staff Captain will indicate to Transport Officers of all Units of the Brigade the exact position of each Unit's Transport Lines.
   Transport Officers will meet the Staff Captain at BERTRANCOURT CHURCH at 9.30 a.m.

4. The Quartermaster's Stores of all Units of the Brigade will be either at MAILLY MAILLET, or AUCHONVILLERS, as most convenient. Application for suitable stores should be made to the Town Majors of these villages.

5. Units billetted in MAILLY MAILLET and AUCHONVILLERS will apply to Town Majors for billets in good time before the arrival of their Units.

6. O.C., 17th Notts & Derby Regt., will place one limber at the disposal of O.C., 117th T.M.Battery, for the move.

7. Reports of Relief Complete and Completion of all moves in this Order will be at once reported to Brigade Headquarters.

8. Brigade Headquarters will be at VITERMONT.
   Report centre closes at BERTRANCOURT at 2.30 p.m., reopening at VITERMONT at the same hour.

9. Acknowledge.

                                                L.E.Maxwell. Captain,
                                              Brigade Major, 117th Brigade.
5.9.1916.
Copies issued at 8 p.m. to:-
No.1. 16th Notts & Derby Regt.   7. H.Q., 39th Division.   13. B.M.
   2. 17th   do   do   8. H.Q., 39th Div.R.A.   14. S.C.
   3. 17th K.R.R.Corps.   9. H.Q., 116th Bde.   15. War Diary.
   4. 18th Rifle Brigade.   10. H.Q., 118th Bde.   16. War Diary.
   5. 117th Mach.Gun Coy.   11. H.Q., 144th Bde.   17. Order File.
   6. 117th T.M.Battery.   12. G.O.C.

March and relief table to accompany 117th Brigade Order No.56.

Unit.	Present billet.	To be clear of present billets by	Whom relieving	Route.	Times and places where Guides,144th Bde will meet Units.	Destination.	Remarks.
16th Notts & Derby Regt.	BEAUSSART.	In time to arrive West end of WITH-INGTON avenue by 10 a.m.	4th Gloucester Rgt., & 1 Coy. 6th Gloucester Regt.	Via ROAD Junction.F.12.c. 95.01-Mailly Maillett.-VITERMONT.Via BEAUSSART	10 a.m.W.end of WITHINGTON avenue (1 guide per platoon).	In the line wide 117th Bde.,Order No.55.	All movements EAST of BEAUSSART will be at intervals of 100 yards between platoons.
17th Notts & Derby Regt.	"Z" CAMP, BERTRANCOURT	8 p.m.	—	—	—	Bde.Support AUCHONVILLERS.	
17th K.R.R. Corps.	"Y" CAMP, BERTRANCOURT	In time for head of Battn.to pass Mailly Maillet Church at 2 p.m.	6th Gloucester Regt. less 1 Company.	Ditto	2.p.m. MAILLY MAILLET CHURCH (1 guide per Coy. only).	In the line wide 117th Bde Order No.55.	
16th Rifle Brigade.	"X" CAMP, BERTRANCOURT	2.30 p.m.	—	Via BEAUSSART-ROAD Junction.F.12.c. 95.01.	—	Bde.Reserve, MAILLY MAILLET.	
117th Mch. Gun Coy.	"Z" CAMP, BERTRANCOURT	In time to arrive Cafe JOURDAIN, MAILLY MAILLET at 11.30 a.m.	1½ Sections of 144th Mch. Gun Coy.	Via BEAUSSART-Road Junctn. F.12.c.95.01. Mailly Maillet	11.30 a.m.144th Bde H.Q., Cafe JOURDAIN,MAILLY MAILLET.	6 guns in the line. Reserve Sections - Mailly Maillet. 2 guns in the line. Reserve Sections - Mailly Maillet.	
117th T.M. Battery.	"Z" CAMP, BERTRANCOURT	Ditto	1 Section of 144th T.M. Battery.	Ditto	Ditto	VITERMONT	
117th Bde H.Q.	BERTRANCOURT	2.45 p.m.	—	Ditto	—	H.Q. Q.19.B. 65.35.	

NOTE: Guides for Lewis Guns of 16th Notts & Derby Regiment, and 17th K.R.R.Corps, will be at the same Rendezvous as indicated in table, but one hour before time stated for Battalion Guides.

SECRET.   War Diary app IV   Copy ..15..

AMENDMENT to 117th Infantry Brigade Order No.56.

5.9.1916.

1. The 17th Notts & Derby Regiment will not move to AUCHONVILLERS tomorrow as stated in Brigade Orders Nos 55 and 56, but will take over the Camp in Wood P.18.B.

2. It has now been ruled that AUCHONVILLERS is outside the Divisional Area.

                                    W.S.Maxwell.   Captain,
5.9.1916.   Brigade Major, 117th Brigade.

Copies issued to:-

No.1. 16th Notts & Derby Regt.   7. H.Q., 39th Division.   13. B.M.
   2. 17th   do   do   8. H.Q., 39th Div.R.A.   14. S.C.
   3. 17th K.R.R.Corps.   9. H.Q., 116th Bde.   15. War Diary.
   4. 16th Rifle Brigade.   10. H.Q., 118th Bde.   16. War Diary.
   5. 117th Machine Gun Coy.   11. H.Q., 144th Bde.   17. Order File.
   6. 117th T.M.Battery.   12. G.O.C.

SECRET. War Diary/   Copy No. 19...

117th BRIGADE ORDER No. 57. App V

10.9.1916.

RELIEF. 1. The following Inter-Battalion reliefs will take place on the 12th September:-

(a) The 17th Notts & Derby Regiment will relieve the 16th Notts & Derby Regiment (less one Company now holding their left front sector, who will be relieved by a Company of the 16th Rifle Brigade later) in the Right sub-sector LONG ACRE to N.ALLEY inclusive.

Relief to be complete by 12 Noon.

(b) The 16th Rifle Brigade will relieve the 17th K.R.R. Corps and the left front Company of the 16th Notts and Derby Regiment, in the Left sub-sector NORTH ALLEY (exclusive) to BROADWAY (exclusive).

Relief not to commence till after 1 p.m.

(c) All other details not mentioned to be arranged by C.O's concerned.

(d) Os.C., 117th Machine Gun Coy., and 117th L.T.M. Battery, will also arrange to carry out a relief, but must do so at such time as will not interfere with Battalion reliefs, i.e. between 12 noon and 1 p.m. O.C., 117th L.T.M.Battery will arrange for Three Stokes Guns to be in the line.

(e) All troops moving across the open to or from WITHINGTON and TIPPERARY will do so by platoons at 100 yards interval.

BILLETS. 2. Relieved Battalions will take over billets vacated by relieving Battalions.

REPORTS. 3. Reports of relief complete will be forwarded to Brigade Headquarters. The code word to denote relief complete will be "ZEPPELIN".

4. Acknowledge.

W.E.Maxwell Captain,
Brigade Major, 117th Brigade.

10.9.1916.

Copies issued to:-
1. 16th Notts & Derby Regt.   6. 117th T.M.Battery.   12. 225 Field Co.R.E.
2. 17th   do   do   7. H.Q., 39th Division.   13. G.O.C.
3. 17th K.R.R.Corps.   8. H.Q., 39th Div.R.A.   14. B.M.   15. S.C.
4. 16th Rifle Brigade.   9. H.Q., 116th Brigade.   16. Signal Officer.
5. 117th Machine Gun Coy.   10. H.Q., 118th Brigade.   17. Intell.Officer.
    18 and 19. War Diary.   20. Office Copy.

SECRET.   App VI   N?   Copy No. 11.

117th INFANTRY BRIGADE ORDER No.58.

Reference: 1/20,000 Sheet 57D. S.E.
           1/10,000 Sheet 57D. 1 and 2 (parts of)   14.9.1916.

INFORMATION. 1. 39th Division will co-operate in operations to be carried out on the 15th instant by the Reserve Army.

Action of 117th Infantry Brigade.

2. (a) Vickers Machine Gun, Light Trench Mortar, Lewis Gun, and rifle fire, will be opened on below mentioned zones at 5.35 a.m. For this purpose the Support line will be manned (not the front line). Parapet will be manned adjacent to dugouts so that in case of heavy barrage being put on casualties may be avoided. An Officer will, however, give this order, and resume firing directly barrage lifts or alters. Firing points will be selected by Os.C., Units, so that it is clear and safe as regards our front line.

(b) Targets:

Rifles and Lewis Guns:-
German front line, support line, and reserve line.
Right Battalion on Salient in enfilade in Northerly direction.
Left Battalion on Zone Q.17.b.0.4.-1.4.-9.4.- BEAUCOURT Station to Q.11.c.3.3.-5.5.-Q.11.d. 3½.6.

Vickers Machine Guns:- (eight)
Enfilade on selected targets within limits of zone as above mentioned. Two Companies on each Battalion front will open fire, and six Lewis Guns on each Battalion front.

Light Trench Mortars will select their own targets
No fire of any kind is to be put South of the line Q.17.b.0.4.-1.4.-9.4. on any account, as a raid is being carried out by the 118th Brigade.

-1-

Smoke Arrangements.

3. Smoke ("P" Bombs) will be discharged along the whole of the front held by the Brigade from the front line under the following arrangements:-

(a) Captain COHEN will be in charge of the arrangements.

(b) The 17th Notts & Derby Regiment, and 16th Rifle Brigade, will each detail One Officer and Two N.C.O's to assist Captain Cohen, and generally supervise the arrangements in their own Battalion Sub-Section. Each Battalion front will be divided into lengths of 25 yards in each, of which a party of One N.C.O. (time-keeper), Two Throwers (bombers), One Carrier, will form a Smoke Party, and throw "P" Bombs in accordance with orders laid down as under. It is calculated that each Battalion will require 23 such parties, and each party will throw four "P" Bombs. These bombs will be thrown at 5.55 a.m. Signal to throw bombs will be a bomb thrown from the highest point of WELLINGTON Trench between SOUTH ALLEY and PICCADILLY. As soon as this bomb is thrown the Smoke Barrage will be taken up all down the Brigade front. After the four bombs have been thrown the smoke parties will withdraw to the Support line and get under cover. They will not do so until permission has been obtained from the Battalion Officer in charge.

(c) The 17th Notts & Derby Regiment, and 16th Rifle Brigade, will draw at 10 p.m. TODAY from the Brigade Bomb Store, STOCKTON DUMP (Q.9.c.5.2.) 120 "P" Bombs each. These must be carried up and placed in position by 1 a.m. Parties as in Sub-para (b) must be in position by 5 a.m. The Two Officers from the 17th Notts & Derby Regiment, and 16th Rifle Brigade, will meet Captain Cohen at 4 a.m. at the Right Battalion Headquarters (17th Notts &Derby Regiment) in order to synchronise watches.

Officers' Patrol	4. An Officers' Patrol, consisting of One Officer and 20 Other Ranks, from each front line Battalion, will be held in readiness at Battalion Headquarters to act on orders being received from the Brigade Headquarters.
Observation after the operation.	5. After the operation all existing Observation Posts will be manned, and every effort made to detect movement of troops or abnormal behaviour in the German trenches. Should any such movement be observed report must be sent to Brigade Headquarters at once.
	6. Acknowledge.

[signature] Captain,
Brigade Major, 117th Brigade.

14.9.1916.

Copies sent to :-

1. 16th Notts & Derby Regt.
2. 17th   do   do
3. 17th K.R.R.Corps.
4. 16th Rifle Brigade.
5. 117th Machine Gun Coy.
6. 117th T.M.Battery.
7. Headquarters, 39th Division.
8. 225th Field Company, R.E.
9. B.M.
10. War Diary.
11. War Diary.
12. Order File.

SECRET. W.B.   Copy No. 11

117th Infantry Brigade Order No.59.

14.9.1916.

1. In the event of a successful advance by the Allies in tomorrow's operations, and subsequent days, the enemy in our front may decide:-

   (a) To hold his present position.
   (b) To create a diversion by seizing HAMEL and AUCHONVILLERS RIDGE.
   (c) Withdraw his troops to a rearward line.

2. In the event of (b) instructions have been issued in B.M./917 and B.M./917.a. as to the action of Support and Reserve Battalions who will immediately take up their allotted positions on orders from Brigade Headquarters.

3. (A) The exact position in the FORT WITHINGTON, FORT ANLEY, AUCHONVILLERS Line, which the Support Battalion will take up, will be indicated in ~~Annexure X.X.21X.~~ these orders.

   (B) The Reserve Battalion will be in a position of readiness in the neighbourhood of the Point (P.8.d.9.4.) indicated in B.M./917.

   (C) Support Section of Machine Gun Coy will move to FORT ANLEY, Reserve Section remaining in the neighbourhood of Point P.8.d.9.6.

   (D) Reserve Section, Light Trench Mortars, will move to FORT WITHINGTON, and await orders.

4. In the event of "(c)-para 1.", two wide gaps in enemy wire will be cut in the front of the Brigade. Each Battalion in the front line will be prepared to send forward at short notice a strong fighting patrol into hostile line as detailed in Brigade Order No. 58. Should the hostile line be found unoccupied, patrols will remain therein reporting back immediately.

5. Intense alertness is to be enjoined on all ranks. Officer and N.C.O. Observers will be posted so that German trenches may be kept under constant supervision. Reports, negative or otherwise, to be sent to Brigade Headquarters every hour from 6 a.m. to dark on the 15th instant.

   Further orders will be issued with regard to Night Patrols.

   (P.T.O.)

6. All Units will hold themselves in readiness to move at 20 minutes notice.

7. **Liaison** Officers mentioned in B.M./917 will report to Brigade Headquarters on receipt of orders to move.

8. Two extra Bicycle Runners will be sent to Brigade Headquarters on the order to move, from each Battalion, and one each from L.T.M. Battery and Machine Gun Coy.

9. Brigade Headquarters will remain at VITERMONT.

10. Effect will be given to these orders on the message "Carry out Brigade Order No.59".

11. Acknowledge.

                                                                           Maxwell Captain,

14.9.1916.   Brigade Major, 117th Brigade.

Copies issued to:-
1. 16th Notts & Derby Regt.   8. G.O.C.
2. 17th   do   do   9. B.M.
3. 17th K.R.R.Corps.   10. S.C.
4. 16th Rifle Brigade.   11. War Diary.
5. 117th Machine Gun Coy.   12. War Diary.
6. 117th T.M.Battery.   13. Order File.
7. Headquarters, 39th Division.

SECRET. W.D.   Order No. 12.

Amendment to 117th Infantry Brigade Order No.59.
----

1. **Para. 3(B).** Map reference of Point described in this para. should be P.18.d.9.4.

2. **Para. 3(C).** Map reference of Point described in this para. should be P.18.d.9.6.

                                         Maxwell Captain,
16.9.1916.   Brigade Major, 117th Brigade.

Copies issued to:-
1. 16th Notts & Derby Regt.
2. 17th   do   do
3. 17th K.R.R.Corps.
4. 16th Rifle Brigade.
5. 117th Machine Gun Coy.
6. 117th T.M.Battery.
7. H.Q's, 39th Division.

8. G.O.C.
9. R.A.
10. S.C.
11. War Diary.
12. War Diary.
13. Order File.

SECRET.   Copy No. 8.

117th Infantry Brigade Order No.60.

15.9.1916.

Reference Divisional 39/G.S.S./12/5.

1. A raid will be carried out on the German trenches at Point Q.11.c.8.4. on night of 15th/16th September. No artillery will be used anterior to the entry into the German trenches. A barrage may be put on as the party comes out if desired. The raid will be carried out with SURPRISE as its basis.

2. The strength of the party will not exceed One Officer and 20 men.

3. Wire is in process of being cut at this point. Officer Commanding the party, and 17th Notts & Derby Regiment, will verify the gap before dark.

4. All arrangements are in the hands of O.C., 17th Notts & Derby Regt. Any requirements with regard to artillery will reach Brigade H.Q's before 6 p.m., a brief outline of proposed action to be sent in at the same hour.

5. O.C., 16th Rifle Brigade, will verify gap at about Q.10.d.5½.6. which is being reopened this afternoon, in case it may be desired to send a similar party over at this point.

6. Should Front Line German trenches be untenanted, the party will make its way into the Support trench. It is of the highest importance to obtain an identification.

7. Raid will not take place before 12 mid-night.

8. Brigade Headquarters will remain at VITRAMONT.

9. Acknowledge.

                                                                                    R.E.Makewell   Captain,

15.9.1916.   Brigade Major, 117th Brigade.

Copies issued to:-
   Headquarters, 39th Division.
   O.C., 17th Notts & Derby Regt.
   O.C., 16th Rifle Brigade.
   O.C., "A" Group, R.A.
   G.O.C.
   B.M.
   War Diary.
   War Diary.
   Order File.

SECRET.   App VII   Copy No. 17

117th INFANTRY BRIGADE ORDER No. 62.

18.9.1916.

Reference: 1/40,000 57D. Ed.I.
57D. N.E. 3 and 4 (parts of)

1. In continuance of 117th Brigade Order No.61, the 117th Brigade will be relieved on the 19th instant, in "Y" Ravine Section, by Two Battalions of the 118th Brigade, in accordance with the attached Table "A".

   After relief the Brigade will move in accordance with Table "A".

2. The relief of the 6th Brigade, and the 99th Brigade, by the 117th Brigade will take place on the 20th instant, in accordance with the attached Relief Table "B".

3. Two Sections of the 117th Machine Gun Coy will remain under the orders of the G.O.C., 118th Brigade, in the "Y" Ravine Section. One Section of the 117th Machine Gun Coy will relieve one Section, 6th Machine Gun Coy., and One Section, 117th Machine Gun Coy will relieve One Section, 99th Machine Gun Coy, in the SERRE and HEBUTERNE Sections respectively, on the 20th instant. All details not mentioned in this Order will be arranged by Os.C., Machine Gun Companies concerned.

4. All details of relief on both days not mentioned in these orders will be arranged direct by Commanding Officers with their respective opposite numbers.

5. Units will hand over to the 118th Brigade on relief, and take over from the 6th and 99th Brigades on relief:-

    (i) All Trench Stores.

    (ii) All R.E.Tools and material in excess of Scale laid down in their Mobilization Stores Tables.

    (iii) All Maps, Plans, and Aeroplane Photos, referring to the area handed over or taken over.

    (iv) All work in hand and proposed work.

6. Reports of Relief Complete, and completion of all moves in this Order, will be at once reported to Brigade Headquarters.

(P.T.O.)

7. Brigade Headquarters will remain at VITERMONT on the 19th., moving to SAILLY-AUX-BOIS (J.18.c.5.3) on the 20th.

Report centre will close at VITERMONT at 2 p.m. on the 20th reopening at the same time at SAILLY-AUX-BOIS.

8. Acknowledge.

W.F. Maxwell Captain,
Brigade Major, 117th Brigade.

18.9.1916.

Copies issued at 3 p.m. to:
1. 16th Notts & Derby Regt.
2. 17th do do
3. 17th K.R.R.Corps.
4. 16th Rifle Brigade.
5. 117th Machine Gun Coy.
6. 117th T.M.Battery.
7. Headquarters, 39th Division.
8. C.R.A., 39th Division.
9. Headquarters, 118th Brigade.
10. ditto 116th Brigade.
11. Headquarters, 6th Brigade.
12. ditto 99th Brigade.
13. G. O. C.
14. B. M.
15. S. C.
16. War Diary.
17. War Diary.
18. Order file.

TABLE "A" - March and relief Table for the 19th September, to accompany 117th Brigade Order No.62.

Unit.	Present Location.	By whom relieved.	Relief to be complete or clear of present billets by.	Route.	Guides.	Destination	Remarks.
16th Notts & Derby Regt.	Battn. in reserve Woods P.18.d.	--	10 a.m.	Via ROAD JUNCTION, P.12.c.9.1.-BEAUSSART.	--	BERTRANCOURT "Z" Camp.	
17th Notts & Derby Regt.	Right Battn in the Line - "Y" Ravine Section.	1/4th Black Watch.	2 p.m.	Via WITHINGTON AV. - ENGLEBELIER - MAILLET MAILLET.	As arranged.	BEAUSSART.	
17th K.R.R.C.	Battn.in Support, Mailly Maillet.	--	11 a.m.	Via ROAD JUNCTION, P.12.c.9.1.-BEAUSSART.	--	BERTRANCOURT "Y" Camp.	
16th Rifle Bde.	Left Battn in the Line - "Y" Ravine Section.	1/1st Herts Regt.	2 p.m.	Via TIPPERARY AV. - AUCHONVILLERS Stn. HAILLY MAILLET - P.6.E.6.1.	As arranged.	COURCELLES AUX BOIS.	Not to enter before 3p.m. takes over from 1st KING'S RGT.
117th M.G.Co. (Less 2 Sectns).	In the Line.	--	2 p.m.	Via TIPPERARY AV. - AUCHONVILLERS Stn. - HAILLY MAILLET - BEAUSSART.	--	BERTRANCOURT "Z" Camp.	g Sectns. Tro-s in line under orders of G.O.C. 118 Brigade.
117th T.M.Bty.	In the Line.	--	2 p.m.	Via WITHINGTON AV. - ENGLEBELIER - MAILLY MAILLET.	As arranged.	BEAUSSART.	

NOTE:- 1. The 117th Brigade Headquarters remain at present Headquarters VITERMONT (ENGLEBELMER).
2. Billetting parties from Battalions should be at their respective destinations by 9 a.m. on the 19th, and meet their units as they enter billets.
3. All movements across the open EAST of Line MAILLY MAILLET - ENGLEBELMER will be at intervals of 100 yards between platoons, and 200 yards between Companies.

SECRET.   TABLE "B" - March and relief table for the 20th September, to accompany 117th Brigade Order No.62.

Unit.	Present billet.	Relieving.	Time & place where guides will meet incoming Battns.	Route.	Destination.	Remarks.
16th Notts & Derby Regt.	"Z" Camp, BERTRANCOURT.	In time to meet guides as ordered.	1st K.R.R.C. (99th Bde.) 17th Middlesex Regt. (6th Bde.)	Cross Roads in K.14.a. 11.30 a.m.	Via COURCELLES AU BOIS to X roads in K.14.a.	Right Battn in line HEB-UTERNE Sectn.
17th Notts & Derby Regt.	BEAUSSART.	ditto		COLINCAMPS. 2.p.m.	Any convenient.	Right Battn in Line SERRE Section.
17th K.R.R.C.	"Y" Camp, BERTRANCOURT.	ditto	1st R.Berkshire Regt. (99th Bde.)	Cross Roads in K.14.a. 10 a.m.	Via COURCELLES AU BOIS to X roads in K.14.a.	Left Battn in line HEB-UTERNE Sectn.
16th Rifle Bde.	COURCELLES AU BOIS.	ditto	13th Essex Regt. (6th Bde.)	COLINCAMPS. 11 a.m.	From COUR-CELLES to COLINCAMPS Via COURCELLES.	Left Battn in Line, SERRE Sectn.
117th M.G.Co. (less 2 Sectns).	"Z" Camp, BERTRANCOURT.	ditto	As arranged between Os.C.,117th, 6th M.G.Coy. and 99th M.G.Companies, not to interfere with Battn. reliefs.	1 Section to COLINCAMP. 1 Section to Cross Roads in K.14.a.	1 Section SERRE Sectn. 1 Section, HEBUTERNE Section.	H.Q.'s at COURCELLES AU BOIS.
117th T.M. Bty.	BEAUSSART.	ditto	As arranged between Os.C.,117th and 6th T.M.Btys, not to interfere with Battn.reliefs.	Any convenient.	SERRE Section. 6 guns in the Line.	H.Q.'s and 2 reserve guns at COURCELLES AU-BOIS.
117th Bde H.Q.'s.	VITERMONT ENGLEBELMER.		6th T.M. Battery.	Via MAILLY MAILLET and COURCELLES AU-BOIS.	SAILLY-AU-BOIS. J.18.c.5.3.	

NOTE: All movements EAST of Line COLINCAMPS - SAILLY-AU-BOIS will be by platoons at four minutes interval, and Companies at 20 minutes interval.

SECRET   A/b/b VIII   ND   Copy No. 14

117th INFANTRY BRIGADE No. 63.   25.9.1916.

Reference: 1/10,000 Map Sheet 57D. SE 1 and 2 (parts of)
           Sheet 57D. NE 3 and 4 (parts of)

1. Certain Corps of the Reserve Army are to attack the Ridge running N.W. of COURCELETTE to the SCHWABEN Redoubt at ZERO Hour on "Z" day.

2. 39th Division will carry out the following operations:-

   (a) Deliver feint attack on the Front Q.10.d.6.7. to K.35.a.2.2. at ZERO – 10 minutes on "Z" day.

   (b) Assist the Main Operation with Artillery fire, Left Group, R.F.A., covering Brigade front, will fire at selected targets throughout the day. Heavy, Medium, and Stokes, Trench Mortars will co-operate.

   (c) Discharge Smoke on the Fronts now held by the 118th and 116th Brigades commencing at ZERO minus 11 minutes.

3. All Brigade and Battalion O.P's will be manned from ZERO hour onwards, and any abnormal movement will be at once reported to Brigade Headquarters.

4. VICKERS Guns will carry out bursts of fire throughout the day on all roads and communications in rear of the Brigade Section. At least 12 Guns are to be employed, and suitably emplaced for day firing. Battle Emplacements will on no account be used.

5. In anticipation of Hostile Artillery fire and Trench Mortar fire being directed against our trenches, as many men as possible should be kept under cover.

6. There will be no R.E. parties tomorrow.

7. ZERO hour and "Z" day will be notified later.

8. Acknowledge.

                       G.S. Maxwell, Captain,
                    Brigade Major, 117th Infantry Brigade.

25.9.1916.
Copies issued at 3.30 p.m. to:-
1. 16th Notts & Derby Regt.   9. O.C., Left Group, R.A.
2. 17th   do   do   10. H.Q's, 39th Division.
3. 17th K.R.R.Corps.   11. G. O. C.
4. 16th Rifle Brigade.   12. B. M.
5. 117th Machine Gun Coy.   13. S. C.
6. 117th T.M.Battery.   14. War Diary.
7. 5th Field Coy., R.E.   15. War Diary.
8. East Anglian Field Coy.R.E.   16. Order File.

SECRET.

Copy No. 18

117th INFANTRY BRIGADE
DEFENCE SCHEME (PROVISIONAL).

1. BOUNDARIES.

2. NEIGHBOURING TROOPS.

3. DEFENSIVE SYSTEM.

4. DISTRIBUTION OF TROOPS (See Appendix "A").

5. PRINCIPLES of DEFENCE.

6. GAS.

7. MISCELLANEOUS.

APPENDICES.

A. Distribution of Troops.
B. VICKERS Machine Guns.
C. Artillery; Heavy, Medium and Light Trench Mortars.
D. S.O.S. Signals, and Retaliation Scheme.
E. Bomb, S.A.A. and Ration Stores; Water arrangements; Trench Railways.
F. Signal and Cable Communications.
G. MEDICAL Arrangements.

SECRET.   29.9.1916.

117th INFANTRY BRIGADE.

PROVISIONAL DEFENCE SCHEME while the 117th BRIGADE is holding the SERRE and HEBUTERNE Sections.

Reference: 1/10000 Sheets 57D. N.E. 3 and 4 (parts of) and 57D. S.E. 1 and 2 (parts of).
1/40000 Sheet 57D.

BOUNDARIES. 1. The Boundaries of the Brigade Section are as follows:-

On the SOUTH. FLAG Trench - K.34.b.½.9½. - thence WESTWARDS to WATERLOO BRIDGE - SOUTHERN AVENUE (inclusive to SERRE Section) - COLINCAMPS (inclusive to REDAN Section). All inclusive.

On the NORTH. K.11.c.2.0. - K.16.b.5.8½. - Road Junction at K.16.a.9.8½. - Road Junction at K.16.a.2.7. - K.9.d.2.2. - 5 Cross Roads K.15.a.9½.9. - along HEBUTERNE - SAILLY AU BOIS Road to SAILLY AU BOIS (all inclusive to HEBUTERNE Section).

The Dividing Line between the SERRE and HEBUTERNE Sections is as follows:-

Junction of Front Line and NAIRNE Street Communication Trench K.23.d.3.4. - along NAIRNE Street to K.22.d.3.1. - thence due West to Road at K.20.c.0.0. - thence to Green Line at K.19.c.1.6. (all inclusive to SERRE Section).

The Boundaries of the BATTALION Sub-sections are as follows:-

RIGHT Sub-section (SERRE Section).

    Southern Boundary: As above.
    Northern Boundary: WARLEY AVENUE inclusive to Right Sub-section.

LEFT Sub-section (SERRE Section).

    Southern Boundary: WARLEY AVENUE (exclusive).
    Northern Boundary: As above.

(contd).

Sheet 2.

RIGHT Sub-section. (HEBUTERNE Section).

   Southern Boundary: As above.

   Northern Boundary: JENA, LABOUR, PASTEUR Avenue.

LEFT Sub-section. (HEBUTERNE Section). JENA (inclusive) PASTEUR (inclusive) ex

   Southern Boundary: As above.

   Northern Boundary: As above.

NEIGHBOURING TROOPS. 2. On the RIGHT: 116th Brigade, 39th Division.

                     Headquarters at BEAUSSART.

      On the LEFT: Brigade of 33rd Division.

                     Headquarters at SAILLY AU BOIS.

DEFENSIVE SYSTEM. 3. Comprises:-

   (a) Front Line System of Fire, Support and Reserve Trenches.

   (b) A Second Line including the following posts:-
FORT SOUTHDOWN (K.21.c.8.4.) with obligatory garrison of one Platoon and one Machine Gun.
FORT BRIGGS (K.22.d.3.4.) with obligatory garrison of one Platoon and two Machine Guns.
HEBUTERNE Defences (K.15.b. and 16.a.) with obligatory garrison of two platoons and six Machine Guns).
This Line is known as the YELLOW Line.

   (c) A Third Line, known as GREEN Line which runs through COLINCAMPS and SAILLY AU BOIS.

DISTRIBUTION OF TROOPS. 4. Distribution of troops is shewn in APPENDIX "A".

PRINCIPLES OF DEFENCE. 5. (a) In case of attack the Front Line System will be held at all costs.
Troops will not fall back from any one line to any other, but all Defences will be held to the last, whether the garrisons are outflanked or not.

   (b) Should the enemy obtain a footing in our trenches he will be counter-attacked immediately.
All Commanders are responsible that plans for immediate local counter-attack are prepared and

(contd)

sheet 3.

known to all.

Counter-attack parties are as hitherto, to be told off every night, and so dispersed as to be in the Company Commander's hands, i.e. in dug-outs close to his Headquarters.

Similarly, Battalion Commanders will use their Support and Reserve Companies in like manner.

All counter-attacks will be launched without waiting for orders from, but reports of action taken will be sent to, the next Higher Authority.

(c) All approaches across the open to the Front Line from Support and Reserve Lines must be thoroughly reconnoitred, and it must be borne in mind that an immediate counter-attack across the open is almost bound to succeed, whilst a bombing attack down trenches is often liable to fail.

GAS.   6. Orders for GAS ALERT, and action to be taken in case of Hostile Gas Attacks have recently been issued to all Units.

MISCELLANEOUS.   7. All information regarding covering Artillery, Trench Mortars, Bomb and S.A.A. Stores, Water, Trench Tramways, S.O.S. Signals, Retaliation Schemes, Vickers Machine Guns, CABLE Lines, and MEDICAL Arrangements, will be found in the Appendices. (see Index).

K.E. Maxwell   Captain,
Brigade Major, 117th Infantry Brigade.

29.9.1916.

Copies sent to:-
No. 1, 16th Notts & Derby Regt.
 2. 17th   do   do
 3. 17th K. R. R. Corps.
 4. 16th Rifle Brigade.
 5. 117th Machine Gun Coy.
 6. 117th T.M. Battery.
 7. 5th Field Coy., R.E.
 8. East Ang. Field Coy., R.E.
 9. H.Q's, 39th Division.
 10. G.R.A., 39th Division.
 11. O.C., Left Group, R.A.
 12. H.Q'S, 116th Brigade.
 13. Brigade on Left.
 14. G.O.C.
 15. B.M.
 16. S.C.
 17. Bde Signal Officer.
 18. War Diary.
 19. War Diary.
 20. Order file.

APPENDIX "A"

DISTRIBUTION and LOCATION of UNITS of 117th INFANTRY BRIGADE and UNITS attached to 117th Infantry Brigade.

SERRE Section.

RIGHT Battalion:

Front Line:	Two platoons.
MONI and ROB ROY:	Three platoons.
DUNMOW, BLENAU and LEGEND:	Seven platoons.
BASIN WOOD and SACKVILLE Street:	Four platoons.
Battalion Headquarters:	LEGEND Trench (K.28.d.0.0.)

LEFT Battalion.

Front Line:	Two platoons.
JONES Street and ROB ROY:	Four platoons.
MONK Trench:	Three platoons.
DUNMOW and ROLLAND:	Eight platoons.
Battalion Headquarters:	Junction of ROLLAND and EXGENA. (K.28.b.4½.2.)

HEBUTERNE Section.

RIGHT Battalion.

Front Line:	One platoon and seven posts.
JONES Trench:	Two platoons.
KNOX Street:	Two platoons.
CABER Trench and BRISQUX:	Three platoons.
VAUBAN and FORT BRIGGS:	Four platoons.
DU GUESCLIN:	Three platoons.
VERCINGETORIX:	One platoon.
Battalion Headquarters:	VERCINGETORIX (K.22.c.3.7.)

LEFT Battalion.

Front Line:	Nine posts.
Main Fire Trench:	Nine platoons.
BUGEAUD and VILLON:	One platoon.
CARENCY:	Two platoons.
HEBUTERNE Defences; and VERCINGETORIX:	Four platoons.
Battalion Headquarters:	HEBUTERNE (K.15.b.9.8.)

(contd).

Sheet 2. (Appendix "A")

__MACHINE GUN COMPANY.__   Headquarters at COURCELLES (J.29.B.0.2.)

Under Orders of O.C., 117th MACHINE GUN COMPANY are the following:-

__SERRE Section:__   Seven guns - 6th Machine Gun Coy.
Four guns - 117th Machine Gun Coy.

__HEBUTERNE Section:__   Five guns - 99th Machine Gun Coy.
Five guns - 99th Machine Gun Coy. (In reserve at HEBUTERNE).
Three guns - M.M.G.Battery.
Four guns - 117th Machine Gun Coy.

For actual positions see Appendix "B".

__LIGHT TRENCH MORTAR BATTERY.__   Headquarters at COLINCAMPS (K.30.d.9.3.)

For actual positions and Offensive, Defensive, and

Proposed Emplacements see Appendix "C".

__ATTACHED UNITS:__

East Anglian Field Coy.,R.E. (Working in SERRE Section).   )
Headquarters: COURCELLES (J.29.B.0.6.)   )

5th Field Coy, R.E. (Working in HEBUTERNE Section)   )
Headquarters: COIGNEUX (J.3.c.5.6.)   )

252nd Tunnelling Coy., R.E. (In charge of TUNNELS in SERRE and)
HEBUTERNE Sections).   )
Headquarters: BEAUSSART.   )

Detachment XIII Corps Cavalry Regiment. (Working in SERRE Section))
Headquarters: COURCELLES.   )

117th Brigade Headquarters is in GRAVEL PIT, SAILLY-AU-BOIS
(J.18.c.5.3)

APPENDIX "B".

VICKERS MACHINE GUN EMPLACEMENTS in SERRE and HEBUTERNE Sections.

SERRE Section.

    117th Machine Gun Coy. occupy: Nos. 8, 9, 10, 11.

    6th Machine Gun Coy. occupy: Nos. 1, 2, 3, 4, 5, 6.

HEBUTERNE Section.

    3rd Bty, M.M.G's occupy: V.12, V.13, V.14.

    99th Machine Gun Coy occupy: V.15, V.11, V.10, V.9, V.8, V.5.

    117th   ditto   occupy: V.1, V.2, V.6, V.7.

Machine Gun Emplacements - SERRE Sector.

No. 1. - about K.28.d.3.0.

Open emplacement situated in MAITLAND 5 yards from Junction of same with BLENAU.

Dug-out. (Shallow)   1 Alternative emplacement.

No. 2. - about K.28.d.6.0.

Open emplacement. Situation about 20 yards N. of FLAG in a small trench connecting FLAG with BLENAU.

Dug-out. (Deep)   1 Alternative emplacement.

No. 3. - K.29.a.4½.1.

Emplacement in small offshoot of WORLEY about 100 yards East of Junction of WORLEY and MONK.

Dug-out, deep, being constructed.

No. 4. - K.28.b.9½.0.

Open emplacement - situated in MONK Trench about 200 yards South of the Junction of EXCELM and MONK. Field of fire unlimited sweeping everything to the East and N.East.

Enemy front and support line visible as also is SERRE.

Dug-out, deep, being constructed.   1 Alternative emplacement.

No. 5. - K.28.b.9½.2.

Open emplacement - situated in MONK Trench about 20 yards South of the Junction of EXCELM and MONK.
Unlimited field of fire to the East and S.East, also covering SERRE.

Dug-out, (Deep)   1 Alternative emplacement.

No. 6. - K.23.c.2½.½.

Open emplacement - situated in CAMPION 10 yards South of Junction with JORDAN.
Field of fire East to N.East covering ground for 100 yards in front of gun, then dead ground to within 100 yards of enemy front line trenches, but covers everything into and beyond SERRE.
Shallow dug-out, new deep dug-out and emplacement being made.
Two alternative emplacements.

(contd)
p t o

Sheet 2 (Appendix "B".

No. 9. K.28.b.6.6½.

In loop trench off MONK near Ration Dump about 50 yards N. of A in STAFF COPSE.

Deep dug-out is being made.   1 Alternative emplacement.

No.10. - K.28.b.2½.0.

Open emplacement being made. Covered combined dug-out and emplacement, accommodation for N.C.O. and 4 O.R. situated in ROLLAND about midway between Junction of JORDAN and NAIRNE.

Field of fire E. to N.E. covering TOUVENT Farm ridge and STAFF COPSE, followed by about 150 yards dead ground, but also covering enemy second and third line defences around SERRE.

2 Alternative emplacements, and one Aeroplane emplacement. Dug-out.

No.11. - K.27.b.5½.8½.

Situated in PALESTINE trench. Emplacement 20 yards North of Junction of PALESTINE with NORTHERN. Strong concrete emplacement with trench mounting.
Field of fire unlimited to the E. and N.E.

2 deep Dug-outs.   2 Alternative emplacements, one of which is concrete.

Machine Gun Emplacements - HEBUTERNE Section.

No.V.1. -K.23.a.90.15.   Open emplacement in recess off WRANGLE Avenue. Deep dug-out in course of construction.

No.V.2.   Open emplacement off WAGRAM between KNOX Street and VALENTIN. Deep dug-out in course of construction.

No.V.5. - K.16.d.5.5.   Open emplacement. Deep dug-out.

No.V.6.   Open emplacement in LAFAYETTE, 50 yards S. of its junction with AUERSTADT.
Deep Dug-out.   2 Alternative emplacements.

No.V.7. - K.22.d.44.   Open emplacement in FORT BRIGGS.
2 Alternative emplacements. 1 deep and 1 shallow Dug-out.

No.V.8. - K.22.a.2.3.   Covered emplacement.
Deep dug-out.   Alternative open emplacement.

No.V.9. - K.16.c.4.0.   Covered emplacement.
Deep dug-out.   Alternative open emplacement.

No.V.11. - K.16.c.1.7.   Splinterproof emplacement.
Deep dug-out in course of construction. Holds no men at present.

No.V.12. - Covered emplacement at K.16.a.70.35.
Deep dug-out shared with V.13.   Night firing position K.16.C.1.1. with deep dug-out 30 yards from gun.

No.V.13. - K.16.a.75.40.   Open emplacement. Shares dug-out with V.1

No.V.14. - K.16.b.0.7.   Open emplacement. Deep dug-out in course of construction - holds 4 men at present.
Alternative covered emplacement at K.16.b.1.8. with small dugout.

No.V.15. - K.16.b.0.0. Covered emplacement with tunnel leading to it.
Open emplacement very close, but no deep dug-out.

RIGHT Sub-section OFFICER lives in dug-out about K.34.b.3½.8½. near Right Battn H.Q's, and has command of Guns Nos.1,2,3,4,5 and 6.
LEFT Sub-section OFFICER lives in dug-out in LE CATEAU 15 yards West of ROLLAND. Has command of Guns Nos 7,8,9,10 and 11.

APPENDIX "C".

ARTILLERY; HEAVY, MEDIUM and LIGHT TRENCH MORTARS.

The following Batteries comprising LEFT GROUP cover present Front and fire on Zones described below:-

Battery.	Unit covered.	Zones.	Defence Lines.
C/179.	Right Battalion, SERRE Section.	K.29.b.20.20. K.35.a.80.70.	K.35.a.9.7½. K.35.a.9.9½. K.29.d.2½.5. K.29.b.1½.0.
D/36.	Both Battalions, SERRE Section.	K.23.d.80.35. K.35.a.80.70.	K.29.d.40.40. K.29.b.70.20. K.29.b.90.50. K.30.d.10.90.
C/186.	Left Battalion, SERRE Section.	K.23.d.90.50. K.29.b.20.20.	K.23.d.85.50. K.23.d.80.10. K.29.b.40.70. K.29.b.30.35.
A/184 & ½ C/184.	Right Battalion, HEBUTERNE Section.	K.17.d.25.35. K.23.d.90.50.	K.24.c.80.50. K.24.a.60.30. K.23.d.70.30. K.23.b.55.40. K.17.d.3.1.
B/184 & ½ C/184.	Left Battalion, HEBUTERNE Section.	K.17.d.20.55. K.17.b.05.25.	K.17.b.05.20. K.17.b.05.25.

HEAVY TRENCH MORTARS.

SERRE Section: One (9.4') Emplacement K.29.c.48.
Two (9.4') Emplacements K.23.c.18 and K.22.B.8.1.

MEDIUM TRENCH MORTARS.

SERRE Section: Two (2") Emplacements K.29.c.3.6.

HEBUTERNE Section: Three (2") Emplacements.
Two at K.17.c.2.1.
One at K.23.A.5.2.

LIGHT TRENCH MORTARS.

The Light Trench Mortars are all in the SERRE Section.

There are Six guns (Stokes) in the Line, i.e:-

(1) in WARLEY Trench near MATTHEW COPSE, (K.29.c.4½.9¾)

(2) in ROB ROY between GREY and BLENAU Streets,)
(K.29.c.4½.5))
Four in Reserve in MONK Trench K.28.B.75.35.)
K.28.b.8½.3.)

Nos 1 and 2 are Offensive Emplacements.

The following Offensive and Defensive Emplacements are also under construction:-

(Contd.- p.t.o.)

OFFENSIVE.

1. EXCEMA Trench K.29.a.7.3½.

2. WARLEY Street K.29.a.5½.9.

3. BLENAU Trench K.29.c.7½.3¾. (not yet commenced).

DEFENSIVE.

1. Junction of LE CATEAU and ROB ROY, K.29.a.5.4.

NOTE:- The remaining Two Guns are in Billet of H.Q's at COLINCAMPS until such time as more emplacements are completed.

APPENDIX "D".

S.O.S. SIGNALS and RETALIATION SCHEME.

S.O.S. SIGNALS.

1. Until further orders the S.O.S. Signal in the Reserve Army will be:-
One Red Rocket, one Blue Rocket, fired in quick succession, and repeated until the artillery opens fire.

2. The S.O.S. Signal will only be sent up at points where the enemy's Infantry is attacking.

3. The Artillery will open fire as soon as they see one Red and one Blue rocket.

4. Red and Blue Rockets will be distributed at the rate of at least 15 each per Battalion. Each Coy H.Q's should be supplied with Rockets, and also any isolated portions of the Front Line.

RETALIATION SCHEME for SERRE and HEBUTERNE Sections.

NOTE: This Scheme cancels previous schemes and comes into force at 1 p.m. September 29th.

2. ARTILLERY at disposal:-

SERRE Section.

Unit.	Objective.	Rate of fire.
C/179.	Trench system in Battery Zone.	½ round per Gun per minute for 20 minutes. All H.E.
1 H.T.M.	Located Minenwerfer emplacements.	Three rounds only.
1 M.T.Ms.	ditto	10 rounds per mortar at rate of 1 round every two minutes.
3 L.T.Ms.	Ditto and German trench system within range.	6 rounds per gun per minute.

HEBUTERNE Section.

A/184.	Trench system in Battery Zone.	½ round per Gun per minute for 20 minutes. All H.E.
2 H.T.Ms.	Located Minenwerfer emplacements.	Three rounds each only.
2 M.T.Ms.	ditto	10 rounds per Mortar at rate of one round every two minutes.

3. On receipt of CODE word and time from Left Group H.Q's, Guns and Trench Mortars open fire, on targets described above in para 2.

4. The Battalion in whose Sub-section retaliation is required will send the CODE message to BRIGADE H.Q's by priority wire, at the same time sending Duplicate message to the other Battalion in the same Section, and vice versa.

(P.T.O.)

Appendix "D" (contd)

5. Immediately retaliation is demanded, or message from other Battalion in same Section received, all trenches in the line of fire of the Heavy Trench Mortars will be cleared.

   Thus if the Left Battalion, HEBUTERNE Section, want retaliation, they send at once to BRIGADE H.Q'S CODE word for the day, say "LOTUS", sending duplicate to Right Battalion, HEBUTERNE Section, On receipt of this, Right Battalion clears trenches in the line of the Heavy Trench Mortars.

6. On arrival of the CODE message at the Brigade, a copy will be sent at once to O.C., Left Group, R.F.A., who will send Code message with Time to Group Artillery and the Trench Mortars in the Section concerned, and fire will be opened at the time given in this message.

7. The 117th Trench Mortar Battery in the SERRE Section will invariably be warned by the Left Battalion, SERRE Section, and will stand by until such time as Artillery, Heavy and Medium Trench Mortars, open fire; as soon as this is heard, fire will be opened, to conform with scheme.

APPENDIX "E"

WATER SUPPLY ARRANGEMENTS, TRENCH TRAMWAYS, and BOMB, S.A.A. &
RATION STORES.

WATER SUPPLY.

The Main Supply is based on a 4" line running from HEBUTERNE along
VERCINGETORIX and SACKVILLE Street, as far as GREY Street. The
Pump at HEBUTERNE supplying this line at present delivers about
700 gallons per hour.

From this line a 2" branch supplies a 600 gallon Tank at SUSSEX
FORT. Another 2" branch connects up with the LA SIGNY FARM -
OBSERVATION WOOD - STAFF COPSE System.

This latter system is not in working order, water being supplied
to OBSERVATION WOOD through a 2" pipe running from the SUCRERIE
(K.33.c.).

A subsidiary system consisting of a 2" pipe running from HEBUTERNE
and supplied by the same pump as the 4" line, follows the same
route as far as AUERSTAEDT trench, and supplies Tanks at the
CEMETERY, JENA and VILLARS trenches.

The water supply is in working order, but a careful check must

be kept on the R.E. Water Patrols.

TRENCH TRAMWAYS.

SERRE Section.

A trench railway starts at the COLINCAMPS end of RAILWAY AVENUE,
and runs along that trench to EUSTON where it ends.

A second Railway begins at EUSTON, and runs over the open past
LA SIGNY FARM and OBSERVATION WOOD to STAFF COPSE.

A line branches off this Railway at LA SIGNY FARM, and runs S.E.
to CHARING CROSS in rear of SACKVILLE Street to Right Battn H.Q's.

HEBUTERNE Section.

The line runs from R.E. Dump, HEBUTERNE (K.9.d.1.1.) to road
junction K.15.b.7.6., and then along the VERCINGETORIX Trench, and
Right Battn. H.Q's.

These railways are in working order.

Section.	Position of Battn Store.	Boxes in Store. S.A.A.	Mills.	R.G.	Distributed in front lines and reserves. S.A.A.	Mills.	R.G.
SERRE.							
Right Battn.	K.34.b.3.8½.	70	55	9	86	593	91
Left Battn.	OBSERVATION WOOD K.28.b.3.3.	70	83	4	285	263	57
HEBUTERNE.							
Right Battn.	VERCINGETORIX, K.22.a.2.3.	60	130	20	167	312	21
Left Battn.	K.16.a.1.6.	80	211	70	212	237	10

DISPOSITION of S.A.A. and BOMBS.

P.T.O.

Appendix "E" (contd).

RESERVE RATIONS (IRON).

K.28.c.1.2.	2000
K.28.c.2.4.	1000
K.34.a.2.9.	120
DUNMOW.	260.
BRIGGS Fort.	240
JUNCTION Trench.	320
K.16.a.2.7.	100
Total	4040.

These are not up to establishment at present as a considerable number were consumed by 2nd Division by order.

These are being made up.

RESERVE WATER SUPPLY.

Tanks for storing water are distributed at various points throughout the pipe line system (see above).

In addition there are petrol tins held in charge by all battalions which would be used in case of necessity.

APPENDIX "F".

SERRE and HEBUTERNE SECTIONS - SIGNAL COMMUNICATIONS.

SERRE Section.

Lines from COURCELLES (J.29.b.8.4.)

East Anglian Field Co., R.E.   R.E.1.   D.5 Airline.

Local Artillery, Centre Group, R.F.A. R.A.1.   D.3 Airline.

Machine Gun Coy.   M.G.1.   D.5 Airline.

O.P.   Visual tree in orchard D.5 Airline.

Brigade on Left.   See HEBUTERNE Section.

To Left Battalion. K.28.b.4.2.   H.B.38.39 Corps buried all the
way to A Dug-out, thence as H.B.70.71 to B Dug-out and
L. Battalion. The portion from COURCELLES to K of H.B.70.71
is not used.
  H.B.54.55, Corps buried through to B dug-out. Same
number throughout.
  F.1. to L.M. (K.33.b.5.0.) L and R Battalions, D.5
metallic pair to K.30.b.8.7. where one leg is labelled H.B.73
and buried, the other being trenched. Both meet at CENTRAL
Avenue, and go on as a pair to L.M. The line to the L.Batt-
alion from L.M. is labelled F.2., while there is a lateral
between Left and Right Battalions labelled F.1. Fullerphone
line.

To Right Battalion. K.34.b.2.9.   H.B.58 and 59 Corps buried all
the way through P dug-out and L.M.
  H.B.50 and 51 Corps buried all the way to P. dug-out,
thence through L.M. as H.B.56 and 57.
  H.B.60 and 61 Corps buried to L.M. only.

There is a line K.M.1 from K dug-out to K dug-out, joined
to H.H.11 to R.Bde.

HEBUTERNE Section.   Brigade H.Q's, SAILLY QUARRY (J.18.c.5.3.)

Division. SQDL 1 Phone pair, armoured cable, buried from Office to
pole outside the Dell exchange, thence connected through
to ACHEUX.

SQDL 2 used as one line for Sounder, armoured cable, buried
from Office to pole outside the Dell exchange, thence connected through to ACHEUX.

Support Battalion in the Dell SQ.99. Single comic air line.

Artillery, Left Group in Quarry SQ.98, D3 airline. metallic pair.

Brigade on Left (J.18.d.2.5) Labelled in Office 3 KSQ 6, Corps buried
to Junction Box (J.B.) 4 and onwards as D5 metallic pair
airline. From Office to J.B. 3, leaving as 3 K 6 to
J.B.4. This box is the limit of patrol from this Office
for linesmen.

Forward Lines to PDE in HEBUTERNE (K.15.b.5.7.) Labelled in Office
3 KSQ 4. Corps buried. From Office to J.B.3, leaving as
3 K 3 to J.B.4, leaving as 4K3 to J.B.5, leaving as 5K3
to J.B.6, leaving as 6K3, and so labelled in PDE. (Could
be bridged over to SQ 96 for communication with Left
Battalion.

To Left Battalion. (K.16.a.2.7.) Corps buried to A dug-
out (K.15.d.8.7.) labelled in Office 3KSQ1. From Office
to JB3, leaving as 3K1 to JB4, leaving as 4K1 to JB5,

(contd)
P.T.O.

Sheet 2 (Appendix "F")

leaving as 5KM to A dug-out. Leaves as ASN1 and so
enters Left Battn. Buried from A to Pelissier, the
remainder being D5 metallic, trenched.

To Right Battalion (K.22.c.3.6.) Corps buried, through
A dug-out, labelled in Office 3KSQ2. From Office to JB3,
leaving as 3K2 to JB4, leaving as 4K2 to JB5, leaving as
5K3 to A dug-out, leaving as ASD1 to Saalfield O.P.
(K.16.c.0.3) and entering Right Battn to SDRB1, buried
all the way.

PDE to Left Battn. D5 metallic pair airline. SQ.96.

PDE to Advanced 5th Field Coy., R.E. in Hebuterne,
SQ.97. D5 metallic pair.

SQ.100 to PDE, Left and Right Battns, used for Fullerphone.
Enters PDE and is then bridged to the two Battns, a tee
being left for use in PDE. Metallic D5 poled to K.15.a.2.1,
the remainder trenched.

Lateral Line Left Battn to Right Battn. Leaves Left Battn as ASN2,
D5 metallic trenched to Sonis O.P. (K.16.a.9.2.) and is
buried to A dug-out, leaving as ASD3, buried to Saalfield
(K.15.d.) and is buried to Right Battn as SDRB3. At
A dug-out is a tee off leading to O.P.A. Advanced Artill-
ery Exchange (call H1) situated at K.21.b.1.1., labelled
AOPA3. Outside OPA there is a tee off AOPA3 labelled
OPAOPL1 to Fort Grosvenor (K.21.a.) which it enters as
Sq.95.

Lateral Line KYB, Left Battn to Right Battn of Bde on Left. Buried,
crosses Welcome and Wood Streets.

Lines to COURCELLES buried. 3KSQ8 to JB3, leaving as 2K2 to JB2,
leaving as 2K3 to L, leaving as KL32 to K, and is bridged
over to HB 81-85 to Courcelles.

SQDL4 via the Dell and enters Courcelles as DLCL 5 and 6.

3KSQ11, via JB4,3,2, and 1 (labelled 1K1 to K poles) to
the Dell, via Bus, and enters Courcelles as BUCL 12.10

VISUAL COMMUNICATION.

There is a station at COURCELLES Bde H.Q's in a tree (J.29.b.2.8.)
which can work to Advanced Bde H.Q's at K.27.d.8.1. From a station
at this point the front line can be seen and messages can therefore
be sent DD from the front and then transmitted to the station at
J.29.b.2.8. The Right Battn H.Q's can also send DD messages to
the same station.※

※ This station is the Div.O.P. situated about 100 yards further up
Southern Trench from Advanced Bde H.Q's.

Messages can be sent from tree at J.29.b.2.8. forward to K.27.d.8.1.

PIGEONS.

Right and Right Centre Battalions.

Four Pigeons arrive at COURCELLES every other day and Pigeoners
from Right and Right Centre Battns call for them accordingly.

Left and Left Centre Battalions.

Draw four pigeons each every other day from the Advanced
Machine Gun H.Q's in HEBUTERNE which are deposited there by
the Corps.

APPENDIX "G".

MEDICAL ARRANGEMENTS.

SERRE Section.

   Right Battalion.

      Battn Aid Post: Junction of FLAG Avenue and SACKVILLE Street.
                                                                  (K.24.b.7½.8.)

      Advanced Dressing Station: COLINCAMPS.

      Motor Ambulances clear from EUSTON DUMP.

   Left Battalion.

      Battn Aid Post: OBSERVATION WOOD (K.28.b.3.3.)

      Advanced Dressing Station: COLINCAMPS.

      Motor Ambulances clear from EUSTON DUMP.

HEBUTERNE Section.

   Right Battalion.

      Battn Aid Post is at K.22.d.3.4.

   Left Battalion.

      Battn Aid Post is at K.16.a.5.5.

Advanced Dressing Station for both Battalions is at K.15.B.2.6.
There is also a Dressing Station at J.16.d.8.8.   Ambulances are
at the latter point, but they can clear from the former by
daylight.

SECRET.

Copy No. 14

117th INFANTRY BRIGADE ORDER No.64.

30.9.1916.

Reference:- 1/10000 Sheet 57D. N.E. 3 and 4 (parts of)
1/20000 Sheet 57D. N.E.

1. (a) Battalions of the 117th Infantry Brigade, and Guns of the 117th Machine Gun Company, holding the SERRE Section, will be relieved today by Units of the 99th Infantry Brigade in accordance with the attached relief table.

    (b) The 117th Trench Mortar Battery will be relieved tomorrow, October 1st., under arrangements to be notified later.

2. The relieving Battalions will not pass Eastern edge of COLINCAMPS before 4 p.m. All details of relief not mentioned in this order will be arranged direct between Commanding Officers.

3. Units will hand over on relief:-

    (i) All Trench Stores.

    (ii) All R.E. tools and materials in excess of scale laid down in Mobilization Table.

    (iii) All maps, plans, panorama and aeroplane photographs, referring to area handed over.

    (iv) All reserves of supplies, Grenades and S.A.A., authorised for Trenches and Keeps.

4. Acknowledge.

Captain,
Brigade Major, 117th Infantry Brigade.

30.9.1916.

Copies issued at 10.30 a.m. to:-
No.1, 16th Notts & Derby Regt.
   2. 17th   do   do
   3. 17th K.R.R.Corps.
   4. 16th Rifle Brigade.
   5. 117th Machine Gun Coy.
   6. 117th T.M.Battery
   7. East Anglian F.Coy.,R.E.
   8. H.Q's, 39th Division.

No.9. Left Group, R.A.
  10. C.R.A., 39th Div.
  11. G. O. C.
  12. B. M.
  13. S. C.
  14. War Diary.
  15. War Diary.
  16. Order file.

RELIEF TABLE to accompany 117th Brigade OPERATION ORDER. NO. 64.

Item.	Date.	Unit.	Relieved by.	Guides.	Destination.	Route.	Remarks.
1.	30/9/16.	17th NOTTS & DERBY Regt.	1st ROYAL BERKS Regt.	As arranged direct between C.O's.	BERTRANCOURT "Z" Camp.	Any convenient.	
2.	30/9/16.	16th RIFLE BRIGADE.	1st K. R. R. Corps.	ditto	COURCELLES.	ditto.	
3.	30/9/16.	Guns of 117th M.Gun Coy. in SERRE Section.	99th M.Gun Coy. (part of)	ditto	COURCELLES	ditto	
4.	1/10/16.	117th T.M. Battery.	99th T.M.Bty. (part of)	ditto	Not yet known.		

All movements in the open East of COLINCAMPS will be at 10 minutes interval between platoons, and 20 minutes between Companies.
Units will arrange to send forward the usual billetting parties, and
The Code word is "SPIDERS" to be used to denote Relief Complete.
Reports on arrival in billets will also be sent in.
Brigade Headquarters will remain at SAILLY AU BOIS QUARRY.

SECRET. KW VI   W.D.   Copy No. 17.

117th INFANTRY BRIGADE ORDER No. 65.

                                                              30.9.1916.
Reference 1/10000 Sheet 57D. N.E. 3 and 4 (parts of).
           1/20000 Sheet 57D. N.E.
           1/40000 Sheet 57D.

1. (a) Battalions of the 117th Infantry Brigade, and Guns of the 117th
       Machine Gun Coy., holding the HEBUTERNE Section, will be re-
       lieved tomorrow, October 1st., by Units of the 6th Infantry
       Brigade in accordance with the attached table.

   (b) The 117th Trench Mortar Battery will be relieved in the SERRE
       Section by part of the 99th Trench Mortar Battery in accordance
       with the attached table.

   (c) All details of relief not mentioned in this ORDER will be ar-
       ranged direct between Commanding Officers.

2. Units will hand over on relief:-

      (i) All Trench Stores.
     (ii) All R.E. tools and materials in excess of the scale laid
          down in Mobilization Table.
    (iii) All Maps, Plans, Panorama and Aeroplane Photographs, De-
          fence Schemes, etc., referring to the area handed over.
     (iv) All reserves of supplies, grenades, and S.A.A., authorised
          for Trenches and Keeps.

3. The 17th Notts & Derby Regiment, 16th Rifle Brigade, and 117th
   Machine Gun Coy., will act as described in the attached table.

4. The CODE word "AJAX" will be wired to Brigade H.Q.'s to denote
   Relief Complete. Reports on arrival in Billets will also be
   sent in.

5. The 117th Infantry Brigade Report Centre will close at SAILLY AU
   BOIS QUARRIES at 5 p.m., reopening at the same hour at BERTRANCOURT.

6. Acknowledge.

                                        B.E.Maxwell. Captain,
30.9.1916.   Brigade Major, 117th Infantry Brigade.
Copies issued at 3.30 p.m.to:-
No.1. 16th Notts & Derby Regt.   No.7. H.Q's, 39th Division.
   2. 17th   do   do   8. C.R.A., 39th Div.
   3. 17th K.R.R.Corps.   9. O.C., Left Group, R.A.
   4. 16th Rifle Brigade.   10. H.Q's, 6th Brigade.
   5. 117th Machine Gun Coy.   11. H.Q's, 99th Brigade.
   6. 117th T.M.Battery.   12. H.Q's, 99th Brigade.
      No.13. 5th Fld Coy., R.E.   No.17. War Diary.
         14. G. C. C.   18. War Diary.
         15. B. M.   19. Order file.
         16. S. C.

S E C R E T.   MARCH and RELIEF Table to accompany 117th Brigade OPERATION ORDER No.65.

Item.	Date.	Unit.	Present location.	Relieved by.	Guides.	Destination.	Route.	Remarks.
1.	1/10/1916.	16th Notts & Derby.	Right Battalion, HEBUTERNE Sectn.	13th ESSEX Regt.	Platoon & HQ guides to be at Road Junc. in SAILLY AU BOIS (J.18.B.3.2) at 2 pm.	BEAUSSART.	via HEBUTERNE SAILLY AU BOIS & COURCELLES.	
2.	Do.	17th Notts & Derby.	Billets, "Z" Camp, BERTRANCOURT.	-	-	Remains at "Z" Camp, BERTRANCOURT.	-	
3.	Do.	17th K.R.R. Corps.	Left Battalion, HEBUTERNE Sectn.	1st KING'S Regt. A Battn. of 99th Brigade.	As for Item 1., but at 10.30 a.m.	"Y" Camp, BERTRANCOURT.	Via HEBUTERNE SAILLY AU BOIS & COURCELLES. Direct road to BERTRANCOURT.	To be clear of COURCELLES by 10 a.m. All arrangements to be made between OsC.
4.	Do.	16th Rifle Bde.	Billets, COURCELLES. 4 Guns in Line,	-	-	"X" Camp, BERTRANCOURT	-	
5.	Do.	117th M.G.Co.	HEBUTERNE Sectn. 4 Guns in billets, COURCELLES.	Guns of 6th M.G. Coy.	As arranged, vide Remarks Column.	"Z" Camp, BERTRANCOURT	Via HEBUTERNE SAILLY AU BOIS & COURCELLES.	M.G.Cos. Relief to be complete by Noon. Relieved guns to join remainder-COURCELLES. All arrangements to be made between OsC.
6.	Do.	117th T.M.Bty.	In Line, SERRE Section.	Guns of 99th T.M. Battery.	Ditto.	"Z" Camp, BERTRANCOURT	via COLINCAMPS and COURCELLES.	T.M.Bty. Relief to be complete by Noon.
7.	Do.	117th Inf.Bde. H.Q's.	SAILLY AU BOIS QUARRIES. J.18.c.5.3.	5th Inf. Brigade H.Q's.	-	BERTRANCOURT Bde H.Q's.	via COURCELLES.	

NOTE:- 1. All movements in the Open East of SAILLY AU BOIS and COLINCAMPS will be at 10 minutes interval between platoons, and 20 minutes between Companies.

2. Units will arrange to send forward the usual billetting parties.

39th Division.

B. H. Q.

117th INFANTRY BRIGADE

OCTOBER 1916

Appendices attached:-

Brigade Orders.
Report on Operations 9th October 1916.
Report on Operations 21st October 1916.
Maps: Tracings etc.

B.M./148

To /
　　Headquarters,
　　　　39th Division.

Herewith WAR DIARIES of Brigade Headquarters, and Units of this Brigade, for the month of October, 1916.

[signature]

　　　　　　　　　　　　　　　　Brigadier General,
1.11.1916.　　　　　Commanding 117th Infantry Brigade.

Army Form C. 2118

WAR DIARY
or
INTELLIGENCE SUMMARY

(Erase heading not required.)

Instructions regarding War Diaries and Intelligence Summaries are contained in F.S. Regs., Part II. and the Staff Manual respectively. Title Pages will be prepared in manuscript.

Place	Date	Hour	Summary of Events and Information	Remarks and references to Appendices
BERTRAN-COURT.	Oct. 1.		Brigade is relieved in HEBUTERNE Section by 6th Brigade, and 117th Trench Mortar Battery in SERRE Section by 99th Trench Mortar Battery. Brigade, less 16th Rifle Brigade, now in billets at BERTRANCOURT, 16th Rifle Brigade at COURCELLES.	
	2nd		On verbal orders from 39th Division, 117th Brigade Order No.66 is issued for Brigade Head-quarters and two Battalions to move on 2nd October to billets at HEDAUVILLE, and for Brigade less these Units to move to MARTINSART WOODS on the 3rd.	App. 1.
			The 17th Notts & Derby Regt., and 16th Rifle Brigade, move to billets at HEDAUVILLE. 117th Brigade Order No.67 issued for move of rest of Brigade to MARTINSART WOODS. On orders from 39th Division, Brigade Headquarters does not move until the 3rd.	App. 2.
SENLIS.	3rd		Units of Brigade, less 17th Notts & Derby Regiment, and 16th Rifle Brigade, move to MARTINSART WOODS. Brigade Headquarters move to SENLIS.	
MARTINSART.	4th		Brigade Headquarters move to dug-outs at W.6.d.10. South of MARTINSART. 117th Infantry Brigade Order No.69 issued for Brigade to relieve 55th Infantry Brigade in THIEPVAL Section on the 5th. 1/1st Cambs Regt., and 11th Royal Sussex Regiment, being attached from the 118th and 116th Brigades respectively.	App. 3.
PASSERELLE de MAGENTA.	5th		Brigade relieves 55th Infantry Brigade in THIEPVAL Section in accordance with 117th Brigade Order No.69. Three Battalions in the Line, one in Brigade Support, and two in Brigade Reserve. 7th Brigade is on the right, and 118th on the left. Brigade Headquarters moves into dug-outs at PASSERELLE de MAGENTA between MESNIL and THIEPVAL WOOD.	
	6th		Nothing unusual. Enemy artillery active throughout the day.	
	7th		Enemy artillery active throughout the day. At 6.15 p.m. small enemy bombing and flammenwerfer attack on SCHWABEN REDOUBT, which was easily repulsed. No Infantry attack. Our artillery barraged until 7.45 p.m.	
	8th		At 5 a.m. enemy attacked our front line from Point 10 to Point 22 held by the 17th Notts & Derby on the right, and 16th Notts & Derby in the centre, and succeeded in entering our trenches at Point 27. The enemy were driven out almost immediately leaving 25 prisoners in our hands.	App. 4.

1875 Wt. W593/826 1,000,000 4/15 J.B.C. & A. A.D.S.S./Forms/C.2118.

WAR DIARY or INTELLIGENCE SUMMARY

Army Form C. 2118

Page 2.

(Erase heading not required.)

Place	Date	Hour	Summary of Events and Information	Remarks and references to Appendices
PASSERELLE de MAGENTA	8th (contd)		Their casualties were severe, ours slight. The remainder of the day was quiet, but their artillery was very active during the night.	
	9th	4.30 a.m.	At 5am 4.30 a.m. three Companies of the 16th Notts & Derby Regiment assaulted the front face of the SCHWABEN REDOUBT between R.19.d - 99 - 49 - 39. The Right Company reached its objective between Points 99 and 69, but eventually had to withdraw. The Centre Company failed entirely to reach objective, but the Left Company succeeded in advancing its bombing block about 60 yards. Our casualties were heavy, 13 Officers being killed wounded or missing, and approximately 200 Other Ranks. See App.8 for full report of operation. At 6.55 p.m. S.O.S. signal was reported, but on investigation proved to be false. The rest of the day was exceptionally quiet.	App. 4 to 8.
SENLIS.	10th		The 117th Brigade relieved by the 118th Brigade in the THIEPVAL Section. 17th K.R.R.Corps moved to billets NORTH and SOUTH BLUFFS, AUTHUILLE; 16th Rifle Brigade to dug-outs near PIONEER Road, W.9.b. and d.; 17th Notts & Derby Regt., 117th Machine Gun Coy., and 117th T.M.Battery to MARTINSART Woods; 16th Notts & Derby Regt. to SENLIS. Brigade Headquarters at SENLIS.	App. 9.
	11th		Cleaning up and inspections, etc., under Battalion arrangements.	
	12th		Training under Battalion arrangements, one Company, 17th Notts & Derby Regiment, permanent working party NAB Valley Railway. The 17th K.R.R.Corps took over the line held by the 1/1st Herts Regiment, 118th Brigade, who were to attack the SCHWABEN REDOUBT. The attack was postponed for 24hours, but the 17th K.R.R.Corps remained in the line. A carrying party of 420 men provided by 16th Rifle Brigade at night.	
	13th		Working parties amounting to 420 men and 10 Officers provided by 17th Notts & Derby Regiment, carrying party of 410 men provided by 16th Rifle Brigade, 16th Notts & Derby Regiment attended demonstration of trench digging.	
	14th		118th Infantry Brigade captured the remainder of SCHWABEN REDOUBT. The 17th K.R.R.Corps remained under Orders of G.O.C., 118th Brigade, and 16th Rifle Brigade were placed at his disposal.	

Army Form C. 2118

WAR DIARY
or
INTELLIGENCE SUMMARY

(Erase heading not required.)

Page 3.

Instructions regarding War Diaries and Intelligence Summaries are contained in F. S. Regs., Part II. and the Staff Manual respectively. Title Pages will be prepared in manuscript.

Place	Date	Hour	Summary of Events and Information	Remarks and references to Appendices
SENLIS.	15th		17th K.R.R.Corps take over captured line from Units of 118th Brigade. Orders received to relieve 118th Brigade in RIVER Section, THIEPVAL, on 16th., and 117th Brigade Order No.73 issued accordingly.	App.10.
PASSERELLE de MAGENTA.	16th		Enemy Counter-attack on SCHWABEN REDOUBT repulsed by 17th K.R.R.Corps. The Brigade relieves 118th Brigade in RIVER Section, and 12th R.Sussex Regiment relieve 17th K.R.R.Corps. We have two Battalions of Notts & Derby Regiment in front line, 16th Rifle Brigade in Support, and 17th K.R.R.Corps in reserve. The 116th Infantry Brigade is on our right, and 189th on our left. Brigade Headquarters move to PASSERELLE de MAGENTA.	
	17th		Nothing abnormal.	
	18th		Usual artillery activity. 117th Infantry Brigade Order No.74 issued for minor operation in conjunction with attack by 116th Infantry Brigade on STUFF Trench.	App.11.
	19th		The minor operation postponed 24 hours. Weather conditions bad, operations postponed a further 24 hours. 117th Infantry Brigade Orders Nos 75 and 76 issued for relief of 17th Notts & Derby Regiment by 16th Rifle Brigade.	App.12 and 13.
	20th		At about 5 a.m. the enemy makes an attack on trenches and bombing posts held by 17th Notts & Derby Regiment. The attack, which was prepared by an intense bombardment, was completely unsuccessful. A report is attached.	App.14.
			The 17th K.R.R.Corps relieve 14th Hampshire Regiment in the SCHWABEN REDOUBT, and come under orders of G.O.C., 116th Infantry Brigade. Vide 117th Infantry Brigade Order No.77.	App.15.
			Owing to the relief of 17th Notts & Derby Regiment by 16th Rifle Brigade, the Orders for the minor operation to be carried out on 21st are varied, the consolidating parties company being detailed from the latter Unit.	
	21st		The enemy counter-attacked the front held by 17th K.R.R.Corps at about 5 a.m. after intense artillery preparation. The attack, which was made with picked troops, was repulsed with heavy losses. 93 prisoners, including 4 officers, remained in our hands, and at least 50 Germans were killed. Our losses were approximately 3 Officers, and 20 Other Ranks.	App.16.

Army Form C. 2118

WAR DIARY
or
INTELLIGENCE SUMMARY

(Erase heading not required.)

Page 4.

Instructions regarding War Diaries and Intelligence Summaries are contained in F. S. Regs., Part II. and the Staff Manual respectively. Title Pages will be prepared in manuscript.

Place	Date	Hour	Summary of Events and Information	Remarks and references to Appendices
PASSERELLE de MAGENTA.	21st (contd)		The minor operation detailed in previous operation orders was carried out, ZERO time being 12.6 p.m. Point 16 was captured in about five minutes, Point 47 was also taken, and a bombing block established. Owing to lack of cover, and difficulty of ascertaining its position on the ground, the attack on Point 38 was not pressed. Report appended.	App. 17.
			The 116th Infantry Brigade on our right having attacked and captured STUFF Trench, the Divisional front is contracted, and 117th Infantry Brigade Order No.78 is issued accordingly. We now hold from R.19.d.9.9. to the River ANCRE, with three Battalions in the line, the 17th K.R.R.C. on the right, the 16th Rifle Brigade in the Centre, and the 16th Notts & Derby Regiment on the left. The 17th Notts & Derby Regiment are in support.	App. 18.
	22nd		Brigade on our right relieved by 56th Infantry Brigade. 19th Division now on our right, and front redistributed. Dividing line between REDOUBT and RIVER Sections is now R.19.d.99 - 92.	
			Enemy artillery active against our front.	
			Our casualties during 21st and 22nd amount to nearly 270.	
			117th Infantry Brigade Order No.79 issued for relief of 17th K.R.R.Corps by 4/5th Black Watch from 118th Infantry Brigade on 23rd, and of 16th Rifle Brigade by another Battalion of the 118th Brigade on 24th.	App. 19.
	23rd		17th K.R.R.Corps relieved by 4/5th Black Watch, and become Battalion in Brigade Reserve. 117th Machine Gun Coy., and 117th Trench Mortar Battery, relieve their opposite numbers in 116th Brigade in SCHWABEN REDOUBT.	
			A General Attack is to take place on the 25th. The 118th Brigade, reinforced by one Battalion, 116th Brigade, and one Battalion, 117th Brigade, is to carry out the attack on the objective allotted to 39th Division. The 16th Notts & Derby Regiment is to carry out a subsidiary attack up the Valley of the River ANCRE. 117th Infantry Brigade Orders issued accordingly.	
			A very misty day up to past mid-day. The Attack postponed 24 hours, and 117th Infantry Brigade Order No.82 issued. 16th Rifle Brigade to be relieved in RIVER Centre Sub-section by 17th Notts & Derby Regiment. 16th Rifle Brigade then become Battalion in Brigade Reserve, displacing	App. 21.

1875 Wt. W593/826 1,000,000 4/15 J.B.C. & A. A.D.S.S./Forms/C. 2118.

Army Form C. 2118

WAR DIARY
or
INTELLIGENCE SUMMARY

Page 5.

(Erase heading not required.)

Instructions regarding War Diaries and Intelligence Summaries are contained in F.S. Regs., Part II. and the Staff Manual respectively. Title Pages will be prepared in manuscript.

Place	Date	Hour	Summary of Events and Information	Remarks and references to Appendices
PASSERELLE de MAGENTA.	23rd (contd)		17th K.R.R.Corps, who move up into Support.	
	24th		Wet, going heavy. 17th Notts & Derby Regiment relieve 16th Rifle Brigade in River Centre Sub-Section. 117th Infantry Brigade Order issued for relief of the Brigade on 25th by the 116th Infantry Brigade.	App.22.
PIONEER Road.	25th		The Brigade is relieved by 116th Infantry Brigade, and moves to the BLUFFS and PIONEER Road with Brigade Headquarters in PIONEER Road. The relief worked smoothly.	
			The G.O.C. addresses 17th K.R.R.Corps, and congratulates them upon their defeat of the German Counter-attack on the SCHWABEN REDOUBT on the 21st. This Battalion has received congratulations from the II Corps, and the Reserve Army.	
	26th		Orders received to take over the line from 116th Brigade on the 27th, and 117th Infantry Brigade Order No. 84 issued accordingly.	App. 23.
PASSERELLE de MAGENTA.	27th		We relieve 116th Infantry Brigade in the RIVER Section in accordance with 117th Infantry Brigade Order No. 84.	
	28th		A quiet day. The following Brigade Orders are issued:- 117th Infantry Brigade Orders Nos 85, 86 and 87, with regard to the General Attack originally to have taken place on the 25th. No.85 gives Divisional Objectives, No.86 details of Subsidiary Attack to be carried out by 16th Notts & Derby Regiment, and No.87 Orders for 116th and 117th T.M.Batteries to be under command of O.C., 117th Trench Mortar Battery. 117th Infantry Brigade Orders Nos 80 and 81 are cancelled.	See 23rd. App. 24, 24a. and 24b.
SENLIS.	29th		Brigade is relieved by 118th Brigade, and moves to MARTINSART Woods, and SENLIS, with Brigade Headquarters at SENLIS. (See 117th Infantry Brigade Order No. 88)	App.25.
	30th		Rest, cleaning equipment, and kit. 17th K.R.R.Corps bathe.	
	31st.		750 men found for working parties.	

[signature]
Brigadier General,
Commanding 117th Infantry Brigade.

SECRET.   Copy No. 13

117th BRIGADE ORDER No. 66.

1.10.1916.

Reference: 1/40000 Sheet 57D.

1. The following moves will take place tomorrow:-

   The 117th Brigade Headquarters, 17th Notts & Derby Regiment, and 16th Rifle Brigade, will move independently from present billets to HEDAUVILLE.

   The 17th Notts and Derby Regiment, and 16th Rifle Brigade, will be clear of present billets by 2 p.m.

   The 117th Brigade Headquarters will be clear of present billets by 3 p.m.

   In each case ROUTE will be via BERTRANCOURT and FORCEVILLE.

2. The 16th Notts & Derby Regiment, and 17th K.R.R. Corps, 117th Machine Gun Coy., and 117th Trench Mortar Battery, will remain where they are tomorrow, but will move to MARTINSART WOODS on October 3rd. Further orders regarding this move will be issued later.

   Brigade Transport will remain in BEAUSSART until further orders.

3. Billetting parties from the 17th Notts & Derby Regiment, and 16th Rifle Brigade, will meet the Staff Captain at HEDAUVILLE Church (P.34.a.5.0) at <u>11 a.m. tomorrow.</u>

4. The 117th Infantry Brigade Report Centre will close at BERTRANCOURT at 3 p.m. tomorrow, reopening at HEDAUVILLE at the same hour.

5. Acknowledge.

                                            W.G. Maxwell   Captain,
                                          Brigade Major, 117th Infantry Brigade.

1.10.1916.

Copies issued at 9.30 p.m. to:-

    No.1. 16th Notts & Derby Regt.   7. H.Q's, 39th Division.
       2. 17th   ditto   8. Bde Signal Officer.
       3. 17th K.R.R.Corps.   9. G.O.C.
       4. 16th Rifle Brigade.   10. B.M.
       5. 117th Machine Gun Coy.   11. S.C.
       6. 117th T.M.Battery.   12. War Diary.
                                          13. War Diary.
                                          14. Order file.

SECRET.   AAp II   W.D   COPY No. 12

117th INFANTRY BRIGADE ORDER No. 67.   2.10.1916.

Reference 1/40000 sheet 57D.

1. The following moves will take place tomorrow, October 3rd:-

   (a) The 16th Notts & Derby Regiment, 17th K.R.R.Corps, 117th Machine Gun Company, and 117th Trench Mortar Battery, will move independently to MARTINSART WOODS (in squares W.2. and W.3.). In each case route will be via BEAUSSART, Cross Roads in P.12.c., Road Junction in P.23.d., Cross Roads in Q.25.a., thence from ENGLEBELMER via Road running through squares Q.25.b., Q.25.d., Q.31.b., Q.32.c., Q.32.d. to MARTINSART.

   (b) After passing BEAUSSART Units will move at intervals of 200 yards between Companies and 100 yards between Platoons.

   (c) Units will pass the Road Junction (J.33.d.5.0.) in the following order at times stated below:-

16th Notts & Derby Regiment	1.30 p.m.
17th K. R. R. Corps	2.15 p.m.
117th Machine Gun Coy	2.45 p.m.
117th Trench Mortar Battery	3. p.m.

   (d) The 117th Brigade Headquarters will march from BERTRANCOURT to FORCEVILLE at 10.30 a.m.

2. Billeting parties from the 16th Notts & Derby Regiment, 17th K.R.R.Corps, 117th Machine Gun Coy., and 117th Trench Mortar Battery, will meet the Staff Captain at MARTINSART CHURCH (W.3.a.8.2.) at 11 a.m. tomorrow.

3. The 17th Notts & Derby Regiment, and 16th Rifle Brigade, will remain at HEDAUVILLE.

4. The 117th Infantry Brigade Report Centre will close at BERTRANCOURT at 10.30 a.m. tomorrow, reopening at FORCEVILLE at the same hour.

5. Acknowledge.

                                            Captain,
                           Brigade Major, 117th Infantry Brigade.

2.10.1916.

Copies sent at 6.30 p.m. to:-
No. 1. 16th Notts & Derby Regt.
    2. 17th   ditto
    3. 17th K. R. R. Corps.
    4. 16th Rifle Brigade.
    5. 117th Machine Gun Coy.
    6. 117th T.M.Battery.
    7. H.Q's, 39th Division.
    8. Bde Signal Officer.
    9. G. O. C.
   10. B. M.
   11. S. C.
   12. War Diary.
   13. War Diary.
   14. Order file.

SECRET.   App III   Copy No. 21
W.D.

117th INFANTRY BRIGADE ORDER No. 69.

4.10.1916.

Reference: Sheet 57D. 1/40000.
           57D. S.E. 1/20000.
           St. PIERRE DIVION Trench Map.

1. The 117th Brigade, and Two Battalions from the 116th and 118th Infantry Brigades, will relieve the 55th Infantry Brigade in the THIEPVAL Section tomorrow, October 5th., under the following arrangements, in accordance with the attached table.

   All details not mentioned in these orders will be arranged direct between Commanding Officers concerned.

   Trench Stores, etc., will be taken over in the usual manner.

2. ADVANCE PARTIES.

   The Advance Parties mentioned in the table will consist of Company Commanders and Company Officers (numbers at the discretion of Commanding Officers), and the requisite number of Guards and Bombing Posts (all of whom should be selected bombers) to take over dangerous posts during the hours of daylight.

   The posts to be so relieved by the Advance Parties are as follows:-

   Right Battalion: Pts. 45 and 15.
   Centre Battalion: Pts. 27, 99, 61, 39, 19.
   Left Battalion: Pts. 36 and 47.

   In all cases spare men for extra guards or posts will accompany these advance parties, as they will be required should the situation change during the night 4th/5th. (Attention is called to Paras. 4 and 5 re Rations, Bombs and Mills Cups, etc.)

   The Advance Parties from the 17th K. R. R. Corps, 1/1st Cambs. Regiment, and the Battalion from the 116th Bde., will be more in the nature of billetting parties, and are necessary since no guides will be available for these Battalions from the 55th Bde.

3. MACHINE GUNS and LIGHT TRENCH MORTARS.

   The 117th Machine Gun Coy., and 117th T.M. Battery, will act in accordance with the attached table. They will detail two men and a proportion of N.C.O's to each Gun or Mortar position, to help personnel of the 55th Machine Gun Company and Trench Mortar Battery, and get to know the Lie of the Land before changing Guns

(P.T.O.)

- 2 -

or Mortars on the morning of the 6th.

They will proceed to the various Gun positions as soon as possible after arrival in the Trenches.

The remainder of the Personnel from the 117th Machine Gun Coy., and 117th Trench Mortar Battery, will be accommodated with their guns and mortars at the Headquarters of the 55th Machine Gun Coy., and 55th Trench Mortar Battery, respectively.

4. RATIONS.

In addition to the Emergency Ration, Two Days' Rations will be carried by each Officer and man of the three Front Line Battalions, 117th Machine Gun Company, and the 117th Trench Mortar Battery.

Orders re drawing these will be issued later.

5. BOMBS.

(a) Each man of the Companies who will be in the Front Line will carry TWO bombs (detonated). Immediately on arrival in the Front Line these Bombs ARE TO BE AT ONCE COLLECTED, and placed in Sandbags, and dumped in Dug-outs.

Care must also be taken to provide the Guards and Bombing Posts to go on ahead in a similar manner. Bombs on wheels can be used - those that are used will be replaced in the usual manner.

(b) All available Very Pistols will be carried up, and 50 rounds of Very Ammunition carried by the owner of each pistol.

(c) Every Bombing Post is to be provided with a proportion of Mills Cups on a basis of one for two men of the post.

Every Bombing Post will carry up in sandbags 50 Mills Rifle Grenades and Cartridges. Notification regarding the drawing of these will be issued later.

6. O.C., 17th K.R.R.Corps, will arrange to hold in readiness Two Working Parties of 100 men each. These may be required at any minute by day or night, and must be told off before going into the trenches.

7. On taking over trenches all Units in the Front Line will ensure that liaison exists between all other Units on their Right and

/Left.

- 3 -

Left/.

Battalion Commanders will also ensure that they have liaison between the Battalion Headquarters on their Right and Left, and that a proportion of their Runners know the Routes to Brigade H.Q's.

8. <u>RUNNERS</u>.

The 17th K.R.R.Corps, and 1/1st Cambridgeshire Regiment, will each detail EIGHT Guides per Front Line Battalion, i.e. 32 Guides. These Guides will meet the respective Front Line Battalions at the Rendezvous stated for Platoon Guides in the attached table. They will accompany the respective Battalions to the Front Line, returning to their Battalions as soon as the Battalion in question has taken over.

9. <u>DRESS</u>.

(a) All Runners of Front Line Battalions will work without Equipment or Rifles until further orders.

(b) Front Line Battalions will not carry packs. Rations and Waterproof Sheet will be carried in the haversack, and three pairs of Socks in breast pockets.

10. An Administration Order regarding Cooking and Ration Arrangements, Position of First Line Transport, Water, Supply of Bombs and S.A.A., Trench Stores, etc., will be issued by the Staff Captain.

11. Battalions will report RELIEF COMPLETE, and ARRIVAL in BILLETS, by wire or runner, using the Code Word "CRAIGROY".

12. The 117th Infantry Brigade Report Centre will close at ARRET (W.3.D.1.0) at 3 p.m. tomorrow, reopening at Brigade Headquarters Q.29.d.45.50. at the same hour.

13. <u>Acknowledge</u>.

W.G.Maxwell. Captain,
Brigade Major, 117th Infantry Brigade.

4.10.1916.

Copies issued at 9.30 p.m. to:-
No. 1. 16th Notts & Derby Regt.
    2. 17th   ditto
    3. 17th K.R.R. Corps.
    4. 16th Rifle Brigade.
    5. 117th Machine Gun Coy.
    6. 117th T.M.Battery.
    7. H.Q's, 116th Brigade.
    8. H.Q's, 118th Brigade.
    9. H.Q's, 55th Brigade.
   10. H.Q's, 7th Brigade.
   11. 1/1st Cambs Regt.
   12. Battn of 116th Bde.
13. No.3 Coy.Train,A.S.C.
14. H.Q's, 39th Division.
15. C.R.A., 39th Division.
16. C.R.E., 39th Division.
17. G.O.C.
18. B.M.
19. S.C.
20. Bde Signal Officer.
21. and 22. War Diary.
23. Order file.

SECRET.

RELIEF TABLE.

To accompany 117th Infantry Brigade Order No. 69.

Item.	Date.	Unit.	Relieving.	Sub-section or Locality.	Guides for Advance Party.	Platoon Guides for Unit.	Remarks.
1.	5/10/1915.	16th Notts & Derby.	7th Buffs.	THIEPVAL Centre.	55th Bde H.Q's. 8 a.m.	Cross Roads at W.15.b. 75.35. 12 noon.	
2.	do.	17th Notts & Derby.	6th Berks.	THIEPVAL Right.	Crucifix Corner 9 a.m.	Crucifix Corner, 2 p.m.	
3.	do.	17th K.R.R.C.	--	Battn in Bde Support. All Coys in LEIPSIC Salient (HINDENBURG and LEMBERG Trenches) Battn H.Q. WOOD Post X.1.c.5.65.	Advance Parties to be sent on early to find exact accommodation and Guide in Companies, as they arrive. Head of Battalion not to pass Cross Roads W.15.B.75.35. before 2 p.m.		
4.	do.	16th R.B's.	R.West Kent Regt.	THIEPVAL Left.	Point where Tramway leaves the road at Q.35.d.40. 99. 8 a.m.	Point where Tramway leaves the road at Q.35.d.40.99. 2 p.m.	
5.	do	117th M.G.C.	55th M.G.C.	--	M.G.Coy arrives LANCASHIRE DUMP (Q.35.c.3.2.) at 8 a.m. where guide of 55th M.G.C. will meet them.	--	Guns will be carried up to THIEPVAL Dugouts on 5th. Guns of 55th Bde not actually relieved till 6th.
6.	do	117th T.M.By.	55th T.M.Bty.	--	T.M.Batty arrives LANCASHIRE DUMP 9.30 a.m. where guide from 55th T.M.B. will meet them.	--	Mortars will be carried to 55th T.M.B. H.Q. on the 5th. Guns of 55th T.M.Batty will not be actually be relieved till the 6th.

(P.T.O.)

- 2 -

Item.	Date.	Unit.	Relieving.	Sub-section or Locality.	Guides for Advance Party.	Platoon Guides for Unit.	Remarks.
7.	5/10/1916.	1/1st Cambs.	--	Battn in Bde Reserve in North Bluff Q.36.c.7.8. and South Bluff W.6.A.	Advance Parties to be sent on early to find exact accommodation and guide in Companies as they arrive. Head of Battalion not to pass Cross Roads W.16.B.75.35. before 5 p.m.		
8.	do.	Battn of 116th Brigade.	--	To be notified later.			
9.	do.	117th Brigade H.Q's.	55th Brigade H.Q's.	Brigade H.Q's, Q.29.D.45.50.	Will arrive at 55th Brigade Headquarters at 3 p.m.		

NOTE: All movements North East of Line AVELUY and MARTINSART will be at intervals of 200 yards between Companies, and 100 yards between Platoons. These intervals will be increased at the discretion of O.C., Units, after passing this Line.

SECRET.   Copy No. 22

117th INFANTRY BRIGADE ORDER No. 70.

7.10.1916.

Reference: Trench Map 1/5000.
           Trench Map 1/10000.

1. The following Operation will be carried out by the 117th Infantry Brigade at an hour and date to be notified later, which will depend entirely on the state of the going. Three Companies of the 16th Notts & Derby Regiment will assault and occupy the whole of the remainder of the SCHWABEN Redoubt.

2. OBJECTIVE Points. R.19.d.99 - R.19.d.6.9. - R.19.b.6.2. - R.19.d. 4.9. - 3.9. - 19 Central.

3. INFORMATION.

   It is believed that there are two German Dug-outs about Point 99, some Dug-outs in Communication Trench leading from Points 49 and 69, and at least three between Points 39 and 19. All of these are in Square R.19.d. There is probably a Machine Gun between Points 49 and 39.

4. PLAN of ATTACK.

   During the previous night three patrols will peg out tapes to indicate assembly positions, as near to the hostile line as possible, running roughly on a Front R.20.c.1.9. - R.19.d.6.8./-3.8./- R.19.9½.8. - each tape will be long enough for the assembly of each Company on a Two Platoon Front in four waves, and square to its objective. Previous to ZERO hour the Companies will assemble as noiselessly as possible on the assembly tapes. At ZERO they will advance direct to the assault, the leading waves taking care to get well past each objective and into the open beyond, leaving the second waves to deal with the dug-outs that are found, and which form the enemy's strong points.

   The 4th Company, 16th Notts & Derby Regiment, will still hold the bombing blocks as at present, and form the Point d'appui for the attack.

5. CONSOLIDATION.

   Two Sections, 234th Field Company, R.E., will be placed at the disposal of O.C., 16th Notts & Derby Regiment, and assemble in

/Dug-outs

P.T.O.

- 2 -

Dug-outs near Point 65, and Company Headquarters.

6. ARTILLERY AND TRENCH MORTARS.

The 18th and 39th Divisional Artillery will open a Barrage on German Communication Trench running through LUCKY WAY - 19.b.6.4. - 9.5. - MAISEY LANE - STRASBURG Trench. They will not open fire until 0.10. Stokes Mortars will open intense fire at extreme range down the STRASBURG Trench and Point 64. On the objectives being gained one Stokes Mortar will be pushed up to Point 27. Any other targets upon which it is required to bring fire to bear will be arranged direct between O.C., 117th Trench Mortar Battery, and O.C., 16th Notts & Derby Regiment.

7. MACHINE GUNS.

O.C., 117th Machine Gun Company, will barrage all the trenches mentioned in the Artillery Programme. On the objective being gained, two Guns each will be pushed up to Points 99 and 39.

O.C., 117th Machine Gun Company, will fire at selected targets in consultation with the Brigade Staff.

Supporting fire from the 116th Infantry Brigade will be arranged.

8. STORES.

One Company, 17th K.R.R.Corps, will be placed at the disposal of O.C., 16th Notts & Derby Regiment, to carry up Bombs, and R.E. Stores, to Company Headquarters in SCHWABEN Redoubt. 100 Rations and 50 tins of Water will also be dumped there.

9. SUPPORTING BATTALION.

O.C., 17th K.R.R.Corps, will move up two Companies to take over the positions vacated by the assaulting Companies of the 16th Notts & Derby Regiment in THIEPVAL.

O.C., 1/1st Cambridgeshire Regiment, will move up two Companies to take over Dug-outs vacated by 17th K.R.R.Corps in LEIPSIC Salient.

10. COMMUNICATION.

Assaulting troops will carry Red Flares, as it is hoped to arrange for Contact Patrol. Four baskets of Pigeons will be sent to 16th Notts & Derby Headquarters by Brigade Signalling Officer, who will also arrange Visual from that point rearwards.

11 ADVANCED AID POST. will be established at Advanced Battalion Headquarters, and a RELAY POST established in MARTIN'S LANE about

(contd)

- 3 -

R.25.b.9.8.

12. CAPTURED PRISONERS will be sent to Brigade Headquarters at PASSERELLE de MAGENTA.

13. Synchronisation of Watches will be notified later.

14. BRIGADE HEADQUARTERS will remain at PASSERELLE de MAGENTA, but a Liaison Officer from the Brigade will be at 16th Notts & Derby Headquarters.

15. Acknowledge.

F.G.Maxwell Captain,
Brigade Major, 117th Infantry Brigade.

8.10.1916.

Copies issued to:-

No.1. 16th Notts & Derby Regt,	13. H.Q's, 116th Brigade.
2. 17th ditto	14. 234th Field Coy.,R.E.
3. 17th K.R.R.Corps.	15. 225th ditto
4. 16th Rifle Brigade.	16. 1/1st Cambs. Regt.
5. 117th Machine Gun Coy.	17. 13th Gloucesters.
6. 117th T.M.Battery.	18. G.O.C.
7. H.Q's, 39th Division.	19. B.M.
8. ditto.	20. S.C.
9. C.R.A., 39th Division.	21. Bde Signal Officer.
10. C.R.A., 18th Division.	22. War Diary.
11. H.Q's, 7th Brigade.	23. War Diary.
12. H.Q's, 118th Brigade.	24. Order file.

SECRET.   Copy No. 22
              117th INFANTRY BRIGADE.
                                         8.10.1916.

1. The Operations described in 117th Infantry Brigade Order No.70 will take place tomorrow morning, 9th October.

2. ZERO hour will be at 4.30 a.m.

3. Watches will be synchronised at 11.30 p.m. tonight, 8th October, at Headquarters, 16th Notts & Derby Regiment, THIEPVAL CHATEAU, by an Officer of the Brigade Staff. All Units taking part in the Operations will send an Officer Representative for this purpose. The Brigade Staff Officer will remain at the Headquarters of the 16th Notts & Derby Regiment throughout the operations.

4. Reference Para.6 of 117th Brigade Order No. 70. Our artillery barrage will not be opened until 0.20.

5. In the event of rain falling to any great extent between now and ZERO hour, Operations will be postponed.
   The final decision as to whether Operations will take place or not will be wired Priority to Brigade Headquarters by O.C., 16th Notts & Derby Regiment; The word "EGGS" being used to denote that Operations will take place, and the word "COAL" being used to denote Operations will not take place.

6. The word "COAL" will be wired to Units taking part in the Operations if Operations are cancelled.

7. Acknowledged.

                              W.S. Maxwell   Captain,
8.10.1916.   Brigade Major, 117th Infantry Brigade.

Copies issued at 7 p.m. to:-

No.1. 16th Notts & Derby Regt.   13. H.Q's, 116th Brigade.
   2. 17th   ditto   14. 234th Field Coy., R.E.
   3. 17th K.R.R.Corps.   15. 225th   ditto
   4. 16th Rifle Brigade.   16. 1/1st Cambs Regt.
   5. 117th Machine Gun Coy.   17. 13th Gloucesters.
   6. 117th T.M.Battery.   18. G.O.C.
   7. H.Q's, 39th Division.   19. B.M.
   8.   ditto   20. S.C.
   9. C.R.A., 39th Division.   21. Bde Signal Officer.
  10. C.R.A., 18th Division.   22. War Diary.
  11. H.Q's, 7th Brigade.   23. War Diary.
  12. H.Q's, 118th Brigade.   24. Order file.

SECRET.

18th DIVISIONAL ARTILLERY ORDER NO. 23.

by Brig. Gen. S.F. Metcalfe, D.S.O.

Reference $\frac{1}{5000}$ Trench Maps.

(1) On the morning of the 9th inst., at dawn (about 4.30 a.m.) three companies of the 16th Notts & Derby Regt. will assault and occupy the whole of the remainder of SCHWABEN Redoubt.

(2) OBJECTIVES.

R.19.d.9.9. - R.19.d.6.9. - R.19.b.6.2. - R.19.d.4.9.

R.19.d.3.9. and 19 central.

(3) During the night patrols will peg out tapes to indicate assembly positions, as near to the hostile line as possible, running roughly on a front R.20.c.1.9. - R.19.d.6.8. - 3.8. R.19.c.9½.8. Previous to zero hour the companies will assault as noiselessly as possible on the assembly tapes. At zero, they will advance direct to the assault, the leading waves taking care to get well past each objective and into the open beyond leaving the second waves to deal with the dug-outs that are found and which form the enemy' strong points.

(4) The 18th Div. Artillery and 39th Div. Artillery will assist in the operation by barraging approaches from 20 minutes after zero time.

(5) Tasks of 18th Div. Artillery 18-pdrs will be as under:-

82nd Brigade enfilade HANZALINE from R.19.b.6.4. to R.14.c.0.1. and approach from R.19.b.9.6. to R.19.b.95.30.

83rd Brigade enfilade STRASBURG LINE from R.19.a.9.1. to ST. PIERRE DIVION.

84th Brigade will shell LUCKY WAY from R.20.a.5.1. to R.20.b.2.7. and trench running from R.20.a.6.2. to R.20.a.8.8.

85th Brigade will enfilade STUFF Trench from R.20.a.5.1. to R.20.b.6.5.

(6) 4.5" Howitzers will be distributed as follows:-

D/82 ----- R.19.a.6.3. - 5.4. - 4.5.

D/84 ----- R.20.a.3.2. - 5.1. - 6.2.

(7) In order to avoid a sudden outburst of fire which would inevitably draw the enemy's barrage, Brigades will start firing in succession at the following times:-

82nd Brigade 0.22.
83rd Brigade 0.26.
84th Brigade 0.20.
85th Brigade 0.24.

-2-

(8) Brigades will barrage approaches allotted to them by sudden bursts of fire at irregular intervals. Ammunition will be expended approximately at the following rates:-

From 0.20 to 0.30 ----- 1 round per gun per minute.
From 0.30 to 0.45 ----- 2 " " " " "
From 0.45 to 1.00 ----- 1½ " " " " "
From 1.00 to 2.00 ----- 1 " " " " "
From 2.00 to 3.00 ----- ½ " " " " "

Namely, approximately 150 rounds per gun.

(9) From 3 hours after zero, fire will be kept up according to circumstances.

(10) Brigades should be prepared to return to normal barrage front should occasion arise to do so.

(11) From dawn onwards, Observing Officers of 82nd & 83rd Brigades should be prepared to engage any parties which may be visible in vicinity of areas allotted to them.

(12) The fire of 83rd and 85th Brigades has been crossed with the object of obtaining better enfilade fire on their respective objectives, and with a view to establishing a different barrage from that to which the enemy is now accustomed.

(13) Watches will be synchronised at 11.0 p.m. to-night. Zero time will be communicated later.

(14) 39th Div. Artillery are co-operating by enfilading MAISIE LANE, and by bringing fire to bear on STRASBURG LINE.

(15) Please acknowledge.

                                                Major, R.A.,
                                    Brigade Major, 18th Div. Artillery.
8/10/16.

Issued at 9.0 p.m.

Copies to:-
117th Infantry Brigade.
39th Div. Artillery.
82nd Brigade
83rd   "
84th   "
85th   "
File.

App VII

War Diary

SECRET.

Copy No. 3

8/10/1916.

ARTILLERY ORDER NO. 37.
==*=*=*=*=*=*=*=*=*=*

1. In co-operation with an attack by the 39th Division to-morrow, 9th October, to complete the capture of the SCHWABEN REDOUBT, the action of the II Corps H.A. will be as follows:-

    (a) 0.20 - 3 hours.   4 - 60-pdrs search LUCKY WAY between R 14 d 9.3 - R 20 a 7.3.
    (within safety limits).
    4 - 60-pdrs search STUFF TRENCH from R 20 b 8.5 - 0.2.
    (within safety limits).
    4 - 60-pdrs search R 14 d 1.6 - R 20 a 6.5. (within safety limits).
    40 rounds per hour each task.

2. From 0.20 - 0.40 every hostile battery known to shell the area of operations will be neutralized.
From 0.40 Onwards there will be neutralizing fire as called for.

3. ZERO hour is 4.30 a.m. on the 9th.

4. Acknowledge. ✓

Issued at 11.55 p.m.

               Major. R.A.
            S.O.R.A. II Corps.

Copy No. 1 to R.A. Reserve Army.
       2 to 'G' II Corps.
       3 & 4 to 39th Division.
       5 to 39th Divisional Artillery.
       6 to II Corps. H.A.
       7 to 11th Divisional Artillery.
       8)
       9) Retained.
      10)

H.Q. 117 Bde.

Passed for information

9/10/16.

REPORT on OPERATIONS carried out on the morning of the 9th
October, 1916.

In accordance with orders an attack was made having for its objective the front face of the SCHWABEN Redoubt between R.19.d. - 99 - 69 - 49 - 39.

Three Companies of the 16th Notts & Derby Regiment were employed each of whom had the following objectives:- On the Right - Strong Point at 99; in the Centre-from Point 69 to 49, thence to the junction of HANSA Trench; on the Left - Point 39 working Westwards. During the night the assembly positions of the three Companies were successfully taped out which left the assaulting troops about 150 yards to cover. The assembly was carried out without difficulty except for a little shelling. The Companies attacked in depth. The assault was carried out at 4.30 a.m. under cover of darkness, and without artillery barrage. It was hoped by this means that the intervening space between the assembly positions and the German trenches would be crossed before the enemy had time to put a barrage down on "No man's Land", previous experience having shewn that it was very quickly available and very accurately placed in between our front line running from 15 to 45 and the German trenches. The assaulting waves had, however, not gone more than half the distance before Machine Gun and Rifle fire was opened as they rose the crest. The enemy barrage was not put down till 4.38 although there was some intermittent shelling. The Right Company succeeded in reaching its objective, and passing between Points 99 and 69 made good the German trench, but in so doing they received a large number of casualties. The Centre Company on arriving at the front line of the German trenches found that there was a considerable amount of wire in front of it. The Left Company were held up just South of Point 39 with a heavy Machine Gun and Rifle fire. It should be stated that the German line cannot be be seen from our lines, nor is it under artillery observation. On the Right a Bombing fight ensued, the enemy pushing up considerable numbers of men. This fight lasted about an hour when our

/bombs

were exhausted. All enemy bombs which could be found were utilised and some were brought up from Point 27 by the Battalion Bombers of the 17th Notts & Derby Regiment. The enemy eventually forced the party back and Point 99 was lost. The Centre Company failed entirely to reach the objective; they were heavily fired on and bombed, and therefore retired into shell holes in close proximity to the German lines and kept up a heavy fire. On the Left the course of the fight was similar to that of the Right, except that the Bombing Block previously held was advanced some 60 or 70 yards.

The tactical result achieved was nil, with the exception of the slight advance mentioned above. Our position is otherwise the same as when the assault started.

It appears to me necessary to employ at least a Battalion and a half in order to make good this objective. If I had to carry out the Operation over again I should suggest that it will be necessary, notwithstanding the destruction of dug-outs, to deal with the German trenches with heavy artillery on previous days. I should carry out the assault under an intense barrage from field artillery. This presents difficulties because the trench is not observable from the ground, but I have no doubt it could be done successfully. To carry out the bombardment of the trenches it will be necessary to withdraw the Forward Stops.

It is satisfactory to know that a large number of Germans were killed especially about Point 99 which was fully occupied, and the dug-outs therein bombed. A good number of German dead can be seen lying about on the Forward Blocks as especially on the Right they advanced to the counter attack. Our own casualties were heavy, and amount to 13 Officers and 200 Other Ranks. With the exception of two Officers killed, the others were only wounded.

9.10.1916.

Brigadier General,
Commanding 117th Infantry Brigade.

SECRET.   App. IX   WD   Copy No. 22

117th INFANTRY BRIGADE ORDER No.71.

9.10.1916.

Reference: Sheet 57D. 1/20000
            57D. S.E. 1/20000.
            St. PIERRE DIVION Trench Map.

1. The 117th Infantry Brigade will be relieved tomorrow morning, the 10th instant, by the 118th Brigade in the THIEPVAL Section, under the following arrangements, and in accordance with the attached table. All details not mentioned in these Orders will be arranged direct between Commanding Officers concerned.

    Trench Stores, detail of work, all paper trench maps recently issued shewing trenches on our front, exact description of trenches handed over, full detail of Water, S.A.A., Bomb and Ration supplies, etc., will be handed over in the usual manner.

2. ADVANCE PARTIES.

    The 118th Brigade will send forward Advance Parties to take over all Bombing Blocks in the front line before the arrival of the remainder of their Units.

    Battalion Commanders will ensure that these posts are correctly placed, and full detail regarding the posts handed over.

    For further arrangements regarding Guides for these Advance Parties, etc., see attached table.

3. MACHINE GUNS and LIGHT TRENCH MORTARS.

    The relief of the 117th Machine Gun Company, and the 117th Trench Mortar Battery, will be in accordance with the attached table but all details of relief will be arranged between Commanding Officers of those Units with their Opposite Numbers direct. A proportion of N.C.O's and men from the 118th Brigade will arrive this afternoon, and will be attached to each Gun and Mortar position in order that they may get to know the lie of the land.

4. Destinations after Relief Complete will be in accordance with the attached table.

5. O.C., 16th Notts & Derby Regiment, will arrange for a hot meal to be served at some convenient place en route to SENLIS.

6. Evacuation of Wounded. O.C., 117th F. A. Corps, will ensure that all wounded in the SCHWABEN Redoubt are evacuated before the relief

/takes

- 2 -

takes place.

7. Battalions will report Relief Complete and Arrival in Billets, by wire or runner, using the Code Word "CORRIEHALLOCH" to denote Relief Complete.

8. Units will arrange to send forward the usual billetting parties. Representatives from those Units billetting in MARTINSART Wood will meet the Staff Captain at the Town Major's Office, MARTINSART, at 10 a.m. tomorrow for the allocation of billets.

9. The 117th Infantry Brigade Report Centre will close at PASERELLE de MAGENTA at 6 p.m., reopening at SENLIS at the same hour.

10. Acknowledge.

Captain,
Brigade Major, 117th Infantry Brigade.

9.10.1916.

Copies issued at 4.30 p.m. to:-

No. 1. 16th Notts & Derby Regt.
2. 17th ditto
3. 17th K. R. R. Corps.
4. 16th Rifle Brigade.
5. 117th Machine Gun Coy.
6. 117th T.M.Battery.
7. 1/1st Cambs Regt.
8. H.Q's, 116th Brigade.
9. H.Q's, 118th Brigade.
10. H.Q's, 7th Brigade.
11. No.3 Train, A.S.C.
12. H.Q's, 39th Division.
13. ditto
14. C.R.A., 39th Division.
15. C.R.A., 18th Division.
16. C. R.E., 39th Division.
17. Bde Signal Officer.
18. G. O. C.
19. B.M.
20. S.C.
21. War Diary.
22. War Diary.
23. Order file.

SECRET.

117th INFANTRY BRIGADE.

MARCH and RELIEF Table to accompany the 117th Brigade Order No. 71

Item.	Date.	Unit.	Relieved by.	Sub-section or Locality.	Guides for advance Party.	Platoon Guides.	Destination after relief.	Route.	Remarks.
1.	10/10/1916.	16th N & Derby/less 1 Coy.Attd. 17 K.R.R.C. and 1 Coy. 17th K.R. R.C.	1/1st Cambs.	Battn in Bde Support - LEIPSIC Salient Redoubt & WOOD Post.	—	As arranged	SENLIS.	Any convenient.	All arrangements to be made direct with O.C.1/1 Cambs. Relief to be complete by 12 noon.
2.	do	17th Notts & Derby.	1/1st Herts.	THIEPVAL Right.	Crucifix Corner. 8 a.m.	Crucifix Corner. 10 a.m.	MARTINSART Wood.	Any convenient.	—
3.	do	17th K.R.R.C. ✶	4/5th B.Watch.	THIEPVAL Centre.	Cross Road at W.16.b.75.35. 8 a.m.	Cross Roads at W.16.b.75.35. 10.30 a.m.	BLUFFS North and South AUTHVILLE. Dug-outs near	Any convenient.	Relieves 1/1 Cambs Regt.
4.	do	16th R.Bde.	6th Cheshires.	THIEPVAL Left.	Point where tramway leaves Road at Q.35.d.40.99.	Point where tramway leaves Road at Q.35.d.40.99.	Pioneer Road. W.9.b. and d.	Any convenient.	—
5.	do	117th M.G.C.	118th M.G.C.	—	As arranged.	As arranged.	MARTINSART Wood.	Any convenient.	Arrangements to be made direct with O.C.118 MGC.
6.	do	117th T.M.Bty.	118th T.M.Bty.	—	As arranged	As arranged.	ditto	Any convenient.	Arrangements to be made direct with O.C.118 TMB.
7.	do	117th Bde H.Q.	118th Bde H.Q.	—	—	—	SENLIS.	Any convenient.	—

NOTE: All movements N.E. of line AVELUY and MARTINSART will be at intervals of 200 yards between Companies and 100 yards between Platoons. These intervals will be decreased at the discretion of Os.C. Units after passing East of this Line.

✶ (less one Company) and one Company 16th Notts & Derby Regt.

SECRET.

App X

W.D.

Copy No. 19

AMENDMENT TO 117th BRIGADE ORDER No. 73.

ITEMS 1 and 2 of the RELIEF TABLE.

In Column "Platoon Guides for Unit" -

in Item 1 for 12 noon read 2 p.m., and

in Item 2 for 2 p.m. read 12 noon.

[signature] Captain,
Brigade Major, 117th Infantry Brigade.

16.10.1916.

Copies issued to all recipients of 117th Brigade Order No.73.

SECRET.   Copy No. 19.

117th INFANTRY BRIGADE ORDER No.73.
15.10.1916.

References: 1/10000 Sheet 57D. S.E. 1 and 2 (parts of).

1. The 63rd Division will relieve the 39th Division in the Line North of the ANCRE by 12 noon on the 16th October.

2. The 116th Brigade will be relieved tomorrow by the 116th and 117th Infantry Brigades as follows:-

    (a) The 116th Infantry Brigade will relieve on a front from R.20.d. 0.1. to R.19.c.8.2. inclusive. This Section will be known as the REDOUBT SECTION.

    (b) The 117th Infantry Brigade will relieve on the line from R.19. c.8.2. exclusive to the River ANCRE. This Section will be known as the RIVER SECTION.

    All reliefs must be complete by 7 p.m.

    (c) The dividing line between the REDOUBT and RIVER SECTIONS is the line R.19.c.7.5 - R.19.c.9.8 - R.19.d.0.3 - and thence South along the middle of the former "No Man's Land".

3. One relief, the 117th Infantry Brigade will take over the following dispositions:-

    RIGHT FRONT Battalion: 17th Notts & Derby Regiment.

        Two Companies from R.19.c.9.8 - 8.6 - 4.7 - 4.5 - 3.5, and old German front line trenches within the boundary described in Para 2(c).

        Two Companies in PAISLEY AVENUE and PAISLEY DUMP.

        NOTE: One Company will probably be pushed up as soon as arrangements can be made to Dug-outs in old German line about R.25.b.2.8.

        Battalion Headquarters at R.19.c.9.1.

    LEFT FRONT Battalion: 16th Notts & Derby Regiment.

        Two Companies from R.19.c.1.3. to the River ANCRE.

        Two Companies in PAISLEY AVENUE and PAISLEY DUMP.

        Battalion Headquarters in PAISLEY AVENUE.

    Battalion in Brigade SUPPORT: 16th Rifle Brigade.

        NORTH and SOUTH BLUFFS, AUTHUILLE.

    Battalion in Brigade RESERVE: 17th K.R.R. Corps.

        Dug-outs in PIONEER Road.

P.T.O.

117th MACHINE GUN COMPANY:

Six guns now in vicinity of HAMEL will remain.

Ten guns of the 118th Machine Gun Company will be relieved by eight guns. Remaining two guns, and 117th M.G.Company H.Q's will be at NORTH BLUFF.

117th TRENCH MORTAR BATTERY: Will have four guns in the line with the 17th Notts & Derby Regt. Battery H.Q's and Reserve Guns will be at NORTH BLUFF.

117th BRIGADE HEADQUARTERS: Will be at BASSEVILLE de MAGENTA.

(a) The Relief will take place in accordance with the attached table, and all details not mentioned in this order will be arranged direct between C.Os concerned.

(b) Commanding Officers, Company Commanders, an Officer from the 117th M.G.Coy., and Officer from the 117th T.M.Battery, and a proportion of N.C.O's, will report at 118th Brigade H.Q's, BASSEVILLE de MAGENTA, at 9 a.m. tomorrow, for preliminary reconnaissance of the line. Guides will be provided.

(c) Advance parties consisting of Bombing Posts, etc., from the two front line Battalions will rendezvous at the 118th Brigade H.Q's at 10 a.m.

(d) The leading Platoon of the 17th Notts & Derby Regiment will arrive at 12 noon at the point where the tramway leaves the Road at A.35.d.40.99, where platoon guides will meet them. The 16th Notts & Derby Regiment will arrive at the point described above at 2 p.m., where guides will also be provided. The 117th Machine Gun Coy., and 117th T.M.Battery, will arrange all details of relief with their opposite numbers. In all cases relief must be complete before 7 p.m., 16th instant.

5. The carriage of Bombs, Very Pistols, Mills Cups, Rifle Grenades, will be the same as ordered in Brigade Order No.69.

Dress for the front line Battalions will be as ordered in Brigade Order No.69.

6. Trench Stores, Detail of work, and all particulars regarding the Section will be taken over as usual.

7. Transport lines and Quartermaster's Stores will remain where they are at present.

8. Units will report RELIEF COMPLETE by wire or runner using the

/Code

- 3 -

Code word "GREEN".

9. 117th Infantry Brigade Report Centre will close at SENLIS at 3 p.m. tomorrow, reopening at PASERELLE de MAGENTA at the same hour.

10. Acknowledge.

[signature] Captain,

15.10.1916.   Brigade Major, 117th Infantry Brigade.

Copies issued to:- 11.55 am 15/10

No.1. 16th Notts & Derby Regt.
   2. 17th   ditto
   3. 17th K. R. R. Corps.
   4. 16th Rifle Brigade.
   5. 117th Machine Gun Coy.
   6. 117th T.M.Battery.
   7. H.Q's, 116th Brigade.
   8. H.Q's, 118th Brigade.
   9. No.3 Coy Train, A.S.C.
 10. H.Q's, 39th Division.
 11. H.Q's, 39th Division.
 12. C.R.A., 39th Division.
 13. C.R.E., 39th Division.
 14. H. O. C.
 15. B. M.
 17. S. C.
 18. Bde Signal Officer.
 19. War Diary.
 20. War Diary.
 21. Order file.
 22. 225th Field Coy.,R.E.

SECRET.

RELIEF TABLE.

To accompany 117th Brigade Order No. 73.

Item	Date.	Unit.	Relieving.	Sub-section or Locality.	Guides for Advance Party.	Platoon Guides for Unit.	Route.	Remarks.
1.	16/10/1916.	16th Notts & Derby.	Part of 1/5th Cheshires.	RIVER Section Left.	C.35.d.40.99. 10 a.m.	C.35.d.40.99. 12 noon.	Any convenient.	
2.	do.	17th Notts & Derby.	Part of 1/6 Cheshires.	RIVER Section Right.	ditto	C.35.d.40.99. 2 P.M.	ditto	
3.	do.	17th K.R.R.C.	--	Battn in Brigade Reserve, PIONEER Road.				After being relieved by Battn of the 116th Brigade will proceed by any convenient route to destination.
4.	do.	16th R.E.	--	Battn in Brigade Support, AUTHUILLE BLUFFS.				Remains at AUTHUILLE BLUFFS.
5.	do.	117th M.G.C.	10 guns,118 M.G.Coy.	RIVER Section.				All details of this relief to be arranged direct. Relief to be complete by 7 p.m. 6 Guns at HAMEL remain where they are.
6.	do.	117th T.M.B.	Guns of 118 T.M.Bty.	RIVER Section.				All arrangements of relief to be made direct. Four guns to be placed in the line with the RIGHT Sub-section.
7.	do.	117th Bde. H.Q's.	118th Bde H.Q's.	PASSRELLE de LAGENTA.	--	--	Any convenient.	

NOTE:- 1. All movements North East of line AVELUY and MARTINSART will be at intervals of 200 yards between Companies, and 100 yards between Platoons. These intervals will be increased at the discretion of O.C., Units, after passing this line.

2. LEWIS GUNS will move up with their Battalions.

SECRET.   App XI   Copy No. 19

117th INFANTRY BRIGADE ORDER No 74.
                                                                18.10.1916.

Reference:- 1/5000 Map St. PIERRE DIVION and GRANDCOURT.
            1/20000, 57D. S.E.

1. Under order from 39th Division the 117th Infantry Brigade, in conjunction with the operation on STUFF Trench (to be carried out by the 116th Brigade) will push forward along the trenches on its front.

2. It is proposed to capture and hold Points 38 and 16, pushing out a Bombing Block 100 yards along PAISLEY Lane, or such less distance as is convenient.

3. Strong points are to be constructed at Points R.19.c.62.90 - R.19.c. 36.90. Trench 38 to 16 will be cleared. The second blocks we now hold between 45 and 16 and just West of Point 47 will be held as Supporting Points.

4. One Company, 17th Notts & Derby Regiment, will be utilised as the attacking party, and a second Company held in readiness to consolidate the line.

5. Artillery. It may be possible to arrange co-operation by certain elements of the 39th Divisional Artillery. Any such arrangements will be communicated later.

6. The Two VICKERS Guns at Point 86 are placed at the disposal of O.C., 17th Notts & Derby Regiment, for any action he may think necessary. The VICKERS Guns in RIVER Left Section will create a barrage on the German front and second line trenches, and communication trenches. They will not fire East of the line 97 - 90 - 04.

7. Six STOKES Guns are placed at the disposal of O.C., 17th Notts & Derby Regiment, for intense bombardment and barrage.

8. The operation will be carried out at ZERO, which will be notified later, plus 10.

9. The Reserve Company of the 17th Notts & Derby Regiment now at PAISLEY Avenue will move up into Dug-outs in the old German Front Line about R.25.b.2.8., and be in position in these dug-outs one hour before ZERO.

10. As soon as the Company of the 17th Notts & Derby Regiment has vacated dug-outs in PAISLEY Avenue, the O.C., 16th Rifle Brigade, will send forward one Company from North and South Bluffs to take over these dug-outs.

                                                                (P.T.O.)

11. Prisoners of War will be sent to Brigade Headquarters, PASERELLE de MAGENTA, and thence to the Prisoners of War Collecting Station at G.35.d.4.8., under as small an escort as possible.

12. **Medical arrangements.** The Advanced Aid Post is at R.25.b.2.9. Stretcher and Walking cases will proceed via old German Front Line to JOHNSTONE'S Post, A.D.S. O.C., 17th Notts & Derby Regiment, will have call on the Company of the 16th Rifle Brigade at PAISLEY Avenue, for Relay Stretcher Bearing Parties, if required.

13. A Contact Patrol Aeroplane will fly over the area of attack from ZERO hour on October 19th. Five N.C.O's and men per Platoon will be detailed to carry three Flares each.
    Flares will be lit by the leading Infantry at ZERO plus one hour, and again at ZERO plus two hours.
    A supply of Flares will be sent up this evening.

14. OsC., 16th Notts & Derby Regiment, 17th Notts & Derby Regiment, 16th Rifle Brigade, and 117th Machine Gun Coy., will each send an Officer to Brigade Headquarters at 12 noon tomorrow to synchronise watches. Synchronisation with O.C., 117th Trench Mortar Battery, will be made direct by O.C., 17th Notts & Derby Regiment, at his Battn Headquarters.

15. Brigade Headquarters will remain at PASERELLE de MAGENTA.

16. Acknowledge.

W.E.Maxwell Captain,
Brigade Major, 117th Infantry Brigade.

18.10.1916.

Copies issued at 1/hrs to:-

No.1. 16th Notts & Derby Regt.	12. C.R.A., 39th Division.
2. 17th do do	13. A.D.M.S., 39th Division.
3. 17th K. R. R. Corps.	14. 225th Coy., R.E.
4. 16th Rifle Brigade.	15. G. O. C.
5. 117th Machine Gun Coy.	16. B. M.
6. 117th Trench Mortar Bty.	17. S. C.
7. H.Q's, 116th Brigade.	18. Bde Signals Officer.
8. H.Q's, 118th Brigade.	19. War Diary.
9. H.Q's, 189th Brigade.	20. War Diary.
10. H.Q's, 39th Division.	21. Order file.
11. ditto	

SECRET.   App XII   WD   Copy... 20

117th INFANTRY BRIGADE ORDER No.75.

                                                        19.10.1916.

Reference: 1/5000 St.PIERRE DIVION Trench Map.
           1/20000 57D. S.E.

1. The Operations which were to have taken place today are postponed for 24 hours.

2. If Operations are postponed again tomorrow, the 16th Rifle Brigade will relieve the 17th Notts & Derby Regiment in RIVER Right Sub-section, completing the relief by 4 p.m. If on the other hand the Operations take place tomorrow the following arrangements will be carried out:-

(a.) The Two Companies of the 17th Notts & Derby Regiment (the Assaulting Company and Supporting Company) as detailed in 117th Brigade Order No.74, will remain in their present positions, and carry out the assault as directed in the above quoted Order. The Support Company now in dug-outs in old German Front Line about R.25.b.2.8 and 2.9 will be relieved by 11 a.m. tomorrow by a Company of the 16th Rifle Brigade, and proceed after relief to dug-outs in SOUTH BLUFFS, AUTHUILLE. O.C., 16th Rifle Brigade, will also send up another Company to dug-outs in old German Front Line and Support Line, about R.25.b.2.6. and 4.6. These Two Companies of the 16th Rifle Brigade will then come under orders of O.C., 17th Notts & Derby Regiment.

(b) Thus at 11 a.m. tomorrow the positions of the 17th Notts & Derby Regiment, and 16th Rifle Brigade, will be as follows:-

One Company, 17th Notts & Derby Regt., holding line from Point 13.95.86.5.7.

One Company,   ditto   holding line from Point 91-84-1.5-5.0.

One Company,   ditto   In dug-outs in PAISLEY Avenue.

One Company,   ditto   in SOUTH BLUFFS, AUTHUILLE.

Battalion Headquarters, ditto   R.25.b.2.8.

Two Companies, 16th Rifle Brigade, under orders of O.C., 17th Notts & Derby Regiment, in dug-outs in old German Front Line about R.25.b.2.8 - 2.9 - 2.6 - 4.6.
Two Companies, 16th Rifle Brigade, and Battalion Headquarters, at North and South BLUFFS, AUTHUILLE.

                                                        P.T.O.

3. O.C., 16th Rifle Brigade, will arrange to relieve rest of the 17th Notts & Derby Regiment, as soon after the conclusion of the operations as possible, and the Company of the 17th Notts & Derby Regiment at PAISLEY Avenue will move to NORTH or SOUTH BLUFFS. After being relieved the Battalion Headquarters, and all four Companies of the 17th Notts & Derby Regiment, will be at NORTH and SOUTH BLUFFS, AUTHUILLE.

4. The Commanding Officers and of the 17th Notts & Derby Regiment, and 16th Rifle Brigade, will arrange all further details of relief direct. Should the Operations prove successful, the O.C., 16th Rifle Brigade, may find it necessary to move his reserve Company from PAISLEY Avenue to the old German Front Line.

5. All other arrangements for the Operations tomorrow will be as stated in 117th Brigade Order No. 74.

6. Acknowledge.

W.E.Maxwell   Captain,

.10.1916.
                                Brigade Major, 117th Infantry Brigade.

Copies issued at 5.30 p.m. to:-

No.1. 16th Notts & Derby Regt.
  2. 17th   ditto
  3. 17th K.R.R.Corps.
  4. 16th Rifle Brigade.
  5. 117th Machine Gun Coy.
  6. 117th T.M.Battery.
  7. H.Q's, 116th Brigade.
  8. H.Q's, 118th Brigade.
  9. H.Q's, 119th Brigade.
 10. H.Q's, 39th Division.
 11. B.C's, ditto.

 12. C.R.A., 39th Division.
 13. C.R.E., 39th Division.
 14. A.D.M.S., 39th Div.
 15. 225th Field Coy., R.E.
 16. G.O.C.
 17. B.M.
 18. S.C.
 19. Bde Signal Officer.
 20. War Diary.
 21. War Diary.
 22. Order file.

SECRET.   XVII   WD   Copy No. 20

117th INFANTRY BRIGADE ORDER No. 76.
                                                          19.10.1916.

1. Reference 117th Infantry Brigade Order No. 75. Operations for tomorrow, the 20th October, have been postponed. The postponement will probably be for 24 hours.

2. The 16th Rifle Brigade will therefore relieve the 17th Notts & Derby Regiment in the RIVER Right Sub-section tomorrow, the 20th October.
   All details of relief will be arranged direct between Commanding Officers concerned.
   The relief to start at 7 a.m., and should be complete by 12 noon. The 16th Rifle Brigade will hold this Sub-section in the same manner as now held by the 17th Notts & Derby Regiment.

3. After relief the 17th Notts & Derby Regiment will be located at NORTH and SOUTH BLUFFS, AUTHUILLE.

4. The Code Word "EDINBURGH" will be wired to Brigade Headquarters to denote completion of relief.

5. Acknowledge.

                                          C. Maxwell, Captain,
19.10.1916.   Brigade Major, 117th Infantry Brigade.

Copies issued at   to:-

No. 1. 16th Notts & Derby Regt.   12. C.R.A., 39th Division.
    2. 17th   ditto   13. C.R.E., 39th Division.
    3. 17th K.R.R. Corps.   14. A.D.M.S., 39th Division.
    4. 16th Rifle Brigade.   15. 225th Field Coy., R.E.
    5. 117th Machine Gun Coy.   16. G.O.C.
    6. 117th T.M. Battery.   17. B.M.
    7. H.Q's, 116th Brigade.   18. S.C.
    8. H.Q's, 118th Brigade.   19. Bde Signal Officer.
    9. H.Q's, 189th Brigade.   20. War Diary.
   10. H.Q's, 39th Division.   21. War Diary.
   11.   ditto   22. Order file.

117th INFANTRY BRIGDE.

REPORT on the German attack on Point 16 on the morning of the 20th October.

During the whole of yesterday, the 19th instant, the German Artillery fire on the front held by the RIVER Right Battalion was more intense than usual, and was kept up during the night of the 19th/20th. Just before 5 a.m. the fire grew more intense, attention being specially directed to Points 45, 86, 94 and 91. At about 5 a.m. the alarm was given that the Germans were attacking from the direction of Point 38 towards Points 45, also across "No man's land" from the trench running between Points 16 and 38, and from Point 16. Accordingly the S.O.S. Signal was sent up, and all ranks stood to. It would appear that his intention was to cut off our posts at the POPE'S NOSE. His attack, which we met with heavy rifle and rifle grenade fire, was a half-hearted one, and in no cases did he succeed in reaching our trenches or bombing blocks. It appeared that the Germans required a considerable amount of urging, and it seemed as if they were being kicked up out of their trenches, as a man or two got up and then got back again. His losses, however, must have been severe, and one Platoon Commander states that he dropped a rifle grenade in the middle of a group of six, and knocked them all out. Our Lewis Guns are reported to have done good work.

Our Artillery were somewhat slow in taking up the S.O.S. Signal but their barrage seemed to be effective when it started. The S.O.S. Signal was apparently not seen by the Left Artillery Brigade, possibly owing to the mist in the Ancre Valley. This requires adjustment.

It was noticed that the Germans employed the following ruse: a party of one or two Germans would wave their hands looking as if they wished to surrender, thus inducing our men to shew themselves as targets for the snipers who lay ready waiting.

Our casualties were not excessive, practically all being caused by the German barrage.

(Sd) W.G.MAXWELL, Captain
Brigade Major for Brigadier General
Commanding 117th Infantry Brigade.

20.10.1916

SECRET.   AMc XV   W.D.   Copy No. 19

117th INFANTRY BRIGADE No. 77.
20.10.1916.

Reference: 1/5000 St. PIERRE DIVION Trench Map.
1/20000 57D. S.E.

1. The 17th K.R.R.Corps will relieve the 14th Hampshire Regiment in the SCHWABEN REDOUBT today. Arrangements must be made to send forward advance Parties to reconnoitre the line to be taken over. Battalion Headquarters of the 14th Hampshire Regiment are in BULGAR Trench. After relief the 17 K.R.R.C. will come under orders of G.O.C., 116th Brigade.

2. Guides from the 14th Hampshire Regiment will be at the derelict tank at the Eastern end of BLIGHTY VALLEY at 3 p.m. today.

3. The 17th K.R.R.Corps will move up via CRUCIFIX Corner and BLIGHTY Valley.

4. All details of relief, intervals, etc., to be arranged direct between C.O.s concerned.

5. Machine Guns, and Light Trench Mortars, of the 116th Brigade, will remain in their present positions in SCHWABEN REDOUBT.

6. O.C., 17th K.R.R.Corps, will see that each man carries up two bombs, and that a proportion of No.23 Rifle Grenades, Mills Cups, and S.O.S. Signals, are also carried up.

7. The Code Word "CANDLES" will be sent by wire or runner to denote completion of relief.

8. Acknowledge.

R F Maxwell Captain,
20.10.1916.   Brigade Major, 117th Infantry Brigade.

Copies issued at 11 a.m. to:-

No. 1. 16th Notts & Derby Regt.   12. C.R.A., 39th Division.
    2. 17th   ditto   13. C.R.E., 39th Division.
    3. 17th K.R.R. Corps.   14. G.O.C.
    4. 16th Rifle Brigade.   15. B. M.
    5. 117th Machine Gun Coy.   16. S.C.
    6. 117th T.M. Battery.   17. Bde Bombing Officer.
    7. 14th Hampshire Regt.   18. Bde Signals Officer.
    8. H.Q's, 116th Brigade.   19. War Diary.
    9. H.Q's, 118th Brigade.   20. War Diary.
   10. H.Q's, 39th Division.   21. Order file.
   11.   ditto

SECRET.   Copy No.....

117th INFANTRY BRIGADE.

20.10.1916.

1. 117th Brigade Order No.74 will be carried out tomorrow, October 21st., with the following variations:-

    One Company, 17th Notts & Derby Regiment, already detailed, will carry out the assault as laid down in the Order.

    One Company, 16th Rifle Brigade, will replace the Second or Consolidating Company of 17th Notts & Derby Regiment, and remain in close support, and be under the orders of the Assaulting Company Commander. On the objectives being gained, the consolidating parties will move up.

    It is to be also understood that this Company will reinforce the 17th Notts & Derby Company, if it is necessary, for the capture of any given point.

2. All other arrangements will be made direct by Os.C., 16th Rifle Brigade, and 17th Notts & Derby Regiment.

3. Para.9. The Reserve Company, 16th Rifle Brigade, will move up to Dug-outs in German Front Line about R.25.b.2.8. one hour before ZERO.

4. The deepening of the Trench between Point 45 and our Bombing Bloc at the POPE'S NOSE is to be energetically carried on with tonight, as must also the consolidation of shell slits in this vicinity and the deepening of trench between 45 and 64.

5. ACKNOWLEDGE.

                                              T.G. Maxwell   Captain,

20.10.1916.   Brigade Major, 117th Infantry Brigade.

Copies issued at 3.30 p.m. to:-

All recipients of 117th Infantry Brigade Order No.74.

117th INFANTRY BRIGADE.

Report on OPERATIONS carried out by one Company of the 17th NOTTS and DERBY Regiment, supported by the 16th RIFLE BRIGADE, on the 21st October, 1916.

Reference: St. PIERRE DIVION, 1/5000 Map.

GENERAL.

The object of this attack was to capture the trenches known as the POPE'S NOSE, Points 16 and 38, R.19.c.

The difficulty of the operation was greatly increased by the obliteration of trenches caused by the German bombardment during the attack on the SCHWABEN REDOUBT in the early hours of the morning.

Places of assembly were rendered unrecognisable, and it was almost impossible to identify the actual points which formed the objective of the attack.

The conditions were not very favourable for observation owing to a slight mist, but valuable reports were nevertheless received.

SPECIAL.

(a) Composition of Assaulting Party.

Under command of Captain LE PREVOST, 17th NOTTS & DERBY REGIMENT.

Divided into three groups:-
    Two consisting of One Officer, and 20 Other Ranks, each.
    One consisting of One Officer, and 20 Other Ranks.

Intention:-

One party to seize point 16, and then form three blocks in the three trenches leading away from that point.

One party to seize Point 47, then Point 38, and block (a) MAISIE LANE and (b) R.19.c.20.83.

One party to make good the trench running from Point 16 to Point 38.

(b) Assembly.

Owing to the condition of the trenches the time of assembly as originally fixed was abandoned, and the various parties were sent up so as to arrive at their assembly points as short a time as possible before the hour for the assault.

The estimates of time were accurate, and the plan worked well.

(c) Time.

The operation was timed to commence with a Light Trench Mortar Bombardment at 12.16 p.m.: this was begun punctually to the minute.

(d) The Assault.

(1) Point 16.

The leading squad rushed in, the enemy fought stubbornly for five minutes, and then withdrew.

A machine gun with a broken tripod was captured here.

The Block Party moving up STORY TRENCH found 9 or 10 of the enemy in a dug-out. One or two were killed, three slightly wounded by

/Contd.

a Mills Bomb. Seven of them were taken prisoners.

Point 16 was ultimately consolidated, and blocks were established at R.19.c.½.7. and R.19.c.0.5½.

(ii) Point 38.

Point 47 was first rushed and taken; the party then moved on towards Point 38 but owing to lack of cover were badly hit by shrapnel and machine gun fire, the latter seeming to come from about R.19.c.4.½. 9½. in MAISIE LANE.

Eventually the advance had to be given up, and a block was established ten to fifteen yards beyond Point 47.

Point 38 was strongly held for a time by the enemy, who suddenly retired, probably in order to give their guns opportunity to shell Points 38 and 47.

A considerable volume of shrapnel fire was opened on these points by the German guns soon after their Infantry had withdrawn.

(iii) Trench from Point 16 to Point 38.

This could not be identified, nor could WEST K.O.Y.L.I.

(e) Reports.

Many reports of the capture of POPE'S NOSE were received between 1 p.m. and 3 p.m., chiefly from Artillery and Brigade O.P's.

Actual confirmation as to the capture of Points 16 and 47 was received from the O.C., 16th Rifle Brigade, dispatched at 2.40 p.m., and received here at 3.25 p.m.

(f) Subsequent measures.

Detachments of R.E., and of the 13th Battalion GLOUCESTER Regiment (Pioneers), were sent up immediately on receipt of the above message.

The R.E. were to consolidate Point 16, the Pioneers Point 47, and a new trench was to be constructed on either side of each captured point for a distance of 50 yards.

(g) Stokes Guns.

These were most useful in the attack on Point 16. The guns helping in the attack on Point 38 were unlucky.

(h) Enemy Artillery.

The fire encountered from the enemy's artillery was stronger than had been expected in view of our preliminary bombardment, and of the operations carried out on the right.

October 22nd.,1916.

SECRET.   XVIII   Copy No. 20

117th INFANTRY BRIGADE ORDER No. 78.
------------------------------------   20.10.1916.

Reference: 1/5000 St PIERRE DIVION Trench Map.
           1/20000 Sheet 57D. S.E.

NOTE: The following Orders are contingent on the capture of STUFF Trench.

1. (a) The 17th K.R.R.Corps are now holding the REDOUBT Left Sub-section, and will be under the orders of the Brigadier General Commanding the 116th Infantry Brigade for defensive purposes until after the capture of STUFF Trench. The exact hour will be notified later. After the capture of STUFF Trench, the 17th K.R.R.Corps will again come under the orders of the 117th Infantry Brigade, and will hold the line from R.19.d.9.9. exclusive as far as the present boundary of the REDOUBT and RIVER Sections.

   (b) The dividing line between the REDOUBT and RIVER Sections will then be the line R.19.d.9.9 - R.19.d.9.2, and thence the line of the Crucifix - Thiepval - line of Apple trees - Road to R.31.c. 5.5 - 1.2 - 0.0 - W.6.d.5.5 - W.5.d.8.0.

   (c) The RIVER Section will thus be divided into three Sub-sections, viz:-

   RIVER Right: From R.19.d.9.9. to R.19.a.7.5. inclusive.

        Battalion H.Q's - In some convenient dug-outs South of
            Point 7.2. in MARTIN'S Lane. Reconnaissance to be
            carried out as early as possible tomorrow morning,
            and information sent to Brigade Headquarters giving
            the exact location.

   RIVER Centre: From line running through R.19.a.7.5 - R.19.c.9.8 -
            R.19.d.2.2. to R.19.c.0.6.

        Battalion H.Q's - R.25.b.2.8.

   RIVER Left: Old British Front Line Q.24.d.9.9 - 30 to the River
            ANCRE.

        Battalion H.Q's - PAISLEY Avenue.

2. (a) 116th Infantry Brigade will be relieved in the REDOUBT Section by the 56th Infantry Brigade, 19th Division, on the night of the 22nd/23rd. Relief to be complete by 9 p.m.

   (b) 118th Infantry Brigade Headquarters will move to PAISLEY DUMP, Q.30.c.7.3., by 9 p.m., 22nd October.

3. The 34th Machine Gun Company will relieve the guns of the 117th Machine Gun Company WEST of the ANCRE by 10 a.m. on the 22nd October. On relief the guns of the 117th Machine Gun Company will rejoin their Unit, but O.C., 117th Machine Gun Company, will arrange to relieve those guns of the 116th Machine Gun Company in the SCHWABEN REDOUBT

P.T.O.

West of the line 99.92, by 12 noon, 22nd October.

4. Completion of all moves and reliefs will at once be wired or sent by runner to Brigade Headquarters.

5. Two Stokes Mortars will be withdrawn from RIVER Centre Sub-section, and come into action to support the RIVER Right Sub-section.

6. The 117th Infantry Brigade Headquarters will remain at PASSRELLE de MAGENTA.

7. ACKNOWLEDGE.

J.G. Maxwell Captain,
Brigade Major, 117th Infantry Brigade.

20.10.1916.

Copies issued at   p.m. to:-

No.1. 16th Notts & Derby Regt.
2. 17th   ditto
3. 17th K. R. R. Corps.
4. 16th Rifle Brigade.
5. 117th Machine Gun Coy.
6. 117th T.M. Battery.
7. H.Q's, 116th Brigade.
8. H.Q's, 118th Brigade.
9. H.Q's, 189th Brigade.
10. H.Q's, 39th Division.
11.   ditto.
12. C.R.A., 39th Division.
13. C.R.E., 39th Division.
14. A.D.M.S., 39th Division.
15. 225th Field Coy., R.E.
16. G.O.C.
17. B.M.
18. S.C.
19. Bde Signal Officer.
20. War Diary.
21. War Diary.
22. Order file.

SECRET.

117th INFANTRY BRIGADE ORDER No. 79.

Copy No. 22

22.10.1916.

Reference: 1/20000 Map 57D. S.E.
1/5000 St. PIERRE DIVION Trench Map.

1. (a) The 17th K.R.R. Corps will be relieved tomorrow morning, 23rd October, in the RIVER Right Section by the 4/5th Black Watch, who are spending the night at NORTH and SOUTH BLUFFS, AUTHUILLE. The 4/5th Black Watch will be under the orders of the G.O.C., 117th Infantry Brigade, until an hour to be notified later, on the 24th October.

    After relief the 17th K.R.R. Corps will proceed by any convenient route to Dug-outs in PIONEER Road.

   (b) The 16th Rifle Brigade will be relieved in the River Centre Section by 10 a.m. on the 24th October by a Battalion to be detailed by the Brigadier General Commanding the 118th Infantry Brigade.

    The location of the 16th Rifle Brigade after relief will be notified later.

   (c) The 17th Notts & Derby Regiment now in THIEPVAL and old German Line will return to NORTH and SOUTH BLUFFS by 11 a.m. tomorrow morning. The Four Officers and 150 Other Ranks of the 17th Notts & Derby Regiment, now acting as Common Supports to the Battalions holding the RIVER Right Section and RIVER Centre Section, will remain where they are tomorrow, but will rejoin their Battalion by 10 a.m. on the 24th.

   (d) All Machine Guns and Stokes Mortars in the RIVER Right and RIVER Centre Sections will be relieved by guns and mortars of the 118th Brigade by 10 a.m. on the 24th October.

   (e) All arrangements for the above reliefs will be made direct between Commanding Officers concerned.

2. On the 24th October, on completion of the reliefs described above, the Brigadier General, Commanding the 118th Infantry Brigade, will assume command of the RIVER Right and Centre Sections.

3. The Code Word "NARCISSUS" will be wired to Brigade Headquarters to denote completion of reliefs.

P.T.O.

4. The 117th Infantry Brigade Headquarters will remain at PASSERELLE de MAGENTA.

5. ACKNOWLEDGE.

                                   W.E. Maxwell. Captain,
                            Brigade Major, 117th Infantry Brigade.

22.10.1916.

Copies issued at 8 p.m. to:-

No.1. 16th Notts & Derby Regt.
   2. 17th ditto
   3. 17th K. R. R. Corps.
   4. 16th Rifle Brigade.
   5. 117th Machine Gun Coy.
   6. 117th T.M. Battery.
   7. H.Q's, 116th Brigade.
   8. H.Q's, 118th Brigade.
   9. H.Q's, 189th Brigade.
10. H.Q's, 39th Division.
11. H.Q's, ditto
12. C.R.A., 39th Division.
13. C.R.A., 18th Division.
14. C.R.E., 39th Division.
15. A.R.M.S., 39th Division.
16. 225 Field Coy., R.E.
17. 4/5th Black Watch.
18. H.O.C.
19. B.M.
20. S.C.
21. Bde Signals Officer.
22. War Diary.
23. War Diary.
24. Order file.

SECRET.   Copy No. 10

117th INFANTRY BRIGADE ORDER No. 80.

23.10.1916.

Reference:
1/20000 Map Sheet 57D. S.E.) Cancelled by No 85
1/5000 St PIERRE DIVION.   )

1. (a) The RESERVE ARMY attained all its objectives on the 21st October.

   (b) A General Attack will take place on the 25th October.

   (c) The objective of the 39th Division will be the Line River ANCRE from the Bridge at R.8.c.4.5. to our present Line.

2. The 118th Infantry Brigade, reinforced by a Battalion from the 116th Infantry Brigade, and by the 17th K. R. R. Corps, will carry out the Attack. The Third Objective for this Brigade is the Trenches about R.13.d.78 and 69, the line of Trenches R.19.a.1.8 - Q.24.b.7.7 - 8.4 - 7.2 - Q.24.d.4.8 and the Trench Q.24.b.6.4 - 2.6. Three Battalions will carry out this attack.

   On the attainment of the final objective, St. PIERRE DIVION will be captured. SERB Road, HANSA Road, and the valley of the ANCRE, will be cleared up by the two Battalions in Brigade Reserve of the 118th Infantry Brigade working up the valley.

3. The 16th Notts & Derby Regiment will carry out a Subsidiary Attack up the Valley of the River ANCRE as far as the Trench Q.24.b.6.4 - Q.24.b. 2.6. (inclusive).

   A separate Order for this attack will be issued later.

4. The Reliefs and Movements of Units of the Brigade on the 23rd, 24th, and 25th October, will be shewn on the attached table.

5. Throughout the day the 16th Rifle Brigade, 117th Machine Gun Coy. (less Guns in the line and section detailed to move forward with the Assaulting Battalion), and the 117th Trench Mortar Battery, will be ready to move at half an hour's notice.

6. (a) The First Line Transport of the 16th Notts & Derby Regiment, and the 17th K. R. R. Corps, will be formed up about R.16.a.8.8. by ZERO plus two hours, ready to move forward as ordered by 39th Division Headquarters, on the capture of St. PIERRE DIVION.

   (b) An Advanced Divisional Dump will be formed at LANCASHIRE DUMP (Q.35.c.3.3.) with reserves of S.A.A., Grenades, Stokes Ammunition, and Rations.

                                                                    P.T.O.

- 2 -

7. A Hot Meal will be issued to the 16th Notts & Derby Regiment, at NORTH BLUFFS, before their Departure to the Assembly positions.

8. Not more than Two Officers per 100 men will accompany their Units into action: 25% of N.C.O's and Specialists will also remain behind. These Officers, N.C.O's, and Specialists, will remain with their First Line Transport.

9. ZERO hour will be notified later.

10. 117th Infantry Brigade Headquarters will remain at PASSERELLE de MAGENTA.

11. ACKNOWLEDGE.

Captain,
Brigade Major, 117th Infantry Brigade.

23.10.1916.

Copies issued at 8 p.m. to:-

No. 1. 16th Notts & Derby Regt.
2. 17th   ditto
3. 17th K.R.R. Corps.
4. 16th Rifle Brigade.
5. 117th Machine Gun Coy.
6. 117th T.M. Battery.
7. H.Q's, 116th Brigade.
8. H.Q's, 118th Brigade.
9. H.Q's, 189th Brigade.
10. H.Q's, 39th Division.
11. H.Q's,   ditto
12. C.R.A., 39th Division.
13. C.R.A., 18th Division.
14. C.R.E., 39th Division.
15. A.D.M.S., 39th Division.
16. 225 Field Coy., R.E.
17. G.O.C.
18. B.M.
19. S.C.
20. Bde Signals Officer.
21. War Diary.
22. War Diary.
23. Order file.

SECRET. TABLE shewing MOVEMENTS of UNITS of the 117th INFANTRY BRIGADE on the 23rd., 24th., and 25th
OCTOBER. (To accompany 117th INFANTRY BRIGADE ORDER NO. 30).

Unit.	Location on 23rd October.	Movements on 24th October.	Movements on 25th October.
16th Notts & Derby Regt.	RIVER Left.	Is relieved by 17th Notts & Derby Regt. in RIVER Left. Relief to be complete by 6 p.m. After relief proceeds to NORTH BLUFFS.	Advances from NORTH BLUFFS to Assembly Positions at 2 a.m. Carries out assault (see Body of Order).
17th Notts & Derby Regt.	NORTH and SOUTH BLUFFS.	Relieves 16th Notts & Derby Regt. in River Left Section. Relief to be complete by 6 p.m. Battn. H.Q's and Reserve Coy: PAISLEY Avenue.	Remains in RIVER Left Sub-section.
17th K.R.R. Corps.	PIONEER Road Dug-outs.	Moves from PIONEER Road Dug-outs to DUG-OUTS South of AUTHUILLE in W.C.A. and C.※ PIONEER Road Dug-outs to be vacated by 12 noon.	Arrives NORTH BLUFFS at 3 a.m. Comes under orders of G.O.C., 118th Inf.Bde as Battalion in Brigade Reserve.
15th Rifle Brigade.	RIVER Centre.	Is relieved by 1/1st HERTS Regt. in RIVER Centre Sub-section. Relief to be complete by 10 a.m. After relief proceed to Dug-outs in PIONEER Road.	Remains at PIONEER Road Dug-outs.
117th M.G. Company.	In the Line.	GUNS in RIVER Right and Centre Sub-sections are relieved by Guns of the 118th M.G.Coy. Relief to be complete by 10 a.m. After relief proceed to Reserve in NORTH BLUFFS.	Remains at NORTH BLUFFS. One Section follows up 15th Notts & Derby Regt., and takes up positions on captured objective.
117th T.M. Battery.	In the Line.	As for 117th Machine Gun Company.	Remains at NORTH BLUFFS.

NOTE:- Throughout these Operations the 117th BRIGADE HEADQUARTERS, and REPORT CENTRE, will remain at ASSERELLE de MAGENTA.

※ CENTRAL BLUFFS.

SECRET.　　　　　　　　　　　　　　　　　　　　　　　　　　　Copy No. 18

117th INFANTRY BRIGADE ORDER No. 81.
23.10.1916.

Reference: 1/20000 Map, Sheet 57D. S.E,)
1/5000 St PIERRE DIVION.)

1. Reference 117th Infantry Brigade Order No.80.

    The 16th Notts & Derby Regiment will carry out a Subsidiary Attack on the left flank of the 118th Infantry Brigade.

2. OBJECTIVES. To clear the Valley of the River ANCRE in the neighbourhood of the enemy dug-outs about Q.24.b.2.3. and Q.24.b.5.4. A 2nd party to push on as far as a line Q.24.b.6.6. - 2.3., and hold it.

3. PLAN. The Battalion will assemble in the neighbourhood of MILL Road, Q.24.c.00.30 - 65 - 95., and in line of old trenches about BURGHEAD. The advance will not take place until the Infantry of the 118th Brigade have reached their Second Objective (see attached map). Efforts will be made to arrange a signal from the neighbourhood of 2nd parallel about Point Q.24.d.45.55., but direct observation from neighbourhood of assembly is essential.

4. TANKS will be used. ~~Their routes are shown in attached map.~~ Co-operation with No. 3 Tank is all important. Attention is drawn to the pamphlet issued today to the four Battalions of the Brigade regarding Tanks and Signals.

5. One Section, 117th Machine Gun Company, will be placed at the disposal of O.C., 16th Notts & Derby Regiment, ready to move forward to captured positions.

6. Artillery arrangements will be made to deal with the Machine Guns (with Shaft Battle Emplacements) at Q.24.D.25.79.

7. O.C., 117th Machine Gun Company, will arrange to bring covering fire to bear on Q.24.D.25.79 - 48 - St. PIERRE DIVION, from his guns in THIEPVAL Wood. He will also tell off a gun to snipe active machine guns at these points. Proposals will be submitted by 12 noon tomorrow.

8. The Staff Captain will arrange direct with O.C., 16th Notts & Derby Regiment, to make a DUMP of Bombs, and Rations, at a point in SPEYSIDE.

9. Each man of the attacking Battalion will carry 100 rounds of S.A.A., and Four Bombs. Packs will not be worn.

10. ZERO hour will be notified later.

11. Acknowledge.

W.E. Maxwell.　　　Captain,
23.10.1916.　　　　　　　　　　　　　　　　　　Brigade Major, 117th Infantry Brigade.
　　　　　　　　　　　　　　　　　　　　　　　　　　　　　　　　　　　　　　P.T.O.

- 2 -

Copies issued to:-

No. 1. 16th Notts & Derby Regt.
    2. 17th   ditto
    3. 17th K. R. R. Corps.
    4. 16th Rifle Brigade.
    5. 117th M.G.Coy.
    6. 117th T.M.Battery.
    7. H.Q's, 116th Brigade.
    8. H.Q's, 118th Brigade.
    9. H.Q's, 189th Brigade.
  10. H.Q's, 39th Division.
  11. H.Q's,   ditto
AQ — 12. C.R.A., 39th Division.
  13. C.R.A., 18th Division.
  14. C.R.E., 39th - ditto
  15. A.D.M.S., 39th Division.
  16. 225th Field Coy. R.E.
  17. G.O.C.
  18. B.M.
  19. S.C.
  20. Bde Signal Officer.
  21. War Diary.
  22. War Diary.
  23. Order file.

SECRET. Copy No. 21

117th INFANTRY BRIGADE ORDER No. 82.

23.10.1916.

Reference: 1/20000 Map Sheet 57D. S.E.
1/5000 St. PIERRE DIVION.

1. Reference Operation Orders Nos. 80 and 81. Operations are postponed for 24 hours.

2. The 16th Rifle Brigade will be relieved in the RIVER Centre Section tomorrow by the 17th Notts & Derby Regiment. Relief will commence at 8 a.m. After relief the 16th Rifle Brigade will proceed to PIONEER Road Dug-outs.

3. The 17th K.R.R. Corps will vacate PIONEER Road Dug-outs by 11 a.m. tomorrow, and will proceed to NORTH and SOUTH BLUFFS, taking over there from the 17th Notts & Derby Regiment.

4. The guns of the 117th Machine Gun Company, and 117th Trench Mortar Battery, in the RIVER Right and Centre Section, will not be relieved tomorrow.

5. The Command of the RIVER Right and Centre Sections will remain with the 117th Infantry Brigade until further orders.

6. ACKNOWLEDGE.

Captain,
Brigade Major, 117th Infantry Brigade.

23.10.1916.

Copies issued to:-

No. 1. 16th Notts & Derby Regt.
2. 17th ditto
3. 17th K.R.R.Corps.
4. 16th Rifle Brigade.
5. 117th Machine Gun Coy.
6. 117th T.M.Battery.
7. H.Q's, 116th Brigade.
8. H.Q's, 118th Brigade.
9. H.Q's, 189th Brigade.
10. H.Q's, 39th Divsion.
11. H.Q's, ditto
12. C.R.A., 39th Division.
13. C.R.E., 39th Division.
14. C.R.A., 18th Division.
15. A.D.M.S., 39th Division.
16. 225th Field Coy., R.E.
17. G.O.C.
18. B.M.
19. S.C.
20. Bde Signal Officer.
21. War Diary.
22. War Diary.
23. Order file.
24. 4/5th Black Watch.

SECRET.   Map XXV   W.D.   Copy No. 23

117th BRIGADE ORDER No. 83.

24.10.1916.

Reference: 1/20000 Map Sheet 57D. S.E.
            1/5000 St. PIERRE DIVION.

1. The 117th Infantry Brigade will be relieved tomorrow in the RIVER Section by the 116th Infantry Brigade, in accordance with the attached table. All details of relief not mentioned in this Order will be arranged direct between Commanding Officers concerned.

2. Os.C., Units, will ensure that all wounded are evacuated from the trenches before the arrival of Units of the 116th Infantry Brigade.

3. Commanding Officers will pay special attention to the handing over of all bombs, Mills rifle grenades, and S.O.S. rockets, and will indicate to the relieving C.O's the exact places where such stores exist. Exact dispositions of the way the line is held, the areas to be avoided, the shelled areas, and all information regarding the various Sub-sections will be similarly handed over.

4. Quartermasters' Stores, and Transport Lines, will remain as at present.

5. O.C., 16th Rifle Brigade, will place two limbers at the disposal of the 117th Trench Mortar Battery, to be at LANCASHIRE DUMP by 12 noon tomorrow, for the purpose of relief.

6. The 117th Infantry Brigade Report Centre will close at PASSERELLE de MAGENTA at 6 p.m., reopening at Dug-outs in PIONEER Road, about W.3.d.6.2. at the same hour.

7. Acknowledge.

                                            B.E. Maxwell Captain,
24.10.1916.   Brigade Major, 117th Infantry Brigade.

Copies issued at 5 p.m. to:-
No. 1. 16th Notts & Derby Regt.   13. C.R.E., 39th Division.
    2. 17th   ditto   14. C.R.A., 16th Division.
    3. 17th K.R.R.Corps.   15. A.D.M.S., 39th Division.
    4. 16th Rifle Brigade.   16. 225th Field Coy., R.E.
    5. 117th Machine Gun Coy.   17. 4/5th Black Watch.
    6. 117th T.M.Battery.   18. G.O.C.
    7. H.Q's, 116th Brigade.   19. B.M.
    8. H.Q's, 118th Brigade.   20. S.C.
    9. H.Q's, 189th Brigade.   21. Bde Signal Officer.
   10. H.Q's, 39th Division.   22. War Diary.
   11. H.Q's, 39th Division.   23. War Diary.
   12. C.R.A., 39th Division.   24. Order file.

SECRET.

RELIEF TABLE to accompany 117th Infantry Brigade Order No.63.

It.No.	Date.	Unit.	From.	To.	Relieved by.	Route.	Advance Party Guides.	Platoon and other Guides for Units.	Remarks.
1.	24/2/1918	15th Notts & Derby R.	RIVER Left Sub-section.	Huts in Jonnber road.	2/4th of 116 Inf.Brigade.	via PAISLEY - LANCASHIRE Dumps.	1 p.m. LANCASHIRE Dump.	2 p.m. LANCASHIRE Dump.	
2.	do.	17th Notts & Derby R.	RIVER Centre Sub-section.	SOUTH BLUFFS part CENTRE BLUFFS.	ditto	O.G.L.-dist 70-PAISLEY - LANCASHIRE Dumps.	11 a.m. LANCASHIRE Dump.	12 noon LANCASHIRE Dump.	After passing ft 70, 17th N.&D. R't may take most convenient route.
3.	do.	17th S.W.B.	Remains in NORTH BLUFFS and part of CENTRE BLUFFS. SOUTH BLUFFS to be vacated by 2 p.m.						
4.	do.	10th S.W.B.	Remains in DUG-OUTS in BUNKER Row.						
5.	do.	Last RIVER Right Sub-section.	SEMLIN.	2/4th of 116 LIGHT Valley Inf.Brigade.	Derelict Tank 183 ? 0000 Post.	9 a.m. Derelict Tank N.End of BLIGHTY Vly.	10 a.m. Derelict Tank N.End of BLIGHTY Vly.		
6.	25/2/1918	RIVER Sub-section.	Huts in Jonnber road.	118th M.G. Company.	ditto	3 p.m. LANCASHIRE Dump.	Guides for each Gun position from 118th. LANCASHIRE Dump.		
7.	26/2/1918				116th T.M.	ditto		Guides for each Gun position from 116th. LANCASHIRE Dump.	

SECRET.   AAp XXIV   W.D   Copy No. 23.

117th INFANTRY BRIGADE ORDER No. 85.

27.10.1916.

Reference: 1/10000 Sheets 57D. N.E. and S.E.
1/5000 St. PIERRE DIVION Trench Map.

NOTE: This Order cancels 117th Infantry Brigade Order No. 80 of 23.10.1916.

1. (a) The Reserve Army will attack on "Z" day. ZERO hour will be notified.

   (b) The II Corps is to attack Northwards and to capture MIRAUMONT, the Line of the MIRAUMONT - BEAUCOURT SUR ANCRE Road to the South of the Bois D'HOLLANDE, and thence Westwards to the Crossings of the River ANCRE.

   (c) The V Corps is attacking EASTWARDS North of the ANCRE with a view to seizing the Line BEAUREGARD DOVECOTE (L.28.c.) - SERRE (inclusive).

   (d) The main objective of the 39th Division is the Line of the River ANCRE from R.8.c.2.0. to Q.24.b.1.3., and the crossings at the MILL (P.13.a.2.7) and BRIDGE ROAD (Q.18.b.85.40). This objective is to be gained by ZERO plus 1 hour, 40 minutes. The Dividing Line between the 19th Division and the 39th Division is the Line R.19.d.9.9 - R.14.c.2.1 - R.8.c.3.3.

   The Dividing Line between the 39th Division and the 63rd Division is the Line of the River ANCRE.

   The 63rd Division is to reach the General Line of the BEAUCOURT Road at ZERO plus 50 minutes.

   One Company, 63rd Division, has been detailed to clear up the MOUND and the Railway Embankment in Q.13.c.

2. (a) The Attack of the 39th Division will be carried out by four Battalions of the 118th Infantry Brigade, and one Battalion from each of the 116th and 117th Infantry Brigades.

   The 16th Rifle Brigade is detailed in Support of the 118th Infantry Brigade.

   (b) A Subsidiary Attack will be carried out by one Battalion (16th Notts & Derby Regiment) of the 117th Infantry Brigade, and one Section of the 117th Machine Gun Company.

   A separate Order for this attack, with Map shewing barrages, etc., is being issued.

   (c) Movements of Units of the 117th Infantry Brigade on "Y" and "Z" days are shewn on the attached table.

3. (a) The area of attack of the 118th Infantry Brigade is as follows:-

   This attack will be divided into three subsidiary objectives:-

   OBJECTIVE "A": Group of Trenches R.19.b.9.7. - R.19.b.8.6 - 6.4 - 2.4 - 3.6, and the Line R.19.a.6.5 - R.19.c.3.8 - R.19.c.1.6.   To be captured by ZERO plus 4 minutes.

   OBJECTIVE "B": Line of the SERB ROAD from R.13.d.6.3 - R.19.a.6.8 - 4.5 - 0.4 - R.24.b.9.0 - 95.0.0. - Q.24.d.8.7.   To be captured by ZERO plus 18 minutes.

   OBJECTIVE "C": The Line of the GRANDCOURT - St.PIERRE DIVION - HAMEL Road from R.13.b.3.5 to Q.24. b.1.1.   To be captured by ZERO plus 28 minutes.

P.T.O.

- 2 -

    (b) The objectives of the 16th Notts & Derby Regiment are:-

        (i) The Dug-outs Q.24.b.2.3 - 5.4.
        (ii) The Line Q.24.b.6.6. - 2.8.

4. The 16th Rifle Brigade has been allotted to the 118th Infantry Brigade. They will be located at NORTH BLUFFS, coming under the orders of G.O.C., 118th Infantry Brigade at 3 a.m. "Z" Day.

5. (a) The following is the action of the Light Trench Mortar Batteries of the 116th and 117th Infantry Brigades:-

    16 Stokes Mortars will be emplaced from R.19.c.6.6. to Left of 2nd PARALLEL, and bombard enemy trenches from ZERO until ZERO plus 28, the bombardment ceasing progressively from the right.

    A separate order will be issued for this Operation.

    (b) The 117th Machine Gun Company (less one Section attached to the 16th Notts & Derby Regiment, and one Section in Divisional Reserve) will enfilade the front of attack from ZERO to ZERO plus 25, gradually switching West in front of advancing infantry.

    A Special Order will be issued with regard to timings and zones of fire.

6. Owing to the wide front to be covered in the attack, and the limited amount of artillery available, it is most important that the fire of all Machine guns, and Stokes Mortars, should be utilised to the fullest extent to assist the barrage.

7. The 17th Notts & Derby Regiment, and the 17th K.R.R.Corps, will detail two and one TANK GUARDS respectively. Each TANK GUARD will consist of One N.C.O. and Two Men. These Guards will report to O.C., TANKS, at 6 p.m. on "Y" day, at 118th Brigade Headquarters, PAISLEY DUMP.

8. Transport Orders will be issued by the Staff Captain.

9. The remaining two Battalions of the 117th Infantry Brigade (17th Notts & Derby Regiment, and 17th K.R.R.Corps) and one Section of the 117th Machine Gun Company, will be in Divisional Reserve, and ready to move at half an hour's notice.

    One Officer and two Cyclist runners from each of these Battalions will report to 117th Brigade Headquarters one hour before ZERO.

10. (a) No man will carry more than 150 rounds of S.A.A.
    (b) Steps will be taken to ensure that every man has his iron rations on him before "Z" day.

11. 117th Infantry Brigade Headquarters will remain at PASSERELLE de MAGENTA.

12. ACKNOWLEDGE.

                                                W.E.Maxwell   Captain,

28.10.1916.   Brigade Major, 117th Infantry Brigade.

Copies issued at 12.30 p.m. to:-

No.			
1.	16th Notts & Derby Regt.	11. H.Q's, 39th Div.	21. S.C.
2.	17th ditto	12. H.Q's, ditto	22. Bde Sigs Offcr.
3.	17th K.R.R.Corps.	13. C.R.A., ditto	23. War Diary.
4.	16th Rifle Brigade.	14. C.R.E., ditto	24. War Diary.
5.	117th Machine Gun Coy.	15. C.R.A., 18th Div.	25. Order file.
6.	117th T.M.Battery.	16. A.D.M.S., 39th Div.	
7.	H.Q's, 116th Brigade.	17. 225 Field Coy., R.E.	
8.	H.Q's, 118th Brigade.	18. No.3 Coy., Div.Train.	
9.	H.Q's, 189th Brigade.	19. G.O.C.	
10.	H.Q's, 56th Brigade.	20. B.M.	

SECRET. TABLE shewing movements of Units of the 117th INFANTRY BRIGADE on "Y" and "Z" days (to accompany 117th Infantry Brigade Order No.6C).

Item.	Unit.	"Y" Day.	"Z" Day.	Remarks.
1.	15th Notts & Derby Regiment.	SOUTH BLUFFS.	Vacates SOUTH BLUFFS at 3 a.m. and moves to assembly positions.	
2.	17th Notts & Derby Regiment.	PIONEER Road DUG-OUTS.	Remains.	After ZERO "Z" Day becomes Divl Reserve.
3.	17th K.R.R.Corps.	PIONEER Road HUTS.	Remains.	ditto
4.	16th Rifle Brigade	NORTH BLUFFS.	Remains. Comes under Orders of G.O.C., 118th Inf.Bde at 3 a.m.	
5.	117th Machine Gun Company.	(a) 8 Guns to be emplaced in RIVER Left Sub-section for barrage fire "Z" day by 2 p.m. (b) One Section - SOUTH BLUFFS. (c) One Section - PIONEER Road HUTS.	(a) remains and fires on barrage lines as ordered. (b) accompanies 16th Notts & Derby Regt to assembly positions from SOUTH BLUFFS. (c) remains.	The Section at PION+ EER Road HUTS becomes M.G.Section in Divl Reserve after ZERO "Z" Day.
6.	117th Trench Mortar Battery.	8 Mortars to be emplaced in accordance with Special Orders by 2 p.m.	Remains and fires on barrage lines as ordered.	

SECRET.   Copy No. 21

                    117th INFANTRY BRIGADE ORDER No. 86.
                    -------------------------------------   28.10.1916.

Reference: 1/20000 Map Sheets 57D. N.E. and S.E.
           1/5000 St. PIERRE DIVION Trench Map.

  NOTE: This Order cancels 117th Brigade Order No. 81.

1. Reference 117th Brigade Order No. 85. The 16th Notts & Derby Regt
   will carry out a Subsidiary Attack on the Left Flank of the 118th
   Brigade on "Z" Day.

2. Objectives. To clear the valley of the River ANCRE in the neighbourhood of the enemy dug-outs about Q.24.b.2.3 - 5.4. A Second Party
   will push on as far as the Line Q.24.b.6.6 - 2.8, and hold it.

3. Plan.

   (a) The Battalion will assemble in the neighbourhood of MILL Road,
       Q.24.d.00.80, Q.24.c.6595, and in Line of old trenches about
       BURGHEAD.

   (b) Orders for the assembly will be issued later.

   (c) The Advance will not take place until the Infantry of the 118th
       Brigade have reached their Second Objective (see attached Map).

   (d) The Line of Advance of the Right Company will be so planned
       that the Dug-outs at Q.24.b.2.3 - 5.4. will be approached from
       Q.24.b.4.1. to 6.2., i.e. so as to get on top of the Bank and
       aim at cutting them off from about Q.24.b.6.4.

4. Artillery barrages and advance on objectives of the 118th Infantry
   Brigade will be as follows (see also attached Map):-

   The artillery barrage both frontal and enfilade will lift at an
   average rate of 50 yards a minute on the Right, and 25 yards a
   minute on the Left. The Line of barrage being being continuous
   across the whole front.

   The initial Lift off each Objective will be 100 yards, and the
   barrage will remain for four minutes from 0.18' to 0.22' on a Line
   100 yards beyond Objective B as shewn on the attached map.

   An enfilade barrage will be placed on the Line of the HAMEL - St.
   PIERRE DIVION - GRANDCOURT Road from Q.24.b.1.1 to R.13.b.3.5., and
   on HANSA Road from ZERO hour onwards.

   This barrage will lift off the above at ZERO plus 22'.

5. Tanks will be used. Their routes are shewn on the attached Map.
   Co-operation with No.3 Tank is all-important. Attention is drawn
   to the pamphlet issued regarding Tanks and Signals. It is to be
   impressed on all ranks of the attacking Battalion that on no
   account are Infantry to wait for the TANKS.

6. One Section, 117th Machine Gun Company, will be placed at the disposal of O.C., 16th Notts & Derby Regiment, ready to move forward
   to the captured positions.

7. Each man of the attacking Battalion will carry 150 rounds of S.A.A.
   and four Bombs. Packs will not be worn. One day's ration in addition to the Emergency Iron Ration will be carried. Four N.C.O's
   and Four Privates in each Platoon will carry four flares each. Six
   sets of S.O.S. Rockets will be carried forward.

                                                                    P.T.O.

- 2 -

8. A Contact Patrol Aeroplane will fly over the area of attack from ZERO hour onwards.

   The leading Infantry will light flares one hour after ZERO, and every subsequent hour, or any time the aeroplane sounds a Klaxon or lights a White Light. These flares must not be placed in the open.

9. Medical arrangements. An Advance Aid Post will be established in SPEYSIDE about C.30.B.1.9. Wounded will be evacuated from this Aid Post to A.D.S., PAISLEY Avenue, A.D.S., LANCASHIRE DUMP.

10. The arrangement for the synchronisation of watches will be notified later.

11. The 117th Infantry Brigade Headquarters will remain at PASSERELLE de MAGENTA.

12. ACKNOWLEDGE.

W.E. Marinell Captain,

28.10.1916.
                                    Brigade Major, 117th Infantry Brigade.

Copies issued at   to:-

No.1 18th Notts & Derby Regt.	13. C.R.A., 18th Division.
2. 17th ditto.	14. 225 Field Coy. R.E.
3 17th K.R.R.Corps.	15. G.O.C.
4 16th Rifle Brigade.	16. B.M.
5 117th Machine Gun Coy.	17. S.C.
6 117th Trench Mortar Bty.	18. Bde Signals Officer.
7 H.Q's, 116th Brigade.	20. Bde Bombing Officer.
8 H.Q's, 118th Brigade.	21. War Diary.
9 H.Q's, 39th Division.	22. War Diary.
10 H.Q's, ditto	23. Order file.
11.C.R.E., ditto	
12 C.R.A., ditto	

SECRET. Copy No. 13

117th INFANTRY BRIGADE ORDER No. 87.

28.10.1916.

Reference: 1/5000 St. PIERRE DIVION Trench Map.

1. Reference 117th Infantry Brigade Order No.85.

   In accordance with Divisional Order No.66 the Light Trench Mortar Batteries of 116th and 117th Infantry Brigades will cover the front of the Infantry Attack with STOKES MORTAR fire.

2. The objectives and lifts are as follows:-

   OBJECTIVE "A": Group of Trenches R.19.b.9.7. - R.19.b.9.6 - 6.4 - 2.4 - 5.6, and the Line R.19.a.6.3 - R.19.c.3.8 - R.19.c.1.6.   To be captured by ZERO plus 4 minutes.

   OBJECTIVE "B": Line of the SERB ROAD from R.13.d.6.9 - R.19.a.6.8 - 4.5 - 0.4 - Q.24.b.9.0 - 95.0.0. - Q.24.d.8.7.   To be captured by ZERO plus 18 minutes.

   OBJECTIVE "C": The Line of the GRANDCOURT - St.PIERRE DIVION - HAMEL Road from R.13.b.3.5 to Q.24.b.1.1.   To be captured by ZERO plus 28 minutes.

3. Mortars are allotted to objectives as follows:-

   116th T.M.Bty: 2 Guns at Point 16.   ) For
   116th T.M.Bty: 2 Guns at West K.O.Y.L.I.   )) OBJECTIVE "A".
                  Junction with 2nd PARALLEL.)

   116th T.M.Bty: 2 Guns from Point 24.d.7.4. to) For
                  Point 24.d.3.5.   ) OBJECTIVE "B".
   117th T.M.Bty: 4 Guns from ditto   ditto.   )

   117th T.M.Bty: 4 Guns from Point 24.d.2.7. to) For
                  Point 24.c.9.7.   ) OBJECTIVE "C".

   All Mortars open fire at ZERO at varying rates of fire according to the length of time given to reach each objective.

   Mortars for "A" OBJECTIVE cease fire at 0 plus 4.

   Mortars for "B" OBJECTIVE cease fire at 0 plus 18.

   Mortars for "C" OBJECTIVE cease fire at 0 plus 28.

   Care must be taken that the Guns firing on the extreme left do not endanger the Subsidiary Attack to be carried out by the 16th Notts & Derby Regiment. This Attack leaves its assembly trenches at 0 plus 18 minutes. The targets for these Guns should therefore be divided, i.e. up to 0 plus 18 minutes on enemy front and support lines, for 0 plus 18 minutes onwards on to support lines and beyond.

4. **Ammunition.**

   4 Guns for OBJECTIVE "A": 40 rounds a gun.   Dumped in Tunnel No.7.

   6 Guns for OBJECTIVE "B": 60 rounds a gun,) To be selected
) by O.C., 117th
   4 Guns for OBJECTIVE "C": 80 rounds a gun) T.M.Battery.

P.T.O.

- 2 -

5. O.C., 117th Trench Mortar Battery, will command both Batteries, and make arrangements for emplacements today.

6. Working parties to be found from Reserve Company, 16th Rifle Brigade.

7. ACKNOWLEDGE.

                                         B.Morwill   Captain,

28.10.1916.   Brigade Major, 117th Infantry Brigade.

Copies issued at 3.30 p.m. to:-

No.		No.	
1.	16th Notts & Derby Regt.	8.	H.Q's, 39th Division.
2.	116th T.Mortar Battery.	9.	H.Q's, ditto
3.	117th T.Mortar Battery.	10.	G.O.C.
4.	117th Machine Gun Coy.	11.	B.M.
5.	H.Q's, 116th Brigade.	12.	S.C.
6.	H.Q's, 118th Brigade.	13.	War Diary.
7.	H.Q's, 189th Brigade.	14.	War Diary.
		15.	Order file.

SECRET. Copy No. 22

117th INFANTRY BRIGADE ORDER No. 88.

28.10.1916.

Reference: 1/20000 Map Sheet 57D. S.E.
1/5000 St. PIERRE DIVION Trench Map.

1. The 117th Infantry Brigade will be relieved tomorrow in the RIVER Section by the 118th Infantry Brigade, in accordance with the attached table.

    All details of relief not mentioned in this Order will be arranged direct between Commanding Officers concerned.

2. Os.C., Units, will ensure that all wounded are evacuated from the trenches before the arrival of Units of the 118th Infantry Brigade.

3. Commanding Officers will pay special attention to the handing over of all Bombs, Mills Rifle Grenades, and S.O.S. Rockets, and will indicate to the relieving C.O's the exact places where such stores exist. Exact dispositions of the way the line is held, the areas to be avoided, the shelled areas, and all information regarding the various Sub-sections will be similarly handed over.

4. Quartermasters' Stores, and Transport Lines, will remain as at present.

5. O.C., 16th Notts & Derby Regiment, will place two limbers at the disposal of the 117th Trench Mortar Battery, to be at LANCASHIRE DUMP by 12 noon tomorrow for the purpose of relief.

6. The Code Word "LUXOR" will be wired to Brigade Headquarters to denote completion of relief.

7. The 117th Infantry Brigade Report Centre will close at PASSERELLE de MAGENTA at 5 p.m., reopening at SENLIS at the same hour.

8. ACKNOWLEDGE.

T.G. Maxwell Captain,
Brigade Major, 117th Infantry Brigade.

28.10.1916.

Copies issued at   to:-

No. 1. 16th Notts & Derby Regt.
2. 17th   ditto
3. 17th K.R.R.Corps.
4. 16th Rifle Brigade.
5. 117th Machine Gun Coy.
6. 117th T.M. Battery.
7. H.Q's, 116th Brigade.
8. H.Q's, 118th Brigade.
9. H.Q's, 189th Brigade.
10. H.Q's, 39th Division.
11. H.Q's,   ditto
12. C.R.A., ditto
13. C.R.E., 39th Division.
14. C.R.A., 18th Division.
15. A.D.M.S., 39th Division.
16. 225th Field Coy., R.E.
17. No.3 Coy., Divl Train.
18. G.O.C.
19. B.M.
20. S C.
21. War Diary.
22. War Diary.
23. Bde Signal Officer.
24. Order file.

SECRET.

RELIEF TABLE to accompany 117th INFANTRY BRIGADE ORDER No. 88.

Item	Date.	Unit.	From.	To.	Relieved by.	Route.	Advance Party Guides.	Platoon & other Guides for Units.	Remarks.
1.	29/10/1916.	16th Notts & Derby Regt.	Battn in Bde Support, THIEPVAL.	MARTINSART Woods (takes over billets vacated by 1/1st Cambs Regt.)	1/1st Cambs Regiment.	Any convenient.	1 p.m. Lancashire Dump.	2 p.m. Lancashire Dump.	
2.	do.	17th do.	RIVER Centre Sub-section.	SENLIS (takes over billets vacated by 4/5 Black Watch)	4/5th Black Watch Regiment.	Any convenient after passing R.25.c.7.0.	11 a.m. R.25.c.7.0.	12 noon. R.25.c.7.0.	
3.	do.	17th K.R.R.C.	RIVER Right Sub-section.	SENLIS (takes over billets vacated by 1/1st Herts).	1/1st Herts Regiment.	ditto	8 a.m. R.25.c.7.0.	9 a.m. R.25.c.7.0.	
4.	do.	16th Rifle Brigade.	RIVER Left Sub-section.	MARTINSART Woods (takes over billets vacted by 1/6th Cheshires).	1/6th Cheshire Regiment.	Cheshire Dump-Paisley Dump.	11 a.m. Lancashire Dump.	12 noon. Lancashire Dump.	
5.	do.	117 M.G.C. (less 2 Stns) & 2 Sections 116 M.G.C.	RIVER Section.	SENLIS.	118th M.G.C.	Any convenient.	Guides for each Gun Position.	10 a.m. Lancashire Dump.	See below. (Note 2).
6.	do.	117th T.M.Bty.	RIVER Left and Centre Sub-sections. PASSERELLE de MAGENTA.	MARTINSART Woods.	118th T.M.B.	ditto	Guides for each Gun Position.	10 a.m. Lancashire Dump.	
7.	do	117th Bde H.Q's.		SENLIS.	118th Bde H.Q's.	ditto	--	--	

NOTE:
1. Intervals of 20 minutes between Companies and 10 minutes between Platoons will be observed N.E. of the line OVILLERS - AUTHUILLE - MESNIL. These intervals may be increased at the discretion of C.O's.

2. The remaining two Sections of the 117th Machine Gun Company now resting at PIONEER ROAD HUTS will rejoin the rest of the Company as it marches to SENLIS. The two Sections of the 116th Machine Gun Company after relief will be under the orders of the G.O.C., 116th Infantry Brigade.

SECRET.   Copy No. 7.

117th INFANTRY BRIGADE ORDER No. 89.
                                                           31.10.1916.

Reference: 1/10000 BEAUMONT, 57D. S.E. 1 and 2, parts of.

1. Reference 117th Infantry Brigade Order No.85, dated 27/10/1916, para. 5(b).

   The programme described in para 3 below will be carried out by the 117th Machine Gun Company (less one section, Divisional Reserve, and one section under orders of O.C., 16th Notts & Derby Regiment) on "Z" day.

2. The Gun Groups will be in their positions with their Guns and S.A.A. by 2 p.m. on "Y" day, and all Guns for barrage fire will be carefully laid during the hours of daylight on "Y" day.

3. The Guns will fire as follows, and adhere strictly to their programmes:-

   GROUP "A" (4 Guns with fire positions at Q.30.b.3.3.)

   Programme: (a) From ZERO to ZERO plus 8, Guns will barrage on the Line Q.24.d.8.7 - Q.24.b.85.15 - STONY Trench - SERB Road.

   (b) At ZERO plus 8, all guns of the Group will gradually switch Westwards to the Line St. PIERRE DIVION - MILL Trench - JUNCTION of HANSA Line and MILL Road (R.13.b.4.5) actually reaching this Line with their barrage at ZERO plus 15.

   (c) Group will fire on this Line from ZERO plus 15 to ZERO plus 22. Fire will cease at ZERO plus 22.

   (d) Group will remain in Gun positions (under cover) after ZERO plus 22, and await further orders.

   GROUP "B" (3 Guns with fire positions at Q.29.b.5.8).

   Programme: (a) From ZERO to ZERO plus 22, Guns will barrage on the Line St. PIERRE DIVION - MILL Trench - JUNCTION of HANSA Line and MILL Trench (R.13.b.4.5).

   (b) At ZERO plus 22 Guns will cease fire, pack up and proceed by road via SOUTHERN CAUSEWAY to the Trench Railway Junction at the East side of the CAUSEWAY about Q.30.c.45.15, where they will await orders. The arrival at this point will be immediately notified to Brigade Headquarters.

   GROUP "C" (One Gun with fire position at Q.24.a.5.0).

   This Gun will fire using direct observation on the Trench running from Q.24.b.6.4 to Q.24.b.3.6 from ZERO to ZERO plus 25, or later if necessary, and will cover the advance of the 16th Notts & Derby Regiment.

   This Gun will remain in position after the advance.

4. One Officer of the Machine Gun Company will be with each Group, and carefully supervise the firing of the Group. O.C., 117th Machine Gun Company, will be with Group "B".

5. Arrangements for the synchronisation of watches will be notified later. The very greatest care must be exercised in obtaining the exact synchronisation with the Officers in charge of each Group.

                                                           P.T.O.

- 2 -

6. Arrangements regarding the Forward Parking of Machine Gun Company Limbered Wagons will be notified later.

7. ACKNOWLEDGE.

W E Maxwell Captain.
31.10.1916.   Brigade Major, 117th Infantry Brigade.

Copies issued at 8 p.m. to:-

No. 1. 16th Notts & Derby Regt.
    2. 117th Machine Gun Company.
    3. ditto
    4. ditto
    5. ditto
    6. 117th T.M. Battery.
    7. H.Q's, 39th Division.
    8. H.Q's,   ditto
    9. H.Q's, 116th Brigade.
   10. H.Q's, 118th Brigade.
   11. G.O.C.
   12. B.M.
   13. S.C.
   14. War Diary.
   15. War Diary.
   16. Order file.

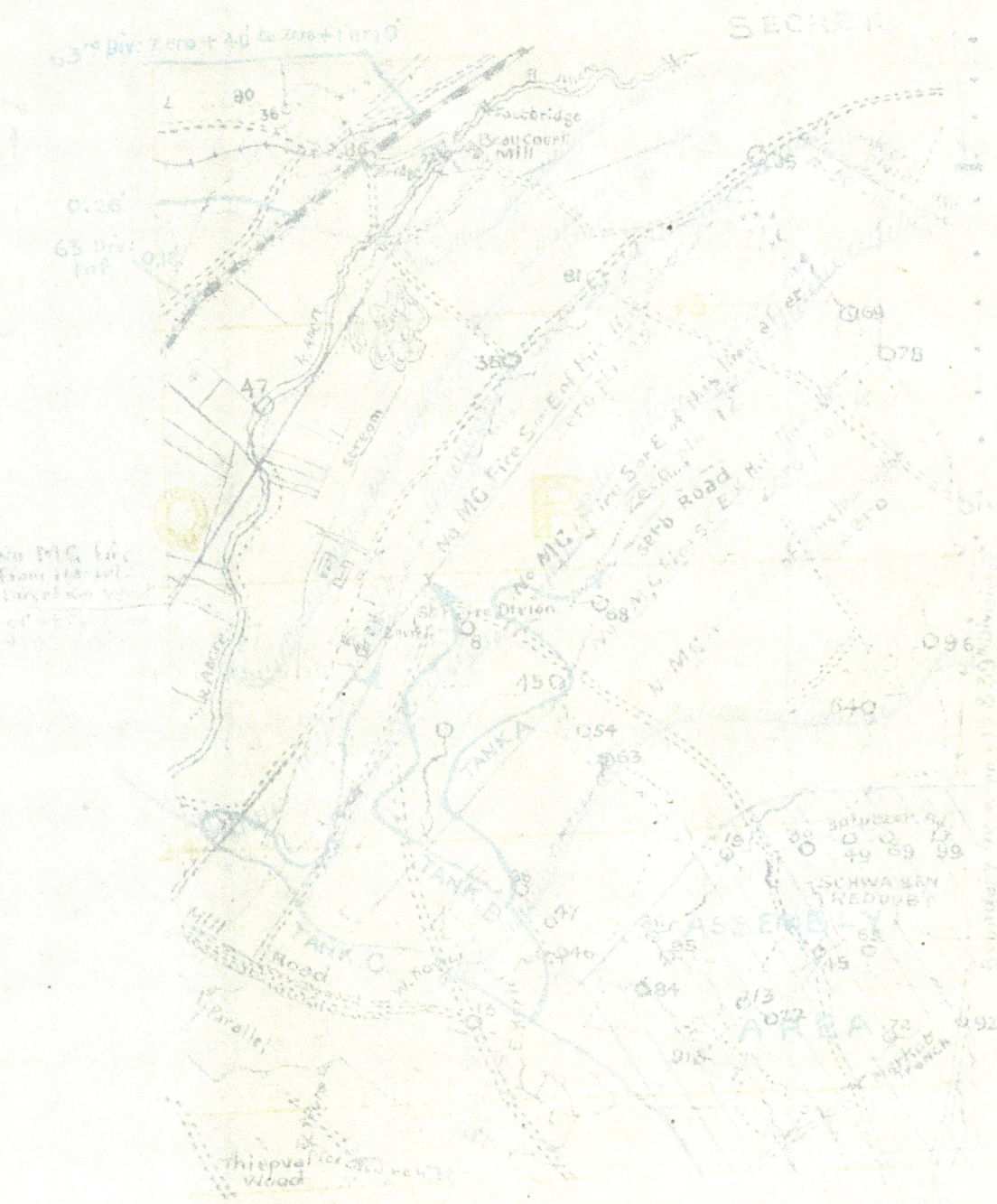

116. (116) ✓

■ = 1 Platoon. 11th R. Sussex
■ = 1 Coy. Do.
■ = 1 Plat. = 13th R. Sussex
■ = 1 Coy Do.

■ = 1 Plat. 12th R.S.
■ = 1 Coy Do.

■ = 1 Plat. 14th Hants
■ = 1 Coy. Do.

• T.M. Emplacements
⊙ M.G. Do.
Bn. H.Q. ♇

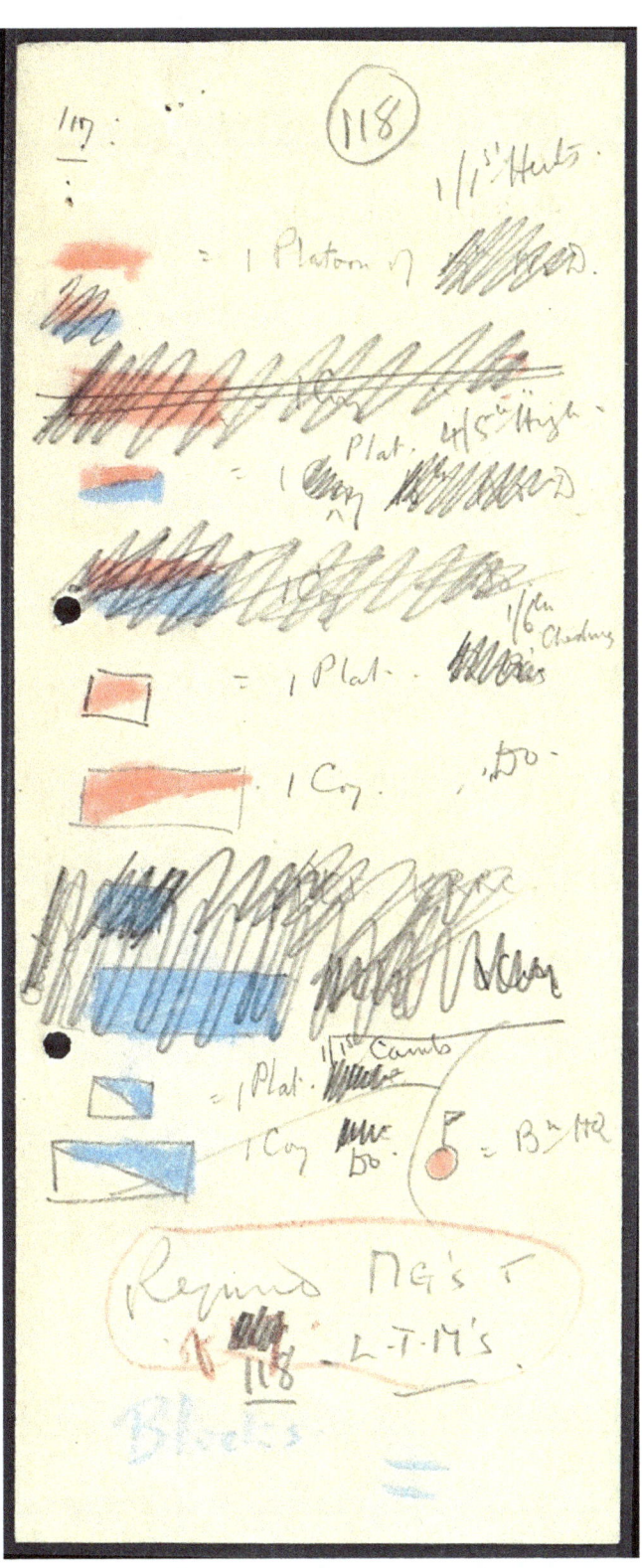

"A" Form.
MESSAGES AND SIGNALS.

Army Form C.2121 (in pads of 100).

Prefix	Code	m.	Words	Charge	This message is on a/c of:	Recd. at......m.
Office of Origin and Service Instructions.			Sent			Date
Secret			At......m.		......Service.	From
Special D.R.			To			By
			By		(Signature of "Franking Officer.")	

TO — 39th Div'n

Sender's Number.	Day of Month.	In reply to Number.	AAA
BM/.435	6/10.		

Herewith Advance Distribution map shewing the Distribution of this Brigade. It is regretted that the Exact positions of the 1/1st Cambs is not shewn. The positions of MGuns & L.TMs will be shewn tomorrow. There are 16 of the former and 7 of the latter in the line.

It will be seen that at present the 16th R&D are holding the Bombay block between 27 and 99. This is being handed over to the 17th R&D tomorrow. The front line marked in in blue is exactly as taken over from 55th Inf Bde 18th Div'n

From — 117th Brigade
Place —
Time — 10.25 pm.

(Z) WMarwell Capt

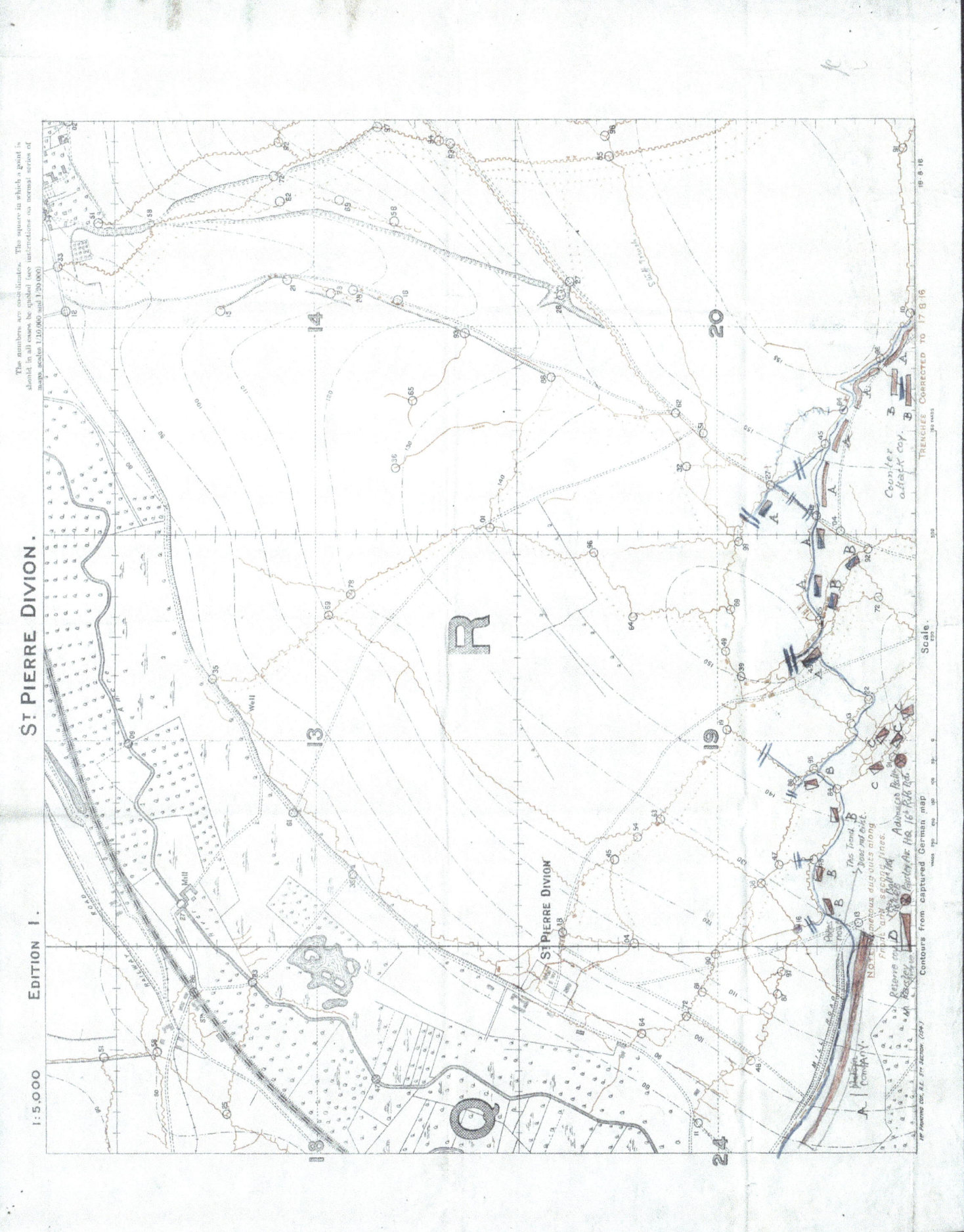

THIEPVAL. SECRET.

EDITION 4.
CANCELLING ALL PREVIOUS ISSUES

Contours from Captured German Map.
TRENCHES CORRECTED TO 17-9-16

Scale - 1:5,000

The numbers are co-ordinates. The square in which a point is situated is in all cases to be quoted (see instructions on normal series of maps, scales 1/10,000 and 1/20,000).

23-8-16

Signs:
- Bombing Block
- Kitchen
- M.G.
- Dug Outs
- Snipers
- Trench Mortar
- Batt'n H.Q.

Office Copy

39/G/36/4.

II Corps.

With reference to II Corps message No.G. 2690 of this date, the following line was taken over from the 18th Division:-

R.20.d.1.0. - R.20.c.9.2. - 6.4 - 4.5 - 2.7 - 1.5 -
R.19.d.6.5 - 4.5 - 2.2 - 1.3 - R.19.c.9.5 - 8.6 - 8.4 -
4.5 - 10.45 - thence along old British front line; with blocks at R.20.c.15.85, R.19.d.42.63, R.19.d.2.5,
R.19.c.95.78, 72.60, 45.55, 10.45.

Thr same line is now held by this Division with the single exception of the block at R.19.d.45.55 which was advanced to R.19.d.42.62 in the attack of the morning of Oct. 9th 1916.

Oct 12th 1916.

Major-General,
Commanding 39th Division.

"C" Form (Original).
MESSAGES AND SIGNALS.

Army Form C. 2123.
(In books of 50's in duplicate.)

Prefix	Code	Words	Received From	Sent, or sent out At	Office Stamp
					C 12.X.16 TELEGRAPHS
Charges to collect			By	To	
Service Instructions				By	

Handed in at .... Office 9.46 m. Received 9.50 m.

TO 39 Div

Sender's Number	Day of Month	In reply to Number	AAA
G2690	12th		

Kindly report exact line taken over by you from 18th Div also exact line now held in this sector aaa The reason for any difference in the two lines should be given

981/9.52/p

FROM 2nd Corps
PLACE & TIME 9/50 am

* This line should be erased if not required.
Wt. 432—M437 500,000 Pads. H W V 5 16 Forms C.2123.

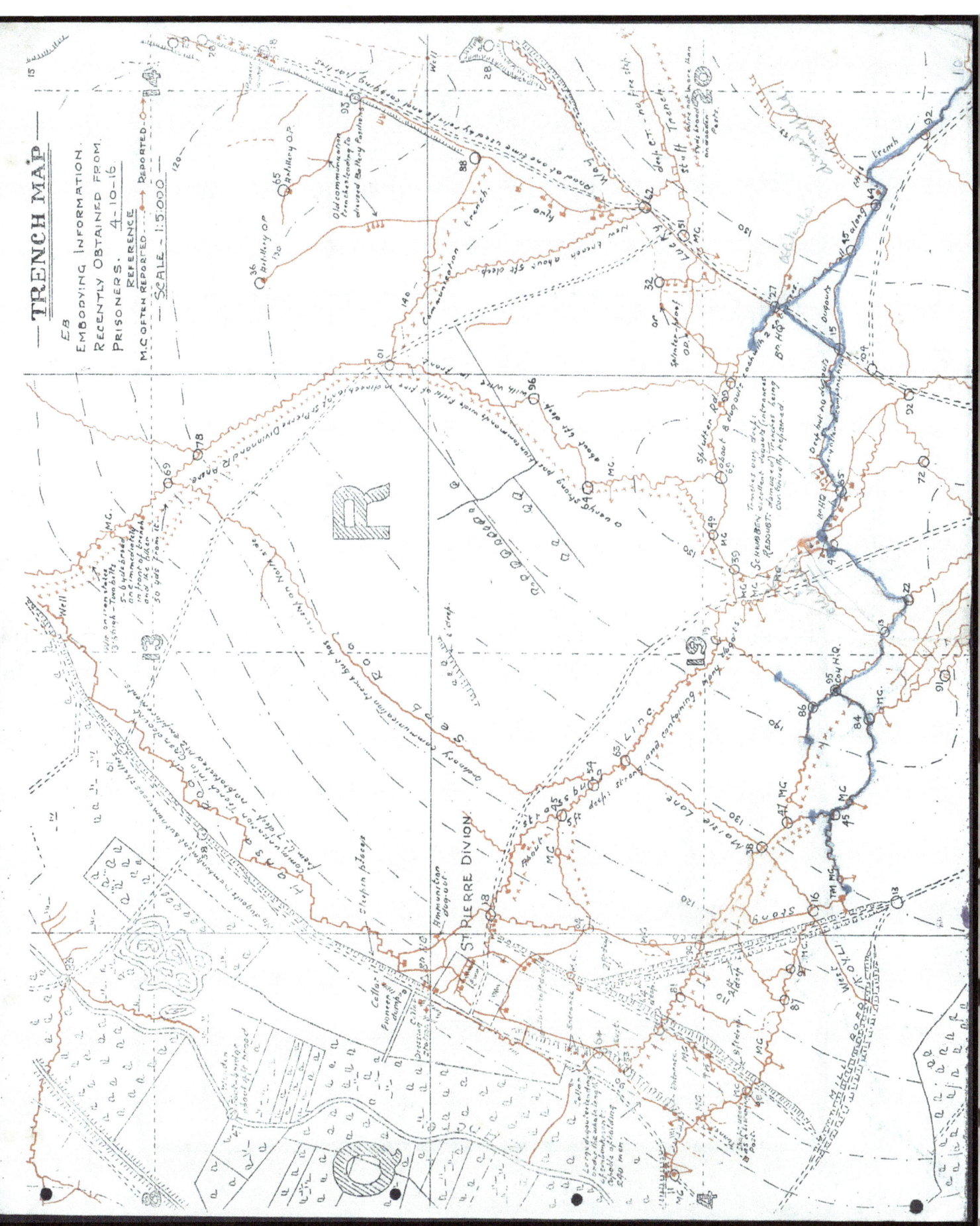

"A" Form.
MESSAGES AND SIGNALS.
Army Form C. 2121.

Prefix......... Code.........m.	Words	Charge	This message is on a/c of:	Recd. at .... m.
Office of Origin and Service Instructions.	Sent		Service.	Date
Special DR	At .... m.		39/G/36/4	From
	To		(Signature of "Franking Officer.")	By
	By			

TO { 39th Division

| Sender's Number | Day of Month | In reply to Number | AAA |
| BM/469 | 10/10/16 | | |

Herewith Disposition Map AAA A similar map has been handed over to 118 Brigade AAA The Bombing Block shown between pt 45 and 39 is not quite so far North as shown but it is hard to determine exact position. It was advanced 70 or 80 yards in the attack yesterday.
The Bombing Block at the Pope nose is also nearer Pt 45 than shown.
It is regretted that this map could not be sent earlier but exact information has been difficult to obtain.
A complete Census of Dugouts has been made but time has not permitted of these being shown on this map. The papers have been handed over to 118 Bde

From   117th Brigade
Place
Time   1pm

The above may be forwarded as now corrected. (Z)   W.S. Marawa Capt
                                      Censor.   Signature of Addresser or person authorised to telegraph in his name.

39th Division.

B. H. Q.

117th INFANTRY BRIGADE

NOVEMBER 1 9 1 6

Attached:-

Brigade Orders.

Report on Operation 13th November.

Army Form C. 2118

WAR DIARY
or
INTELLIGENCE SUMMARY

(Erase heading not required.)

Instructions regarding War Diaries and Intelligence Summaries are contained in F.S. Regs., Part II. and the Staff Manual respectively. Title Pages will be prepared in manuscript.

Place	Date	Hour	Summary of Events and Information	Remarks and references to Appendices
SENLIS.	1st Nov.		Working Parties and rest. The weather again becomes wet. On October 31st 117th Infantry Brigade Order No. 89 was issued detailing the Programme to be carried out by the 117th Machine Gun Company under Order No. 85.	App. 1.
	2nd		Amendment to 117th Infantry Brigade Order No. 85 is issued, also 117th Infantry Brigade Order No. 90 for relief of 118th Machine Gun Company by 117th Machine Gun Company in the RIVER Section on the 3rd. A wet morning clearing towards mid-day with prospect of a frosty night.	App. 2. App. 3.
PASSERELLE de MAGENTA.	3rd		Brigade relieved 118th Infantry Brigade in RIVER Section in accordance with 117th Infantry Brigade Order No. 91. Three Battalions in front line, 17th K.R.R.Corps in Support. Enemy indulged in fairly heavy shelling during relief. Casualties Nil. Brigade Headquarters moves into Dug-outs at PASSERELLE de MAGENTA.	App. 4.
	4th		Nothing unusual happened.	
SENLIS.	5th		Brigade is relieved by 116th Infantry Brigade, and moves to MARTINSART Woods and SENLIS, with Brigade Headquarters at SENLIS (See 117th Infantry Brigade Order No. 92). Amendment to 117th Infantry Brigade Order No. 85 is issued. Two Sections of 117th Machine Gun Company not relieved in accordance with Order No 92.	App. 5.
PASSERELLE de MAGENTA.	6th		Brigade relieved 116th Infantry Brigade in RIVER Section in accordance with 117th Infantry Brigade Order No. 93. Three Battalions front line, 16th Rifle Brigade in Support. Brigade Headquarters moves into Dug-outs at PASSERELLE de MAGENTA.	App. 6.
	7th		Weather continues bad. High wind, heavy rain. 117th Infantry Brigade Order No. 94 issued for relief of Brigade by 118th Infantry Brigade.	App. 7.
PIONEER Road.	8th		Brigade relieved by 118th Infantry Brigade. 16th Notts & Derby Regt move to SOUTH BLUFFS, 16th Rifle Brigade NORTH BLUFFS, two Battalions to PIONEER ROAD. Brigade H.Q's at PIONEER Rd.	
	9th		Rest. Improvement in weather.	

1875 Wt. W593/826 1,000,000 4/15 J.B.C. & A. A.D.S.S./Forms/C. 2118.

Army Form C. 2118

WAR DIARY
or
INTELLIGENCE SUMMARY

(Erase heading not required.)

Page 2.

Instructions regarding War Diaries and Intelligence Summaries are contained in F. S. Regs., Part II. and the Staff Manual respectively. Title Pages will be prepared in manuscript.

Place	Date	Hour	Summary of Events and Information	Remarks and references to Appendices
PIONEER Road. SENLIS.	10th		117th Infantry Brigade Order No. 95 issued for move to MARTINSART WOODS and SENLIS.	App. 8.
	11th		Brigade moves in accordance with Order No.95. 16th Notts & Derby Regiment and 16th Rifle Brigade in MARTINSART WOODS, other Battalions in SENLIS. Two Sections Machine Gun Company relieve 118th Machine Gun Company in accordance with Order No. 95. Brigade Headquarters at SENLIS. Weather - morning dull, afternoon fine drizzle. 117th Infantry Brigade Order No 96 issued.	App. 9.
	12th		The Brigade moves to assembly positions in RIVER Section. Brigade H.Q's at NORTH BLUFFS.	
NORTH BLUFFS.	13th		In accordance with Brigade Order No. 85 (and amendments) the Brigade attacked German Lines South of the River ANCRE. Full account appended. Brigade Headquarters moves to PAISLEY Dump. 117th Infantry Brigade Order No. 97 issued.	App.10. and 10a
PAISLEY DUMP.	14th		117th Infantry Brigade Order No. 98 issued. Brigade is relieved by the 95th Infantry Brigade in accordance with Order No. 98 and proceeds to WARLOY. Brigade Headquarters at WORLOY.	App.11.
WARLOY.	15th		117th Infantry Brigade Order No.99 issued and Brigade moves, 16th Notts & Derby Regt., 17th Notts & Derby Regt., and 17th K.R.R.Corps to GEZAINCOURT, 15th Rifle Brigade, 117th Trench Mortar Battery, and 117th Machine Gun Coy., to BEAUVAL. Brigade H.Q's to GEZAINCOURT.	
GEZAINCOURT	16th		Instructions for entrainment of 117th Infantry Brigade issued.	App.12.
BOLLEZEELE	17th 18th		Brigade Headquarters moves to BOLLEZEELE. Brigade moves to area BOLLEZEELE- VOLKERINCKHOVE - MERKEGHE. 17th Notts & Derby Regiment to TATINGHEM.	
	20th		Brig.General R.D.F.OLDMAN, D.S.O. proceeded to England on 10 days' leave. Lieut.Colonel C. HERBERT-STEPNEY, 16th Notts & Derby Regiment, took over command temporarily.	
	21st		Brigade Training.	
	22nd		Inspection of Brigade by Lieut.General Sir SYLMER HUNTER WESTON, K.C.B., D.S.O., Commanding the VIIIth Corps, vide 117th Infantry Brigade Order No. 101.	App.13.

Army Form C. 2118

WAR DIARY
or
INTELLIGENCE SUMMARY

(Erase heading not required.)

Page 3.

Place	Date	Hour	Summary of Events and Information	Remarks and references to Appendices
LLEZEELE	23rd to 30th		Brigade Training.	
	December 1st, 1916.			

[signature]
Brigadier General,
Commanding 117th Infantry Brigade.

SECRET.   Copy No. 15

117th INFANTRY BRIGADE ORDER No. 89.

31.10.1916.

Reference: 1/10000 BEAUMONT, 57D. S.E. 1 and 2, parts of.

1. Reference 117th Infantry Brigade Order No.85, dated 27/10/1916, para. 5(b).

    The programme described in para 3 below will be carried out by the 117th Machine Gun Company (less one section, Divisional Reserve, and one section under orders of O.C., 16th Notts & Derby Regiment) on "Z" day.

2. The Gun Groups will be in their positions with their Guns and S.A.A. by 2 p.m. on "Y" day, and all Guns for barrage fire will be carefully laid during the hours of daylight on "Y" day.

3. The Guns will fire as follows, and adhere strictly to their programmes:-

    GROUP "A" (4 Guns with fire positions at Q.30.b.3,3.)

    Programme: (a) From ZERO to ZERO plus 8 Guns will barrage on the Line Q.24.d.8.7 - Q.24.b.85.15 - STONY Trench - SERB Road.

    (b) At ZERO plus 8 all guns of the Group will gradually switch Westwards to the Line St.PIERRE DIVION - MILL Trench - JUNCTION of HANSA Line and MILL Road (R.13.b. 4.5) actually reaching this Line with their barrage at ZERO plus 15.

    (c) Group will fire on this Line from ZERO plus 15 to ZERO plus 22. Fire will cease at ZERO plus 22.

    (d) Group will remain in Gun positions (under cover) after ZERO plus 22, and await further orders.

    GROUP "B" (3 Guns with fire positions at Q.29.b.5.8).

    Programme: (a) From ZERO to ZERO plus 22 Guns will barrage on the Line St.PIERRE DIVION - MILL Trench - JUNCTION of HANSA Line and MILL Trench (R.13.b.4.5).

    (b) At ZERO plus 22 Guns will cease fire, pack up and proceed by road via SOUTHERN CAUSEWAY to the Trench Railway Junction at the East side of the CAUSEWAY about Q.30.c.45.15, where they will await orders. The arrival at this point will be immediately notified to Brigade Headquarters.

    GROUP "C" (One Gun with fire position at Q.24.a.5.0).

    This Gun will fire using direct observation on the Trench running from Q.24.b.6.4 to Q.24.b.3.6 from ZERO to ZERO plus 25, or later if necessary, and will cover the advance of the 16th Notts & Derby Regiment.

    This Gun will remain in position after the advance.

4. One Officer of the Machine Gun Company will be with each Group, and carefully supervise the firing of the Group. O.C., 117th Machine Gun Company, will be with Group "B".

5. Arrangements for the synchronisation of watches will be notified later. The very greatest care must be exercised in obtaining the exact synchronisation with the Officers in charge of each Group.

P.T.O.

- 2 -

6. Arrangements regarding the Forward Parking of Machine Gun Company Limbered Wagons will be notified later.

7. ACKNOWLEDGE.

W E Maxwell Captain,

31.10.1916. Brigade Major, 117th Infantry Brigade.

Copies issued at 8 pm to:-

No. 1. 16th Notts & Derby Regt.
2. 117th Machine Gun Company.
3.   ditto
4.   ditto
5.   ditto
6. 117th T.M.Battery.
7. H.Q's, 39th Division.
8. H.Q's,   ditto
9. H.Q's, 116th Brigade.
10. H.Q's, 118th Brigade.
11. G.O.C.
12. B.M.
13. S.C.
14. War Diary.
15. War Diary.
16. Order file.

SECRET.   COPY No. 16

AMENDMENT to 117th INFANTRY BRIGADE ORDER No. 85.
                                                               2.11.1916.

I. (a). <u>PARA.7.</u> Delete "6 p.m. on 'Y' day", and substitute "5.30 a.m. on 'Z' day".

   At end of para add: "These men will assist to start the Tanks".

(b). <u>PARA.11.</u> Delete para and substitute "117th Brigade Headquarters will move to AUTHUILLE North Bluffs at ZERO minus 3 hours".

(c). <u>ATTACHED TABLE.</u> <u>Item 2.</u> "Z" day. Delete "remains" and substitute "arrives NORTH BLUFFS at ZERO minus one hour"."

<u>Item 3.</u> "Z" day. Delete "remains" and substitute "arrives SOUTH BLUFFS at ZERO minus one hour".

<u>Item 4.</u> "Z" day. Delete "remains. Comes under orders of G.O.C., 118th Infantry Brigade, at 3 a.m." and substitute "Leaves NORTH BLUFFS for THIEPVAL Dug-outs" at ZERO, and comes under orders of G.O.C., 118th Infantry Brigade."

<u>Item 5.(c)</u> "Z" day. Delete "remains" and substitute "arrives CENTRAL BLUFFS at ZERO minus one hour".

<u>Item 6.</u> Under Column "Unit" under words 117th Trench Mortar Battery add "116th Trench Mortar Battery. Both Batteries under command of Captain H.R. STEVENS, M.C."

Under Column "Y day" delete "8" and substitute "16".

Under "Column of remarks" insert sentence "After completion of their tasks the 116th and 117th Trench Mortar Batteries will rendezvous at the East end of SOUTHERN CAUSEWAY, and await orders".

Add following FOOTNOTE: "Headquarters of 117th Infantry Brigade will be at AUTHUILLE North Bluff from ZERO minus 3 hours".

                                    W.S. Maxwell   Captain,
2.11.1916.   Brigade Major, 117th Infantry Brigade.

Copies issued at 12 noon to:-

No.1. 16th Notts & Derby Regt.   9. H.Q's, 116th Brigade.
   2. 17th   ditto   10. H.Q's, 118th Brigade.
   3. 17th K.R.R.Corps.   11. G.O.C.
   4. 16th Rifle Brigade.   12. B.M.
   5. 117th Machine Gun Coy.   13. S.C.
   6. 117th T.M.Battery.   14. Bde Signals Officer.
   7. H.Q's, 39th Division.   15. War Diary.
   8. H.Q's,   ditto   16. War Diary.
                                    17. Order file.

SECRET.   Copy No. 16

117th INFANTRY BRIGADE ORDER No. 90.

2.11.1916.

1. The 117th Machine Gun Company will relieve the 118th Machine Gun Company in the RIVER Section tomorrow morning, November 3rd., under arrangements to be made direct between Commanding Officers concerned.

   After relief the 118th Machine Gun Company will take over billets in SENLIS vacated by the 117th Machine Gun Company.

2. Guides from the 118th Infantry Brigade for each Gun position will rendezvous at LANCASHIRE DUMP at 10 a.m.

3. A statement of the amount of S.A.A. taken over at each Gun position, and a statement of all Reserve Machine Gun S.A.A., will be sent to 117th Infantry Brigade Headquarters as soon after the relief as possible.

4. After relief the 117th Machine Gun Company will come under the orders of G.O.C., 118th Infantry Brigade.

5. Completion of relief will be wired to 117th and 118th Infantry Brigade Headquarters, the Code word "TABLE" being used.

W.E. Maxwell Captain,
Brigade Major, 117th Infantry Brigade.

2.11.1916.

Copies issued at 3 p.m. to:-

No. 1. 16th Notts & Derby Regt.　　　9. H.Q's, 116th Brigade.
　　2. 17th   ditto　　　　　　　　10. H.Q's, 118th Brigade.
　　3. 17th K.R.R.Corps.　　　　　　11. G.O.C.
　　4. 16th Rifle Brigade.　　　　　12. B.M.
　　5. 117th Machine Gun Company.　 13. S.C.
　　6. 117th Trench Mortar Battery.14. Bde Signals Officer.
　　7. H.Q's, 39th Division.　　　　15. War Diary.
　　8. H.Q's,   ditto　　　　　　　16. War Diary.
　　　　　　　　　　　　　　　　　　17. Order file.

SECRET.   Copy No. 23

117th INFANTRY BRIGADE ORDER No. 91.

2.11.1916.

Reference: 1/20,000 Map, Sheet 57D. S.E.
           1/5000 St. PIERRE DIVION Trench Map.

1. The 117th Infantry Brigade will relieve the 118th Infantry Brigade in the RIVER Section tomorrow, November 3rd., in accordance with the attached table.

   All details of relief not mentioned in this Order will be arranged direct between Commanding Officers concerned.

2. Os.C., Battalions holding front line will ensure that a proportion of No.23 Rifle Grenades are carried up.

3. 117th Machine Gun Company, and 117th Trench Mortar Battery, will relieve in accordance with the attached table.

4. O.C., 16th Notts & Derby Regiment, will place two limbers at the disposal of the 117th Trench Mortar Battery.

5. Quartermasters' Stores, and Transport Lines, will remain as at present.

6. The Code Word "TWENTY" will be wired to denote Relief Complete.

7. The 117th Infantry Brigade Report Centre will close at SENLIS at 4 p.m. reopening at PASSERELLE de MAGENTA at the same hour.

8. ACKNOWLEDGE.

                                                        Captain,
                                    O/c Brigade Major, 117th Infantry Brigade.

2.11.1916.

Copies issued at 11.30 p.m. to:-

No. 1. 16th Notts & Derby Regt.   13. C.R.E., 39th Division.
    2. 17th   ditto   14. C.R.A., 18th Division.
    3. 17th K.R.R.Corps.   15. A.D.M.S., 39th Division.
    4. 16th Rifle Brigade.   16. 225th Field Coy., R.E.
    5. 117th Machine Gun Coy.   17. No.3 Coy., DivTrain.
    6. 117th Trench Mortar Bty.   18. G O.C.
    7. H.Q's, 116th Brigade.   19. B.M.
    8. H.Q's, 118th Brigade.   20. S.C.
    9. H.Q's, 189th Brigade.   21. Bde Signals Officer.
   10. H.Q's, 39th Division.   22. War Diary.
   11. H.Q's, 39th Division.   23. War Diary.
   12. C.R.A., 39th Division.   24. Order file.

R E L I E F   T A B L E   to accompany 117th Infantry Brigade Order No. 91.

Ref.	Date.	Unit.	From.	To.	Relieving.	Route.	Guides.	Remarks.
1.	3/11/1916.	16th Rifle Brigade.	MARTINSART Woods.	RIVER Right Sub-section.	1/6th Cheshire Regiment.	AUTHUILLE – Pt. R.25.c.7.0.	Time: 10 a.m. Pt.R.25.c.7.0.	--
2.	do.	17th Notts & Derby.	SENLIS.	RIVER Centre Sub-section.	1/1st Herts Regiment.	Any convenient.	Nil	Head of leading Coy at O.G.L.,Pt.2.d. at 12 noon.
3.	do.	16th Notts & Derby.	MARTINSART Woods.	RIVER Left Sub-section.	4/5th Royal Highlanders.	LANCASHIRE Dump – PAISLEY Dump.	Nil	Head of leading Coy arriv. LaNCS Dump 2 p.m.
4.	do.	17th K.R.R.C.	SENLIS.	THIEPVAL. Battn in Brigade Support.	1/1st Cambs Regiment.	AUTHUILLE – THIEPVAL Road – Pt.R.25.c.7.0.	Time: 2 p.m. Pt.R.25.c.7.0.	--
5.	do.	117th M.G.C.	SENLIS.	RIVER Section.	118th M.G.Coy.	Any convenient.	Guides for each Gun position. 10 a.m. LANCASHIRE Dump.	
6.	do.	117th T.M.B.	MARTINSART Woods.	RIVER Section.	118th T.M.Bty.	Any convenient.	To be arranged between Os.C., Batteries concerned.	H.Q.118 TM Bty – LANCS Dump.
7.	do.	117th Bde H.Q's.	SENLIS.	PASSERELLE de MAGENTA.	118th Bde H.Q's.	Any convenient.	--	--

NOTE:- After passing the line OVILLERS – AUTHUILLE – MESNIL intervals of 20 minutes between Companies, and 10 minutes between Platoons will be observed. These intervals may be increased at the discretion of Commanding Officers.

SECRET.   Copy No. 24

117th INFANTRY BRIGADE ORDER No. 92.

4.11.1916.

Reference:
   1/20000 Map, Sheet 57D. S.E.
   1/5000 St. PIERRE DIVION Trench Map.

1. The 117th Infantry Brigade will be relieved tomorrow in the RIVER Section by the 116th Infantry Brigade, in accordance with the attached table.

   All details of relief not mentioned in this Order will be arranged direct between Commanding Officers concerned.

2. Commanding Officers will pay special attention to the handing over of all Bombs, Mills Rifle Grenades, and S.O.S. Rockets, and other trench stores, and will indicate to the relieving Commanding Officers the exact places where such stores exist.

   Exact dispositions of the way the line is held, the areas to be avoided, the shelled areas, and all information regarding the various sub-sections, will be similarly handed over.

3. Two Sections of the 117th Machine Gun Company will not be relieved, and will come under the orders of the G.O.C., 116th Infantry Brigade, on completion of relief.

4. Quartermasters' Stores, and Transport Lines, will remain as at present.

5. O.C., 17th K.R.R.Corps, will place two limbers at the disposal of the Trench Mortar Battery, to be at LANCASHIRE DUMP at 12 noon, for the purpose of relief.

6. The Code Word "LEDBURY" will be wired to Brigade Headquarters to denote completion of relief.

7. The 117th Infantry Brigade Report Centre will close at PASSERELLE de MAGENTA at 4 p.m., reopening at SENLIS at the same hour.

8. Relief to be complete by 5 p.m.

9. ACKNOWLEDGE.

                                                       Captain,
                                           Brigade Major, 117th Infantry Brigade.

4.11.1916.

Copies issued at 8 p.m. to:-

No. 1. 16th Notts & Derby Regt.   13. C.R.A., 39th Division.
    2. 17th   ditto   14. C.R.E., 39th Division.
    3. 17th K.R.R.Corps.   15. C.R.A., 18th Division.
    4. 16th Rifle Brigade.   16. A.D.M.S., 39th Division.
    5. 117th Machine Gun Coy.   17. 225th Field Coy., R.E.
    6. 117th Trench Mortar Battery.   18. No.3 Coy., Div.Train.
    7. H.Q's, 116th Brigade.   19. G.O.C.
    8. H.Q's, 118th Brigade.   20. B.M.
    9. H.Q's, 190th Brigade.   21. S.C.
   10. H.Q's, 57th Brigade.   22. Bde Signals Officer.
   11. H.Q's, 39th Division.   23. War Diary.
   12. H.Q's, 39th Division.   24. War Diary.
                                          25. Order file.

SECRET. R E L I E F   T A B L E to accompany 117th INFANTRY BRIGADE ORDER No. 92.

Item	Date	Unit	From	To.	Relieved by.	Route.	Advance Party Guides.	Platoon and other Guides for Units.	Remarks.
1.	5/11/1916.	16th Notts & Derby.	RIVER Left Sub-section	SENLIS. Takes over billets vacated by 11 Royal SUSSEX.	11th Royal SUSSEX Regt.	PAISLEY Dump - LANCASHIRE Dump.	11 a.m. LANCASHIRE Dump.	12 noon. LANCASHIRE Dump.	
2.	do.	17th Notts & Derby.	RIVER Dentre Sub-Sn.	MARTINSART Wds. Takes over billets vacated by 13 R.SUSSEX	13th Royal SUSSEX Regt.	Any convenient after passing Pt.R.25.c.7.O.	Pt.R.25.c.7.O.	12 noon.	
3.	do.	17th K.R. R.Corps.	Battn in Bde Support, THIEPVAL.	MARTINSART Wd. Takes over billets vacated by 14th HANTS.	12th Royal SUSSEX Regt.	Any convenient.	1 p.m. LANCASHIRE Dump.	2 p.m. LANCASHIRE Dump.	
4.	do.	16th Rifle Bde.	RIVER Right Sub-section	SENLIS. Takes over billets vacated by 12th R.SUSSEX	14th HANTS Regt.	Any convenient after passing Pt.R.25.c.7.O.	Pt.R.25.c.7.O. 8 a.m.	Pt.R.25.c.7.O. 9 a.m.	
5.	do.	117th MGC (2 sections only)	RIVER Section.	SENLIS.	2 Sections 116 M.G.C.	Any convenient.			All details with regard to relief to be arranged between C.O's concerned.
6.	do.	117th T.M.Bty.	RIVER Section.	MARTINSART Woods.	116th T.M.Bty.	ditto			All details with regard to relief to be arranged between C.O's concerned.
7.	do.	117th Bde H.Q's.	PASSERELLE de MAGENTA.	SENLIS.	116th Bde H.Q's.	ditto			

NOTE: 1. Intervals of 20 minutes between Companies, and 10 minutes between platoons, will be observed N.E. of the line OVILLERS - AUTHUILLE - ESKIIL. These intervals may be increased at the discretion of Commanding Officers.
2. All Units proceeding to MARTINSART WOODS will detail a small billetting party to meet the Asst.Staff Captain at the Huts at 11.30 a.m. when accommodation will be allotted.

SECRET.   Copy No....

AMENDMENT to 117th INFANTRY BRIGADE ORDER No. 85.

1. Reference Para. 1(d), Sub-para. 3.

    There is a clerical error.

    This Para. should read as follows:-

    "The 63rd Division is to reach the General Line of the BEAUCOURT Road at One hour plus 50 minutes", and not "ZERO plus 50 minutes" as stated.

2. ACKNOWLEDGE.

                                        A.E. Fetherstonhaugh Captain,
                                        f/Brigade Major, 117th Infantry Brigade.

5.11.1916.

Copies issued to all recipients of 117th Infantry Brigade Order No. 85.

SECRET. Copy No. 25

117th INFANTRY BRIGADE ORDER No. 93.

6.11.1916.

Reference: 1/20000 Map, Sheet 57D. S.E.
          1/5000 St. PIERRE DIVION Trench Map.

1. The 117th Infantry Brigade will relieve the 116th Infantry Brigade in the RIVER Section today, November 6th., in accordance with the attached table.

   All details of relief not mentioned in this Order will be arranged direct between Commanding Officers concerned.

2. The 117th Machine Gun Company, and 117th Trench Mortar Battery, will relieve in accordance with attached table.

3. O.C., 17th Notts & Derby Regiment, will place two limbers at the disposal of the 117th Trench Mortar Battery.

4. Quartermasters' Stores, and Transport Lines, will remain as at present.

5. The Code Word "CROOME" will be wired to denote Relief Complete.

6. The 117th Infantry Brigade Report Centre will close at SENLIS at 6 p.m. reopening at PASSERELLE de MAGENTA at the same hour.

7. ACKNOWLEDGE.

                                              Captain,

                            Brigade Major, 117th Infantry Brigade.

6.11.1916.

Copies issued at 3.15 a.m. to:-

No.1. 16th Notts & Derby Regt.	14. C.R.E. 39th Division.
2. 17th ditto	15. C.R.A., 18th Division.
3. 17th K.R.R.Corps.	16. A.D.M.S., 39th Division.
4. 16th Rifle Brigade.	17. 225th Field Coy.,R.E.
5. 117th M.G.Coy.	18. 227th Field Coy.,R.E.
6. 117th T.M.Battery.	19. No.3 Coy.,Div.Train.
7. H.Q's, 116th Brigade.	20. G.O.C.
8. 118th Brigade.	21. B.M.
9. 190th Brigade.	22. S.C.
10. 57th Brigade.	23. Bde Signals Officer.
11. 39th Division.	24. War Diary.
12. 39th Division.	25. War Diary.
13. C.R.A., 39th Division.	26. Order file.

SECRET.

RELIEF TABLE to accompany 117th Infantry Brigade Order No. 93.

Item	Date.	Unit.	From	To	Relieving.	Route.	Advance Party Guides.	Platoon and other Guides for Units.	Remarks.
1.	6/11/1916.	16th Notts & Derby Rgt.	SENLIS.	RIVER LEFT Sub-section.	11th Royal SUSSEX.	LANCASHIRE Dump - PAISLEY Dp.	Nil	Nil.	Head of leading Coy arrive LANCS.DUMP 12 noon.
2.	do.	17th Notts & Derby Rgt.	MARTINSART Woods.	RIVER CENTRE Sub-section.	13th Royal SUSSEX.	Any convenient.	Reserve Coy. LANCS.DUMP 2 p.m.	3 Front Coys LANCS. DUMP 3 p.m.	---
3.	do.	117th K.R.R. Corps.	MARTINSART Woods.	RIVER RIGHT Sub-section.	14th HANTS Regt.	AUTHUILLE - Pt.R.25.c.7.0	Reserve Coy. Pt.R.25.c. 7.0 - 2 pm.	3 Front Coys. Pt.R.25.c.7.0. 3.30 p.m.	
4.	do.	16th Rifle Brigade.	SENLIS.	THIEPVAL. Battn in Bde Support.	12th Royal SUSSEX.	ditto	Nil	Pt.R.25.c.7.0. 12 noon.	Relief to be complete by 2 p.m.
5.	do.	117th M.G.C. (2 sections)	SENLIS.	RIVER Section.	116th MGCoy. (2 Sections)	Any convenient.	Guides for each Gun position 2 p.m. LANCASHIRE Dump.		Times of relief to be arranged between C.Os.
6.	do.	117th T.M. Battery.	MARTINSART Woods.	RIVER Section.	116th T.M. Battery.	ditto	Guides for each Gun position concerned 2 p.m. LANCASHIRE Dump.	ditto	ditto
7.	do.	117th Bde H.Q's.	SENLIS.	PASSERELLE de MAGENTA.	116th Bde. H.Q's.	ditto	---	---	---

NOTE: Intervals of 20 minutes between Companies, and 10 minutes between Platoons, will be observed N.E. of the line OVILLERS - AUTHUILLE - MESNIL. These Intervals may be increased at the discretion of Commanding Officers.

SECRET.   Copy No. 24

117th INFANTRY BRIGADE ORDER No. 94.

7.11.1916.

Reference: 1/20000 Map, Sheet 57D. S.E.
           1/5000 St. PIERRE DIVION Trench Map.

1. The 117th Infantry Brigade will be relieved tomorrow, the 8th instant, in the RIVER SECTION by the 118th Infantry Brigade.

2. Commanding Officers will pay special attention to the handing over of all Bombs, Mills Rifle Grenades, S.O.S. Rockets, and other trench stores, and will indicate to the relieving Commanding Officers the exact places where such stores exist.

   Exact disposition of the way the line is held, the areas to be avoided, the shelled areas, and all information regarding the various Sub-sections, will be similarly handed over.

3. The 117th Machine Gun Company, and 117th Trench Mortar Battery, will be relieved in accordance with attached table.

4. O.C., 16th Rifle Brigade, will place two limbers at the disposal of the Trench Mortar Battery, to be at LANCASHIRE DUMP at 4 p.m. for the purpose of relief.

5. The Code Word "BELVOIR" will be wired to Brigade Headquarters to denote Relief Complete.

6. All N.C.O's in charge of Salvage Dumps will send in returns to this Office of the amount of Salvage at their Dumps by 10 a.m., 9th instant.

7. The 117th Infantry Brigade Report Centre will close at PASSERELLE de MAGENTA at 6 p.m., and will reopen at PIONEER Road (about W.3.d.6.2.) at the same hour.

8. ACKNOWLEDGE.

                                                    Captain,
                                    Brigade Major, 117th Infantry Brigade.

Copies issued at 8.30 p.m. to:-

No. 1.	16th Notts & Derby Regt.	14. C.R.E., 39th Division.
2.	17th ditto	15. C.R.A., 18th Division.
3.	17th K.R.R.Corps.	16. A.D.M.S., 39th Division.
4.	16th Rifle Brigade.	17. 225th Field Coy., R.E.
5.	117th Machine Gun Coy.	18. 227th Field Coy., R.E.
6.	117th Trench M.Battery.	19. No.3 Coy., Div.Train.
7.	H.Q's, 116th Brigade.	20. G.O.C.
8.	118th Brigade.	21. B.M.
9.	189th Brigade.	22. S.C.
10.	56th Brigade.	23. Bde Signals Officer.
11.	39th Division.	24. War Diary.
12.	39th Division.	25. War Diary.
13.	C.R.A., 39th Division.	26. Order file.

SECRET.   R E L I E F   T A B L E to accompany 117th INFANTRY BRIGADE ORDER No. 94.

Item.	Date.	Unit.	From.	To.	Relieved by.	Route.	Advance Party Guides.	Platoon and other Guides for Units.	Remarks.
1.	8/11/1916.	16th Notts & Derby Rgt.	RIVER LEFT Sub-section.	S.BLUFFS. Takes over from 4/5 Royal Highlanders.	1/1st HERTS.	Any convenient.	12 noon. LANCASHIRE Dump.	1 p.m. LANCASHIRE Dump.	
2.	do.	17th Notts & Derby Rgt.	RIVER CENTRE Sub-section.	PIONEER Road HUTS Takes over from 1/1st HERTS.	4/5th Royal Highlanders	do.	2.30 p.m. Reserve Coy. LANCS. Dump.	3.30 p.m. 3 Front Companies. LANCASHIRE Dump.	
3.	do.	17th K.R.R. Corps.	RIVER RIGHT Sub-section.	PIONEER Road HUTS Takes over from 1/6th CHESHIRES.	1/1st CAMBS.	do.	Pt.R.25.c.7.0. Reserve Coy., 2.30 p.m.	Pt.R.25.c.7.0. 3 Front Companies. 3.30 p.m.	
4.	do.	16th Rifle Brigade.	Battn in Bde Support. THIEPVAL.	N BLUFFS and HUTS W.10.d.8.5. Takes over from 1/1st CAMBS.	1/6th CHESHIRES.	do.	--	Pt.R.25.c.7.0. 12 noon.	
5.	do.	117th M.G. Company.	RIVER SECTION.	PIONEER Road HUTS.	118th M.G.Coy.	do.	Guides for each Gun position. 2 p.m. LANCASHIRE Dump.		
6.	do.	117th T.M. Battery.	RIVER SECTION.	PIONEER Road HUTS	118th T.M.Bty.	do.	ditto		
7.	do.	117th Bde H.Q's.	PASSERELLE de MAGENTA.	PIONEER Road Dug-outs. W.c.d.6.2.	118th Bde H.Q's.	do.	--	--	

NOTE: 1. Intervals of 20 minutes between Companies, and 10 minutes between Platoons, will be observed N.E. of the line OVILLERS - AUTHUILLE - MESNIL. These intervals may be increased at the discretion of Commanding Officers.
2. All Units of the 117th Infantry Brigade will send Advance Parties to their respective destinations to take over the billets, by 11 a.m.
3. Advance Parties of Units proceeding to PIONEER Road HUTS will meet the Asst. Staff Captain at 11 a.m. at the HUTS, where accommodation will be allotted.

SECRET.   Copy No. 20

117th INFANTRY BRIGADE ORDER No. 95.
                                                           10.11.1916.

Reference: 1/20000 Map, Sheet 57D. S.E.

1. The 117th Infantry Brigade will move to billets in SENLIS and MARTIN-SART Woods tomorrow, 11th instant, in accordance with the attached table.

2. Two Sections, 117th Machine Gun Company, will relieve two Sections, 118th Machine Gun Coy., in the RIVER SECTION tomorrow.

   All details of relief to be arranged between Os.C. concerned.

3. All Units will be clear of their present billets by 2 p.m.

4. The Quartermasters' Stores, and Transport Lines, will remain as at present.

5. Reports of arrival in billets will be reported immediately to 117th Brigade Headquarters.

6. The 117th Infantry Brigade Report Centre will close at PIONEER Road (about W.3.d.6.2) at 3 p.m., reopening at SENLIS at the same hour.

7. ACKNOWLEDGE.

                                    N.C. Fotheringham   Captain,
10.11.1916.   A/Brigade Major, 117th Infantry Brigade.

Copies issued at 8 p.m. to:-

No. 1. 16th Notts & Derby Regt.   13. 225th Field Coy., R.E.
    2. 17th   ditto   14. 227th Field Coy., R.E.
    3. 17th K.R.R.Corps.   15. No.3 Coy., Div. Train.
    4. 16th Rifle Brigade.   16. G.O.C.
    5. 117th Machine Gun Coy.   17. B.M.
    6. 117th T.Mortar Battery.   18. S.C.
    7. H.Q's, 116th Brigade.   19. Bde Signals Officer.
    8.   118th Brigade.   20. War Diary.
    9.   39th Division.   21. ditto
   10.   39th Division.   22. Order file.
   11. C.R.A.,39th Division.
   12. C.R.E.,39th Division.

SECRET.

SECRET.

MOVEMENT TABLE to accompany 117th Infantry Brigade Order No. 95.

Item.	Date.	Unit.	From.	To	Take over from.	Route.	Remarks.
1.	11/11/1916	16th Notts & Derby Regt.	SOUTH BLUFFS.	Huts, MARTINSART Woods.	1/1st HERTS Regiment.	Any convenient.	
2.	do.	17th Notts & Derby Regt.	PIONEER Road.	SENLIS.	4/5th BLACK WATCH. (billets).	Pioneer Road - Northumberland Avenue.	
3.	do.	17th K.R.R. Corps.	ditto	ditto	1/6th CHESHIRE Regt. (tents).	ditto	
4.	do.	16th Rifle Brigade.	NORTH BLUFFS & Huts N.10.d.8.5.	Huts, MARTINSART Woods.	1/1st CAMBS Regiment.	Any convenient.	
5.	do.	117th M.G.Coy. (2 Sections)	PIONEER Road.	SENLIS.	118th M.G.Coy. (2 sections).	Pioneer Road - Northumberland Avenue.	
6.	do.	117th M.G.Coy. (2 Sections)	PIONEER Road.	RIVER Section.	118th M.G.Coy. (2 sections).	Any convenient.	Details of relief to be arranged between Os.C., concerned will come under orders of G.O.C., 116th Bde on completion of relief.
7.	do.	117th T.M.Bty.	MARTINSART.	Huts, MARTINSART Woods.	--	ditto	
8.	do.	117th Bde H.Q's.	PIONEER Road.	SENLIS.	118th Bde H.Q's.	ditto	

NOTE: 1. Units proceeding to SENLIS will, detail advance parties to take over billets, to report at Town Major's Office by 11 a.m.
2. Units proceeding to MARTINSART WOOD Huts will detail advance parties to meet the Asst.Staff Captain at the Huts at 11 a.m. when accommodation will be allotted.

SECRET.   Copy No......

117th INFANTRY BRIGADE ORDER No. 96.

                                                             11.11.1916.

Reference: 1/10000 Sheets 57D. N.E. and S.E.
           1/5000 St. PIERRE DIVION Trench Map.

Reference 117th Infantry Brigade Order No. 85, the following are the Orders for Assembly, etc:-

1. Movements of 117th Infantry Brigade on "Y" and night of "Y/Z" days are shewn in the attached table.

2. Liaison Officers will report as follows at ZERO minus One Hour:-

   39th Div. H.Q's: Capt. P.H.COLERIDGE, 16th Notts & Derby Regt.

   189th Bde H.Q's: 2nd.Lt.E.S.ESAM,   ditto

   118th Bde H.Q's: Lieut. F.P.HOLMES,   ditto.

   Each Officer will have his servant with him as an Orderly.

3. (a) One section, 117th Machine Gun Company, will on relief move from RIVER Section to Dug-outs on HAMEL Road just North of PASSERELLE de MAGENTA, ready for action on "Z" day.

   One Section from RIVER Section to AUTHUILLE NORTH BLUFFS, by 4 p.m. "Y" Day.

   One Section will move with 16th Notts & Derby Regiment.

   One Section remains in THIEPVAL Wood for action on "Z" Day.

   (b) 116th and 117th Trench Mortar Batteries will emplace their Guns by 5.30 p.m. on "Y" day, and remain in RIVER LEFT Section. Os.C., Batteries, will arrange to give their men a hot meal at 8 p.m. on "Y" Day, and tea at 3 a.m. on "Z" Day. Cooking to be done at PAISLEY AVENUE.
   Teams will be in position by ZERO minus One and a half hours.

4. (a) The O.C., 17th Notts & Derby Regiment, will detail one Officer and nine men as a guard on the AVELUY - AUTHUILLE Road at the Southern exit of AUTHUILLE. This guard will stop all vehicles other than those belonging to the 39th Division. Guard to mount at ZERO minus 9 hours.

   (b) In addition to the Guards already ordered in Brigade Order No. 85, One Officer, 17th Notts & Derby Regiment, will report to O.C., TANKS, at 118th Infantry Brigade Headquarters, at 5.30 p.m. on "Y" Day.
   The guards will help to start the Tanks, and the Officer will see that the Tanks start from their place of assembly at ZERO. After this duty is performed he will return to his Unit.

5. Os.C., 17th K.R.R.Corps, and 17th Notts & Derby Regiment, will detail bearer parties as follows:-

   17th K.R.R.Corps.   2 Officers, 5 N.C.O's, 50 men, for A.D.S.,
                        LANCASHIRE Dump.

   17th Notts & Derby   2 Officers, 5 N.C.O's, 50 men, for A.D.S.,
   Regiment.   PAISLEY Dump.

   Parties to report at ZERO hour to M.O., i/c Stations.

6. Transport.

   Cooks Wagons may be taken forward as follows, and they must accompany Units moving into position.

                                                                /They

They will return to the transport rendezvous at W.16.a.8.8. or Bde Transport Lines as the case may be. (See 117th Bde Admin.Order No.5.)

(i) From THIEPVAL. To leave THIEPVAL at ZERO minus 2 hours, halt at AUTHUILLE at ZERO minus one hour, then proceed via BLACK HORSE Bridge.

(ii) From PAISLEY Dump. Dixies by trolley to PASSERELLE de MAGENTA, thence by transport as in para (iii) at ZERO minus 1½ hours.

(iii) PASSERELLE de MAGENTA. To be clear by ZERO minus 1½ hours.

7. No halts, except usual ten minutes halt before each clock hour, will be made West of River ANCRE and South of PASSERELLE de MAGENTA.

8. Os.C., Units, will arrange to give their men hot tea, soup, or rum, as late as assembly hours and return of transport will permit.

9. All Units must be in their assembly positions at ZERO minus 1½ hours, and a report sent to Brigade Headquarters by ZERO minus 1 hour 15 minutes that assembly is complete.

10. Watches will be synchronised as follows:-

"Y" Day.

At 6 p.m. an Officer of the Brigade Staff will be in MARTINSART Woods for synchronisation of 16th Notts & Derby Regiment and 16th Rifle Brigade; and at Brigade Headquarters, SENLIS, for synchronisation of 17th Notts & Derby Regiment and 17th K.R.R.Corps, at that hour.

Os.C., 117th Machine Gun Company, and 117th and 116th Trench Mortar Batteries, will each send an Officer at 6 p.m. to 118th Brigade Headquarters, and synchronise there.

"Z" Day.

At 5.30 a.m. by telephone (using Code Word) to 16th Notts & Derby Regiment.

Os.C., 117th Machine Gun Company, and 117th and 116th Trench Mortar Batteries, will each send an Officer at 4 a.m. to 118th Brigade Headquarters, and synchronise there.

11. O.C., 16th Notts & Derby Regiment, will arrange to draw 50 White Star Grenades.

12. 117th Brigade Headquarters will be at NORTH BLUFF from ZERO minus 3 hours onwards.

13. In acknowledging these orders Os.C., Units, will state whether all the orders are clearly understood, and all amendments due to postponement, etc., duly noted.

O.W. Fetherstonhaugh Captain,

11.11.1916.   a/Brigade Major, 117th Infantry Brigade.

Copies issued at 11.30 p.m. to:-

No.1. 16th Notts & Derby Regt.
　2. 17th   ditto
　3. 17th K.R.R.Corps.
　4. 16th Rifle Brigade.
　5. 117th Machine Gun Coy.
　6. 117th Trench Mortar Bty.
　7. H.Q's, 116th Brigade.
　8.   118th Brigade.
　9.   189th Brigade.
　10.   56th Brigade.
　11.   39th Division.
　12.   39th Division.
13. C.R.A., 39th Division.
14. C.R.E., 39th Division.
15. C.R.A., 18th Division.
16. A.D.M.S., 39th Division.
17. 225th Field Coy., R.E.
18. 227th   ditto
19. No.3 Coy., Div.Train.
20. G.O.C.
21. B.M.   22. S.C.
23. Bde Signals Officer.
24 & 25. War Diary.
26. Order file.

TABLE to accompany 117th INFANTRY BRIGADE ORDER No. 96.

Item.	Unit.	From.	To.	Route.	Remarks.
1.	16th Notts & Derby Regt.	MARTINSART Woods.	ASSEMBLY Positions.	PIONEER Road - AVELUY - HAMEL Road and NORTHERN CAUSEWAY.	To pass road junction at W.16.b.8.8. at ZERO minus 5 hours, and to be NORTH of PASSERELLE de MAGENTA by ZERO minus 4 hours.
2.	17th Notts & Derby Regt.	SENLIS.	PAISLEY AVENUE.	BOUZINCOURT - AVELUY - BLACK HORSE BRIDGE - AUTHUILLE - PAISLEY Dump.	To pass road junction at W.16.b.8.8. at ZERO minus 3 hours 30 minutes, and to be EAST of R.ANCRE by ZERO minus 2 hours 30 minutes.
3.	17th K.R.R. Corps.	SENLIS.	SOUTH BLUFF.	BOUZINCOURT - AVELUY - BLACK HORSE BRIDGE.	To pass road junction at W.16.b.8.8. at ZERO minus 2 hours 15 minutes and to be EAST of R.ANCRE by ZERO minus 1 hour 15 minutes.
4.	16th Rifle Brigade.	MARTINSART Woods.	THIEPVAL.	PIONEER Road - AVELUY - HAMEL Road - BLACK HORSE BRIDGE and THIEPVAL Avenue.	To pass road junction at W.16.b.8.8. at ZERO minus 4 hours 15 minutes and clear of BLACK HORSE Bdge by ZERO minus 3 hours 30 minutes.
5.	117th Mch. Gun Coy.	RIVER Section. SENLIS.	See body of Order No.96.	Any convenient.	2 Sections, 117th M.G.Coy. will be relieved by 2 Sections, 118th M.G. Coy. by 2 p.m. on "Y" Day. ✻
6.	116th T.M.Bty. 117th T.M.Bty.	MARTINSART Woods.	See body of Order No.96.	Any convenient.	
7.	117th Bde H.Q.	SENLIS.	AUTHUILLE NORTH BLUFFS.	Any convenient.	To be established by ZERO minus 3 hours.

✻ Arrangements for relief to be made between Os.C. concerned.

SECRET. APP. X   WD   Copy No 21

117th INFANTRY BRIGADE ORDER No. 97.

13.11.1916.

Reference: 1/10000 Sheets 57D. N.E. and S.E,
1/5000 St. PIERRE DIVION Trench Map.

1. The 118th Infantry Brigade will consolidate and hold the line R.14.c.0.1 - R.13.b.3.5 - R.13.a.98.98.

   Its Battalions will be disposed as follows:-

   4/5th Black Watch: R.14.c.0.1. to Point 78.

   1/st Herts Regt: Point 78 to R.13.b.3.5., i.e. HANSA Line.

   1/1st Cambs Regt: HANSA Road, Post BEAUCOURT HILL and at Point 83. Remainder in SERB Road, and a line running from R.13.d.7.8 to 3.8.

   1/6th Cheshire Regt: In St. PIERRE DIVION on a line from 1.8. to 6.8. in SERB Road.

2. The 117th Infantry Brigade will be disposed as follows:-

   16th Notts & Derby Regt: In PAISLEY AVENUE.

   17th Notts & Derby Regt: One Company in RIVER LEFT Sub-section.
                                One Company in MILL Road, and about Q.24.c.9.7., i.e. today's assembly positions of 16th Notts & Derby Regiment.
                                One Company about Point 87 and 97 in German Front Line.
                                One Company in PAISLEY AVENUE.

   17th K.R.R.Corps: In old German Dug-outs about Q.24.d.6.7. and Q.24.b.5.4., i.e. German Front and Support Lines.
                                Care must be taken not to interfere with the Battalion of the 118th Infantry Brigade in St. PIERRE DIVION.

   16th Rifle Brigade: In old RIVER RIGHT and CENTRE Sub-Sections.

                                Two Companies in SCHWABEN REDOUBT.
                                One Company in old RIVER CENTRE Sub-Section.
                                One Company and Battalion H.Q's in old RIVER CENTRE Sub-section.

   117th Machine Gun Coy: One Section where they are at present in St. PIERRE DIVION Area.
                                One Section in SANDY BLUFF.
                                Two Sections and Headquarters in PAISLEY AVENUE, or NORTH BLUFF if they will not interfere with Battalion of 116th Inf.Bde.

   117th Trench Mortar Bty: Four guns remain where they are at present in St. PIERRE DIVION.
                                Four guns in PAISLEY AVENUE.

3. Rations will be brought up to LANCASHIRE DUMP for all Units except 16th Rifle Brigade, which will be taken to Point 70. The 17th K.R.R. Corps will send carrying party to LANCASHIRE DUMP on being informed that the rations have arrived.

4. The above moves will take place on receipt of these Orders, and arrival of Units in locations stated will be reported by Code Word "CHATSWORTH".

5. The 117th Infantry Brigade Headquarters will be in PAISLEY AVENUE.
6. ACKNOWLEDGE.

13.11.1916.

                                            Captain,
                                a/Brigade Major, 117th Infantry Brigade.

B.M./215.

To /
　　Headquarters,
　　　　39th Division.

I forward herewith Report of O.C., 16th Notts & Derby Regiment, and my own Diary of events, which lead to the capture of St. PIERRE DIVION. A certain number, about 15, White Star Bombs were used and were necessary. At the time of relief of my Brigade there were a few Germans still in some of the tunnels over which sentries had been placed. In all these localities a Gas Bomb was placed before leaving, as there was a difficulty in the dark in making certain that every entrance would be taken over.

　　　　　　　　　　　　　　　　　　　　Brigadier General,
16.11.1916.　　　　　　　　　Commanding 117th Infantry Brigade.

117th INFANTRY BRIGADE.

REPORT on OPERATIONS carried out on NOVEMBER 13th.,1916, by the 16th NOTTS & DERBY Regiment.

THE ASSEMBLY was carried out quietly in accordance with orders in very misty weather.

The three Companies advanced to the assault at the scheduled time under cover of an excellent barrage fire.

There was no enemy barrage - only a little desultory shelling.

Both on right and left the advance met opposition from enemy's bombers interspersed with desultory rifle fire. No great difficulty, however, was met with in entering the German front line.

THE LEFT COMPANIES proceeded to work along the face of the BLUFF posting sentries over dug-outs. Before reaching the second objective they encountered a heavy bombing attack. The enemy were, however, driven eventually into their dug-outs by bombs and rifle fire, and sentries posted over them.

THE RIGHT COMPANY on entering the enemy front line trench met with a severe bombing attack from the right from Point Q.24.d.5.8.

The advance was held up, and at 6.35 a.m. I ordered up the Reserve Company to assist them. Their arrival cleared the situation.

Two platoons of the Reserve Company assisted the Right Company and blocked the front line dug-outs. The other two platoons advanced via Point Q.24½d.5.4. along the top of the BLUFF to the German Battalion Headquarters which they reached just in time to prevent the exit of a number of Germans.

Leaving sentries on all dug-outs, this party advanced as far as Point 61 in the HANSA LINE, and then returned to assist in clearing the dug-outs.

The total number of prisoners taken and sent in amounts to about 13 Officers, including a Battalion Commander, and 720 Other Ranks.

Our casualties consisted of:-
    1 Officer killed.   4 Other Ranks killed.
                       15   ditto   missing (probably wounded).
                       49   ditto   wounded.
    1   68

Difficulty was experienced in the mist in recognising the objective allotted to the Battalion, and the Battalion advanced a considerable distance beyond their objective, and took the whole of the village of ST. PIERRE DIVION as far as and including the German Battn H.Q's.

Two Officers and ten Other Ranks of the 4/5th Black Watch assisted. The remainder of this Battalion apparently lost direction in the mist, and failed to reach their final objective.

The 1/6th CHESHIRES Regiment also apparently lost direction to their right, and took no part in the capture of ST. PIERRE DIVION.

All ranks of the Battalion displayed a keen soldierly spirit, and worked admirably together, although we had 150 newly joined men in the ranks.

I would like to especially mention the work of the Artillery. The barrage was wonderfully accurate, enabling our men to advance to within 20 yards of it.

The enemy wire was completely cut although a few days previously it formed a very considerable obstacle.

                                        C. HERBERT STEPNEY, Lieut. Colonel
14.11.1916.   Commanding 16th Notts & Derby Regiment.

117th INFANTRY BRIGADE.

REPORT on OPERATIONS carried out on November 13th., 1916.

No.	From.	Time.	Remarks.
1.	O.C. 16th Notts & Derby Regt.	6.20 am.	Reports – "Men advanced to attack. Hostile artillery fire very slight".
2.	~~O.C. 16th Notts & Derby Regt.~~	6.23 am.	Reported No.1 to 39th Division (verbal)
3.	O.C. 16th Notts & Derby Regt.	6.35 am.	Reports – "2 wounded men say that 16th Notts & Derby Regt. have got in alright on left, and are bombing up and doing well. No report from Right".
4.	ditto.	6.37 am.	Reports – "6 prisoners brought back to Battn Headquarters from the Left".
5.		6.38 am.	Reported Nos 3 & 4 to 39th Division".
6.	O.C. Notts & Derby Regt.	6.40 am.	Reports – "Right Company seems to be hung up, and Reserve Company has been sent up".
7.	ditto.	6.43 am.	Reports – "Capt. ILLINGWORTH reports that on the Left 1st Objective taken, and that they are half way to 2nd objective.
8.	G.O.C.	6.44 am.	One Company, 17th Notts & Derby Regt. and one Company, 17th K.R.R.Corps ordered to "stand to".
9.	39th Division.	6.46 am.	Permission given to send up one Company from 17th Notts & Derby Regt.
10.		6.55 am.	One Company, 17th Notts & Derby Regt. ordered to report to O.C., 16th Notts & Derby Regt., at Battn Headquarters at once. O.C. 16th Notts & Derby Regt. informed. O.C. 17th Notts & Derby Regt. ordered to send up 20 boxes Grenades by the Company.
11.		7.6 am.	O.C. 17th Notts & Derby Regt. ordered to move the remainder of Battn up to Battn H.Q's, 16th Notts & Derby Regt. O.C. 16th Notts & Derby Regt. informed.
12.	G.O.C.	7 am.	Informed 39th Division that the whole of 17th Notts & Derby Regt. would be sent up to 16th Notts & Derby Regt.
13.	O.C. 16th Notts & Derby Regt.	7.10 am.	Reports – "Wounded man says a few 4/5th Black Watch seen on top of Bluff".
14.	G.O.C.	7.15 am.	Informed 118th Brigade, also 39th Division, of No. 13.
15.	O.C. 16th Notts & Derby Regt.	7.17 am.	Reports – "10 more prisoners now coming in. Right Company has reached its objective. A lot more prisoners to come when the dug-outs are cleared".
16.	G.O.C.	7.19 am.	Informed 39th Division of No. 15.
17.	O.C. 17th Notts & Derby Regt.	7.26 am.	Reports – "One Company has left, and the others now going.

- 2 -

18.	O.C. 16th Notts & Derby Regt.	7.27 am.	Reports - "151 prisoners are now passing my Battn H.Q's, and more coming in."
19.		7.29 am.	Reported No. 16 to 39th Division.
20.	O.C. 17th Notts & Derby Regt.	7.31 am.	Reports - "3 Companies have now left, and O.C. and H.Q's are just leaving".
21.	16th ditto	7.34 am.	Reports - "3 Officers among the prisoners".
22.	ditto	7.45 am.	Reports - "Companies report all objectives taken".
23.	G.O.C.	7.55 am.	O.C. 16th Notts & Derby Regt. asked to find out if connection has been established with 4/5th Black Watch.
24.	O.C. 117th T.M. Battery.	8.2 am.	Reports - "Battery withdrawn and now at South CAUSEWAY".
25.	O.C. 16th Notts & Derby Regt.	8.6 am.	Reports - (i) 1 Officer and 15 more prisoners. (ii) 17th Notts & Derby Regt. have arrived at his Battn H.Q's.
26.	ditto	8.12 am	Reports - "102 more prisoners passed - more to come".
27.	G.S.O.1.	8.17 am	Reports that HANSA Line is held.
28.	G.O.C.	8.17 am	Orders to O.C. 16th Notts & Derby Regt. to send one Company, 17th Notts & Derby Regt. across to help, and that Objective Trench is to be strongly garrisoned and consolidated.
29.	O.C. 16th Notts & Derby Regt.	8.24 am	Reports - "4/5th Black Watch seem on top of bank, but they did not come down. The Germans appear to be on our right. We are not in touch with Brigade on our right".
30.	G.O.C.	8.25 am	Orders to O.C. 17th Notts & Derby Regt. to send out an Officer's Patrol of one platoon to move to top of bank, thence in an Easterly direction and gain touch with Brigade on our right.
31.	O.C. 17th Notts & Derby Regt.	8.45 am.	Reports - "Patrol detailed in No. 30 has gone out".
32.	39th Division	8.50 am	G.294 received.
33.	G.O.C.	9.15 am	Machine Gun Section ordered to go up to front objective.
34.	39th Division	8.57 am	G.295 received.
35.	O.C. 16th Notts & Derby Regt.	9 am.	Reports - "In touch with 4/5th Black Watch. At least another 600 prisoners. Require more men to deal with them".
36.	G.O.C.	9.15 am	Orders O.C. 17th Notts & Derby Regt. to send remaining two Companies across to help
37.	G.O.C.	9.15 am	Orders O.C. 16th Notts & Derby Regt. to move his Battn H.Q's forward as soon as possible. O.C. 17th Notts & Derby Regt. to remain in H.Q's vacated by 16th Notts & Derby Regiment.

- 3 -

38. 39th Division.	9.15 am.	G.296 received.
39. O.C. 117th M.G. Company.	9.15 am.	Reports - "Guns North of River assembled in trenches 100 yards East of 118th Brigade H.Q'S, near Brigade Bomb Store".
40. O.C. 17th Notts & Derby Regt.	9.32 am.	Reports - "1 Company, 3 platoons, 17th Notts & Derby Regt. have gone up to 2nd objective".
41. G.O.C. 39th Division.	9.45 am.	G.O.C., Division, sanctions sending up 2 Companies, 17th K.R.R.Corps.
42. O.C. 16th Notts & Derby Regt.	9.50 am.	Reports he is in touch with 1/1st Herts and 1/6th Cheshires, but there seems to be some bombing on his right. He is consolidating the SUMMER HOUSE LINE.
43. 39th Division.	9.55 am.	G.296 received.
44. G.S.O.1.	10.6 am.	Reports - "G.O.C., 118th Infantry Brigade is sending 2 Companies, 14th Hants Regt. down STRASBURG LINE, 2 Companies down German SUPPORT and FRONT LINE, to clear up and reinforce 1/6th Cheshires and 4/5th Black Watch respectively".
45. G.O.C.	10 am.	Orders to O.C. 117th Trench Mortar Bty to move four STOKES Guns up into the line Q.24.b.6.2. - 2.6. 50 men of 17th K.R.R.Corps given him to carry ammunition.
46. G.O.C.	10.am.	Issues following orders to 17th K.R.R. Corps:- 1. Move your Battalion up to line of MILL Road and occupy assembly trenches of 16th Notts & Derby Regiment. 2. 50 men will go to PAISLEY DUMP and carry up STOKES Ammunition, thereafter remaining with you. 3. Before moving across to GERMAN Trenches refer to me if the line still holds, otherwise use your own discretion.
47. O.C. 17th Notts & Derby Regt.	10.20 am	Reports - "Another 150 prisoners passed Battn H.Q's".
48. ditto	10.25 am	Reports that Officer's Patrol has returned and that 16th Notts & Derby Regt. and 4/5th Black Watch in touch at Q.24.d.8.7.(?).
49. 39th Division	10.40 am	G.297 received.
50. O.C. 16th Notts & Derby Regt.	11 am.	Reports from SUMMER HOUSE the whole of St. Pierre Divion occupied by 16th Notts & Derby Regt. He is consolidating from SUMMER HOUSE to Q.18.d.9.4. 1/6th Cheshires carry on from there consolidating up MILL Trench. 1/1st Cambs appear to be working on their right. Colonel Stepney is making his H.Q's in ST. PIERRE DIVION at old German Battn H.Q's. Evacuation of prisoners continues

* Telephone Line

51.	O.C. 117th Trench Mortar Battery.	11.15 am.	Reports moving into line from PAISLEY 10.45 am.
52.	39th Division.	1.15 pm.	Situation Report (No.G.301).
53.	G.S.O.1.	1.45 pm.	Reports 1 Battn reorganise THIEPVAL. 1 Battn - PAISLEY AVENUE. 1 Battn - RIVER LEFT Sedtion. 1 Battn - Dug-outs, St. PIERRE DIVION.
54.	G.O.C.	2.10 pm.	Orders to O.C. 117th Machine Gun Company to assemble two sections at Brigade H.Q's, NORTH BLUFF.

SECRET.   Copy No. 17.

117th INFANTRY BRIGADE ORDER No.98.

14.11.1916.

Reference: 1/40000 Map Sheet 57D.
1/40000 Map ALBERT (Combined Sheet).

1. The 117th Infantry Brigade will be relieved by the 96th Infantry Brigade today, the 14th instant, in accordance with the attached table.

2. Commanding Officers will pay special attention to the handing over of all Bombs, Mills Rifle Grenades, S.O.S. Rockets, Water and Ration Dumps, and other trench stores, and will indicate to relieving Commanding Officers the exact places where such stores exist.

    The exact dispositions of the way the line is held, the areas to be avoided, the shelled areas, and all information regarding the various Sub-sections will be similarly handed over.

3. Os.C., 16th Rifle Brigade, and 16th Notts & Derby Regiment, will each place a Limber at the disposal of O.C., 117th Trench Mortar Battery. (vide Administration Order No.S.C./425 of today's date.

4. Units on relief will march independently 200 yards between Companies.

5. There will be a bus at BLACK HORSE BRIDGE at 6 p.m. to bring on any men, such as guides, who may be left behind. These will not exceed four per Battalion.

    O.C., 16th Rifle Brigade, will detail an Officer to proceed in charge of this party.

6. Transport Orders will be issued by the Staff Captain.

7. Reports of arrival in Billets will be reported immediately to Brigade Headquarters at WARLOY.

8. The 117th Infantry Brigade Report Centre will close at PAISLEY DUMP at 6 p.m., reopening at WARLOY

9. ACKNOWLEDGE.

                                            R.S. Fetherstonhaugh Captain,
14.11.1916.   a/Brigade Major, 117th Infantry Brigade.

Copies issued to:-

No.1. 16th Notts & Derby Regt.   10. H.Q's, 39th Division.
   2. 17th   ditto   11.   39th Division.
   3. 17th K.R.R.Corps.   12. No.3 Coy., Div.Train.
   4. 16th Rifle Brigade.   13. G.O.C.
   5. 117th Machine Gun Coy.   14. B.M.
   6. 117th Trench Mortar Bty.   15. S.C.
   7. H.Q's, 116th Brigade.   16. Bde Signals Officer.
   8.   118th Brigade.   17. War Diary.
   9.   96th Brigade.   18. War Diary.
                                        19. Order file.

SECRET.

RELIEF TABLE to accompany 117th INFANTRY BRIGADE ORDER NO. 92.

Item.	Date.	Unit.	From.	To.	Relieved by.	Route.	Guides.	Remarks.
1.	4/11/1916.	16th Notts & Derby Regt.	PAISLEY Avenue.	ARLOY.	15th LANCS. Fusiliers.	AVELUY - ALBERT - MILLENCOURT - HENENCOURT.	LANCASHIRE Dump. 3.30 p.m.	After guides have met incoming Unit, 17th Notts & Derby may move off and meet the Transport in accordance with Admin.Order S.C./425.
2.	do.	17th Notts & Derby Regt.	THIEPVAL Dug-outs.	do.	16th LANCS. Fusiliers.	ditto	CRUCIFIX CORNER 4 p.m.	
3.	do.	17th K.R.R. Corps.	German.Front and Support Line near ST.PIERRE DIVION.	do.	2nd INNIS- KILLING Fusiliers.	ditto	North CAUSEWAY 5.15 p.m.	
4.	do.	16th Rifle Brigade.	RIVER RIGHT and CENTRE Sub-sectns.	do.	16th NORTHUM- BERLAND FUSRS.	ditto	CRUCIFIX CORNER 5 p.m.	
5.	do.	117th M.G. Company.	RIVER Section.	do.	96th M.G. Company.	ditto	LANCASHIRE Dump. 5.15 p.m.	
6.	do.	117th T.M. Battery.	PAISLEY Avenue.	do.	--	ditto	LANCASHIRE Dump. 5.15 p.m.	
7.	do.	117th Bde H.Q's.	PAISLEY Dump.	do.	96th Inf. Bde H.Q's.	ditto	--	

To Headquarters,
    39th Division.
    ----------------   B.M./215.

   The following are the few further details as to the use of Gas bombs
   on the 13th instant.   About 15 were used in all.

1. In one case where the enemy were using the dug-out to snipe from,
   a bomb was dropped in from on top.   Immediately two Germans rushed
   out foaming at the mouth, and had to be removed on stretchers and
   undoubtedly died.   In another, a dug-out was bombed, and about two
   hours afterwards entered - there were four dead Germans in it.

2. The only details available as to the action of the Tank are that
   it arrived at the German First Line before the attacking Infantry,
   where it subsided into a dug-out and failed to get out.   It was
   surrounded by a party of the enemy.   A Corporal of the 16th Notts
   & Derby Regiment perceived this, and collecting a party went to
   its help, and drove the enemy into their dug-outs, eventually
   capturing them.
   It is understood that the Officer and one man of the Tank crew
   were killed.

                                                    Brigadier General,
18.11.1916.   Commanding 117th Infantry Brigade.

SECRET.   Copy No....

117th INFANTRY BRIGADE ORDER No.100.

Reference: 1/100,000 Map 5.a. HAZEBROUCH.

The 117th Infantry Brigade will be in VIII Corps Reserve in the Area:-

    BOLLEZEELE, MERCKEGHAM, VOLKERINCKHOVE, TATINGHEM.

1. The 17th Notts & Derby Regiment will be attached to the Second Army Central School at TATINGHEM.

2. Detraining Stations and Billetting Areas are as shewn in table given below.

3. The administration of the 39th Divisional School will be carried out by the 117th Infantry Brigade.

4. Reports of arrival in new billets to be reported to Brigade Headquarters.

5. The 117th Infantry Brigade Headquarters will close at GEZAINCOURT at 8 a.m. on the 17th instant, and will open at BOLLEZEELE on arrival.

6. ACKNOWLEDGE.

                                (Sgd) A.J.S.Fetherstonhaugh, Captain,
16.11.1916.   A/Brigade Major, 117th Infantry Brigade.

TABLE

Unit.	Detraining Station	Billetting Area.
117th Bde Headquarters.	ESQUELBECQ.	BOLLEZEELE.
16th Notts & Derby Regt.	)	HERCKEGHEM.
17th K.R.R.Corps.	) ditto.	VOLKERINCKHOVE.
16th Rifle Brigade.	)	
17th Notts & Derby Regt. attached 2nd Army School.	ST. OMER.	TATINGHEM.
117th Machine Gun Coy.	ESQUELBECQ.	BOLLEZEELE.
117th Trench Mortar Bty.	ditto.	ditto.

App 13. M.S.

Copy No.... 10

117th INFANTRY BRIGADE ORDER No. 101.

21.11.1916.

Reference 1/40000 Map of France, Sheet 27.

1. Lieut.General Sir AYLMER HUNTER WESTON, K.C.B., D.S.O., Commanding the VIII Corps, will inspect the 117th Infantry Brigade at 2.30 p.m. tomorrow, the 22nd November.

2. (a) The 117th Infantry Brigade, less 117th Machine Gun Company and 117th Trench Mortar Battery, will be formed up on the Divisional Training Area about G.4.Central, facing South East in line of close columns by the right, with 12 paces interval between Battalions, by 2 p.m. Officers will take post in Review Order.

   (b) The Corps Commander will be received with a GENERAL SALUTE, the Brigade Commander giving all executive words of command to the Brigade.

   (c) The Band of the 13th Gloucester Regiment will attend the Inspection.

4. (a) In the case of all Battalions, Companies will be equalised, sized, and told off into Platoons, as laid down in Chapter IV, Sec.55, para 1, "Ceremonial".

   (b) Section Commanders below the rank of Sergeant, Pioneers, Signallers, and Lewis Gunners, will be in the ranks. Lewis Guns will not be on parade.

   (c) First Line Transport will not parade.

5. All ranks will be dressed in Marching Order.

6. Adjutants will meet the Brigade Major at about G.4.Central at 10 a.m. tomorrow morning, the 22nd instant, when all details will be arranged.

7. All parades for tomorrow morning will be cancelled.

8. ACKNOWLEDGE.

H S Fetherstonhaugh Captain,
a/Brigade Major, 117th Infantry Brigade.

21.11.1916.

Copies issued at 8 p.m. to:-

No.1. 16th Notts & Derby Regt.	No.7. 39th Division.
2. 17th ditto	8. ditto.
3. 17th K.R.R.Corps.	9. B.M.
4. 16th Rifle Brigade.	10. War Diary.
5. 117th Machine Gun Company.	11. ditto
6. 117th Trench Mortar Bty.	12. Order file.

39th Division.

B. H. Q.

117th INFANTRY BRIGADE

DECEMBER 1916

Appendices attached:-
    Brigade Orders.

117th. Infantry Brigade.
Date 1 JAN 1917
No B.M./476

To/
Headquarters,
   39th Division.

Herewith WAR DIARIES for Brigade Headquarters, and Units of this Brigade, for the month of December, 1916.

                                          Brigadier-General.
                              Commanding 117th Infantry Brigade.

1.1.1917.

Army Form C. 2118.

WAR DIARY
or
INTELLIGENCE SUMMARY.
(Erase heading not required.)

Instructions regarding War Diaries and Intelligence Summaries are contained in F. S. Regs., Part II. and the Staff Manual respectively. Title pages will be prepared in manuscript.

Place	Date	Hour	Summary of Events and Information	Remarks and references to Appendices
BOLLEZEELE.	Decr. 1st			
	2nd		BRIGADE AT REST.	
	3rd			
	4th			
	5th		Brigade Order No. 103 issued for inspection of Brigade on March next day.	I
	6th		Brigade inspected on the march by Gen.Sir.Hubert Plumer., G.C.M.G., K.C.B., Comdg II Army.	
	7th		Brigade Order No. 104 issued for inspection of Brigade by Corps Commander on Decr. 8th.	II
			Training.	
	8th		Brigade inspected by Sir.Aylmer Hunter Weston., K.C.B., D.S.O., Comdg VIII Corps.	
	9th		Brigade Order No. 105 issued for moves in connection with the relief of the 38th Division by the 39th Division on the 13th and 14th. 17th Notts & Derby.R. to remain at TATINGHEM.	III
			1/1st Cambs.R. to be attached to 117th Infantry Brigade till 17th Notts & Derby.R. rejoin. 117th Machine Gun Coy and 117th Trench Mortar Battery move by march route to HERZEELE.	
	10th		16th Notts & Derby.R. and 16th Rifle Brigade moved by train to POPERINGHE. Brigade Order	
	11th		No. 106 issued giving further details of relief.	IV
POPERINGHE.	12th		Brigade Headquarters and 17th K.R.Rif.C. moved by train to POPERINGHE. 117th Machine Gun Coy, 117th Trench Mortar Battery, 16th Notts & Derby.R., and 16th Rifle Brigade move by train	

Army Form C. 2118.

WAR DIARY
or
INTELLIGENCE SUMMARY.

(Erase heading not required.)

Instructions regarding War Diaries and Intelligence Summaries are contained in F. S. Regs., Part II. and the Staff Manual respectively. Title pages will be prepared in manuscript.

Place	Date	Hour	Summary of Events and Information	Remarks and references to Appendices
POPERINGHE.	Decr. 12th contd.		and march route to SUPPORT CENTRE SECTION, Canal Bank.	
CANAL BANK (West)	13th		Brigade Headquarters, 17th K.R.Rif.C. and 1/1st Cambs.R. move to SUPPORT CENTRE SECTION Canal Bank, 117th Trench Mortar Battery, 117th Machine Gun Coy, 16th Notts & Derby.R., and 16th Rifle Brigade move into front line. 118th Infantry Brigade on our left; 116th Infantry Brigade on our right.	
	14th		All quiet on Brigade front.	
	15th		All quiet on Brigade front.	
	16th		Brigade Order No. 107 regarding Inter-Battalion relief on 17th instant.	V
	17th		Inter-Battalion relief took place. The 1/1st Cambs.R. relieving 16th Rifle Brigade; 17th K.R.Rif.C. the 16th Notts & Derby.R.	
	18th		All quiet on Brigade Front.	
	19th		All quiet on Brigade Front.	
	20th		Brigade Order No. 108 for Inter-Battalion relief. 1/1st Cambs.R. by 16th Rifle Brigade; 17th K.R.Rif.C. by 16th Notts & Derby.R. on 21st instant.	VI
	21st		Inter-Battalion relief carried out. Brigade Order No. 109 issued for relief of 1/1st Cambs.R. by 17th Notts & Derby.R. arriving by train from TATINGHEM.	VII

T2134. W1. W708—776. 500000. 4/15. Sir J. C. & S.

Army Form C. 2118.

WAR DIARY
or
INTELLIGENCE SUMMARY.
(Erase heading not required.)

Instructions regarding War Diaries and Intelligence Summaries are contained in F.S. Regs., Part II. and the Staff Manual respectively. Title pages will be prepared in manuscript.

Place	Date	Hour	Summary of Events and Information	Remarks and references to Appendices
CANAL BANK (West)	Decr. 22nd		All quiet on Brigade front.	
	23rd		118th Infantry Brigade relieve 116th Infantry Brigade.	
	24th		At 2 a.m. enemy shelled front and support line, causing some casualties. Brigade Order No. 110 issued for Inter-Battalion relief on 25th instant. 17th K.R.Rif.C. to relieve 16th Notts & Derby.R.; 17th Notts & Derby.R. the 16th Rifle Brigade.	VIII
	25th		At 3 p.m. an arranged bombardment of enemy's line by artillery and 117th Trench Mortar Battery carried out. Enemy's retaliation did some damage and caused some casualties. Inter-Battalion relief carried out.	
	26th		All quiet on Brigade front.	
	27th		All quiet on Brigade front.	
	28th		Brigade Order No. 111 issued for Inter-Battalion relief. 16th Notts & Derby.R. to relieve 17th K.R.Rif.C.; 16th Rifle Brigade to relieve 17th Notts & Derby.R.	IX
	29th		All quiet on Brigade front.	
	30th		All quiet on Brigade front.	
	31st		Enemy bombared Left Sub-section. No damage done.	

Brigadier-General.
Commanding 117th Infantry Brigade.

Copy No. 13

117th INFANTRY BRIGADE ORDER No. 103.

5.12.1916.

Reference: 1/40,000 Map of France, Sheet 27.

1. General Sir Herbert Plumer, G.C.M.G., K.C.B., Commanding Second Army, will inspect the 117th Infantry Brigade on the March tomorrow, WEDNESDAY, December 6th., in accordance with the attached March Table

2. The Brigade Starting Point, at 9.40 a.m., is the Road Junction at A.24.d.8.5.

    The Divisional Starting Point, at 10 a.m., is the Forge in B.19.d.

3. (a) Dress will be Marching Order (Packs) and Steel Helmets.

    (b) Parade will be as strong as possible, and Parade States will be handed to the Brigade Major at the Brigade Starting Point at 9.35 a.m.

    (c) Transport, fully loaded, (less Baggage Waggons) will march in rear of each Unit. Dinners will be cooked in the Field Kitchens on the march.

    (d) Attention is drawn to Sect.25, Field Service Regs., Part 1, regarding distances behind Units.

4. The Army Commander will be about 100 yards S.W. of the Mill, in G.12.A. at 10.35 a.m.

5. Watches will be synchronised at 9.30 a.m. at the Brigade Starting Point (A.24.d.8.5.) An Officer from each Unit will attend for this purpose.

6. ACKNOWLEDGE.

W. E. Maxwell Captain,
Brigade Major, 117th Infantry Brigade.

5.12.1916.

Copies issued at 8 p.m. to:-

No. 1. 16th Notts & Derby Regt.
2. 17th K.R.R.Corps.
3. 16th Rifle Brigade.
4. 117th Machine Gun Coy.
5. 117th Trench Mortar Battery.
6. H.Q's, 39th Division.
7. H.Q's, 39th Division.
8. G.O.C.
9. B.M.
10. S.C.
11. Brigade Sigs.Officer.
12. Brigade Bombing Officer.
13. War Diary.
14. War Diary.
15. Order file.

MARCH TABLE to accompany 117th INFANTRY BRIGADE ORDER No. 103.

Unit.	Time head of Unit to pass Brigade Starting Point.	Route to be taken to Brigade Starting Point.	Route for March.	Remarks.
117th Infantry Brigade Headquarters.	9.40 a.m.		FORGE in B.19.d. - MILL in G.12.A - Road Junction at G.11.d.7.1. - VOLKERING - HOVE - MERCKGHEM - BOLLEZEELE.	
16th Notts & Derby Regiment.	9.43 a.m.	Via LEWERCKERVOIT - Road Junction G.5.A.4.9 - BOLLEZEELE.		
17th K.R.R.Corps.	9.48 a.m.	Via BOLLEZEELE.		
16th Rifle Brigade.	9.53 a.m.			
117th Machine Gun Company.	9.58 a.m.	Via BOLLEZEELE.		
117th Trench Mortar Battery.	10.1 a.m.			

REAR PARTY of 1 N.C.O. and 6 men will be found by the 17th K.R.R.CORPS.

The FIRST HALT will be ordered from the head of the Column: Subsequent halts will be at the usual 10 minutes to clock hour.

Copy No. 11

117th INFANTRY BRIGADE ORDER No.104.

Ref:- 1/20,000 Sheet 27 N.W.   6.12.1916.

1. Reference this Office B.M./297 of the 4th instant, Lieut.General Sir Aylmer Hunter-Weston, K.C.B.,D.S.O., Commanding the VIII Corps, will inspect the 117th Infantry Brigade on FRIDAY, December 8th.,1916, in accordance with the attached Programme.

2. (a) Battalions will be formed up in close column by the right, in accordance with the attached plan, facing the entrance to the field in which they are parading, and will receive the Corps Commander with a General Salute when he arrives within 25 yards of the Battalion. Companies should be sized. Those men of Headquarter Companies not shewn in War Establishment will parade with their Companies:

    (b) The 117th Machine Gun Company, and the 117th Light Trench Mortar Battery, will parade fully equipped with full establishment of ammunition, ready for action at short notice.

    (c) Lewis Guns will be drawn up to go in rear of each Battalion.

    (d) First Line Transport, fully loaded, will be formed up for inspection in rear of each Battalion, and will leave the field as soon as it had been inspected.

    (e) After the Inspection of each Battalion close order drill will be carried out.

    (f) Officers and mens billets and messes will be inspected on the conclusion of each Unit.

    (g) All ranks will be in marching order, packs and steel helmets, carrying the full amount of ammunition, 120 rounds per man, unless otherwise laid down. Leather Jerkins will not be worn.

3. ACKNOWLEDGE.

W.E.Maxwell Captain,

6.12.1916.   Brigade Major, 117th Infantry Brigade.

Copies issued to:-

No.1. 16th Notts & Derby Regt.   6. H.Q's.,39th Division.
    2. 17th K.R.R.Corps.   7. H.Q's.,39th Division.
    3. 16th Rifle Brigade.   8. G.O.C.
    4. 117th Machine Gun Coy.   9. B.M.
    5. 117th Trench Mortar Battery.   10. S.C.
                                        11 & 12. War Diary.
                                        13. Order file.

Programme for Inspection of 117th Infantry Brigade
by
LIEUT.GENERAL SIR AYLMER HUNTER-WESTON, K.C.B., D.S.O.,
Commanding VIII Corps
on
8th December, 1916.

---

10 a.m.	Meet G.O.C., 39th Division, and Brigadier General Commanding 117th Infantry Brigade at Cross Roads B.19.A.2.0. Inspection of 16th Rifle Brigade in field at B.19.c.7.8.
10.30 a.m.	Close Order Drill by 16th Rifle Brigade.
10.35 a.m.	Inspection of billets and messes at BOLLEZEELE.
11.5 a.m.	Inspection of 117th Machine Gun Company in field at A.29.b.4.0.
11.10 a.m.	Inspection of 117th Light Trench Mortar Battery in field at A.29.b.4.0.
11.15 a.m.	Motor to MERCKEGHEM.
11.25 a.m.	Inspect 17th K.R.R.Corps in field at A.22.c.4.2.
11.55 a.m.	Close Order Drill by 17th K.R.R.Corps.
12 noon.	Inspection of billets and messes in MERCKEGHEM.
12.30 p.m.	Motor to VOLKERINCKHOVE.
12.35 p.m.	Inspect 16th Notts & Derby Regiment in field at G.15.a.2.5.
1.10 p.m.	Close Order Drill by 16th Notts & Derby Regiment.

CEREMONIAL

- Battn. Commander.
- Senior Major.
- Adjutant.
- Company Commander.
  " 2nd in Command.
- Platoon Commander
- Quartermaster.
- Sergeant Major.
- Battn. Q.M.S.
  " Armourer Serge.
- Coy. Sergt. Major.
- Coy. Q.M.S.
- Platoon Sergt.
- M.O.

SECRET.   Copy No. 19

117th INFANTRY BRIGADE ORDER No. 105.

Reference: Sheets 27 and 28.   9.12.1916.

1. (a) The 39th Division will relieve the 38th Division (Welsh) commencing on the 11th December.

   (b) The 117th Infantry Brigade will relieve the 113th Brigade on the 13th and 14th December.

   (c) The moves from present area will be in accordance with the attached Tables "A" and "B". Personnel only will proceed by train.

2. (a) The 17th Notts & Derby Regiment will remain at TATINGHEM until relieved by a Battalion of the 38th Division.

   (b) The 1/1st Cambridgeshire Regiment will be attached to the 117th Infantry Brigade until the 17th Notts & Derby Regiment rejoin the Brigade.

3. (a) Advance Parties of 1 Officer and 20 Other Ranks each from 16th Notts & Derby Regiment, and 16th Rifle Brigade, will proceed to POPERINGHE on the 10th. They will report to Headquarters, 116th Brigade, and will be rationed from there from the 11th instant inclusive.

   Buses for these parties will be at Brigade Headquarters at 9 a.m. on the 10th.

   (b) Advance Party of 1 Officer and 20 Other Ranks, from the 17th K.R.R. Corps, will proceed to POPERINGHE by the first train on the 11th. They will draw rations for the 12th from the 116th Brigade.

   (c) See below.

4. The following Motor Lorries have been applied for to assist in the removal of Quarter Masters' Stores:-

Each Battalion	Four.
117th Machine Gun Coy)	One.
117th T.Mortar Bty.)	
117th Inf.Bde H.Q's.	One.

5. Units will send to Brigade Headquarters by 12 noon tomorrow, the 10th., an inventory in duplicate of all billet stores which will be left behind on vacating present billets.

6. The First Line Transport of each Unit will draw rations from WORMHOUDT STATION for its Unit for the following day as it passes through that place.
   Lewis Gun Detachments, and the 117th Machine Gun Company and 117th Trench Mortar Battery, will do the same.

7. 117th Infantry Brigade Headquarters will close at BOLLEZEELE at 11 a.m. on the 12th December, reopening on arrival in POPERINGHE.

8. ACKNOWLEDGE.

                                              W.T. Maxwell   Captain,
                                         Brigade Major, 117th Infantry Brigade.
9.12.1916.

   (c) Advance Party of 1 Officer, 3 Other Ranks, from 117th Machine Gun Coy., 1 Other Rank from each Battn. Lewis Gun Detachment, 1 Other Ranks from 117th Trench Mortar Bty., will parade at Brigade H.Q's at 8.45 a.m., the 10th., under an Officer to be detailed by 117th Machine Gun Coy., and will proceed by the bus referred to in 3(a) above, to fix billets in HERZEELE. On arrival at HERZEELE the Officer will report to O.C., 39th Divisional Supply Column for particulars as to accommodation.

Copy No.:

Copies issued at 8.15 p.m. to:-

No. 1. 16th Notts & Derby Regt.
2. 17th ditto
3. 17th K.R.R.Corps.
4. 16th Rifle Brigade.
5. 117th Machine Gun Coy.
6. 117th Trench Mortar Bty.
7. H.Q's, 39th Division.
8. ditto
9. H.Q's, 116th Brigade.
10. H.Q's, 118th Brigade.
11. H.Q's, 113th Brigade.
12. 1/1st Cambs. Regt.
13. No.3 Coy. Train.
14. Comdt., 39th Divl. Schools.
15. B.O.C.
16. B.M.
17. S.C.
18. Bde Signals Officer.
19. War Diary.
20. War Diary.
21. Order file.

TABLE "A" to accompany 117th INFANTRY BRIGADE ORDER No. 103.

Unit.	DECEMBER 11th.			DECEMBER 12th.			DECEMBER 13th.		
	From.	To.	Remarks.	From.	To.	Remarks.	From.	To.	Remarks.
16th Notts & Derby Regt.	BOLLEZEELE Station.	Cheesemarket Stn, POPERINGHE to billet in POPERINGHE.	Go in two trains. 1st:11.30 a.m. 2nd:11.40 a.m.	POPERINGHE.	Support Centre Section.	Train from G.8.b. at 4 p.m.	Support Centre Section.	Trenches.	--
17th K.R.R.C.	Remains in present billets.	--	--	BOLLEZEELE Station.	Cheesemarket Stn, Poperinghe to billet in Poperinghe	By trains. 1st:11 am. 2nd:11.10. 3rd:11.20.	Billets, POPERINGHE.	Support Centre Section.	Trains from G.8.b., 4 p.m.
16th Rfe.Bde.	BOLLEZEELE Station.	Cheesemarket Sn, POPERINGHE to billet in POPERINGHE.	(By trains) 1st:11 am 2nd:11.10. 3rd:11.20	POPERINGHE.	Support Centre Section.	Train from G.8.b. 4 p.m.	Support Centre Section.	Trenches.	--
117th Bde. H.Q's.	Remains in present billets.	--	--	BOLLEZEELE Station.	Cheesemarket S.POPERINGHE, to billet in POPERINGHE.	By Train 11.20 am.	Billets, POPERINGHE.	Support Centre Section.	Train from G.8.b. 4 p.m.
1/1st Cambs. Regt.(attd. 117th Inf.Bde.	--	--	--	--	--	--	ELVER-DINGHE & L.Works.	ditto	March Route

NOTE: 1. Each Train on Metre Gauge (BOLLEZEELE to POPERINGHE) will take 250 All Ranks, and each train on Broad Gauge (POPERINGHE Eastwards) 1200 All Ranks.

2. Exact location of Battalions in Support Centre Section will be notified later.

3. Further Orders will be issued regarding all moves for December 13th.

TABLE "B" to accompany 117th INFANTRY BRIGADE ORDER No. 104, shewing movements of 117th MACHINE GUN COY., 117th TRENCH MORTAR Battery, Battalion Transport and Animals, Battalion Lewis Gun Teams and Handcarts.

Unit.	DECEMBER 10th.			DECEMBER 11th.		
	From.	To.	Remarks.	From.	To.	Remarks.
117th Machine Gun Coy.	BOLLEZEELE.	Billets, HERZEELE.	March Route via ESQUEL-BECQ and WORMHOUDT.	HERZEELE.	Billets, POPERINGHE.	March Route. Order of March as on 10th. Leave HERZEELE 10 a.m.
117th Trench Mortar Bty.	BOLLEZEELE.	ditto.	As for 117th Machine Gun Coy.	HERZEELE.	ditto.	ditto
16th Notts & Derby Lewis GunsTeams.						
16th Rifle Brigade Lewis Gun & Teams.	BOLLEZEELE.	ditto.	As for 117th Machine Gun Coy.	HERZEELE.	ditto.	ditto
17th K.R.R.Corps Lewis Guns & Teams.	BOLLEZEELE.	ditto.	As for 117th Machine Gun Coy.	HERZEELE.	ditto.	ditto
				HERCKEGHEM.	HERZEELE.	March Route via ESQUELBECQ & WORMHOUDT to be clear of BOLLEZEELE by 11 a.m.
16th Notts & Derby Transport.				BOLLEZEELE.	POPERINGHE.	March Route. See NOTE 2 overleaf.
17th.K.R.R.Corps Transport.						
16th Rif.Bde.Transport.				BOLLEZEELE.	POPERINGHE.	March Route. See NOTE 2 overleaf.
117th Bde.H.Q's.Transport.				BOLLEZEELE.	POPERINGHE.	ditto

Movements on December 12th and 13th shewn overleaf.

Unit.	DECEMBER 12th.			DECEMBER 13th.		
	From.	To.	Remarks.	From.	To.	Remarks.
117th Machine Gun Coy.	POPERINGHE.	Support Centre Section.	March Route.	Support Centre Section.	Trenches.	
117th Trench Mortar Bty.	ditto	ditto	ditto	ditto	ditto	
16th Notts & Derby						
Lewis Guns & Teams. 16th Rifle Brigade	ditto	ditto	ditto	ditto	ditto	
Lewis Guns & Teams. 17th K.R.R.Corps	ditto	ditto	ditto	ditto	ditto	
Lewis Guns & Teams.	HERZEELE.	POPERINGHE.	March Route via ESQUELBECQ & WORMHOUDT to be clear of HERZEELE by 10 a.m.	POPERINGHE.	Support Centre Section.	March Route.
16th Notts & Derby Transport.	POPERINGHE.	Support Centre Section.	March Route.			
17th K.R.R.Corps Transport.	MERCKEGHEM.	POPERINGHE.	March Route, leave MERCKEGHEM at 7 a.m.			
16th Rifle Brigade Transport.	POPERINGHE.	Support Centre Section.	March Route.			
117th Bde. H.Q's Transport.	POPERINGHE.	ditto	March Route.			

NOTE:
1. Units marching to HERZEELE on December 10th will march in order:- 117th Machine Gun Coy., 117th Trench Mortar Bty., Lewis Guns 16th Notts & Derby Regt., Lewis Guns 16th Rifle Brigade, Lewis Guns 16th Rifle Brigade. Head of column to pass Brigade Headquarters at 10 a.m. Column to be under Command of Captain H.R.STEVENS, M.C.
2. Transport of 16th Notts & Derby Regt., and 16th Rifle Brigade, in this order will be clear of BOLLEZEELE by 7 a.m. on the 11th. Senior Transport Officer to command Column.
3. Transport of 17th K.R.R.Corps and 117th Brigade Headquarters in this order will be clear of BOLLEZEELE by 7 a.m. on the 12th. Transport Officer, 17th K.R.R.Corps, to command Column.
4. More detailed orders regarding the Moves on the 12th and 13th will be issued later.

SECRET.   Copy No. 20

Further AMENDMENTS to 117th Infantry Brigade Order No. 105.

10.12.1916.

TABLE "A".

16th Notts & Derby)   DECEMBER 11th., Column 3.
    Regiment.   )
                      For 11.30 a.m. substitute:-
                           "12.29 arrive 15.16".

                      For 11.40 a.m. substitute:-
                           "12.39 arrive 15.26".

                      DECEMBER 12th., Column 3.

                      For 4 p.m. substitute "4.30 p.m."

16th Rifle Brigade.   DECEMBER 11th., Column 3.
                      Insert "two" between "by" and "trains".
                      For "11 a.m." substitute "11.59 arrive 15.00".
                      For "11.10" substitute "12.19 arrive 15.06".
                      Delete "3rd: 11.20".

                      DECEMBER 12th., Column 3.
                      For "4 p.m." substitute "4.30 p.m."

17th K.R.R.Corps.   DECEMBER 12th., Column 3.
                      Insert "two" between "by" and "trains".
                      For "11 a.m." substitute "12.19 arrive 15.06".
                      For "11.10" substitute "12.29 arrive 15.16".
                      Delete "3rd: 11.20".

117th Brigade H.Q's. DECEMBER 12th., Column 3.
                      For "11.20 a.m." substitute "12.29 arrive 15.16".

NOTE 1.   For "Each train on Metre Gauge (BOLLEZEELE to POPERINGHE) will
          take 250 All Ranks" substitute:-

          "Accommodation of trains on Metre Gauge Railway (BOLLEZEELE to
          POPERINGHE) will be as follows:-
               Dec.11th.   11.59   ...   350 All Ranks.
                           12.19   ...   250   ditto
                           12.29   ...   250   ditto
                           12.39   ...   250   ditto

               Dec.12th.   12.19   ...   275 All Ranks.
                           12.29   ...   250   ditto "

     NOTE: Attention is drawn to para.2 of 39th Divisional In-
            structions, 39/1285/A, dated 9.12.1916. Troops must
            arrive at Entraining Station at least half an hour
            before train departs.

ACKNOWLEDGE.

                                          Captain,
10.12.1916.   Brigade Major, 117th Infantry Brigade.

     Copies issued to all recipients of 117th Infantry Brigade
     Order No.105.

SECRET.   Copy No.....

AMENDMENT to 117th INFANTRY BRIGADE ORDER No. 105.
--- 10.12.1916.

Reference Move TABLE "B".

1. <u>117th Brigade Headquarters Transport.</u>

   The Moves detailed for December 11th. will take place on December 12th., and those detailed for December 12th. will take place on December 13th.

2. <u>17th K.R.R.Corps Transport.</u>

   Insert for DECEMBER 13th:-

   "Move from POPERINGHE to SUPPORT CENTRE SECTION".

3. Acknowledge.

                                              _____ Captain,
10.12.1916.   Brigade Major, 117th Infantry Brigade.

   Copies issued to all recipients of 117th Infantry Brigade Order No. 105.

SECRET.  Copy No. 20.

117th INFANTRY BRIGADE ORDER No. 106.

11.12.1916.

Reference: Sheets 27 and 28.

1. With reference to and in continuation of 117th Infantry Brigade Order No.105. The following more detailed orders are issued regarding the relief of the 113th Infantry Brigade in the Centre Section on the 12th and 13th December.

2. (a) The relief will be carried out in accordance with the attached tables and Line will be taken over exactly as held by the 113th Infantry Brigade. All details not mentioned in this Order will be arranged direct between Commanding Officers.

   (b) Details of Work in progress, Defence Schemes, etc., will be taken over as usual.

3. No formed bodies will move East of ELVERDINGHE - VLAMERTINGHE Road before 4.15 p.m., while holding the Centre Section.

4. The transport of all Battalions, and the 117th Brigade Transport, will be at A.14.b.8.8.

   The transport of the 117th Machine Gun Company will be at A.22.d.8.2.

   Transport Officers, and Quartermasters, will reconnoitre these Lines whilst their Units are in POPERINGHE, and will take over Lines as under:-

16th Notts & Derby Regiment	from 14th Royal Welsh Fusiliers.
1/1st Cambs Regiment	from 13th Royal Welsh Fusiliers.
17th K.R.R.Corps	from 15th Royal Welsh Fusiliers.
16th Rifle Brigade	from 16th Royal Welsh Fusiliers.

5. The following Posts (garrison of 1 N.C.O. and 3 men each) will be taken over by the 16th Rifle Brigade on the 12th December, viz:-

   Post G.8.   (A.1.B.)
   Post G.7.   (A.2.c.)
   Post G.6.   (A.8.B.)
   Post G.5.N. (A.9.D.4.6.)

   A Guide from each Post will be in the Square, POPERINGHE, by the CHURCH, at 11 a.m. on the 12th., for the purpose of guiding the new garrisons to their posts.

6. Three buses are being arranged for to be in the Square, POPERINGHE, at 8.30 a.m., 12th December.

   One each is allotted to 16th Notts & Derby Regt., and 16th Rifle Bde. One is allotted to 117th Machine Gun Coy., and 117th Trench Mortar Battery.

   The above Units will arrange to send Advance Parties of Officer & N.C.O's to reconnoitre the Front and Reserve Lines, and await the arrival of their Units.

   Advance Parties of the 117th Machine Gun Coy., and 117th Trench Mortar Battery, should include No. 1's for each Gun Position.

7. The Command of the Centre Section will pass to G.O.C., 117th Infantry Brigade, as soon as relief is complete on the 13th December.

   Brigade Report Centre will close at POPERINGHE at 3.30 p.m. on the 13th, and reopen at WEST CANAL BANK DUGOUTS (C.19.c.4.3) at 7 p.m.

8. ACKNOWLEDGE.

W.E. Maxwell   Captain,
11.12.1916.   Brigade Major, 117th Infantry Brigade.

Copies issued at 9 a.m. to all recipients of 117th Infantry Brigade Order No.105.

R E L I E F T A B L E to accompany 117th INFANTRY BRIGADE ORDER No.106.

Date.	Unit.	Arrive Asylum Str., YPRES.	Relieving.	Advance Party Guides.	Platoon, Coy., and Section Guides.	Destination.	Remarks.
Dec. 12th.	16th Notts & Derby Regiment.	5.30 p.m.	16th R.Welsh Fusiliers.	113th Bde. H.Qrs. 9.30 a.m.	Meet Batln. at the Asylum Str., YPRES. 5.30 p.m.	Batln in Right Reserve.	
ditto	15th Rifle Brigade.	ditto	14th R.Welsh Fusiliers.	ditto	ditto	Batln in Left Reserve.	
ditto	117th Machine Gun Company.	--	113th Machine Gun Company.	ditto	Essex Fm.Cross Rds. C.25.a.2.8. 5.30 p.m.	Trenches.	To leave POPER- INGHE by March Route in time to arrive at Essex Fm.Cross Roads at 5.30 pm. Co- lumn under Com- mand of Captain STEVENS, M.C.
ditto	117th Trench Mortar Battery.	--	113th Trench Mortar Battery	ditto	ditto	Trenches.	

NOTE: 1. Lewis Gun Teams will leave POPERINGHE at 1 p.m., and proceed by March Route under Senior Lewis Gun Officer to ASYLUM Station, YPRES, and await arrival of Battalions. March with Battalions from YPRES to destination.

2. Transport with Officers' Kits, and Dixies, etc., required for the trenches, will proceed with above party.

P.T.O.

RELIEF TABLE TO ACCOMPANY 117th INFANTRY BRIGADE ORDER No.106.

Date.	Unit.	Arrives ASYLUM Stn., YPRES.	Relieving.	Advance Party Guides.	Platoon and Coy. Guides.	Destination.	Remarks.
Dec. 13th.	16th Notts Derby Regt.	—	13th R.Welsh Fusiliers.	As arranged.	As arranged.	Right Battalion Centre Section.	Relief to be complete by 8 pm. See FOOTNOTE 2.
ditto	17th K.R.R. Corps.	5 p.m.	16th Notts & Derby Regt.	As arranged.	Platoon & Coy Guides from 16th Notts & Day to meet Battn at Asylum Stn, YPRES 5pm	Battalion in Right Reserve.	To be in position by 8 p.m.
ditto	16th Rifle Brigade.	—	15th R.Welsh Fusiliers.	As arranged.	As arranged.	Left Battalion Centre Section.	Relief to be complete by 8 p.m. See FOOTNOTE 2.
ditto	1/1st Cambs. Regiment.	—	16th Rifle Brigade.	—	As arranged.	Battalion in Left Reserve.	To be in position by 8pm. Route from L.Work to be reconnoitred on morning of 13th, also position of Companies.
ditto	117th Bde H.Q's.	5 p.m.	113th Bde H.Q's.	1 Guide from 113th Bde. H.Q's.	—	West Canal Bank Dug-outs. C.19.c.4.5.	Report Centre will open at 7 p.m.

NOTES:
1. NOTES 1 and 2 on Table for the 12th will hold good for the 17th K.R.R.Corps.
2. As far as possible the relief by the 16th Notts. Derby Regiment, and 16th Rifle Brigade, will take place by day.

SECRET.

DISPOSITION TABLE to accompany 117th INFANTRY BRIGADE ORDER No.106.

Brigade Headquarters: West Canal Bank - C.19.c.4.3.

Right Front Battalion: Battn Headquarters - Canal Bank East, C.19.c.5.5.
16th Notts & Derby Regiment.
3 Companies in front line from C.14.d.3½.6⅔ to C.13.B.75.35 (exclusive).
1 Company - Lancashire Farm.

Left Front Battalion: Battn Headquarters - Canal Bank West, C.13.c.1.2.
16th Rifle Brigade.
3 Companies in front line from C.13.b.75.35 (inclusive) to Canal Bank.
1 Company - Colne Valley, Fargate, and Butts 19, 20, 22.

Right Reserve Battalion: Battn Headquarters - Trois Tours B.28.Central.
17th K.R.R.Corps.
1 Company, Canal Bank East, N. of Bridge 4.
1 Company, Canal Bank West, S. of Bridge 4.
2 Companies, Trois Tours.

Left Reserve Battalion: Battn Headquarters - Canal Bank West, C.19.a.1.6.
1/1st Cambs Regiment.
4 Companies, Canal Bank West.

117th Machine Gun Coy: Headquarters - Canal Bank West, C.19.c.2½.6.

117th Trench Mortar Bty: Headquarters - Canal Bank East, C.19.c.2½.8½.

SECRET.   Copy No. 19

117th INFANTRY BRIGADE ORDER No. 107.

16.12.1916.

Reference:- Paper Trench Map, and Sheet No. 28.N.W.

1. The following Inter-battalion reliefs will take place tomorrow, the 17th December. All details of relief will be arranged direct between Commanding Officers concerned. Wherever possible, trench garrison of the front line will be relieved by day. During the day great care is to be exercised, however, that parties larger than a Section do not move up or down Communication Trenches at a time, and large intervals will be kept between all parties.

   The relief is to be complete by 8 p.m.

2. (a) The 17th K.R.R.Corps will relieve the 16th Notts & Derby Regiment in the RIGHT Sub-section. They will also relieve the Right Company of the 16th Rifle Brigade, i.e. they will take over a frontage from C.14.d.3½.6½. to C.13.b.75.35., including trenches C.13.2. and C.13.3.

   (b) The 1/1st Cambridgeshire Regiment will relieve the 16th Rifle Brigade, less the Right Company.

3. Officers Commanding Battalions will hand over all Defence Schemes, work in hand and proposed, and also information regarding their Sub-sections.

   A copy of the statement of work in hand will be forwarded to this Brigade Headquarters by 8 p.m. TONIGHT.

4. In accordance with Corps Orders each Front Line Company will let off one S.O.S. Rocket at 9 p.m. on the 18th instant.

   The Signal Officer will arrange to send Divisional time to the Front Line Battalion Headquarters at 6 p.m. on this day.

5. Completion of relief will be wired in Code to Brigade Headquarters.

6. ACKNOWLEDGE.

                                                    R.E. Maxwell. Captain,
16.12.1916.   Brigade Major, 117th Infantry Brigade.

Copies issued at 12 noon to:-

No. 1. 16th Notts & Derby Regt.	11. 227 Field Coy.,R.E.
2. 17th ditto	12. H.Q's, 115th Brigade.
3. 17th K.R.R.Corps.	13. H.Q's, 116th Brigade.
4. 16th Rifle Brigade.	14. G.O.C.
5. 1/1st Cambs Regt.	15. B.M.
6. 117th Machine Gun Coy.	16. S.C.
7. 117th Trench Mortar Bty.	17. Bde Sigs. Officer.
8. H.Q's, 39th Division.	18. War Diary.
9. H.Q's, 39th Division.	19. do.
10. O.C., Centre Group, R.A.	20. Order file.

SECRET.   Copy No. 19

AMENDMENT to 117th INFANTRY BRIGADE ORDER No.108.
                                                                                    20.12.1916.

Reference 117th Infantry Brigade Order No.108.

1. The 16th Rifle Brigade will relieve the 1/1st Cambridgeshire Regiment in the LEFT Section tomorrow, the 21st instant.

   They will also relieve the Left Company, 17th K.R.R.Corps.

2. The Order regarding the letting off of S.O.S. Rockets at 9 p.m. on the 22nd instant will still hold good for the 16th Rifle Brigade.

3. ACKNOWLEDGE.

                                                    W.E.Maxwell Captain,
                                            Brigade Major, 117th Infantry Brigade.

20.12.1916.

Copies issued to all recipients of 117th Infantry Brigade Order No.108.

SECRET. Copy No. 19.

117th INFANTRY BRIGADE ORDER No. 108.

20.12.1916.

Reference: Paper Trench Map, and Sheet 28.N.W.

1. The following reliefs will take place tomorrow, the 21st December, and on the 22nd December. All details of relief will be arranged direct between Commanding Officers concerned. Wherever possible trench garrisons of the front line will be relieved by day. During the day, however, great care is to be exercised that parties larger than a section do not move up or down communication trenches at a time, and large intervals will be kept between all parties. Tomorrow's relief is to be complete by 8 p.m.

2. (a) The 16th Notts & Derby Regiment will relive the 17th K.R.R.Corps, less their Left Company, in the RIGHT Sub-section, tomorrow, the 21st instant. The Left Company of the 17th K.R.R.Corps will be relieved tomorrow by the 1/1st Cambridgeshire Regiment.

   (b) The 1/1st Cambridgeshire Regiment will be relieved on the 22nd instant by the 16th Rifle Brigade.

   (c) The 17th Notts & Derby Regiment will take over from the 16th Rifle Brigade positions occupied by Left Battalion in Brigade Support on the 22nd instant.

   Hour of arrival of the 17th Notts & Derby Regiment, and arrangements for guides, will be issued later.

   (d) After relief, the 1/1st Cambridgeshire Regiment will rejoin the 118th Infantry Brigade.

3. Officers Commanding Battalions will hand over all defence schemes, work in hand and proposed, and all information regarding their Sub-Sections.

   A copy of the statement of work in hand will be forwarded to Brigade Headquarters by 8 p.m. on each night of the relief.

4. In accordance with Corps Orders, each Front Line Company of the 16th Notts & Derby Regiment will let off one S.O.S. Rocket at 9 p.m. on the 22nd instant. Similarly, the 16th Rifle Brigade Front Line Companies will let off rockets at the same time on the 23rd instant.

   In both cases the Signals Officer will arrange to send Divisional time to Front Line Battalion Headquarters at 6 p.m. on each day.

5. Completion of relief will be wired in Code to Brigade Headquarters.

6. ACKNOWLEDGE.

W.E. Maxwell Captain,
Brigade Major, 117th Infantry Brigade.

20.12.1916.

Copies issued at 8 p.m. to:-

No. 1. 16th Notts & Derby Regt.
2. 17th ditto.
3. 17th K.R.R.Corps.
4. 16th Rifle Brigade.
5. 1/1st Cambs Regt.
6. 117th Machine Gun Coy.
7. 117th Trench Mortar Bty.
8. H.Q's, 39th Division.
9.   ditto.
10. O.C., Centre Group, R.A.
11. 227 Field Coy., RE.
12. H.Q's., 116th Brigade.
13. H.Q's., 115th Brigade.
14. G.O.C.
15. B.M.
16. S.C.
17. Bde Signals Officer.
18. Bde Bombing Officer.
19. War Diary.
20.   ditto
21. Order file.

SECRET.   Copy No. 19

117th INFANTRY BRIGADE ORDER No. 109.

21.12.1916.

Reference: Paper Trench Map, and Sheet 28 N.W.

1. In continuation of 117th Infantry Brigade Order No.108, the 17th Notts & Derby Regiment will relieve the 1/1st Cambridgeshire Regt. in position of Left Battalion in Brigade Support tomorrow evening the 22nd instant.

2. The 17th Notts & Derby Regiment will arrive at the Asylum Station, Ypres at 5.30 p.m. C.C., 1/1st Cambridgeshire Regiment will arrange to send Platoon Guides to meet the 17th Notts & Derby Regiment when they arrive at the Asylum Station. An Officer will be sent with this party. Route from the Asylum to the Canal Bank should be reconnoitred by this Officer tomorrow morning.

3. The transport and Lewis Guns of the 17th Notts & Derby Regiment, which are coming from Tatinghem by March Route, will not arrive till the evening of the 23rd instant, and will proceed to the Brigade Transport Lines at A.14.b.8.8.

   The Lewis Guns will be sent up to the Line, and will relieve the 1/1st Cambridgeshire Lewis Guns on the morning of the 24th inst.

   The 16th Rifle Brigade will provide a guide for the Lewis Guns from the Brigade Transport Lines to Battalion Headquarters of the 17th Notts & Derby Regiment.

4. As soon as the 1/1st Cambridgeshire Regiment are relieved tomorrow evening by the 17th Notts & Derby Regiment, they will proceed by any convenient route to "G" Camp.

5. The 16th Notts & Derby Regiment will arrange to bring up the rations for the 23rd for the 17th Notts & Derby Regiment tomorrow night, and hand them over on the arrival of this Battalion.

6. Completion of relief will be wired by Code to Brigade Headquarters.

7. ACKNOWLEDGE.

W.E.Maxwell Captain,
Brigade Major, 117th Infantry Brigade.

21.12.1916.

Copies issued to:-

No. 1. 16th Notts & Derby Regt.
   2. 17th   ditto
   3. 17th K.R.R.Corps.
   4. 16th Rifle Brigade.
   5. 1/1st Cambs. Regt.
   6. 117th Machine Gun Coy.
   7. 117th Trench Mortar Bty.
   8. H.Q's, 39th Division.
   9.   ditto
  10. O.C., Centre Group, R.A.
  11. 227th Field Coy., R.E.
  12. H.Q's., 116th Brigade.
  13. H.Q's., 115th Brigade.
  14. G.O.C.
  15. B.M.
  16. S.C.
  17. B.S.O.
  18. B.B.O.
  19. War Diary.
  20. War Diary.
  21. Order file.

SECRET.   Copy No. 19

117th INFANTRY BRIGADE ORDER No. 110.

                                                                     24.12.1916.

Reference: Paper Trench Map, and Sheet 28 N.W.

1. Inter-battalion reliefs will take place tomorrow, the 25th December. All details of relief not mentioned in this Order will be arranged direct between Commanding Officers concerned. Wherever possible, trench garrisons of the front line will be relieved by day, starting at 2, p.m. During the day, however, great care is to be taken that parties larger than a section do not move up or down Communication Trenches at a time, and large intervals are to be maintained between all parties.

   The relief is to be complete by 7 p.m. This is most important on account of the intended bombardment for tomorrow night, which will commence at 9 p.m. (Orders for this bombardment will be issued later).

2. (a) The 17th K.R.R.Corps will relieve the 16th Notts & Derby Regiment, plus the Right Company of the 16th Rifle Brigade, in the RIGHT Sub-section.

   (b) The 17th Notts & Derby Regiment will relieve the 16th Rifle Brigade, less their Right Company, in the LEFT Sub-section.

3. Officers Commanding Battalions will hand over all Defence Schemes, work in hand and proposed, and all information regarding their Sub-sections.

4. In accordance with Corps Orders each Front Line Company of the 17th K.R.R.Corps, and the 16th Rifle Brigade, will let off one S.O.S. Rocket at 9 p.m. on the 26th instant.

   The Brigade Signals Officer will arrange to send Divisional time to these Battalions at 6 p.m. on this day.

5. Completion of relief will be wired in code to Brigade Headquarters.

6. ACKNOWLEDGE.

                                          W.E. Maxwell, Captain,
24.12.1916.   Brigade Major, 117th Infantry Brigade.

Copies issued to:-

    No.1. 16th Notts & Derby Regt.   11. H.Q's., 116th Brigade.
       2. 17th   ditto   12. H.Q's., 115th Brigade.
       3. 17th K.R.R.Corps.   13. G.O.C.
       4. 16th Rifle Brigade.   14. B.M.
       5. 117th Machine Gun Coy.   15. S.C.
       6. 117th Trench Mortar Bty.   16. B.S.O.
       7. H.Q's, 39th Division.   17. B.B.O.
       8.   ditto   18. War Diary.
       9. O.C., Centre Group, R.A.   19. ditto
      10. O.C., 227th Field Coy., R.E.   20. Order file.

SECRET.   Copy No. 19

117th INFANTRY BRIGADE ORDER No. 111.

28.12.1916.

Reference: Paper Trench Map, and Sheet 28. N.W.

1. Inter-battalion reliefs will take place tomorrow the 29th December. All details of relief not mentioned in this order will be arranged direct between Commanding Officers concerned.

   Wherever possible trench garrisons of the Front Line will be relieved by day, starting at 2 p.m.

   During the day, however, great care is to be taken that parties larger than a section do not move up or down Communication Trenches at a time, and large intervals are to be maintained between all parties.

2. (a) The 16th Notts & Derby Regiment will relieve the 17th K.R.R.Corps, less their Left Company, in the RIGHT Sub-section.

   (b) The 16th Rifle Brigade will relieve the 17th Notts & Derby Regt. in the LEFT Sub-section, plus the Left Company of the 17th K.R.R. Corps.

   (c) The 17th Notts & Derby Regiment will on relief move to billets and dug-outs at present occupied by the 16th Notts & Derby Regt., and will become Right Battalion in Brigade Support.

   (d) The 17th K.R.R.Corps will on relief move to dug-outs at present occupied by the 16th Rifle Brigade, and will become Left Battalion in Brigade Support.

3. Officers Commanding Battalions will hand over all DEFENCE SCHEMES, work in hand and proposed, and all information regarding their sub-sections.

4. In accordance with Corps Orders each Front Line Company of the 16th Notts & Derby Regiment, and 16th Rifle Brigade, will let off one S.O.S. Rocket at 9 p.m. on the 30th instant.

   The Brigade Signals Officer will arrange to send Divisional time to these Battalions at 6 p.m. on this day.

5. Completion of relief will be wired in code to Brigade Headquarters.

6. ACKNOWLEDGE.

                                                        Captain,
                                    Brigade Major, 117th Infantry Brigade.

28.12.1916.

Copies issued at 8 p.m. to:-

    No. 1. 16th Notts & Derby Regt.   No.11. H.Q's, 118th Brigade.
       2. 17th   ditto   12. H.Q's, 115th Brigade.
       3. 17th K.R.R.Corps.   13. G.O.C.
       4. 16th Rifle Brigade.   14. B.M.
       5. 117th Machine Gun Coy.   15. S.C.
       6. 117th Trench Mortar Bty.   16. B.S.O.
       7. H.Q's, 39th Division.   17. B.B.O.
       8.   ditto   18. War Diary.
       9. O.C., Centre Group, R.A.   19. ditto
      10. O.C., 227th Coy., R.E.   20. Order file.

ROUTINE ORDERS
by
Brigadier General R.D.F. OLDMAN, D.S.O.,
Commanding 117th Brigade.

Thursday, 7.12.1916.

(No Routine Orders published on the 6th December, 1916).

PART I.

Lewis Gun Course. 327. Reference 39th Division No.39/6/131.G. of 4.12.1916. The following have been selected to attend the Lewis Gun Course at the Machine Gun School, LE TOUQUET, assembling on the 11th December, 1916:-

CLASS "C".

26742	Cpl MILWARD, J.	16th Notts & Derby Regt.
41493	L/S BLOOD, W.	17th ditto
200033	Rfn WIDDINGTON, A.	17th K.R.R.Corps.
S18246	" HAMMOND, W.	16th Rifle Brigade.
S18339	" JOHNSON, A.	ditto.

PART II.

Indents. 328. The STAFF CAPTAIN will see Quartermasters of Battalions, and Quartermaster-Sergeants of 117th Machine Gun Coy, and 117th Trench Mortar Battery, at Brigade Headquarters fortnightly on alternate Mondays, at 2 p.m., to discuss outstanding Indents, and any other questions that may arise.

The first meeting will take place on Monday next, the 11th instant.

Band. 329. The 39th Divisional Band will play in VOLKERINCKHOVE on SATURDAY Afternoon, the 9th instant, at 3 p.m.

W.G. Maxwell Captain,
Brigade Major, 117th Infantry Brigade.

7.12.1916.

Copies issued to:-

16th Notts & Derby Regt.   G.O.C.
17th ditto   B.M.
17th K.R.R.Corps.   S.C.
16th Rifle Brigade.   Bde Sigs.Officer.
117th Machine Gun Coy.   Order file.
117th Trench Mortar Bty.

NOTICES.

A SPORTS MEETING will be held by 17th K.R.R.Corps, at MERCKEGHEM, on TUESDAY, the 12th instant. The Programme will include the following event:-
Brigade Half-mile (Flat) - Race open to Units of 117th Brigade.
Prizes: 1st. ... 30 francs.
          2nd. ... 10 francs.
          3rd. ... 5 francs.
Entries to reach 2nd.Lieut.C.G.HAYNES, 17th K.R.R.Corps, by 8 p.m. on SATURDAY, the 9th instant.

ROUTINE ORDERS
by
Brigadier General R.D.F. OLDMAN, D.S.O.,
Commanding 117th Brigade.

Friday, 8.12.1916.

PART I.

Nil.

PART II.

Divine Services.   330. CHURCH OF ENGLAND Services for Sunday, the 10th inst.

At BOLLEZEELE.

9.15 a.m. Holy Communion.

10.30 a.m. Parade Service - 16th Rifle Brigade.
                            117th M.Gun Coy.
                            117th T.M.Bty.
                            117th Bde H.Q's.

At MERCKEGHEM.

11.30 a.m. Parde Service - 17th K.R.R.Corps.
12.15 p.m. Holy Communion.

At VOLKERINCKHOVE.

8. a.m. Holy Communion.
5.30 p.m. Voluntary Service.

ROMAN CATHOLIC Services for Sunday, the 10th inst.

At BOLLEZEELE.

11.45 a.m. Parade Service - 16th Rifle Brigade.
                            117th M.Gun Coy.
                            117th T.M.Bty.
                            117th Bde H.Q's.

At MERCKEGHEM.

10.30 a.m. Parade Service - 17th K.R.R.Corps.

At VOLKERINCKHOVE.

9.30. a.m. Parade Service - 16th Notts & Derby Regt.

Proficiency Pay.   331. No.7138, Pte BALLANTYNE, D., 8th Gordon Highlanders, is granted Proficiency Pay, Class II, from 12.11.1916.

W.E.Maxwell Captain,
Brigade Major, 117th Infantry Brigade.

8.12.1916.

Copies issued to:-

16th Notts & Derby Regt.   G.O.C.
17th   ditto   B.M.
17th K.R.R.Corps.   S.C.
16th Rifle Brigade.   Bde Sigs.Officer.
117th Machine Gun Coy.   Order file.
117th Trench Mortar Bty.

ROUTINE ORDERS
by
Brigadier General R.D.F. OLDMAN, D.S.O.,
Commanding 117th Brigade.

Thursday, 14.12.1916.

(No Routine Orders issued since the 8th December, 1916.

PART I.

Grenade and S.Mortar Course.
332. Reference this Office B.M./A.929 of 6.12.1916. The following were selected to attend the 69th Grenade and Stokes Gun Course which assembled at TERDEGHEM on the 11th instant:-

GRENADE COURSE.
 R.15861 Cpl. NUTT, J. ... 17th K.R.R.Corps.

STOKES GUN COURSE.
 200051 L/C LLOYD, H.E. ... 117th T.M.Battery.
 3649 L/C VEZEY, H. ... ditto

Signalling Course.
333. Reference this Office B.M./A.899 of the 3rd instant. The following were selected to attend the Courses of Instruction at the Second Army School of Signalling which assembled on the 12th instant:-

Course A (12). (Linesmen) 12.12.1916 - 9.1.1917.
 26674 L/C CREE, J.E. 16th Notts & Derby Regt.
 C3512 Rfn INWOOD, A.G. 17th K.R.R.Corps.
 28416 Pte STEVENSON, P.C. 17th Notts & Derby Regt.

Course B. (7). Visual) 12.12.1916 - 9.1.1917.
 28380 Pte WILCOCKSON, D. 17th Notts & Derby Regt.
 B203008 Rfn PEPPER, H. 16th Rifle Brigade.

Sniping Course.
334. Reference this Office B.M./A.938 of the 11.12.1916. The following have been selected to attend the 49th Course at the Second Army School of Sniping which will assemble on the 16th instant:-
 32253 Pte HASTINGS, A. 17th Notts & Derby Regt.
 28563 Rfn BARRELL, R. 17th K.R.R.Corps.
 F937 " WHYTE, W.E. 16th Rifle Brigade.

PART II.

Medals.
335. The G.O.C.-in-C. has, under authority granted by His Majesty the King, awarded the following decoration:-

DISTINGUISHED CONDUCT MEDAL.

22797 Pte J.BETTS ... 16th Notts & Derby Regt.

The G.O.C., Brigade, heartily congratulates the recipient of this Medal.

W.E.Maxwell Captain,
BRIGADE MAJOR, 117th Infantry Bde.

14.12.1916.

Copies issued to:-
16th Notts & Derby Regt. G.O.C.
17th ditto B.M.
17th K.R.R.Corps. S.C.
16th Rifle Brigade. Bde Sig.Officer.
117th Machine Gun Company. Order file.
117th Trench Mortar Bty.

ROUTINE ORDERS
by
Brigadier General R.D.F. OLDMAN, D.S.O.,
Commanding 117th Brigade.

Wednesday, 20.12.1916.

(No Routine Orders issued since 14.12.1916).

PART I.

Anti-gas Course. 336. The under-mentioned Other Ranks attended the Anti-gas Course at the 39th Divisional Schools which assembled on December 13th:-

    70367 L/C SOUTIN, S.)
    70291 Sgt SCOTT, A.) 17th Notts & Derby Regt.
    35948 Cpl BRIERLEY, J.C.)
    C1501 L/C SUTCLIFFE, J.)
      472 " FORD, C.) 17th K.R.R.Corps.

Reference this Office B.M./777 of 14.12.1916.

Grenade and Stokes Mortar Course. 337. Reference this Office B.M./A.959 of 16.12.1916.
The undermentioned N.C.Os. were selected to attend the 70th Grenade and Stokes Mortar Course which assembled at TERDEGHEM on December 18th and will disperse on December 24th:-

GRENADE COURSE.
27484 Cpl HOOKER, E.A.   16th Notts & Derby Regt.

STOKES MORTAR COURSE.
15920 L/C SCOTT, W.H.   117th Trench Mortar Bty.

Divl. Schools. 358. Reference this Office B.M./A.957 of the 15.12.1916.
The following were selected to attend the courses at the 39th Divisional Schools, which assembled on December 17th and disperse on December 24th:-

(a). Physical Training and Bayonet Fighting.

16th RIFLE BRIGADE.

2/Lieut. P.R.L. Charrington   1857 L/Sgt. F. Peters.
S27182 L/Cpl H. Hards   S16255 L/Cpl W. Wolley.
P1220 Cpl C.W. Pennington

17th K.R.Rif. Corps.

R33585 L/Cpl H. Wood   R33953 L/Cpl H. Tily
R24069 Rfn. A. Wood   A732   Rfn. G. Jackson.

(b). Bombing Course.

16th Rifle Brigade.

P105   L/Cpl W. Brooks   P121   L/Cpl G. Haines.
E203011 Rfn. F. Saunders.   S27224 Rfn. W. Davey.
P602   Rfn. A. Oldershaw.   S18167 Rfn. W.T. Hofford.
S27285 Rfn. E. Hitchcock.   S18134 Rfn. A.J. Black.

17th K.R.R.Corps.

2/Lieut. E. Denny.   R33841 Rfn. G.L. Lester.
R33833 Rfn. G. Cox.   R23596 Rfn. A.S. Fisher.
R30182 Rfn. C.J. Draper.   R33577 Rfn. A. Hawes.
R28550 Rfn. J. German.   R26884 L/C W. Rogers.
R25162 Rfn. C.C. Brooks.

- 2 -

        (c) <u>Sniping Course</u>.

S15690 Rfn H. Pyne.	16th Rifle Brigade.
S27220 " E.R.Dorling.	ditto
C3246 " T.H.King.	17th K.R.R.Corps.
R25240 " J.Garwood.	ditto
14315 Pte M. Hart.	16th Notts & Derby Regt.

Sniping Courses. 359. Reference this Office No B.M./A.938 and B.M./A.968. The undermentioned were selected to attend the 49th and 50th Courses at the Second Army School of Sniping:-

<u>49th Course - December 16th</u>.

P937 Rfn WHYTE, W.E.	16th Rifle Brigade.
28563 " BARRELL, R.	17th K.R.R.Corps.
32253 Pte HASTINGS, A.	17th Notts & Derby Regt.

<u>50th Course - December 23rd</u>.

27887 Pte CONTRELL, T.	17th Notts & Derby Regt.
32583 " LOWE, J.	ditto

Machine Gun Course. 360. Reference this Office B.M./905. The following have been selected to attend a Course for C.O's and Seconds-in-Command of Machine Gun Companies at the VIII Corps School which will assemble on Dec.26th and disperse on morning of Dec.30th:-

    Capt. A. Hall Hall)
    Lieut. A.O. Rees.   ) 117th Machine Gun Coy.

Fullerphone Course. 361. The following have been selected to attend a Course of Instruction in the use of the Fullerphone assembling today at "V" Camp, and dispersing on the morning of the 24th:-

4075 Sgt H.Lacey.	17th Notts & Derby Regt.
S29036 " N.V.Harvey	16th Rifle Brigade.
3629 " S.W.Riggs.	17th K.R.R.Corps.
26660 Pte C.H.Hallam.	16th Notts & Derby Regt.

(Reference this Office B.M./A.961 of the 17th instant.)

C.O's Courses. 362. Reference this Office B.M./A.897 and B.M./A.906. The following were selected to attend Courses for Infantry Commanding Officers at the VIII Corps School:-

<u>1st Course</u> (Dec.18th to 24th).

                                                                     Rgt.
Lieut.Col. C.Herbert-Stepney, 16th Notts & Derby
Lieut.Col. E.F.Ward.   17th K.R.R.Corps.

<u>2nd Course</u> (Jan.1st to 7th.

Lieut.Col. H.M.Milward.	17th Notts & Derby Regt.
Lieut.Col. E.M.Snepp.	16th Rifle Brigade.
Major P.N.G.Fielden.	17th K.R.R.Corps.

C.O's Course. 363. Reference this Office B.M./A.972 of the 19th instant. Lieut.Colonel C.HERBERT-STEPNEY has been selected to attend a Course for Commanding Officers at the Second Army Central School, WISQUES, from 31.12.1916 to 6.1.1917.

                                                       W. Maxwell Captain,
20.12.1916.   Brigade Major,117th Inf.Bde.

Copies issued to:

16th Notts & Derby Regt.	117th M.Gun Coy.
17th ditto	117th T.M.Battery.
17th K.R.R.Corps.	G.O.C., B.M.,
16th Rifle Brigade.	S.C., B.Sigs.Off. Order file.

ROUTINE ORDERS
by
Brigadier General R.D.F. OLDMAN, D.S.O.,
Commanding 117th Brigade.

Thursday, 21.12.1916.

PART I.

Machine Gun Course. 364. Reference this Office B.M./A.970 of 18.12.1916.
2nd.Lieut.L.M.HASLER, 117th Machine Gun Company, has been selected to attend the 37th Series of Machine Gun Courses which will assemble at the Machine Gun School, CAMIERS, on December 26th. and disperse on Jan.13th.,1917.

Second Army School. 365. Reference this Office B.M./A.988 of 21.12.1916.
The following have been selected to attend the 7th Course at the Second Army Central School of Instruction which will commence on Monday, December 25th:-

2nd.Lieut. A.S.MELLOR	...	16th Notts & Derby Regt.
27239 Cpl J.JAYES	...	ditto
3292 Sgt T.TURNER	...	17th K.R.R.Corps.
2nd.Lieut. J.B.CAMP	...	16th Rifle Brigade.
P154 C-S-M H.PARKS	...	ditto
2nd.Lieut. G.A.BROOKE	...	117th Machine Gun Coy.

Courses of Instruction. 366. Complaints have recently been received from the Divl. Schools that men are frequently sent to the Sniping Course with bad rifles.
The G.O.C. directs that in future when any man is detailed to attend a Sniping Course, his rifle be first examined and passed by the Armourer Sergeant. Should the rifle be in any way defective, the man will be provided with a good one.

PART II.

Medals. 367. His Majesty the KING OF MONTENEGRO has awarded the SILVER MEDAL for BRAVERY to:-

22797 Pte JACK BETTS ... 16th Notts & Derby Regiment.

The G.O.C., Brigade, heartily congratulates the recipient of the Medal.

Traffic. 368. The following General Routine Order is republished for information:-

G.R.O.430. "Under no circumstances should heavy draught horses be trotted, whether hooked into loaded or empty vehicles, or when at exercise.
An Officer should invariably accompany horses whilst at exercise or when going to or returning from watering."

Mortar Battery. 369. The following have been permanently attached to the 117th Trench Mortar Battery as from the 17th instant:-

16th Notts & Derby Regt.
31091 Pte JOHNSON, C.			31196 Pte BROCKSOPP, J.
71127 " OAKLEY, D.A.			53418 " SAWYER, C.
50615 " POTTAGE, H.			

17th Notts & Derby Regt.
27231 Pte BIRD, E.W.	20294 Pte STANFORD, E.
28914 " GRIFFITHS, J.	30635 " DRAKE, W.H.
46687 " MARSTON, S.	

17th K.R.R.Corps.
28116 Rfn STADDON, F.W.	27742 Rfn WASHTELL, H.H.
C4212 " TYLER, H.	A200038 " BROWN, W.
C3950 " BIRCHMORE, P.	

P.T.O.

- 2 -

16th Rifle Brigade.
S27189 Rfn BAGGE, F.   S18369 Rfn EDWARDS, T.
S14096 " CALANDRA, J. S27317 " CHAPMAN, S.
S17357 " BROWN, J.R.

W.F. Maxwell Captain,
21.12.1916.   Brigade Major, 117th Infantry Bde.

NOTICES.

Found.   A BAY GELDING, about 15 hands, with both hind fetlocks partly white, 168 marked on near hind hoof.

Apply: O.C., 117th Machine Gun Company.

Copies issued to:-

16th Notts & Derby Regt.   G.O.C.
17th   ditto   S.C.
17th K.R.R.Corps.   B.M.
16th Rifle Brigade.   Bde Sigs. Officer.
117th Machine Gun Coy.   Order file.
117th Trench Mortar Battery.

ROUTINE ORDERS
by
Brigadier General R.D.F. OLDMAN, D.S.O.,
Commanding 117th Brigade.

Saturday, 23.12.1916.

(No Routine Orders published on 22.12.1916).

PART I.

Nil.

PART II

Medals. 370. Under authority delegated by the General-Officer Commanding-in-Chief, the General Officer Commanding II Corps has awarded the following decorations to the undermentioned N.C.O's and men for gallantry and devotion to duty:-

THE MILITARY MEDAL.

26563 Cpl. E. JAYNES.	16th Notts & Derby Regiment.
26804 Pte. H. FARNATH.	ditto
25375 Pte. W. FOWKES.	ditto
27620 Pte. J. HOWITT.	ditto
70079 Pte. W. ROOT.	ditto
25592 Sgt. W. WHITEHEAD.	ditto
27479 Pte. W. EAKIN.	ditto
25992 Cpl. A. MITCHELL.	ditto
27198 Cpl. A. RUSHTON.	ditto
25748 L/C. T. W. BARKES.	ditto
7659 Sgt. C. MONKS.	ditto
26208 Cpl. E. SHELDON.	ditto
26089 Cpl. A. BUSH.	ditto

87555 Cpl. W. TREMBATH. No.3 Section, 39th Divl. Signal Coy., R.E.

The G.O.C., Brigade, heartily congratulates the recipients.

War Material. 371. VIII Corps Order No. 616 is republished:-

"1. There is a serious and preventable waste of War Material. This results in :-
(a) Increased demands on shipping which cannot be spared.
(b) Lessening the output of the ammunition which is so necessary to us.
(c) Increasing the National War expenditure which soldiers as well as others will have to pay for by means of increased taxation both during and after the war.

2. It is therefore the duty of every soldier not only to preserve carefully his own equipment, but to collect and hand in any abandoned article which can be repaired or made use of in any other way.
PRACTICALLY EVERY SALVAGE ARTICLE CAN BE PUT TO SOME USEFUL PURPOSE.

3. The following articles are among those urgently required for the output of ammunition :-
All kinds of empty brass cartridge cases, including S.A.A.
All ammunition boxes.
Tubes, friction and V.S.P.
Fuze plugs, covers, cups and adapters.
Cartridge clips.
Copper of any nature.

4. Monthly Salvage Returns will be rendered by Divisions, Heavy Artillery and Corps Troops.

5. This Order will be republished once a month in the Corps.

W.G. Maxwell. Captain,
Brigade Major, 117th Infantry Brigade.

23.12.1916.

ROUTINE ORDERS
by
Brigadier General R.D.F. OLDMAN, D.S.O.,
Commanding 117th Brigade.

26.12.1916.

(No Routine Orders published since 23.12.1916).

PART I.

Staff Course. 372. Reference 39th Division 39/6/140.G. of 18.12.1916.
Captain W.G. MAXWELL, M.C., has been selected to attend the 2nd Staff Course at HESDIN which assembles today.

Signalling Course. 373. Reference this Office B.M./A.984.
The following were today despatched to "Y" Camp to attend the Signalling Course at the 39th Divisional School:-

70143	L/C MILLSON, J.D.	16th	Notts & Derby Regt.
27185	Pte BERRY, R.	17th	ditto
56712	" GREEN, A.	17th	ditto
23277	" COOKE, A.	17th	ditto
24216	Rfn GILKES, H.W.	17th	K.R.R.Corps.
P493	L/C ANSCOMBE, E.F.	16th	Rifle Brigade.
33264	Pte HARRITY, A.W.	117th	Machine Gun Coy.
752	" SMITH, A.	117th	Trench Mortar Bty.

Lewis Gun Course. 374. Reference this Office B.M./A.12.
The undermentioned have been selected to attend the Lewis Gun Course which assembles at LE TOUQUET on December 27th:-

CLASS "C".

216193	Pte CHAMBERS, W.	16th	Notts & Derby Regt.
70229	L/C CLAY, E.E.	17th	ditto
28111	Rfn SHRIMPTON, W.	17th	K.R.R.Corps.
17973	" HACKER, W.	16th	Rifle Brigade.

Sniping Course. 375. Reference this Office B.M./A.25.
The undermentioned have been selected to attend the 51st Course of Instruction at the Second Army School of Sniping:-

	2nd Lieut. ASHCROFT, R.B.	17th	Notts & Derby Regt.
47924	Pte CHAMBERLAIN, S.		ditto
26057	" HEWITT, R.		ditto

Musketry Course. 376. Reference this Office B.M./A.7.
No.25828 L/Sergt J.W.ARCHER, 16th Notts & Derby Regt., has been selected to attend the 16th Course for the Training of Musketry Instructors which will assemble at the Machine Gun School on Dec.30th. and disperse on Jan.10th.,1917.

Captain,
/Brigade Major, 117th Infantry Brigade.

26.12.1916.

Copies issued to:-

16th Notts & Derby Regt.
17th ditto
17th K.R.R.Corps.
16th Rifle Brigade.
117th Machine Gun Coy.
117th Trench Mortar Bty.

G.O.C.
B.M.
S.C.
B.S.O.
Order file.

SECRET.   R O U T I N E   O R D E R S
                                  by
                   Brigadier General R.D.F. OLDMAN, D.S.O.
                       Commanding 117th Brigade.
                                                        29.12.1916

              (No Routine Orders published since Dec.28th.,1916)

                              PART I.

Pigeoners' 377. The following were selected to attend the Pigeoners Course
Course.   which assembled at WATOU on the 29th instant, and which
                  will disperse on January 1st.,1917:-

                  11707 Pte SMITH, E.   16th Notts & Derby Regt.
                  49280 " JACKSON, T.   ditto
                  51049 " OSBORNE, C.   17th Notts & Derby Regt.
                  41572 " BAKER, G.   ditto
                  56506 " DAWSON, H.   ditto
                  70378 " WARE, J.   ditto
                  70041 " JEFFRIES, T.   ditto
                  50637 " RICHARDSON, H.   ditto
                  R32376 Rfn G. MARSHALL.   17th K.R.R.Corps.
                  C1165 " HORTON, W.   ditto
                  S145   " FOXE, F.   16th Rifle Brigade.
                  Z1533 " BERRY, W.   ditto

                  (Reference this Office B.H./A.41.)

General   378. Reference this Office B.H./A.40.
Course.   The following have been selected to attend the Second
                 General Course of Instruction at the 39th Divisional
                 School assembling on December 31st, and dispersing on
                 January 28th.,1917:-
                 2nd.Lieut. STEVENSON, A.   16th Notts & Derby Regt.
                 26965 Sergt. HALLAM, H.   ditto
       (Lieut)   2nd.HUGHES,B.V.   17th Notts & Derby Regt.
                 28088 Sergt WILLIAMS, D.   ditto
                 2nd.Lieut.PARRY, H.   17th K.R.R.Corps.
                 A200002 Cpl. LEAN, W.C.   ditto
                 2nd.Lieut. CAMP, J.B.   16th Rifle Brigade.
                 S27286 Cpl. SANBY, J.C.   ditto.
                 2nd.Lieut.BURROW, A.H.   117th Trench Mortar Bty.
                 1733 L/Cpl. KERSLAKE, S.   ditto

Signalling 379. Reference this Office B.H./A.30.
Course.   The following have been selected to attend the VISUAL,
                 TELEPHONE & FULLERPHONE Course assembling at the Corps
                 Signal School on January 1st.,1917:-
                 51340 Pte BRAKE, F.H.   16th Notts & Derby Regt.
                 70006 " TRAYNER, R.T.   ditto
                 27678 L/C BROOKE, A.   17th Notts & Derby Regt.
                 30546 " RAWSON, A.   ditto
                 24722 Rfn BOURTON, F.H.   17th K.R.R.Corps.
                 28580 " MOORE, A.W.   ditto
                 P.222 " BURRIDGE, E.   16th Rifle Brigade.
                 S18405 " DUFF, R.   ditto
                 7027 Pte NEWELL, R.V.   117th Machine Gun Coy.
                 45601 " BOWYER, E.R.   ditto

                                                          P.T.O.

PART 2 -

Court of Enquiry. 380. In accordance with 39th Division letter 39/Misc/787-10, dated 27th December, 1916, a Court of Enquiry as detailed below will assemble at the Headquarters, 17th K.R.R. Corps, at 10 a.m. on the 31st instant, to investigate the circumstances under which the men named in the margin contracted trench feet, and to ascertain if all necessary preventative measures had been taken in each case.

No.70033, Pte. A. RICHARDSON,
   17th Notts & Derby Regt. (attached 117th Machine Gun Coy)
No.27181, Pte J. SIDMILL,
   16th Rifle Brigade.

All necessary witnesses will be warned to attend by Os.C., Units, concerned.

The proceedings will be forwarded to Brigade Headquarters in duplicate as soon as possible after the closing of the Court.

PRESIDENT.

Captain W.R. LOW. 17th K.R.R.Corps.

MEMBERS.

Lieut. W. DUNKELS. 17th K.R.R.Corps.
2nd.Lieut. T.C.O. WILLIAMS, 16th Notts & Derby Regiment.

29.12.1916.

M.St.Huistonhaugh, Captain,
Brigade Major, 117th Infantry Brigade.

Copies issued to:-

16th Notts & Derby Regt.	G.O.C.
17th ditto	B.M.
17th K.R.R.Corps.	S.C.
16th Rifle Brigade.	B.S.O.
117th Machine Gun Coy.	Order file.
117th Trench Mortar Bty.	

16/RB

ROUTINE ORDERS
by
Brigadier-General R.D.F.OLDMAN,D.S.O.,
Commanding 117th Brigade.

(No Routine orders were published Decr. 30th.1916.)

Decr. 31st.1916.

PART I.

Divl. Schools. 381. Reference this office B.M./A.42 dated 28.12.1916. The following have been selected to attend the undermentioned Courses at the 39th Divisional School, assembling on Decr. 31st.1916.

(a) <u>Physical Training and Bayonet Fighting.</u>

<u>16th Notts & Derby.R.</u>

2/Lieut...A.Medcalf. 41106. L/Cpl.H.Lacey.
13303. L/Cpl.G.T.Kirk.

<u>17th Notts & Derby.R.</u>

2/Lieut.A.Rangdale. 28839. L/Cpl.W.Cheetham.
14380. Sergt...J.Osborne.

<u>17th K.R.Rif.C.</u>

C.624. Cpl.A.J.Dunlop. R10771. Corpl.H.Tristram.

<u>16th Rifle Brigade.</u>

S27208.Cpl.S.Arnold. S25283. L/Cpl.N.Parkin.

(b) <u>Bombing Course.</u>

<u>16th Notts & Derby.R.</u>

2/Lieut.L.A.Gothard.
24222.L/Cpl.A.Gyte.   71102.Pte.F.A.Brooks.
27395. "   A.Page.   26769. " C.Hee.
25639. "   A.Starbrock. 25819. " W.Siddons.
26614. "   H.Mulvy.   26438. " G.R.Parsons.

<u>17th K.R.Rif.C.</u>

2/Lieut.F.D.Thompson.
R17343.Rfn.A.Knibbs.   R32724. Rfn.H.Dorrington.
16314. "   J.Durnford. R31384. " S.Culver.
R31340. " F.Archer.   R34178. " C.B.Short.
R33597. " A.Waller.   R33858. " F.W.Woodcock.

Grenade & Stokes Mortar Courses. 382. Reference this office B.M./A.48 dated 28.12.1916. The following have been selected to attend the 71st Grenade and Stokes Mortar Course which assembles at TERDEGHEM on January 1st, and disperses on January 7th.1917:-

GRENADE COURSE.
2/Lieut.A.Meakin. 16th Notts & Derby.R.
S16953. Cpl. J.Jones. 16th Rifle Brigade.

STOKES MORTAR COURSE.

2/Lieut.S.W.HILL.(16th Notts & Derby.R.)117/TMB.
26678.L/Cpl.H.Crossland.117/Trench Mortar By.

(2)

PART II

Cookery 383. Reference this office S.C./A255 dated 28.12.1916.
Course. The undermentioned man is detailed to attend the
second course at the Second Army School of Cookery
to assemble on January 1st, dispersing on the 14th
January.1917.

        No.4634. Rfn.J.Jennings.   17th K.R.Rif.C.

Farriery 384. Reference this office S.C./A.293 dated 30.12.1916.
Course. The undermentioned man is detailed to attend the
course of Cold Shoeing at the School of Farriery, ABBEVILLE
to assemble on 1st January 1917 and dispersing 28th
February.1917.

        No. 11184. Driver.E.Lowe.   117th Machine Gun Coy.

                                                          Captain.
31.12.1916.   Brigade Major 117th Infantry Brigade.

Copies issued to :-

    16th Notts & Derby.R.   G.O.C.
    17th Notts & Derby.R.   B.M.
    17th K.R.Rif.C.   S.C.
    1 th Rifle Brigade.   B.S.O.
    117th Machine Gun Coy.   Order file.
    117th Trench Mortar Battery.

www.ingramcontent.com/pod-product-compliance
Lightning Source LLC
Chambersburg PA
CBHW080816010526
44111CB00015B/2565